The Fourth Sector:

Adult and Community Education
in Aotearoa/New Zealand

To Bas and Pat for providing the opportunities they never had; to Alison for helping to make the most of those opportunities; to Jack, Hanna and Meg in the trust that they will have greater opportunities.

John

To my family – Catherine, Amanda and Christopher – thanks for your tolerance and encouragement. To my colleagues, present and past, and the many students whose questions have triggered this book, I hope that it helps to generate still more questioning of what the fourth sector stands for in Aotearoa/New Zealand.

Brian

The Fourth Sector:
Adult and Community Education in Aotearoa/New Zealand

Editors
*John Benseman, Brian Findsen
and Miriama Scott*

The Dunmore Press

©1996 John Benseman, Brian Findsen and Miriama Scott
©1996 The Dunmore Press Ltd

First Published in 1996
by
The Dunmore Press Ltd
P.O. Box 5115
Palmerston North
New Zealand

Australian Supplier:
Federation Press
P.O. Box 45
Annandale 2038 NSW
Australia
Ph: (02) 552-220
Fax: (02) 552-1681

ISBN 0 86469 260 9

Text: Times New Roman 9.5/11.5
Printer: The Dunmore Printing Company Ltd,
                   Palmerston North
Cover design: Vanessa Halley

Copyright. No part of this book may be reproduced without written permission except in the case of brief quotations embodied in critical articles and reviews.

Contents

Preface		9
Introduction		11
John Benseman and Brian Findsen		

Part 1: Mapping the Field — 19

1. Looking Back — 21
   James Dakin
2. What do Adult and Community Educators Share in Common? — 38
   Robert Tobias
3. Mapping the Field in the 1990s — 65
   Jennie Harré Hindmarsh

Part 2: Te Kaupapa Akona no nga Iwi o Aotearoa — 77

Introduction — 79
Miriama Scott

4. 'He Hinaki Tukutuku: the Baited Trap'. Whare Wananga: Tensions and Contradictions in Relation to the State — 81
   Maarie McCarthy
5. Striving for Tino Rangatiratanga — 95
   Bronwyn Yates
6. Maori Literacy – The Local Reality — 112
   Huhana Mete

7.	Towards a Sustainable Relationship: Pakeha and Tangata Whenua in Adult and Community Education *Christine Herzog*	127
8.	So, Whose Logic is it Anyway? The Dilemma of Working as a Person of Iwi Descent in a Tertiary Educational Institution *Miriama Scott*	136

Part 3: Learning Contexts — 147

9.	Learning in the Community: Non-formal and Informal Education *Colin Gunn*	149
10.	Workers' Education and Training in a New Environment *Michael Law*	159
11.	Workplace Literacy: Issues and Trends in Aotearoa/New Zealand *Liz Moore*	177
12.	Adult and Community Education in the Universities *Brian Findsen and Jennie Harré Hindmarsh*	193
13.	The Role of Polytechnics in Community Education *Nick Zepke*	210
14.	Community Development *Wendy Craig and Robyn Munford*	223
15.	Continuing Professional Education *John Benseman*	234
16.	Schooling Big Children? School Based Community Education *Julie Barbour*	247

Part 4: Adult Learning Practices — 261

17.	Developing Educational Programmes for Adults *Brian Findsen*	263
18.	Participation in the Fourth Sector *John Benseman*	274
19.	The Experience of Adult Learning *Colleen Mills*	285
20.	The Education of Adult and Community Educators *Brian Findsen*	297

| 21. | Research and Evaluation
John Benseman | 313 |

Part 5: Educating Adults and Social Justice — 325

22.	Bicultural and Treaty Education *David James*	327
23.	The Invisibility of Women's Studies *Margot Roth*	337
24.	Public Issues and Adult Education *Robert Tobias and Judy Henderson*	347

Part 6: Bringing it Together — 363

| 25. | New Zealand Adult and Community Education:
An International Perspective
Joyce Stalker | 365 |

Glossary	381
Glossary of Maori Terms	386
Contributors	390
Index	396

Preface

This book has been a long time coming – not just in its more immediate production but also in terms of its place in the emerging field of Adult and Community Education (ACE) in Aotearoa/New Zealand. It is a book which gathers contributions from a range of people currently engaged in this sometimes amorphous area. It is written by the field for the field. We, as co-editors, are intermediaries in this process.

In 1980 Roger Boshier edited *Towards a Learning Society* which has been a landmark publication in this country, especially given the paucity of written material which is publicly available. While we were conscious of Boshier's shadow, we were also wanting to break new ground. Sixteen years is a long interlude and much has occurred here since the halcyon days of the late 1970s and early 1980s – stronger vocationalism in all aspects of education; the advent of the minimal state and the dismantlement of our social welfare system; increased government control over learning institutions via the Qualification Authority's framework (thinly disguised as freedom of choice for the individual); a harder face to the Treaty of Waitangi claims and principles in tune with self-determination among iwi; a reduction of spending by the state on the field of ACE itself as evidenced by the 1991 budget cuts; a democratic impulse towards Mixed Member Proportional (MMP) representation in Parliament. In short, the social/political/economic climate of the mid-1990s is virtually unrecognisable to an adult educator of the early 1980s.

One intention of this book, therefore, is to bring such current issues and trends within ACE in Aotearoa/New Zealand to the attention of practitioners and analysts in the local scene and internationally.

As we have developed this book, we have been aware of other international texts which have endeavoured to explore the field in their own countries. Mark

Tennant's *Adult and Continuing Education in Australia: Issues and Practices* (1991) and Griff Foley's *Understanding Adult Education and Training* (1995) have explored a wide range of contexts in that country. While there are commonalities between our two countries and their respective ACE developments, this book should serve to remind readers of areas of difference. Across the Pacific, Gordon Selman and Paul Dampier's *The Foundations of Adult Education in Canada* (1991) also provides a useful point of comparison. Again, there are common strands as one might expect from two Commonwealth countries, but the historical roots of each country are very distinctive and map out divergent patterns of development for the field in each nation.

At a day-to-day level for two of the co-editors working in an academic context, it is tiring and frustrating to continually use overseas literature and examples for those who are students in and of the field. While it is appropriate to expose students of ACE to the global picture (since little which happens here is unaffected by international trends), it is just as necessary for us to develop an 'indigenous' literature of our own – one which reflects our reality and history. This literature is 'indigenous' in two ways: the more restricted but very important sense of Maori writers (tangata whenua) sharing their experiences of ACE; the wider meaning of a literature which has a New Zealand stamp to it. This book is also seen as a resource for local students who can look to others' experiences in this country for support and insight.

A special feature of *The Fourth Sector* is its attempt to encompass a bicultural path towards constructing knowledge. It is not easy to translate Maori oral tradition into a written one without losing a good deal in the process. However, we have brought together writings from both Maori practitioners and from Paheha writers on biculturalism in one section. We regret the relative imbalance of the two portions – there is a larger component of Pakeha and a smaller section of Maori. We hope readers will understand the difficulties entailed in presenting a more equitable share in terms of demands on Maori practitioners. Within the Pakeha sections of the book there are those who also engage in dialogue about bicultural dilemmas so that the separateness is more artificial than exists in real life.

International readers of this book may sometimes get lost in the local idiom. While the glossaries will help remove some of the confusion, the nuances related to 'Kiwi' culture may continue to mystify them. Only so much of local culture can be 'explained' – it is necessary to live in and experience this country to unravel some of its idiosyncracies. Nevertheless, we hope overseas readers' journey through this text will be rewarding and that our New Zealand experiences in ACE may throw light on more global issues.

John Benseman, Brian Findsen and Miriama Scott
June 1996

Introduction

As the first book in the field of adult and community education (ACE) which provides a panoramic view of the field written by New Zealanders for New Zealanders for 16 years, there has been the temptation to try to be comprehensive. However, there is more to be written about than can possibly be contained in this text. This burgeoning field has an increasing number of practitioners (some without realising they are part of it) who have little access to others' experiences of ACE. This book is intended to address the gap in this dialogue and to provide fresh perspectives on practice in Aotearoa/New Zealand.

The title for this book was very carefully chosen. Some explanation is required. *The Fourth Sector* reflects the reality of the other three sectors preceding ours, i.e. early childhood education; primary and secondary education (compulsory attendance at school) as the second; higher education (organised formal learning in institutions such as universities and polytechnics) as the third. The fourth sector, which focuses on that learning beyond structured formalised learning, combines with the other three to constitute *lifelong learning*.

We have adopted the term *adult and community education* for various reasons. First, the 'and' between the terms denotes that they are inseparable on many occasions. We use *adult* to distinguish education that is engaged in by persons deemed to be of adult status in societies (each culture will define 'adult' differently). Second, we use *community* to denote that the learning to which we refer is primarily (though not exclusively) driven by and controlled by 'community'. The notion of community (itself problematic) is used to locate the educative processes and practices in this domain (as opposed to formalised hierarchical structures). The term *continuing education* appears to have lost its support in this country as a frequently used synonym for *adult education* except in particular situations (e.g. continuing professional education). It is noteworthy that adult education provision in secondary schools is most commonly known as *community education* rather than *continuing education*. So our preference has been to use the word *community* rather than *continuing* in the title.

In this book we have included at least three chapters which some might argue do not 'fit' into the above parameters. In particular, we include chapters on community education practice within higher education. In Pakeha terms, Jennie Harré Hindmarsh and Brian Findsen look into the role of the universities in the provision of adult and community education; Nick Zepke analyses the parallel role for polytechnics. In the Maori section, Maarie McCarthy explores the relationships between whare wananga and the state. In the experiences of the editors, some higher institutions operate in a collaborative mode with community; some voluntary organisations are more bureaucratic than higher education providers. Hence, the boundary between adult and community education on the one hand and higher education on the other is sometimes blurred. On balance, given the historical importance of universities and polytechnics (community colleges) to serving community education, we have included these institutions in our scope of operation.

There is a rationale for the construction of 'sections' to this book. In the final analysis, any demarcation of sections is arbitrary (since knowledge is socially constructed) but we attempted to develop inner coherence within each section. Also, we decided to separate the 'Maori section' from the rest of the book (rather than integrate chapters throughout) to highlight their significance and interrelatedness. Readers wanting to gain a feel for the special character of Maori ACE could concentrate on this part.

The first section includes three chapters which set a wider Pakeha framework for understanding the historical and conceptual bases for ACE. Adult education historian, James Dakin, provides a necessarily selective view of historical developments of main institutions within the fourth sector, including those transported here from Britain and subsequently modified for the new environment. He highlights in 'Looking Back' (Chapter 1) the place of the Workers' Educational Association (WEA), explains the demise of the National Council of Adult Education (NCAE) and points to a key role for the New Zealand Association for Community and Continuing Education (since renamed) for the future. The next chapter, by Robert Tobias, is a scholarly piece on what it is that community educators share. To answer this question he reviews the conceptual confusion which abounds in this field, introduces sociological perspectives to encourage us to look more analytically at what we do and why; importantly, he makes explicit links between social movements and the fourth sector, including the idea of the field itself being a social movement. Tobias provides a very useful conceptual tool by studying how concepts in use in ACE

Introduction

have themselves been changed according to historical events. In the final phase he attempts to address the distinctive character of ACE in Aotearoa/New Zealand. In 'Mapping the Field in the 1990s' (Chapter 3) Jennie Harré Hindmarsh elaborates on Robert's analysis by concentrating on the existing diversity of provision in this country at local and national levels. There are many distinguishing features of ACE here and her treatment of the Adult Reading and Learning Association (ARLA) and Te Ataarangi, amid other agencies, helps spell out our national idiosyncracies. In a special section on 'Policy Trends and Issues in the 1990s' Jennie highlights several of our current dilemmas, especially those centred around tino rangatiratanga and equity.

For an introduction to Part 2, readers are advised to refer to the separate piece written by Miriama Scott which immediately precedes the chapters on Maori themes.

In Part 3, *Learning Contexts,* we sample a range of environments where the fourth sector has made special impact. The initial chapter in this section by Colin Gunn concentrates on both informal and non-formal learning situations, thus emphasising that considerable adult learning occurs in people's daily lives in ways unorchestrated by 'leaders' of learning. In particular, Gunn portrays the varying degrees of educator and learner control in community organisations using examples from his home context of Nelson. The next two chapters have the workplace as a location of contestation. Michael Law (Chapter 10) analyses historical and international trends in the provision of worker and trade union education and wonders whether previous democratic impulses in worker education have been permanently squashed. In particular, he provides insights into the emergence and demise of the Trade Union Education Authority, associated with the supposed new accord between employers and employees and the current National government's Employment Contracts Act 1991 (ECA).

For Liz Moore, a long-time staff member of ARLA, there are many serious issues around workplace literacy (Chapter 11). While the drive towards 'upskilling' the work force inevitably entails revisiting the place of literacy in the workplace, there are dangers that the kind of literacy in demand is too vocationally-oriented, meeting primarily economic needs. She questions the roles of government, employers and workers in this new arena of workplace literacy.

The next two chapters discuss the respective roles of universities and polytechnics in the fourth sector. Historically, universities' extension departments (now renamed as 'centres for continuing education') have been favoured in terms of government funding (in comparison with other fourth sector providers). Brian Findsen and Jennie Harré Hindmarsh (Chapter 12) concentrate upon centres' current functions and purposes with special reference to issues of curriculum development, marginalisation/mainstreaming and participation trends. They illuminate the complexities of such organisations. Nick Zepke (Chapter 13) traces the connections of polytechnics with ACE pointing to a problematic relationship. He looks into the effects of recent reforms (for instance, those promulgated through *Learning for Life: Two*) and concludes that there are both opportunities and constraints. Through a case study of the Wairarapa Community Polytechnic, he illustrates different forms of community education and prophesies a rocky path for community education in the polytechnic sector.

Adult education and community development have been synonymous terms for some adult educators. Wendy Craig and Robyn Munford, both experienced practitioners in community development, depict the nature of this relationship with respect to empowerment of people and communities (Chapter 14). They provide valuable models of community development – Maori community development (which has links with the chapters by Christine Herzog and David James); feminist ways of working; working-class struggles; women and unpaid work. In whichever model people may adopt to change their lives, the importance of networking and action/reflection are emphasised by these writers. Chapter 15 in this section which focuses on particular contexts within the fourth sector provides a snapshot of the Continuing Professional Education (CPE) scene in New Zealand. John Benseman, for a significant period of time engaged in continuing medical education, attests to the centrality of lifelong learning for capable practitioners. After reviewing three different approaches to CPE (functionalist; conflict; critical), he traverses the issues of curricula design, the effectiveness of CPE, its administration and the status of CPE as a profession. Julie Barbour provides us with insights into community education practice in schools, a sector of the fourth sector which has a high profile in Aotearoa/New Zealand. After setting the scene for community education practice historically, Barbour concentrates most of her chapter on liberal-humanist influences on what happens in school-based community education which have had some contradictory outcomes. She then argues that the New Zealand Qualifications Authority has the potential to exercise considerable control over current creativity in school-based community education and sees the NZQA framework as a major challenge for colleagues to confront.

We have not attempted to describe and analyse every meaningful context in which adult and community education occurs. However, we have tried to be reasonably representative of the diversity of contexts. There is a tendency for each subsector of the field to perceive itself as the centre of the fourth sector universe. Much exists outside each of the above more specific contexts. By illuminating different arenas within the field, we can more readily make useful theoretical and practical connections with other providers or movements.

Introduction

The next part, *Adult Learning Practices*, deals with actual practices in which many fourth sector workers engage. Some practices are more from an *educator's* perspective (programme development; training; research and evaluation), some more from a *learner's* viewpoint (experiencing adult learning; participation) though this distinction is rather arbitrary. We have included this section because so much of our daily work consists of these activities and because in the local context so little has been documented.

In the first chapter of this section, Brian Findsen discusses a range of models imported to New Zealand from abroad and critiques their applicability. He points to the need for programme developers to ask more critical questions in terms of their practice based on emergent models which work in the local environment. He also raises the fundamental issue of the ownership of curriculum and whose interests current programmes are serving. A Freirian model of development is suggested as a means to move beyond 'middle-class' capture and to promote programmes which are more liberatory than the bulk offered from a liberal tradition. The issue of participation, especially in the local context, is discussed by John Benseman. After reviewing participation studies and research he ventures into 'non-participation' arguing that the classic picture of who participates and who does not, has changed since the advent of several providers whose functions have targeted 'underrepresented' groups. Since participation trends have tended to mirror patterns of inequality in society (those who have, get more), this issue should remain to the forefront of the field.

In 'The Experience of Adult Learning' (Chapter 19), Colleen Mills focuses on the individual learner's experience as opposed to generic descriptions of the characterisitics of adult learners which are so plentiful in the literature. She argues that such generalised descriptions tend to mask the realities of the individual learner. Her chapter explores the state of our local knowledge of adults' learning experiences prior to examining three factors which are important to understanding these experiences: different approaches to learning (e.g. deep versus surface); the way learners conceptualise learning itself; and learning style. She concludes by advocating more research to concentrate on the dynamics of places of learning.

Brian Findsen examines the education (usually called 'training') of adult educators in Aotearoa/New Zealand and finds it wanting. Little priority has been given to training in a largely non-professionalised field. Using the report issued by the National Council of Adult Education's working party (1977) as a benchmark, he critically reviews the extent and styles of 'education' undertaken by fourth sector educators. In particular, he addresses two issues concerning training: What is appropriate training (in terms of content and methods)? How are training and professionalisation linked? These questions are also related to the domestication or liberation of fourth sector educators.

The final chapter in the educational practice section focuses on research and evaluation. As with the education of fourth sector educators, John Benseman in his analysis finds that the quantity and quality of research and evaluation work is lacking. The paucity of research reflects several factors, the principal of which is the Cinderella status of the field – therefore, few academic appointments have been made in universities (where research is traditionally a hallmark) and there is considerable fragmentation. Also, research and evaluation have not been highly valued activities, although the current moves towards accountability within fourth sector providers are providing an increased stimulus for evaluation. Given that much of the research and evaluation undertaken in New Zealand has not been publicly available and that funding has been scant, there is much yet to be achieved in these arenas for the future.

The fifth part, *Educating Adults and Social Justice*, is not as well developed as we would have liked, so that much is left unsaid. In partial defence, we point to the social justice issues treated in other chapters which have not been separated into this portion of the book. Should another edition of this book emerge, then this section will receive greater prominence. The lack of chapters here does not reflect a lack of interest from the editors but more readily reflects the fact that people fighting for social justice seldom have the time to sit and write about it!

One of the features of this book, we believe, is that it includes material rarely written about. This is true for the first chapter in this fifth part (Chapter 22) written by David James whose experience in the area of running Treaty of Waitangi workshops for tauiwi has been extensive. David points to the importance of combatting racism at a structural level rather than at the individual (where guilt is often the dominant feeling invoked). He describes in his chapter the way he works with tauiwi to recognise injustice and to effect change. He also addresses the issue of 'cultural safety' which has come to public attention in recent times.

Just as David James has focused on one source of oppression within New Zealand society, Margot Roth (Chapter 23) looks into the development of women's studies in Aotearoa/New Zealand and portrays its marginality. She discusses more specifically the evolution of the Women's Studies Association in the wider context of feminist issues and the goals of the women's movement. She paints a picture of women contesting resources in an uphill fight for full recognition of women's studies as a legitimate area of serious study. Within the fourth sector itself, Margot expresses annoyance at its invisibility and hopes for better treatment to come.

Introduction

In the third chapter of this section, Robert Tobias and Judy Henderson from Christchurch write about their recent research (based on analysis of newspaper coverage of issues) designed to discover trends in movement-based education in their home city between 1983 and 1991. More specifically, the research focuses on public issues and documents ideological struggles as the New Right sought to gain acceptance for its programme and implement its policies. The issues chosen for discussion are economic, employment and trade union issues; social policy and the social services; health and disability. These are linked convincingly to historical/political events over this time period. As a result of their research, these writers argue for a stronger commitment from adult education agencies in raising the public policy issues for debate and discussion.

The final section, *Bringing it Together,* features the views of a recent immigrant academic in adult education, Joyce Stalker. In the final chapter Stalker provides a panoramic view of the fourth sector, analysing the impact of three major international forces – globalisation, market orientation, and fundamentalism – on the adult/community education field in Aotearoa/New Zealand. After reviewing orthodox responses from adult educators (consensus, conflict, interpretive) to practice she proposes a new model of appropriation wherein fourth sector workers can act positively and creatively in dealing with the special circumstances in this country. More particularly, Stalker points to struggles of the Treaty of Waitangi as triggers for new possibilities of thinking and action; the peripheral location of this country provides us with an opportunity for greater creativity in either modifying institutions and practices from abroad or setting up our own pathways. Further, our nation's history and reputation as a social laboratory allows for appropriation of a special kind related to our collective vision for fairness and social justice.

We have endeavoured to present some of the diversity of the fourth sector within a meaningful framework of sections. Having directed our energies to that purpose, it should be emphasised that no sections exist in isolation – knowledge is a living taonga with permeable boundaries. We encourage readers to find links where these are not explicit and hopefully to use this book as a source for further debate and dialogue. The fourth sector is a vibrant entity – we trust the book convinces you of that.

John Benseman and Brian Findsen

Part 1

Mapping the Field

1

Looking Back

James Dakin

The British Heritage and the Mechanics' Institutes

At the time of the first organised British settlements in Aotearoa in the 1840s, and indeed almost a century thereafter, Maori and Pakeha lived to a large extent in separate communities. The oral traditions of the Maori handed down in such institutions of esoteric learning as the whare wananga were scarcely known or accessible to the new settlers. The settlers, with their literary as well as oral traditions, sought to recreate in their new home the institutions with which they had been familiar in the 'old country' and which would help them to preserve and develop their cultural heritage in the new environment. Indeed, the practice of modelling social institutions, including those of adult education, on the institutions of the 'mother country' persisted in New Zealand for many decades.

In Britain in the 1830s, the most widespread institution of adult education was the mechanics' institute. The first British mechanics' institutes were founded in the 1820s in order to further the education of skilled artisans and especially to introduce them to the sciences related to their work. By the late 1830s, however, the institutes were more and more engaged in providing general education for people in clerical and business occupations (Kelly, 1970: 112–129).

The British settlers in New Zealand did not delay in setting up this kind of institution in their adopted country. As early as 1842 there were active mechanics' institutes in Wellington and Auckland. In Nelson then there was a 'literary and scientific institution' which soon assumed the character of a mechanics' institute. In the New Zealand mechanics' institutes generally, despite the title, there was no special provision for skilled artisans. As settlement extended over the country in the following years, institutes of this kind – sometimes under the name of 'athenaeum' or 'literary institute' – were established in almost every substantial centre of population. The existence at various times of more than 100 such institutes has been recorded. Even what is now the ghost town of Macetown in Otago had its athenaeum in the days of the goldrushes (Thompson, 1945: 17–27).

An institute usually owned a building and provided a room for meetings, a library and reading room. The committee of the institute apart from running a library, would each year offer programmes of lectures on a variety of subjects and at times a class or two on subjects such as drawing or Maori language. From about 1860 the institutes ceased to organise classes and after 1870 their lecture programmes dwindled. After the legislation of 1869 and 1875 empowering local bodies and the government to grant subsidies to public libraries, many of the institutes confined their activities to library work and their adult education activity declined. They were always purely local institutions, not affiliated to any larger organisation and not co-ordinated in any formal way (Thompson, 1945: 34–40).

Mutual Improvement Societies

Religious influences were strong but not all-pervading in the proliferation of mutual improvement and kindred societies that took place over the period 1860–1914. Many of the literary and debating societies that appeared in the later part of this period had mutual improvement as one of their major aims. In New Zealand mutual improvement societies followed a pattern of activity that had been developed in societies of the same kind in Britain. A typical society consisted of about 20 young men who clubbed together to further their education mainly by taking turns to write essays and by discussing the subjects treated in them. Many of these societies were closely associated with the churches, especially those of the Methodist, Congregational, Presbyterian and Baptist denominations, whose premises they used. Others were independent and held their meetings in hired rooms or in homes. The Dunedin Mutual Improvement Society formed in the 1860s by a group of young shop workers was of the latter kind. It alienated churchmen by providing a platform for spiritualist lecturers. Many of these societies were active in the suburbs of the cities and in rural areas throughout New Zealand during this period. Despite their links with some with the churches, they were not co-ordinated nationally and seem to have been purely local institutions (Dakin, 1991).

The Beginnings of Technical Education

From the 1850s, in a period when many children did not receive secondary education, technical education for young people and adults was pioneered by a variety of voluntary societies. Later, Education Boards entered the field and a few public institutions such as the Wellington School of Design (1885) were founded. As industry grew towards the end of the century, government was induced to pass the Manual and Technical Instruction Acts of 1895 and 1900. There followed the establishment of technical schools and colleges at whose evening classes adults as well as young people studied not only technical subjects but general subjects such as English and the arts. In 1914 some 7,600 students, including an unspecified number of adults, were enrolled in the evening classes of the eight largest technical colleges (Nicol, 1940).

The Workers' Educational Associations Established

In early 1915, there arrived two emissaries of the Workers' Educational Association of New South Wales who had been encouraged to visit by interested people in New Zealand. The Workers' Educational Association (WEA) had been formed in Britain in 1902 by labour leaders and university teachers for the purpose of organising educational programmes for working people. The two emissaries had come to promote the formation of WEA organisations in New Zealand. In this they were eminently successful and WEA organisations were formed in the four university centres and in Invercargill. The industrial labour movement had suffered severe setbacks with the Waihi miners' strike in 1912 and with the waterfront strike of 1913. Trade union leaders were turning to political action and any other action that would strengthen their movement. A substantial number of trade union leaders lent their support to the WEA. Many university teachers agreed to co-operate. The University of New Zealand was impressed and made a grant of £300 to each of the four university colleges towards the cost of tutorial classes. These were to be run by the WEA district councils, upon which students would be represented, in concert with the colleges. The early tutorial classes were, as in Britain, of two years' duration, limited to 30 students and required written work of students, but in New Zealand these requirements were gradually relaxed (Thompson, 1945: 65–82).

Tutorial classes commenced in all five WEA centres in 1915. The main subjects treated in the early classes were economics, English literature, psychology and modern history. By 1919 some 1,200 students were enrolled in these classes. In later years the range of subjects was broadened, especially by the inclusion of studies in the arts (Shuker, 1984: 43, 53, 76). At the end of

1920, the Canterbury WEA organised a memorable summer school at Oxford, North Canterbury. This school was directed by Professor James Shelley, a brilliant exponent of the arts in education (Carter, 1993: 137–138).

At first the WEA had no national organisation and each district council acted independently in co-operation with its university college. In 1920, the district councils set up a Dominion Council to which they accorded only delegated powers, mainly for the purpose of negotiating with government and convening national conferences. In 1919 the government had assumed responsibility for the making of an annual grant of £2,000 towards the cost of the tutorial work of the WEA. This sum was to be dispensed through the university colleges.

Expansion and Innovation

The government grant enabled the university colleges to appoint full-time tutor-organisers who would work under the WEA district councils. These 'WEA tutors', as they were called, were the first full-time adult educators to be appointed in New Zealand. By 1922 five, and by 1927 seven of these tutors had been appointed (Shuker, 1984: 66). Senior university teachers were also appointed honorary 'directors of tutorial classes' in three centres. In Auckland, a full-time professional director was appointed (Thompson, 1945: 90). Some of these directors, such as Professors Condliffe and Shelley of Canterbury and Professor Hunter of Wellington, both by their teaching and by their performance as administrators, contributed a great deal to the development of the WEA and adult education generally. The tutor-organisers proved particularly effective in propagating the work of the WEA in rural areas. The total enrolment in all courses rose from 1,476 in 1920 to 7,355 in 1930 (Thompson, 1945: Table xiii).

In 1926 Professor Shelley as director in Canterbury devised the famous 'box scheme' which can be considered the first significant New Zealand innovation in adult education. This scheme inspired the setting up of similar schemes in other WEA centres in New Zealand and Australia. It involved the systematic circulation of boxes containing not only lecture notes but books and learning aids such as gramophone records and art prints for study and discussion by registered groups of students. The scheme was a great boon in rural areas at times when the WEA could not afford to engage tutors and pay for their transport (Carter, 1993: 140–141). By 1930, 76 groups with 1,500 members were registered (Thompson, 1945: 102)

Following up a suggestion made by a WEA district councillor, Professor Shelley planned to engage a tutor-organiser and provide him with a motor van in which to take a 'travelling library' and various learning aids around up-country study groups enrolled, or which might be enrolled, with the box scheme. Thanks to a grant of £500 p.a. for five years from the Carnegie Corporation of New York, this scheme was implemented in 1930 and proved a success. The experience gained in this enterprise was later applied in the development of the Country Library Service. In 1930 also the American Carnegie Corporation made an annual grant of £1,500 for five years to the University of Otago to enable its School of Home Science to establish an extension service which would offer lecture-demonstrations to groups of rural women formed under the auspices of the countrywomen's organisations. When the terms of the mobile library and home science schemes expired in 1935, the Carnegie Corporation made available further funding over another five years for a combination of these two schemes entitled the Association for Country Education (Williams, 1978: 26).

Depression and Renewal

At the onset of the Depression of the 1930s, the government grant to the WEA was at first reduced, and then entirely discontinued in 1932. At the same time, trade union contributions were almost halved (Shuker, 1984: 85). By 1933 only four of the seven full-time tutors could be retained. The WEA was saved from collapse only by the generosity of part-time tutors and others working without remuneration and by the timely grant of £10,000 in 1931 and later contributions amounting to £30,000 from the American Carnegie Corporation (Hall, 1970: 64).

When in early 1936 the first Labour government took over the reins of power, the new Minister of Education, Peter Fraser, an erstwhile student in WEA classes, announced that his government was considering 'the co-ordination of adult education of all kinds with systematic government aid' (*The Standard*, Wellington, 23.5.36). The Minister then promoted the Education Amendment Bill which was passed in 1938. It was the first legislation in our history on adult education apart from technical education. It established a Council of Adult Education (CAE) consisting of seven members including two members appointed by the University of New Zealand, two appointed by the Minister, the directors of education and broadcasting and a nominee of the WEA. The Act charged the Council with the primary duty of co-ordinating the activities of adult education organisations and promoting adult education generally. It was to recommend to the Minister the amount of the annual grant to be made to the university for adult education. The Act made it clear that the university must expend adult education monies according to the directions of the CAE. The CAE had no staff and the Registrar of the university acted as its secretary (Dakin, 1988: 8–12).

In 1938 also, the Minister gave his blessing to the opening of the Feilding Community Centre as an experiment in adult education. This project, which was supported directly by the Department of Education and associated with the local high school, was successful and proved to be a source of inspiration for other community centres and other adult education enterprises associated with schools (Dakin 1979: 14–15).

War and Reorganisation

The effects of the Depression had reduced the numbers enrolled in WEA courses from 7,355 in 1930 to under 5,000 in 1934–1936, but by 1939 numbers had risen again to 5,685. It is interesting to compare these numbers with the estimate of 5,000 students over 18 years of age attending evening classes organised under the Manual and Technical Regulations of the Education Department in the years immediately preceding 1939 (Thompson, 1945: 235). As a result of the war, the number of students enrolled in WEA courses fell again, but rose to the record number of 9,494 in 1945 (Hall, 1970: 80). One of the positive results of the country's engagement in the war was the institution in 1942 of the Army Education and Welfare Service (AEWS) which introduced thousands of New Zealanders to adult education.

At the Ministerial Conference on Education in 1944 the Minister, Rex Mason, issued a statement defining the government's position on adult education. He announced that 'the government does not contemplate establishing a state system of adult education or placing existing agencies under a government department' (Mason, 1944: 84). The conference recommended that the CAE appoint a consultative committee to survey existing cultural and educational facilities and to make recommendations for the future organisation of adult education. This committee produced a very thorough report upon which the Adult Education Act of 1947 was largely based (Cocker, 1947). Behind much of the committee's thinking lay the feeling that, important as university tutelage had been and still was, the destiny of adult education lay in separate, independent development. The Act of 1947 established a National Council of Adult Education (NCAE) served by an executive officer, the National Secretary of Adult Education. The NCAE's primary function was 'to promote and foster adult education and the cultivation of the arts'. The reference to the arts indicated that the NCAE was empowered to finance the Community Arts Service which had been launched in 1946 by tutor-organisers of Auckland University College. This service, which was a new departure in adult education, organised tours by performing artists and circulated art exhibitions. It operated mainly in country communities which seldom, if ever, had witnessed the performance or viewed the works of professional artists (Lusty, 1980: 71–78). Another main function of the NCAE was to recommend to the Minister the amount of the annual grant to be made for adult education and to administer and control the expenditure of the monies received.

In each university district, college councils were required to set up regional councils of adult education, at least half the members of which would be nominated by organisations engaged or interested in adult education. This was intended as a step towards independence from the university. The regional councils (still offshoots of the university colleges) were so strongly represented on the 14-member NCAE, however, that in combination they could, and often did, ensure that by far the greatest part of the funds available would be allocated to their own programmes. This meant that there was little possibility of the NCAE itself developing nation-wide services. Local and regional interests were still strong.

Adult Education Spreads its Wings

The Consultative Committee had recommended a progressive expansion of services to be achieved mainly by the employment of additional tutorial staff rather than by making grants to voluntary and other organisations. The government responded favourably to this recommendation. The annual grant to the CAE had been £17,000 in 1946. The NCAE received £35,000 in 1948 and by 1952 its grant exceeded £85,000. Only some £2,500 of this sum was allocated to the National Secretary and his office in Wellington. Almost all the remainder was apportioned among the four regional councils chiefly for the employment of tutorial staff and four directors. In 1948 there had been 37 tutors; by 1951 there were 50 (Dakin, 1988: 29, 35, 38). Some of these tutors functioned as tutor-organisers for particular districts; others were specialist tutors who conducted courses in home science, drama or music. By 1952 three Maori tutors were specialising in the teaching of Maori language and culture. Some tutor-organisers were posted to centres such as Whangarei, Napier, Hawera, Oamaru and Invercargill to which none had been posted before. Most staff were provided with motor transport to enable them to visit outlying centres. By 1955 when the NCAE received the last increase in its government grant, the total number of tutorial classes and discussion groups organised had risen from 840 in 1949 to 1,493. The number of CAS performances and showings had risen from 366 to 680 (Dakin, 1988: 43).

Expansion is Curbed

At this point the NCAE and the regional councils found it very difficult to extend their services without additional funding. In 1956 the NCAE drew on its reserves to finance courses in child development and other subjects for parents in playcentres. The regional council in Wellington and Canterbury developed programmes of 'university extension' courses which were designed to be financially self-supporting and thus cause no drain on funds derived from grants. These courses were more specialised than the usual tutorial class and were often designed to meet the needs of professional groups such as teachers, bank officers and engineers.

There was another reason for developing these courses. At this time, the number of evening classes at secondary schools was increasing apace and some of these classes, especially in the arts, were similar in character to the classes promoted by regional councils. The regional council tutors felt the need to develop courses more related to university disciplines and distinct from those run by the schools. The NCAE itself noted that more and more public money was being expended on these classes at schools, while it could not obtain an increase in its grant from government. The Currie Commission on Education observed that in 1960 approximately £150,000 was spent on 'hobby' (i.e. non-technical) classes in schools. In that year, the NCAE grant was £121,674 (Dakin, 1988: 45). In 1959 growing concern about the way in which the system was working was aggravated by the WEA complaining to the Minister of Education about the allocation of funds under the control of NCAE (Shuker, 1984: 129).

At this time of unease in adult education circles, the publication of the Report of the Committee on New Zealand Universities (the Parry Report) in 1959 forced the NCAE to consider its future. This report recommended that the regional councils place more emphasis on university types of programme, including refreshment and enrichment courses for professional workers. The Parry Report also recommended the changes that led to the dissolution of the University of New Zealand (UNZ) in 1961 and the setting up of the University Grants Committee (UGC) which took over some of the functions of the UNZ. At this time too, the NCAE and the regional councils were becoming concerned about the rising costs of CAS tours, especially those of the ballet and opera companies. In 1960, the government created an Advisory Arts Council which in 1963 was succeeded by the QE II Arts Council. These councils gradually increased their aid to the two companies and to other arts activities and thus helped the NCAE and the regional council to justify their closing down of the CAS (Lusty, 1980: 78–80).

Reorganisation and the Emergence of Technical Institutes

Between 1960 and 1963 the NCAE deliberated on these developments under the chairmanship of Dr F.J. Llewellyn who had experience of adult education affairs in Canterbury and who became Chairman of the UGC in 1961. After receiving recommendations from interested organisations, the NCAE prepared the draft of an Adult Education Bill which was passed by Parliament in October, 1963, unchanged except for an amendment providing that one member of the newly constituted NCAE appointed by the UGC would be selected from a panel of persons nominated by voluntary organisations engaged in adult education (which would include the WEA). The new NCAE had only six members and, significantly, there was no regional representation. Its functions were to advise the UGC and the Director of Education on adult education matters and to advise and assist institutions and organisations engaged in adult education. It could also conduct surveys and experiments and generally take 'overall cognisance of the development of adult education and do whatever it considered desirable to stimulate activity in adult education'. One of the functions of the reformed NCAE was to advise the UGC concerning the amount of the grants it should pay annually to the universities specifically for their adult education work (Dakin, 1988: 55, 59).

Under this new dispensation the universities, now no longer mere colleges, were under no obligation to set up regional councils and were left free to carry out their adult education function as they saw fit. In the event, they converted their adult education organisations into departments of university extension which were staffed by the directors and tutors, thereafter designated lecturers.

In the meantime, there had been significant developments in technical education. The passing of the Apprentices Act of 1948 meant that many apprentices were required to attend evening or day release classes in secondary schools in order to gain qualifications as tradesmen or technicians. The large number of apprentices propelled into these classes organised by the secondary schools overloaded the system (Potter, 1980: 93). In order to solve this problem, the government founded the first technical institutes as tertiary institutions in Auckland and Wellington in the years 1960–1962. The NCAE was in no way involved in the planning of their founding.

Nor was the NCAE involved in the setting up of the Vocational Training Council (VTC) in 1968. This Council included representatives of industry and the technical institutes in its membership and was served by a full-time director and staff. The VTC encouraged different industrial sectors to set up training boards. These boards could receive government grants if they employed training officers. By 1979, some 50 of these officers were employed by boards. Some of the courses promoted by the boards were run in local technical institutes or through the many departments of the Technical Correspondence Institute in Lower Hutt (Dakin, 1980: 48).

Reduced Role of the NCAE

In 1965 Arnold Hely arrived from Australia to take over from the long-serving Bob Martin Smith who had been National Secretary of Adult Education since 1948. Hely had worked as a director of adult education in Wellington and in Adelaide. One of his first concerns was to identify the gaps in provision that had resulted from the recent reorganisation. To this end he convened conferences and instituted surveys, but collapsed and died tragically in 1967. He was succeeded by his recently appointed assistant, David James. James followed up Hely's initiatives, including a project designated to revive the connection of adult education with the trade unions whose support of the WEA had fallen off over the years (Shuker, 1984: 133, 149). This project was the WEA-Trade Union Postal Education Service (TUPES) which provided free tuition by correspondence for members of affiliated trade unions. This service was later taken over by the Trade Union Education Authority which was created in 1986.

During the 1960s the departments of university extension had increased their commitment to more specialised and more advanced courses. Certificate courses of two years' duration involving written work in such subjects as social studies had been developed. In 1970, the new universities of Massey at Palmerston North and Waikato at Hamilton took over the university extension functions in the central regions of the North Island from Victoria University and the University of Auckland. Massey University and the University of Waikato had been established in 1964. Massey had been made the main instrument of extramural university education and its programmes attracted large numbers of adult (especially older) students. Most of the tuition was by correspondence and in residential seminars. By 1984 there was an enrolment of more than 10,000 students for its examinations (Owens, 1985: 74).

The Optimism of the 1970s

The great trade boom of the early 1970s encouraged a drive towards expansion in education generally. In 1970 the National Commission for UNESCO appointed a committee of six to examine the concept of lifelong education and its implications for New Zealand. The members of this 'Lifelong Education Committee' included David James, Denis Garrett (Director of University Extension, Massey University) and R.C. Stuart (Director of the VTC). The recommendations of this Committee were later endorsed by the Educational Development Conference (EDC) of 1973–1974 and promptly implemented by government (Simmonds, 1972: 9). In 1973 an officer for Continuing Education, none other than Garrett, was for the first time appointed at a senior level in the

Department of Education to superintend its adult education activities. At the end of 1973, pilot projects in continuing education were authorised in four Auckland schools (later designated community learning centres). Provision was made for adults to attend classes in secondary schools in the Education Amendment Act (No. 2) of 1974. By 1978 there were over 2,000 adults enrolled in secondary school daytime classes (Department of Education, 1979: 25). In 1973 the Broadcasting Act was amended to make education a function of the NZBC and in 1975 Radio New Zealand's Continuing Education Unit was created. The origin of all these developments can be traced to the recommendations of the Lifelong Education Committee.

The EDC, in which some 60,000 New Zealanders participated and which attracted some 8,000 submissions, gave prominence to the theme of lifelong learning, the idea of education as a community activity and the value of 'continuing education' – the term commonly used in these times and later years for 'adult education' (Holmes, 1974: 9, 136). The EDC gave its blessing to the plan to found a community college, rather than a purely technical institute, as a continuing education facility to serve the community in Hawke's Bay (see Department of Education, 1973). The community college would include both general and technical courses in its programme. The EDC deplored generally any sharp division between vocational and non-vocational education. It favoured a closer relationship between the VTC and the NCAE as well as a revision of the terms of reference of the NCAE (Holmes, 1974: 98, 104). The Education Amendment Act (No. 2) of 1974 made it clear that the term *continuing education* was intended to embrace both vocational and non-vocational education. By 1980, not only was the community college in Hawke's Bay in operation, but other community colleges had been established at Whangarei, Rotorua and Invercargill.

Concern for the Educationally Disadvantaged

In 1976 a UNESCO conference held in Nairobi urged that the highest priority be given to helping educationally disadvantaged groups. The NCAE reacted to the UNESCO challenge and organised two conferences to discuss the issues raised. New Zealand adult educators knew from their own observations and from Boshier's research in 1969 that their adult education agencies were not reaching this section of the population (see Boshier, 1970, 1971). At the second conference the Minister of Education, L.W. Gandar, announced the Government's decision to finance an increase of NCAE staff in order to help it address some of the problems of the educationally disadvantaged. A permanent officer was to organise training to enhance the skills of adult educators of all kinds. An NCAE working party on training which reported in 1977 had prepared the way for this work (Dingwall, 1977). Another two officers were to be employed for three years working on special projects – Maori/Pacific Islands continuing education and broadcasting liaison. At this time, the McKenzie Education Foundation also agreed to fund the employment of a third project officer who was to develop a reading assistance programme for adults (Dakin, 1988: 82–86).

The ground for the Maori/Pacific Islands project had been explored by the Working Party on Maori Adult Education appointed by the NCAE in 1970 (Te Hau, 1972). The project, under the leadership of Ngoingoi Pewhairangi, helped to breathe new life into Maori adult education and resulted in the formation in 1982 of the Te Ataarangi organisation, which today continues to foster Maori language and culture (Higgins, 1993: 2–4). The work of Rosalie Somerville as project officer for adult reading assistance resulted in the formation also in 1982 of a national voluntary organisation (see Hill, 1990), the Adult Reading and Learning Assistance Federation (ARLA). This organisation now employs a national staff and works with over 80 local adult literacy schemes throughout the country.

Exploratory and Pioneering Projects

The Broadcasting Liaison project did not produce such tangible results as the other two projects although the project officer, working with the Continuing Education Unit of Radio New Zealand, did valuable work exploring the possibilities of bringing continuing education to those elements in the population least likely to participate in formal education.

In 1979 the Department of Education itself took steps to fill a gap in provision partly caused by the withdrawal of university extension staff from outlying centres during the 1960s. When instituting its Rural Education Activities Programme (REAP) primarily to assist country schools, the Department appointed community education organisers who would respond to local initiatives and requests by helping to develop educational programmes involving adults and their local organisations. Community education organisers were posted to smaller population centres where there was minimal educational provision for adults and quickly became very active promoters of rural adult education activity throughout the country (Department of Education, 1978: 16; 1979: 26).

During the 1970s, the district councils of the WEA continued to run their tutorial classes and schools programmes – attended by 17,812 in 1977. In the mid-1970s the WEA's national body developed a book discussion scheme which operated throughout New Zealand. Sets of selected books together with critical commentaries by subject specialists were sent out to enrolled groups.

Members of these groups were expected to study the books and meet to discuss the issues raised. In 1982 the scheme offered a choice of more than 200 titles and there were 114 enrolled groups (Shuker, 1984: 148).

Years of Crisis – the 1980s and Beyond

In 1982 the economic repercussions of the second sudden steep rise in oil prices of 1979–1980 were being felt and each Minister in the Government was required to reduce the expenditure of his or her department drastically. In March 1982, the Minister of Education, M.L. Wellington, suddenly proposed to abolish the NCAE, but desisted when the NCAE members agreed to accept a reduction of staff and an annual budget reduced from $302,000 to $113,000. The existing NCAE staff refused to apply for the vacancies advertised at lower rates of pay and were made redundant. The two newly appointed advisory officers struggled, with some initial success, to restore the prestige of the NCAE, but changing membership in the Council, misunderstandings between staff and Council and disaffection in the field persuaded the next Minister, Russell Marshall, that the Council was ineffective. In 1986 he decided to place it in recess rather than reform it (Dakin, 1988: 126–128). It was finally abolished by the Education Amendment Act of 1990.

The Minister set up an Advisory Group which in a report referred to as *He Tangata* (Shallcrass, 1987) recommended that he establish the Committee for Independent Learning Aotearoa/New Zealand (CILANZ, later CLANZ) which would advise him on all aspects of non-formal learning and distribute funds to non-formal groups. Such groups are those in which systematic learning is controlled by the participants rather than by institutions or professionals. The 12 members of CLANZ, after initial appointments by the Minister, were to be elected by registered non-formal groups. The Minister implemented these recommendations, but did not promote an Act of Parliament to entrench the functions and powers of CLANZ. CLANZ could employ no staff (Dakin, 1988: 136–140). In 1989 CLANZ, in accordance with the recommendations of the Advisory Group, established the National Resource Centre Trust which would take over the assets of the NCAE and operate as a co-ordinating body and a centre for the dissemination of information and the promotion of research (*Lifelong Learning in Aotearoa*, March, 1993). Despite its title, the trust has few resources except the former NCAE building in Wellington.

CLANZ was actually appointed in 1988 but its advisory powers were removed in 1991. Its annual allocation for distribution to groups was reduced by 60 per cent to $200,000 in 1992. Its chairperson sounded a note almost of despair: 'We are fighting for our existence. We have had our funding slashed, our range of operations slashed and our effectiveness reduced' (*Dominion*

Sunday Times, 8.3.92). CLANZ carries bravely on, but with no staff or other resources of its own and a loose organisation, it lacks the cohesive force and the voice to cause its claims to be acknowledged.

To cap this tale of woe, one must report that in 1992 all government funding of the WEA was discontinued in spite of the fact that it had been running a programme for 17,500 students in 12 different centres (Snook, 1991: 9; Yiakmis, 1991: 28). Furthermore, in 1992 the National government withdrew funding from the Trade Union Education Authority, which had been created by the Labour government in 1986 and which in 1990 had organisers promoting courses in seven regions of New Zealand (Law, 1993: 23–27 and TUEA brochure, 1990/91).

New Zealand Association for Community and Continuing Education

As these various adult education institutions were weakened or abolished during the 1980s and early 1990s, the NZACCE became more and more important as a protagonist of adult education. This organisation, founded in 1974 as the Association for Community Education, was supported by both professional and voluntary adult educators working in many different sectors of the diverse field. In 1979 it obtained a grant-in-aid from the NCAE for a conference on the development of New Zealand as a multicultural society, which was subsequently attended by some 200 people (Dakin, 1988: 105–106). In preparation for the 1981 election, it produced a publication comprising conference papers addressing the question, 'What's in it for Community and Continuing Education?'. In 1982, the NCAE co-opted a nominee of the NZACCE as a member. The NZACCE reacted against the drastic reduction of the staff and resources of the NCAE in 1983. It virtually declared the newly advertised vacancies 'black'. By 1986, the NZACCE had come round to supporting the NCAE in principle on the understanding that its constitution should be revised (Dakin, 1988: 127–128). With the demise of the NCAE and the failure of CLANZ to make any significant impact on government, the NZACCE is, it seems, destined to fulfil a more important role than ever before.

Overview

A constant underlying theme in most of this account of the development of adult education in New Zealand is the interplay between voluntary and local enterprises and regulative and centralising tendencies of institutions and the professions. In the vocational sector of adult education these tendencies were especially pronounced. Although in the nineteenth century it was local voluntary societies which first organised technical classes, institutions soon emerged with the support of the district education boards and in the twentieth century institutions created by government soon dominated the field, although independent private enterprises did make a contribution to development.

In the non-vocational sector, the vitality and influence of voluntary and local action have been more enduring. In the nineteenth century, all adult education in this sector was organised at local level by voluntary societies such as the mechanics' institutes and mutual improvement societies. There were virtually no associations or federations of these societies even at provincial, let alone national, level. It took external initiative to set up the WEA in 1915 and then only with the assistance of the university colleges. But the action was still essentially voluntary and regional. When the Dominion Council of the WEA came into being in 1920 it was reluctantly conceded minimum powers by the district councils. Even in 1936 the WEA district councils could not agree to the establishment of a national co-ordinating body for all adult education (Dakin, 1988: 5).

In the meantime, the WEA was being allocated government funds which enabled it to use the services of full-time tutors. These tutors soon perceived their growing indispensability and the fragility of voluntary local organisation. In 1924, A.E. Mander, an enterprising tutor working in the Manawatu, realised that he could win local support and operate independently of the WEA organisation (Thompson, 1945: 97–98). The tutors tended to look more and more to their legal employers, the university colleges. With the reorganisation of 1948, the formal association of the tutors with the WEA was ended. Other voluntary organisations as well as the WEA were now represented on the regional councils. Regional resistance to the building up of national services was still strong but this was partly because of the attitude of the university colleges.

By 1959 the government-controlled technical education system was developing a programme of evening classes for adults which was to some extent competing with classes organised by the voluntary organisations such as the WEA and the Country Women's Co-ordinating Committee. In 1964, the universities finally took over complete control of adult education tutorial staff. It seemed as if the institutions and the professionals were ineluctably taking over adult education. After this, however, the NCAE in its reduced role began to explore the uncultivated areas of the adult education field and came to appreciate more fully the potential of voluntary action for pioneering new developments. It supported the individual efforts of Ngoi Pewhairangi and Rosalie Somerville which led to the creation of the new voluntary societies Te Ataarangi and ARLA which were clearly fitted to meet specific needs in New Zealand society.

The enfeeblement and demise of the NCAE was a misfortune for the voluntary societies, but the wide-ranging inquiries instituted by the Interim Advisory Group on Non-formal Education (IAGNE) afforded the societies the opportunity to voice their disenchantment with institutions and professionals. IAGNE in its report *He Tangata* contended that 'no more than 20 per cent of identifiable learning occurs in institutions' (Shallcrass, 1987: 7). Following the recommendations of IAGNE, the government promoted the formation of CLANZ which is an organisation without staff and totally controlled by voluntary groups, but assisted by an independent trust linked to it. The Government has shown no inclination to give either of these bodies adequate support.

In this parlous situation the best prospect for the voluntary societies seems to lie in the growing influence of NZACCE (now renamed as the Adult and Community Education Association Aotearoa/New Zealand), which includes in its membership both voluntary and professional adult educators. Voluntary societies and professionals need to work together.

References

Boshier, R. (Nov. 1970; April 1971), 'The Participants: A Clientele Analysis of Three New Zealand Adult Education Institutions', *The Australian Journal of Adult Education*, part 1, vol. 10, no. 3, pp. 131–142; part 2, vol. 11, no. 1, pp. 20–44.
Carter, I. (1993), *Gadfly: The Life and Times of James Shelley*, Auckland: Auckland University Press.
Cocker, W.H. (chair) (1947), *Further Education for Adults,* Wellington: Council of Adult Education.
Dakin, J.C. (1979), *The Community Centre Story,* Wellington: National Council of Adult Education.
Dakin, J.C. (1980), 'National Bodies and Public Agencies', in Boshier, R. (ed.), *Towards a Learning Society,* Vancouver: Learning Press.
Dakin, J.C. (1988), *Focus for Lifelong Learning,* Wellington: New Zealand Council for Educational Research.
Dakin, J.C. (1991), 'The Prevalence of Mutual Improvement Societies in Adult Education in NZ', *International Journal of Lifelong Education,* vol. 10, no. 3, pp. 243–254.
Department of Education (1973), *A Hawke's Bay Community College: A Feasibility Study,* Wellington.
Department of Education (1978, 1979), *Annual Reports,* Wellington: Government Printer.
Dingwall, A. (chair) (1977), *Report of Working Party on Training of Continuing Educators,* Wellington: NCAE.

Hall, D.O.W. (1970), *New Zealand Adult Education,* London: Michael Joseph.
Higgins, J.P. (1993), 'Te Ataarangi', in *Lifelong Learning in Aotearoa,* no. 4, pp. 2–4.
Hill, K. (1990), *The Adult Literacy Movement in New Zealand,* Wellington: New Zealand Council for Educational Research.
Holmes, F.W. (chair) (1974), *Directions for Educational Development,* Wellington: Government Printer.
Kelly, T. (1970), *A History of Adult Education in Great Britain* (rev. ed.), Liverpool: Liverpool University Press.
Law, M. (1993), 'The Changing World of Worker Education: An Historical Perspective', in *New Zealand Journal of Adult Learning,* vol. 21, no. 1, pp. 7–33.
Lusty, M. (1980), 'Community Arts Service', in Boshier, R. (ed.), *Towards a Learning Society,* Vancouver: Learning Press.
Mason, H.G.R. (1944), *Education Today and Tomorrow,* Wellington: Government Printer.
Nicol, J. (1940), *The Technical Schools of New Zealand: An Historical Survey,* Wellington: New Zealand Council for Educational Research.
Owens, J.M.R. (1985), *Campus Beyond the Walls,* Palmerston North: Dunmore Press.
Potter, B. (1980), 'Technical Education', in Boshier, R. (ed.), *Towards a Learning Society,* Vancouver: Learning Press.
Shallcrass, J.J. (chair) (1987), *He Tangata,* Wellington: Interim Advisory Group on Non-Formal Education.
Shuker, R. (1984), *Educating the Workers?,* Palmerston North: Dunmore Press.
Simmonds, E.J. (chair) (1972), *Report of the Committee on Lifelong Learning,* Wellington: NZ National Commission for UNESCO.
Snook, I. (Dec. 1991), 'Address to Feilding Community Learning Centre', in *Akina,* no. 37, p. 9.
Te Hau, M. (chair) (1972), *Report of the Working Party on Maori Adult Education,* Wellington: NCAE.
Thompson, A.B. (1945), *Adult Education in New Zealand,* Wellington: New Zealand Council for Educational Research.
Williams, B.M. (1978), *Structures and Attitudes in New Zealand Adult Education 1945–75.* Wellington: New Zealand Council for Educational Research.
Yiakmis, J. (Dec. 1991), 'NZWEA Annual General Meeting', in *Akina,* no. 37, p. 28.

2

What do Adult and Community Educators Share in Common?

Robert Tobias

Introduction

A very wide range of people and organisations are involved in facilitating and promoting adult and community learning. They include organisers, administrators, facilitators, tutors, trainers, managers, supervisors, trade unionists, friends, colleagues, coaches, consultants, counsellors, community workers, social workers, health workers, recreation workers, religious workers, salespeople, journalists, politicians and activists of all kinds. They include people who are paid for their work in adult and community education, as well as those who are unpaid. For a few, this work is a central component of their occupations and indeed of their lives; while for very many more it is a secondary, subordinate or marginal component. Not everyone involved in adult and community education identifies with the field; indeed it is probable that only a very small proportion of those engaged in facilitating and promoting adult and community learning are aware of the existence of such a field; and an even smaller proportion call themselves adult or community educators or take the step of joining an association such as the Adult and Community Education Association (Aotearoa/New Zealand). Thus people's commitment to the broad field of adult and community education as opposed to their own areas of special interest varies widely.

… *What do Adult and Community Educators Share in Common?*

For some people and organisations the promotion or provision of adult and community education is an important end in itself; for others, including those based within many formal educational institutions, it forms part of an educational brief which is focused primarily on the formal education of children and young people; while for many more the promotion and facilitation of adult and community learning constitutes a means to other ends. These other ends include the promotion of economic efficiency and productivity, organisational effectiveness, a more effective and participatory democracy, equity, social justice, increased health and safety, the arts and sciences and community development. They include the promotion of an almost infinite variety of personal, organisational and public interests.

In the light of the diversity of aims, purposes, roles, functions and degrees of commitment of the people and organisations involved in facilitating and promoting adult and community learning, the aim of this chapter is to look at some of the different ways in which those engaged in adult and community education have in the past interpreted the nature and scope of the field. We shall also examine some of the forces that have shaped these different understandings, interpretations and perspectives. When we have done this I hope that we will be in a better position to answer the following kinds of questions: Given the diversity, is there anything worthwhile that all those engaged in adult and community learning share in common? If so, what is it? And if not, should we abandon talk of an all-encompassing field of adult and community education embracing everyone engaged in facilitating or promoting adult and community education and rather focus our attention on bringing together those segments of the field that do share something worthwhile in common? And if the latter, how narrow or how broad should the focus be?

Confusions Over Definitions

Confusions over terminology and definitions in the field of adult and community education have a long history. As has been pointed out previously (Harré Hindmarsh, 1992; Tobias, 1992), these confusions can be explained in part by noting that all definitions are contextual: they serve specific social and political purposes within particular historical contexts.

In pre-capitalist, pre-colonial Aotearoa/New Zealand there would have been no need to define or label any specific sphere of human activities as 'adult education' or 'community education'. Within the whanau and hapu there were undoubtedly highly significant institutionalised forms of learning and teaching and people did continue to learn throughout their lives. Within the whanau, much of the learning would have been community based (see National Council of Adult Education, 1972; Walker, 1980). From the mid-nineteenth century, with the gradual incorporation of Aotearoa/New Zealand into the rapidly expanding British imperialist political economy and its colonisation by successive waves of settlers drawn predominantly from Britain, a new hegemony was established.

This new hegemony served to preserve and extend the interests of British and colonial capital and the patriarchal cultural, social, political and economic institutions and traditions that the new settlers – the *tauiwi* – brought with them. This new hegemony was not established without a struggle. Military, political, economic and ideological means have been used to subdue or contain the forces of resistance over the past 150 years (see Walker, 1982; 1990); and the forms and practices of adult and community education as they exist in Aotearoa/New Zealand under capitalism in this final decade of the twentieth century are a product of these struggles. Predictably our understandings, interpretations and definitions of adult and community education have also been shaped by these struggles.

Both adult education and community education are terms which are fraught with ambiguities. The concept of education itself is highly ambiguous and its meaning has shifted historically. To call an activity 'educational' is to ascribe social value to it: to say that someone is 'educated' or 'uneducated' implies a normative and evaluative judgement. However, the social values and the criteria underlying these judgements are not necessarily self-evident. They are in fact strongly influenced by wider economic, social and political forces and by the struggles of groups and movements to shape their destinies.

Similarly, the meaning of the term 'adult' in adult education is seldom clear. Definitions of both 'adulthood' and 'childhood' are historically grounded and as Geoffrey Squires points out, 'There is no point, in a modern industrialised society, at which a person suddenly and unambiguously becomes an adult' (Squires, 1993: 87). Even if there were such a point, there would be those who would question the value and utility of using such a point to demarcate the field of adult education. The term 'adult education' may refer to all forms of education for those beyond the compulsory school-leaving age (post-compulsory education) or for those who have left full-time schooling (post-school education); it may refer to all those forms of education for people who have completed their initial schooling and their initial professional, vocational, academic or technical education and training (post-initial education); or it may refer not to '... *any* kind of education which contingently happens to be open to adults but ... instead something specifically and uniquely related to adulthood in terms of what is taught, how it is taught and how it is organised' (Lawson, 1975: 106).

For the purpose of this book the editors have defined the parameters and scope of the field. In terms of this definition, our focus is on those forms of learning which occur beyond compulsory schooling and beyond highly structured formalised learning. The fourth sector does not usually include early childhood education (the first sector) or compulsory schooling (the second sector) or higher education, i.e. organised formal learning in institutions such as universities and polytechnics (the third sector).

There are several difficulties inherent in such a definition and in particular in delineating the boundaries between adult and community education and the other sectors. A recent Australian definition is no more successful in resolving many of the difficulties but is nevertheless worth quoting in full since it provides an example of a broad and inclusive definition which succeeds in capturing many of the philosophies underlying much of the work undertaken in the fourth sector.

The Australian Senate Standing Committee on Employment, Education and Training states that:

> Adult and community education is an activity oriented towards lifelong learning which:
>
> - makes provision for the recurrent vocational, personal, cultural and social development of people regardless of their employment status, who are beyond the compulsory school age but are not primarily engaged in post-school education and training programmes
> - involves complex but coherent forms of co-operative learning geared to the adult status of its participants and committed to their empowerment through skill acquisition, access to information and introduction to fields of knowledge
> - is not necessarily constrained by the conventions of place, time and teaching/learning methods which may apply in the familiar settings of the school, TAFE college or university
> - is fundamentally a learner-centred and needs-based practice, characterised by active concern for accessibility, democratic processes, social justice and success measured primarily in terms relevant to the needs and aspirations of the individual participants.
>
> (Australian Senate Standing Committee on Employment, Education and Training, 1991: 175)

By way of contrast the Adult and Community Education Association (Aotearoa/New Zealand) has recently adopted a somewhat more narrowly focused definition:

Adult and community education refers to organised learning activities that groups or individuals undertake for their personal, community, cultural or economic development. It touches all other areas of learning but its primary focus is the adult as learner and the community as context.

Programmes are run by community groups and educational institutions; they are usually short-term, part-time programmes not designed primarily to make a profit for the provider. Outcomes are measured primarily in terms relevant to the needs and aspirations of participants.

Adult and community education is responsive to the learner's needs and aspirations. It is flexible in how, when and what it provides. It enables learners to enter and leave when it is appropriate for them to do so.

Adult and community education covers five main fields:
- adult basic education
- second-chance education opening the way to further formal education, training and/or employment
- personal development education which enables an individual to live in a family, group or community
- cultural education which enables a person to participate in the life of their community
- education to facilitate group and community development.

(Adult and Community Education Association (Aotearoa/New Zealand), 1994: 5)

This definition is somewhat more restrictive than the Australian one since it excludes certain types of providers and types of programmes. Moreover, it includes no explicit references to social justice and democratic processes. On the other hand, its more restricted and limited focus does free it of some of the rhetorical ambiguities and contradictions contained in the Australian definition.

Any attempt to define a fourth sector or a field of adult and community education is bound to be problematic and these are but two recent attempts to set the stage. What is important is to examine some of the different ways in which those engaged in the practice or study of adult and community education in the past have understood the nature and scope of their field of practice and to identify some of the forces that have shaped these different understandings, interpretations and perspectives. Before doing so, however, I want to discuss briefly some sociological perspectives on the nature and functions of various forms of adult and community education.

The Nature and Functions of Adult and Community Education

Sociological Perspectives

In a wide-ranging article published 35 years ago examining the contribution of sociology to education, Jean Floud and A.H. Halsey argued that education fulfils a number of functions in society including those of social differentiation and social selection, as well as performing a role in resource allocation. In a short section on adult education they suggest '... that in relation to the technology, the polity, the economy and the social structure of different countries at different times, adult education has had at least four distinguishable functions: remedial, assimilative, mobility-promoting and compensatory' (Floud and Halsey, 1958: 191).

In relation to the economy, they argue that the *remedial function* of adult education arises from the tendency of technological change to outstrip educational reform, thus creating shortages of appropriately skilled labour power. In relation to the polity, they argue, the remedial functions of adult education can be discerned in some programmes established when educational development has lagged behind the extension of civil and political rights to the mass of the population. No programme can unequivocally be seen as fulfilling only one function; nevertheless adult basic education programmes have historically fulfilled a remedial function and in today's terms many community-based programmes, employment-related programmes, computer literacy programmes and, in general, many programmes designed to upgrade people's technological skills can be seen as fulfilling such a function.

The *assimilative function* of adult and community education arises at times when the dominant economic, political, social and cultural patterns and institutions are under threat or when it is perceived as necessary to absorb peoples within the dominant patterns and institutions of society. Historically, many remedial and other adult and community education programmes may be seen as performing assimilative functions. Floud and Halsey argue that in the United Kingdom the assimilation of the working classes had been achieved in part at least through the contact with the élite university culture provided by the Workers' Educational Association (WEA) through the 'great tradition' of liberal non-vocational adult education. In Aotearoa/New Zealand it may be argued that the WEA may also have fulfilled this function to some extent especially in its earliest years. The assimilationist functions of educational policies for Maori over the years have been widely documented. In addition, programmes for prisoners and offenders and programmes for refugees and other immigrants have served an assimilative function, whilst it may also be argued that one of the functions of the ACCESS Training Scheme, established by government in 1988 to assist unemployed persons to find employment or further vocational training, and of the Training Opportunities Programme (TOP) which replaced it in 1991 has been to assimilate unemployed people within the work force.

Third, the function of adult and community education in promoting *social and occupational mobility* is one which, they argue, has often emerged out of the remedial and assimilative functions. They see this function as underlying the vitality of many contemporary forms of credentialled education. Earl Hopper and Marilyn Osborn (1976), using a similar framework, argued on the basis of their interviews with adult students in London that a key function of adult education is that of 'correcting errors' in the processes of social selection within the school system. The provision for the return of adults to secondary and tertiary education, as well as the development of the National Qualifications Framework can be seen to be fulfilling this function.

Fourth, they argue that the '... conception of adult education as a mechanism for the provision of *compensatory experience* is consonant with the sociological view of urban industrial society as one in which, partly because of its high productivity, individuals are especially likely to suffer from deficient or unbalanced satisfaction of intellectual and emotional needs' (Floud and Halsey, 1958: 192).

They propose that the most general hypothesis which needs further exploration is '... that the advance of industrialism shifts the focus of adult education from remedial and assimilative work to the promotion of mobility and the provision of compensatory or "recreative" experience' (Floud and Halsey, 1958: 192).

This model of the functions of adult education has the considerable virtue of describing and attempting to explain various features of the field from within a broad sociological framework. Thirty-five years and a great deal of sociological theorising later, however, it is possible to identify a number of weaknesses in the model. In the first place, it fails to take into account the ways in which the forces of capitalism, and in particular the forces of multinational capitalism, have shaped the predominant forms and practices of adult and community education. It is essentially based on a consensus rather than a conflict model of society and of the political economy.

Second, it may be argued that it grants to adult education a degree of autonomy that may not be warranted. In sociological terms, many of the programmes of adult and community education that have developed in recent years fulfil very similar functions to those of formal schooling, whilst others perform welfarist functions. Indeed, these functions may be more accurately reconceptualised as extensions into the adult years of the cultural reproduction, legitimation, social control and resource and labour market allocation functions of schooling (see Rubenson, 1989; Courtney, 1992: 123–147).

Third, it may be argued that the model fails to take into account our history of colonialism and the impact of this, together with the patriarchal and capitalist structures in shaping the predominant forms and practices of adult and community education. Kjell Rubenson (1989) and others have pointed out that much adult and community education, including much non-formal education, is hegemonic: it does little if anything to challenge the dominant ideologies in society or effect change in the structures of inequality.

Fourth, the model fails to take into account the counter-hegemonic roles that have been performed at certain times by adult and community education. Contradictions exist from time to time in all social formations. These contradictions give rise to tensions which may in turn be exploited by progressive forces to promote counter-hegemonic education and action. The model fails to raise questions concerning the problematic nature of the curriculum of adult and community education and hence draws attention away from the essentially political question of what counts as knowledge. Throughout history there have been individuals, groups and movements that have resisted or challenged the ideologies promoted by dominant classes and groups and who have created their own curricula.

Perspectives and Traditions

Sean Courtney (1989: 17) suggests that adult education has been defined from five different, if overlapping, perspectives. 'First, it has been seen as the work of institutions and organisations. Second, it has been described as a special kind of relationship, as in the concept of andragogy or as in the distinction between adult education and the education of adults. Third, it has been considered a profession or a scientific discipline. Fourth, it has been seen as stemming from a historical identification with spontaneous social movements. Finally, it has been distinguished from other kinds of education by its goals and functions.' In this chapter we shall adapt Sean Courtney's framework as we outline a number of different perspectives or ways of defining and mapping adult and community education in Aotearoa/New Zealand. Each of these perspectives highlights different aspects of the field. In describing these perspectives I have drawn selectively and thematically on the history of adult and community education in this country. In the first chapter of this book Jim Dakin has recounted this history more fully.

Adult and Community Education Seen as Being Linked Closely with a Range of Social Movements

First, adult and community education may be seen as a form of social, cultural and political practice often closely linked with a range of social movements. If one looks at the rise of adult and community education in the nineteenth and early twentieth centuries, much of it can perhaps best be understood from this perspective by locating it within the context of wider social movements (see Kidd and Titmus, 1989).

Some forms of adult and community education have been closely linked with religious movements. Indeed, most of the great religious leaders throughout history were also great adult and community educators. Traditional forms of adult and community education in pre-colonial Aotearoa/New Zealand contained a strong spiritual element. The early Christian missionaries sought to teach adults as well as children, and many of the mutual improvement societies that flourished briefly in the latter part of the nineteenth century were supported or sponsored by churches, whilst others were strongly secular in their orientation (see Dakin, 1991). In many cases religious, economic and political aspirations and goals have been mixed. Such was the case with much of the educational work undertaken in the Maori religious movements of the nineteenth and early twentieth centuries (see Walker, 1980; 1982) and in the work of the women's temperance movement (see Bunkle, 1980).

Adult and community education has also been closely linked with various socialist, labour and trade union movements since the early years of the nineteenth century. In Aotearoa/New Zealand, initial efforts to organise workers were limited. However, from 1888 rapid unionisation took place and international organisations such as the International Workers of the World and the Knights of Labour which were committed to 'organising, educating and directing the power of the masses, without distinction of trade or craft' (Sutch, 1966: 68) were established. In addition, adult and community education has also been closely linked with a number of other social movements. These have included co-operative, feminist, peace and environmental movements (see Lovett (ed.), 1988).

This tradition of linking adult and community education with social and political movements is still very much alive today and Chapter 24 on 'Public Issues and Adult Education' is devoted to a description of trends and patterns in certain forms of movement-based education in Otautahi/Christchurch in the 1980s and early 1990s.

Adult and Community Education Seen, Itself, as a Social Movement

Second, adult and community education itself has at times taken on the characteristics of a social movement. This occurred particularly during the first half of this century at a time when the working class, women and Maori people were largely excluded from universities and indeed from much post-primary education. Within the context of a class-divided society, adult education was seen by some as providing a way forward to the creation of a true democracy and to the achievement of greater social and economic justice (see Colquhoun, July 1979). 'Education for citizenship', 'education for community' and 'education for living' were seen as high priorities by many liberal and socialist reformers (see Williams, 1978: 1–16) and although efforts were made by many educationalists to bring about progressive reforms to the school system, it was also accepted by many that neither the schools nor the university colleges on their own could provide the kinds of education that were necessary to achieve these goals. This was seen rather as the mission of the adult and community education movement, operating with or without the support of the state and with or without the support of educational institutions.

It would of course be a mistake to view the movement as being at any time fully united. It contained a diverse array of people, groups and organisations reflecting different interests, perspectives and points of view. H.M. Richmond and J.B. Condliffe were among those who argued that 'education must above all be concerned with social change' and that adult education should seek to challenge the traditional and conservative 'moulding forces' in society. They stressed the political purpose and nature of adult education. James Shelley, on the other hand, emphasised the importance of lifelong education for personal enlightenment, enrichment, creativity and self-fulfilment, while H.C.D. and Gwendolyn Somerset argued that education should be seen as part of everyday life, that it should be integrated within the community and that close links should be developed between the curriculum and everyday, lived experience (see Williams, 1978: 1–16).

Increasingly the factor that gave a sense of unity and direction to the field was a common commitment to voluntarism, democratic processes and student- or participant-centred approaches to the education of adults. A.B. Thompson in 1945 took a position similar to that of the Somersets arguing that adult and community education should be closely linked with local community development, cultural enrichment and the provision of opportunities for recreation. He argued that, 'The aim of adult education ... is to bring form and shape into the community by providing in it the means of achieving the good life' (Thompson, 1945: 288).

Despite these divergent strands, there remained a sense of an adult education movement. Adult and community educators had a social purpose. To borrow a phrase from a later period, they were concerned with education that took place beyond the '... hierarchically structured, chronologically graded "educational system" '(Coombs *et al.*, 1973: 9–11) and, as we have seen, they shared a number of beliefs and commitments. Most forms of vocational and technical education were seen as too narrow and prescriptive to be part of adult and community education. All in the movement were concerned with breaking down élitism, either within the education system itself or within the wider society, and all were concerned to foster lifelong learning for its own sake and/ or for the purposes of everyday living. Within the movement there was also generally a sense of marginality and struggle against the wider forces in society.

This tradition of seeing adult and community education as a broadly-based social movement is also still very much alive today and nowhere is this more strongly evident than at the annual hui of the Adult and Community Education Association of Aotearoa/New Zealand.

Adult and Community Education Identified with the Work of a Limited Number of Organisations

Third, closely parallelling the previous perspective and growing out of it, was the view that adult and community education may be distinguished from other forms of education by the fact that it is organised by a limited number of clearly identifiable adult and community organisations or by clearly identifiable sections of formal educational institutions. Indeed, many of the histories of adult and community education that have been written have focused on one or other of these organisations or on the struggles between them and/or on the struggles of these organisations to obtain state recognition and funding (see, for example, Hall, 1970; Shuker, 1984; Williams, 1978).

From their foundations in 1915, the WEAs have occupied a unique place in our history. At a time during the 1920s and 1930s when very few people received a post-primary education, the WEAs performed a central role, especially in the main centres, in extending educational opportunities to working people. This education took the form of a wide range of classes, discussion groups, lectures and other programmes not intended for degree or diploma purposes. The WEAs were established with the support of the labour movement and a large number of progressive educators, and they very soon developed close links with the university colleges and the University of New Zealand. With an annual grant from the state, the university colleges appointed full-time tutor-organisers who worked for the WEAs. Since these WEA tutors were the first full-time adult educators to be appointed in Aotearoa/New Zealand, it is not surprising that many identified adult education almost exclusively with the work of the WEAs.

This pride of place was, however, not to remain free from challenge for long. Other voluntary organisations, such as the Country Women's Institutes (established in 1921), the Women's Division of Federated Farmers (established in 1925) and the Association for Country Education (established in 1935), were also involved in the education of adults, especially in rural areas. In addition, under the influence of people such as the Somersets (at Oxford and then at Feilding) and J.E. Strachan (at Rangiora) certain secondary schools attempted to break the restrictive academic straitjacket and to establish themselves as community schools serving wider educational interests in their communities. Community centres were established with Education Department support in Feilding in 1938 and then in Christchurch (Risingholme), Dargaville, Westport and elsewhere (see Dakin, 1979).

As noted above, the university colleges had for many years played a key role in supporting adult education in general and the WEAs in particular. In terms of the 1947 Adult Education Act which established a new National Council of Adult Education, the university colleges provided the base for the regional councils of adult education. They thus occupied a central position in the field of adult and community education. They not only disbursed state funds to voluntary organisations in their regions, but also employed most of the organising and specialist tutors. From the early 1960s, following the establishment of independent universities in the main centres and the changes to the National Council of Adult Education brought about by the 1963 Adult Education Act, most of the universities gradually withdrew from their wider adult and community education responsibilities and sought to limit their programmes to those which were considered academically and professionally appropriate to a university. Despite this narrowing of purpose and function, the universities continued to be the largest employers of full-time adult educators in the country.

These then were some of the key adult and community education organisations which existed prior to the 1970s. From the 1970s there was a rapid growth in the number and range of organisations committed to the kinds of ideals referred to earlier. A significant number of schools and polytechnics have become involved, Rural Education Activities Programmes (REAPs) play a key role and the WEAs, the Country Women's Institutes and the Women's Division of Federated Farmers have been joined by Te Ataarangi (formed in the 1970s), the Adult Reading and Learning Association (ARLA) (formed in 1983) and other voluntary organisations. Thus, although the number of organisations has grown, the tradition of identifying adult and community education primarily with the work of a limited range of organisations also lives on today.

Broadening Perspectives on Adult and Community Education

International Developments

In the latter part of the 1960s and early 1970s, major debates on educational policies were being undertaken within the framework of a number of international organisations. These debates were prompted by a number of factors (see Gelpe, 1979; Law, 1993; Lovett *et al.*, 1983; Sissons and Law, 1982). They included the continuation of the Cold War, decolonisation, the growth of international capitalism, changes in systems and methods of capitalist production associated with the increasingly varied applications of new technologies, the increasing power of the mass media, the development of the global economy and increasing internationalisation of the division of labour. They also included an increasing disillusionment with the welfare state compromises of the 1930s and 1940s, increasing questioning of the possibility of solving problems of wealth and poverty, peace and war, the sustainability of the ecosystem within the existing political and economic settlement and the rise of new social movements (see Welton, 1993). All this was happening at a time of rapid expansion of educational provision, increasing recognition of the limits of schooling in both rich and poor countries and upheavals in universities in the course of which fundamental questions were being raised about the nature and purpose of education.

Within this context, UNESCO adopted *lifelong education* as its guiding principle. This became one of the main themes of the International Year of Education in 1970 and the report of its International Commission on the Development of Education was based on this concept (Faure *et al.*, 1972). One of the aims of UNESCO was to persuade governments to shift from an exclusive policy focus on the expansion of formal schooling and to examine educational alternatives from a wider lifelong perspective. At about the same time the Council of Europe adopted *education permanent* as its guiding principle in the field of educational and cultural policy. This notion shared much in common with UNESCO thinking; however, its main aim was to promote cultural democracy and the democratisation of culture (see, for example, Council for Cultural Co-operation, 1971). The OECD was also reviewing educational policies at this time and it too focused on the importance of lifelong learning. Drawing, however, on the Swedish experience, it focused its attention on advocating strategies for post-compulsory education which included alternating periods of study and work throughout life. This strategy was embodied in its central concept of *recurrent education* (OECD, 1973).

As far as adult and community education was concerned, the increasingly widespread recognition of the importance of lifelong education, recurrent education and *permanent education* carried two major implications. In the first place, the necessity to provide opportunities for all adults to continue their learning throughout their lives was increasingly widely acknowledged. Second, it was increasingly accepted by governments that a higher priority should be given to the provision of educational opportunities for those young people and adults whose requirements and interests had not previously been served effectively by secondary and tertiary educational institutions, or indeed by existing adult and community education organisations.

What was new by the 1970s was the increased interest of educational bureaucrats and governments in the provision of adult and community education. This was reflected in the very much larger attendance by representatives of governments at the third UNESCO world conference on adult education held in Tokyo in 1972. This conference for the first time served to set adult education within the mainstream of educational thinking and planning internationally. However, the understandings and interpretations of the nature, purposes and functions of adult education held by the majority of educational bureaucrats and politicians were very different from those held both by the majority of social and educational reformers and by the liberal adult educators who had tended to dominate the field in the immediate past.

One of the main thrusts of the Tokyo conference may be summed up in the following comments and recommendation:

> Experience shows that the provision of more education in most communities tends to favour most the already well educated; the educationally underprivileged have yet to claim their rights. Adult education is no exception to the rule, for these adults who most need education have been largely neglected – *they are the forgotten people*. Thus, the major task of adult education during the Second Development Decade of the United Nations is to seek out and serve these forgotten people.
>
> (UNESCO, 1972: 9)

The Tokyo conference was followed four years later by a further large conference convened once again by UNESCO and held in Nairobi in 1976. This conference adopted a very broad definition of adult education:

> 'Adult education' denotes the entire body of organised educational processes, whatever the content, level and method, whether formal or otherwise, whether they prolong or replace initial education in schools, colleges, technical institutes and universities, whereby persons regarded as adult by the society to which they belong

develop their abilities, enrich their knowledge, improve their technical or professional qualifications and bring about changes in their attitudes or behaviour in the two-fold perspective of full personal development and participation in balanced and independent social, economic and cultural development; adult education, however, must not be considered an entity in itself, but is a subdivision and an integral part of, a global scheme for lifelong education and learning.

(UNESCO, 1976)

The very wide range of recommendations which arose out of this conference were grounded in this broadened interpretation of adult and community education. It was argued that a variety of forms of adult and community education were necessary within the context of educational systems based on principles of lifelong education and that adult and community education had a number of key roles to perform within the political economies of nations.

Internationally the 1970s, then, may be characterised as a period during which international agencies sought to establish and promote the principles of lifelong and recurrent education and to work out policy implications for all educational sectors including adult and community education. In particular, the early and mid-1970s saw an increasing sense of urgency to provide for the educational needs of 'the forgotten people'. Adult and community education was widely seen as having a key role to perform in this. Following the oil crisis of 1974, however, a sustained period of economic growth in many industrialised countries came to an end. This was followed by a series of political defeats of social democratic reform governments and the rise to power of conservative governments driven by revitalised neo-liberal economic doctrines. In many countries the welfare state came under increasing attack on both equity and efficiency grounds and the gaps between rich and poor both within countries and internationally continued to grow.

In the light of this, many of the progressive educational proposals and policies were either put on hold or refashioned to meet the new political and economic imperatives. The principles of lifelong education were reshaped in the 1980s to meet the requirements of the marketplace and the new 'enterprise culture' and this tendency gained momentum following the collapse of the communist regimes in the Soviet Union and Eastern Europe in the late 1980s.

A new vocationalism and credentialism came to dominate the field of adult and community education. In times of high unemployment and increasing impoverishment and exploitation in many parts of the world, many of the demands for equity were reshaped into either welfarist or narrow vocationally-oriented, skills-focused responses. Democratic imperatives for the development of adult education lost ground, as curricula of adult learning around the world came increasingly to be organised around the short-term demands of rapidly changing and highly segmented labour markets, which in turn were shaped by the demands of post-Fordist systems of production and by the demands of multinational capital. In the new 'enterprise culture', employers and private providers came to be seen by many governments as more cost-effective agencies of adult education and training than traditional educational institutions; and voluntary organisations and community groups engaged in adult and community education came to be viewed as agencies to receive state funding only to the extent that they served the narrowly prescribed welfarist or labour market requirements of the state.

Broadening Perspectives on Adult and Community Education in Aotearoa/ New Zealand

As mentioned previously, in Aotearoa/New Zealand prior to the 1970s adult education had been closely identified with non-vocational and non-prescriptive forms of education for adults and in particular with the work of the WEAs and university extension departments. This tradition was not unique to this country, but was common in Europe and North America. Few links existed between adult education on the one hand and technical and vocational education on the other. In particular, the links between the recently established technical institutes and those schools that were engaged in community education and between these organisations and teachers' colleges, universities and voluntary organisations engaged in adult education were weak. In 1968 a national body, the Vocational Training Council (VTC), had been established which was entirely independent of the National Council of Adult Education.

Under the influence of the forces discussed above and the reorientation in international thinking about education, from the early 1970s philosophies of lifelong education and recurrent education began to affect developments in Aotearoa/New Zealand. This movement gained considerable political momentum under the third Labour government between 1972 and 1975 and was supported by the many thousands of people who participated in an Educational Development Conference that was convened by the Minister of Education, Phil Amos.

A sustained critique was mounted of what was perceived as a narrow, university-dominated conception of adult education and of the sharp policy and administrative divisions which existed between non-vocational and vocational education. In an attempt to break down these divisions, the concept of 'continuing education' was increasingly used to cover all forms of post-initial or post-compulsory education. In 1972, a Committee on Lifelong

Education of the New Zealand National Commission for UNESCO recommended the adoption of the term *continuing education*. This was defined as '... the education, both vocational and non-vocational, of those whose main occupational role is no longer that of a student'. The committee thus saw continuing education in terms of post-initial education and went on to state: ' "Continuing education" has tended to supersede the older term "adult education". It is more precise and includes more explicitly the education of those who have left school but are still minors, excluding only those who are undertaking further education before taking up a vocation' (Simmonds (Chair), 1972: 5).

Two years later, in 1974, the final report of the Educational Development Conference extended the definition of continuing education even further. It viewed continuing education in terms of post-full-time school education and described it as: '... education provided for persons who are no longer full-time pupils within the primary and secondary school systems (and) thus encompasses all aspects of education after school, whether full-time, part-time, extramural, on-the-job, vocational or non-vocational' (Educational Development Conference, 1974: 81).

The Labour government of the time acted on this and other recommendations arising from the Educational Development Conference and in that same year brought to parliament a Bill to amend the Education Act. In terms of the Bill, all the work of tertiary institutions including universities, teachers' colleges, technical institutes and community colleges as well as provision for part-time secondary school studies would have been brought within the field of continuing education. Following submissions at the committee stages, however, the Bill was amended to exclude universities and teachers' colleges from its provisions. The final version of the Education Amendment Act of 1974 thus stated that:

> 'Continuing education' means education, including vocational education, provided for persons who are no longer required to attend school under the provisions of this Act and who are not, unless expressly provided for by this Act, enrolled as pupils in any secondary school or department; but this does not include education at a University or University College of Agriculture or Teachers' College.
> (New Zealand Government, 1974)

The new focus on lifelong education and in particular on continuing education, viewed in terms of the provision of a wider range of opportunities for post-compulsory and post full-time school education, resulted in the 1970s in the launching of a number of new initiatives. These included the establishment of a division of continuing education in the department of education, a rapid expansion in the number of technical institutes and a broadening of their roles, the establishment of a number of community colleges and schools-based Community Learning Centres, the establishment of 13 Rural Education Activities Programmes, the Nelson Community Education Service and the Wairarapa Community Action Programme. They also included changes in legislation to allow for adults to return to school, provision for the direct funding of voluntary organisations from Vote Education, the establishment of a number of Industry Training Boards under the Vocational Training Council and the establishment of a number of pilot programmes and projects in Maori education, adult literacy, the use of radio in adult and community education, as well as in the appointment of a training and development officer by the National Council of Adult Education.

By the late-1970s and early 1980s, however, a number of changes were taking place which brought a halt to the progressive movement of a few years earlier which had seen a broadening of the scope of adult and community education. As in many other capitalist countries, from the mid-1970s Aotearoa/ New Zealand witnessed an increasing crisis of capital accumulation and a growth in unemployment. Among other things, the populist National government under the premiership of Sir Robert Muldoon borrowed heavily to finance a series of 'Think Big' projects, whilst at the same time in the early 1980s instituting a wage/price freeze and cutting back on educational expenditure. These cuts, which were particularly severe in their effects on several adult and community education organisations such as the WEAs and the NCAE, together with other policies which sought to redirect priorities within the polytechnics and community colleges to the provision of narrow skills-based labour market programmes, brought to a premature end the progressive era in adult and community education initiated in the early 1970s.

With the election of the fourth Labour government in 1984 there were great expectations of a return to the progressive era of the 1970s. Several important new initiatives were undertaken over the next few years. These included the restoration of some of the state funding that the WEAs and other organisations had lost in the early 1980s, the restoration of funding for more broadly-based programme development in the polytechnics and community colleges, the recognition of paid educational leave for trades unionists, the establishment of the Trade Union Education Authority, the setting up of ACCESS courses for unemployed people, the provision of some equity funding in tertiary institutions and some responses by the state to the pressures from Maoridom for recognition of their rights under the Treaty of Waitangi.

Nevertheless, the high expectations of the mid-1980s were never fulfilled. Elsewhere (Tobias, 1990) I have discussed this in some depth. Here I wish to suggest briefly two reasons for the failure to develop a more progressive overall policy framework for adult and community education. In the first place, the failure was a direct consequence of the rapid rise to political dominance of 'new right' ideologues committed to neo-liberal economic doctrines. They argued strongly for lower levels of taxation, a substantial reduction in the role of the state in the provision of education and other social services and much greater reliance on the marketplace and on market signals in the determination of policy. Within this framework, the long-established linkages between adult education, citizenship and the state were largely severed and replaced by linkages between adult education, the consumer and the labour market. Throughout the 1980s and into the 1990s, 'new right' forces have continued to exercise considerable influence on policy. As in many other countries, this has resulted in the dominance of a new vocationalism and credentialism in adult and community education. However, in 1990–1991 these influences reached a new peak with the election of a national government which initiated a far-reaching attack on all aspects of the welfare state. State funds were once again withdrawn from several adult and community education organisations and the commercialisation and privatisation of adult and community education was taken a stage further (see Tobias, August, 1993).

In the second place, the failures of progressive policies arose out of the divisions and fragmentation within the field of adult and community education itself – divisions, for example, between better-funded institutions and poorly funded voluntary organisations and community groups – which were exacerbated by the increasing competition fostered by market-oriented 'New Right' ideologies.

Making Sense of Diversity in Aotearoa/New Zealand

In the light of all the changes taking place in the early 1970s it appeared at the time that the name, scope and constitution of the National Council of Adult Education (NCAE) would require amendment to reflect the broader perspective. However, the necessary legislation to achieve this was never enacted. Nevertheless, the NCAE did seek to broaden the scope of its work. Between 1975 and 1983 it published a series of *Directories of Continuing Education* which may be seen as signalling the adoption of a wider definition of its functions.

The entries in these directories were organised somewhat differently in each successive issue. However, they are of interest in the present context in that they appear to constitute a succession of attempts to bring a sense of order out of the confusion of diversity of organisations involved in the field. The structure of the directories appears to reflect the influence of writers such as Wayne Schroeder (1970). In the 1977 edition (National Council of Adult

Education, 1977), national, regional and local organisations were described in the following categories:

1. organisations engaged in facilitating, co-ordinating, administering and providing continuing education resources
2. educational organisations directly engaged in continuing education
3. other organisations which direct some of their energies towards continuing education
4. organisations whose continuing education programmes are directed to special groups and, as such, not generally open to the public.

A very different approach was that adopted by the Trade Union Education Task Force (see Law, M. (Chair), 1987: 63–64) which grouped programmes within three different though overlapping clusters: 'labour market', 'institutional' and 'community' education. (See Chapter 3 by Harré Hindmarsh for elaboration of these categories.)

Other approaches have also been taken which have sought to legitimate and establish the case for state-funding of non-prescriptive forms of education. Their focus, therefore, has been somewhat more limited than that which characterised the thinking of the NCAE and other organisations in the somewhat headier days of the 1970s. As part of the wider reform of the entire field of post-compulsory education in the latter part of the 1980s, the Minister of Education in 1989 appointed a Non-formal and Community Education Working Group to make recommendations on this aspect of the field. This group produced two different definitions of non-formal learning and community education. In its draft report it stated that:

> *Non-formal Learning* refers to the way in which learning takes place. It is essentially learner directed and controlled with a blurring of learner/facilitator/tutor roles, accepting that everyone has knowledge and skills to share. *Community education* refers to programmes and activities in which people participate to develop their potential and that of their communities. Normally, such activities are not part of a full-time education programme nor do they lead to recognised educational qualifications. They are in general not specifically employment directed or focused.
> (Non-formal and Community Education Working Group, 1 May 1989: 14)

In its final report however, both definitions were modified significantly and in the latter case broadened substantially. In this report it was stated that:

> *Non-formal learning* refers to a distinct learning process common in community organisations. It is essentially learner directed and controlled. Accepting that learners, tutors, facilitators, akonga, kaiwhakaako, kaiwhakarite, kai awhina all have knowledge and skills to share. This learning is purposeful, structured and takes place in venues and at times selected by the learners ... (and) ... *Community education* is a general term that describes a range of delivery mechanisms and styles. Community education is delivered through community organisations, institutions and sections within institutions, where people participate to develop their potential, that of their communities and to address issues of social concern. Such activities can sometimes be part of a full-time education programme and may lead to recognised educational qualifications. Community education involves such learning experiences as wananga, one to one tutoring, counselling and support, liaison, needs analysis, courses and workshops. Non-formal learning is an important component of community education. *Community development* is an enabling or empowering process that is inseparable from non-formal and community education.
>
> (Non-formal and Community Education Working Group, 7 July, 1989: 11)

Finally, in 1990 a further Non-formal and Community Education Task Force was appointed. This task force developed the following definitions among others:

> *Formal Learning* refers to any purposefully organised learning process which is substantially controlled by the institution in or through which it is delivered. *Non-formal Learning* refers to any purposefully organised learning process which is intended to serve an identifiable group with specific learning objectives and which is substantially controlled by the participants and/or local community. *Informal Learning* refers to learning processes which are ongoing, pervasive and incidental (for example: learning via the media). *Community Education* refers to any purposefully organised learning process, the primary intention of which is community development and action.
>
> (Non-formal and Community Education Task Force, May 1990: 12–13)

These then are some of the key definitions that were used by some of the groups established by the state to advise on policy as part of the major educational reform process that took place in the late-1980s. Elsewhere (Tobias, 1990, 1992 and 1993) I have examined various aspects of this process and the confusions and contradictions of interpretation and understanding of the field of adult and community education that were generated. All I wish to do here is to draw attention to two consequences of the reform process: First, the statutory National Council of Adult Education (NCAE) was disestablished; and second, the broad-based concept of continuing education which had been adopted by the state in the 1970s disappeared from official discourses. Moreover, the concept of adult education failed to reappear except in the name of the independent but minimally-funded National Resource Centre for Adult Education and Community Learning (NRC) which was supposed to take over those functions of the National Council of Adult Education which had not been allocated to the newly created committee – Community Learning Aotearoa/ New Zealand (CLANZ). The fragility of the central structures which took the place of the NCAE and which were intended to promote and support adult and community education was demonstrated in the early 1990s with the substantial funding cuts (see Tobias, August, 1993).

Conclusion

In this chapter I have examined from a critical and historical perspective a range of approaches that have been adopted not only to make sense of the myriad of activities which might count as part of the field of adult and community education, but also to legitimate specific forms and practices of adult and community learning. I have argued that adult and community education has been defined in a number of ways for a variety of purposes. These definitions and understandings have seldom been consensual: they have been and will continue to be used as weapons in ongoing political and ideological struggles. Even the official abandonment of concepts such as 'adult education' over a period of 20 years or more must be understood in the light of these struggles.

More or less explicit philosophical and political commitments have provided and will continue to provide the common ground for many adult and community educators to work together within the context of social and political movements and indeed within the context of adult and community education movements in their own right. With no common institutional ties, however, this common ground has never been very large or stable, as liberals, social reformers and radicals have contested understandings, interpretations and priorities.

Many others reject the search for common philosophical and political commitments and seek common ground in technical instrumentalism through the development of a standardised body of accredited knowledge and the systematised training of practitioners. Their focus is on means rather than ends – on methods and techniques of human resource development, technologies of adult learning, teaching and programme development and on the management of learning. With the rapid expansion and increasing diversification of post-compulsory education and training in recent years certain forms of psychological and 'andragogical' theory and research have been seen as providing the common ground for the increasing professionalisation of adult and community education (see, for example, Collins, 1991; Cunningham, 1989; Welton, 1987; Wilson, 1993).

What, then, do we as adult and community educators share in common? What, if anything, holds us together? Ultimately the answers that we give to these kinds of questions hinge on our positions in the political economy, our understandings of the political, social, cultural and economic forces which shape our lives and practices as adult and community educators, our political and moral principles and convictions and our implicit or explicit 'theories' of adult and community education.

There are those whose 'theories' of adult education are grounded in technical and practical rationality and a consensus model of the political economy. Such theories have considerable appeal to those who seek common ground on the basis of a series of universalistic assumptions about human nature together with the development of a 'technology' of adult learning which may be applied by 'professional' adult educators across a wide range of situations.

These and other similar 'theories' are unlikely to provide a basis for common reflection and action that will include those adult and community educators who are committed to adult and community education for social and political change. Radical adult and community educators are more likely to pursue their common understandings of the field by remaining rooted in the struggles over class, race and gender both here in Aotearoa/New Zealand and internationally, and by drawing on the work of other adult and community educators in the various radical and movement-based traditions.

Having painted a picture which highlights differences of interpretation and understanding, together with the difficulties involved in finding common ground among adult and community educators, perhaps I should conclude on a more positive note. My personal view is that provided there is broad acceptance that a key goal of adult and community educators should be to work towards greater equity and social justice and an explicit recognition and acceptance of differences, there is considerable value in adult and community educators of widely different persuasions and backgrounds coming together to engage in dialogue and undertaking strategic political action and advocacy. Without this, the opportunities and facilities for many adults to pursue their learning interests will be very much the poorer.

References

Adult and Community Education Association (Aotearoa/New Zealand) (1994), 'Adult and Community Education Policy/Resource Working Document', ACEA.
Australian Senate Standing Committee on Employment, Education and Training (1991), *Come in Cinderella: the Emergence of Adult and Community Education*, Canberra: Senate Publications Unit, Parliament of the Commonwealth of Australia.
Bunkle, P. (1980) 'The Origins of the Women's Movement in New Zealand: The Women's Christian Temperance Union 1885–1895', in Bunkle, P. and Hughes, B. (ed.), *Women in New Zealand Society*, Auckland: Allen and Unwin.
Carlson, R. (1980), 'The Foundations of Adult Education: Analyzing the Boyd-Apps Model', in Boyd, R.D., Apps, J.W. and Associates, *Redefining the Discipline of Adult Education*, San Francisco: Jossey-Bass, pp. 174–184.
Collins, M. (1991), *Adult Education as Vocation: A Critical Role for the Adult Educator*, London: Routledge.
Colquhoun, J. (July 1979), 'Education for Social Change', *Industrial Relations Review*, vol. 1, no. 2, pp. 21–25.
Coombs, P.H. et al. (1973), *New Paths to Learning for Rural Children and Youth*, New York: International Council for Educational Development.
Council for Cultural Co-operation (1971), *Permanent Education: Fundamentals for an Integrated Educational Policy*, Strasbourg: Council of Europe.
Courtney, S. (1989), 'Defining Adult and Continuing Education', in Merriam, S.B. and Cunningham, P.M. (eds), *Handbook of Adult and Continuing Education*, San Francisco: Jossey-Bass.
Courtney, S. (1992), *Why Adults Learn: Towards a Theory of Participation in Adult Education*, London: Routledge.
Cunningham, P.M. (1989), 'Making a More Significant Impact on Society', in Quigley, B.A. (ed.), *Fulfilling the Promise of Adult and Continuing Education*, New Directions for Continuing Education, No. 44, San Francisco: Jossey-Bass, pp. 33–46.
Dakin, J.C. (1979), *The Community Centre Story*, Wellington: National Council of Adult Education.
Dakin, J.C. (July–September, 1991), 'The Prevalence of Mutual Improvement

in Adult Education in New Zealand 1870–1915', *International Journal of Lifelong Education,* vol. 10, no. 3, pp. 243–254.

Educational Development Conference (1974), *Directions for Educational Development, Report of Advisory Council on Educational Planning,* Wellington: Government Printer.

Faure, E. *et al.* (1972), *Learning to Be,* Paris: UNESCO.

Floud, J. and Halsey, A.H. (1958), 'The Sociology of Education', *Current Sociology,* vol. 7, no. 3, pp. 165–193.

Gelpe, E. (1979), *Lifelong Education: Principles, Policies and Practices,* Manchester: Department of Adult and Higher Education, University of Manchester.

Hall, D.O.W. (1970), *New Zealand Adult Education,* London: Michael Joseph Ltd.

Harré Hindmarsh, J. (1992), 'Community and Continuing Education in 1992: Trends and Issues', *New Zealand Annual Review of Education,* no. 2, pp. 179–204.

Hopper, E. and Osborn, M. (1976), *Adult Students – Education, Selection and Social Control,* London: Frances Piester.

Kidd, J.R. and Titmus, C.J. (1989), 'Introduction', in Titmus, C.J. (ed.), *Lifelong Education for Adults: An International Handbook,* London: Pergamon Press.

Law, M. (Chair) (1987), *Trade Union Education: Directions for Change – Second Report of the Task Force on Trade Union Education,* Wellington.

Law, M. (1993), 'The Changing World of Worker Education: An Historical Perspective', *New Zealand Journal of Adult Learning,* vol. 21, no. 1, pp. 7–33.

Lawson, K.H (1975), *Philosophical Concepts and Values in Adult Education,* Nottingham: Department of Adult Education, University of Nottingham.

Liveright, A.A. and Haygood, N.(eds) (1969), *The Exeter Papers,* Boston: Center for the Study of the Liberal Education of Adults.

Lovett, T, Clarke, C. and Kilmurray, A. (1983), *Adult Education and Community Action,* London: Croom Helm.

Lovett, T. (ed.) (1988), *Radical Approaches to Adult Education,* London: Routledge.

National Council of Adult Education (1972), *Maori Adult Education – Report of a Working Party,* NCAE, Wellington.

National Council of Adult Education (1975, 1977, 1983), *New Zealand Directory of Lifelong Learning,* NCAE, Wellington.

New Zealand Government (1974), *Education Amendment Act,* Wellington: Government Printer.

Non-Formal and Community Education Working Group (1 May 1989), *Draft Report*, Wellington: Ministry of Education.

Non-Formal and Community Education Working Group (7 July 1989), *Report*, Wellington: Ministry of Education.

Non-Formal and Community Education Task Force (May 1990), *Report*, Wellington: Ministry of Education.

OECD (1973), *Recurrent Education: A Strategy for Lifelong Learning*, Paris: OECD/CERI.

Rubenson, K. (1989) 'The Sociology of Adult Education' in Cunningham, P. and Merriam, S. (eds), *Handbook of Adult and Continuing Education*, San Francisco: Jossey-Bass.

Schroeder, W.(1970), 'Adult Education Defined and Described', in Smith, R.M., Aker, G.F. and Kidd, J.R. (eds), *Handbook of Adult Education,* New York: Macmillan and Adult Education Association of the U.S.A.

Shuker, R. (1984), *Educating the Workers?* Palmerston North: Dunmore Press.

Simmonds, E.J. (Chair) (1972), *Lifelong Education*, Report of a Committee of the New Zealand National Commission for UNESCO, Wellington.

Sissons, L. and Law, M. (1982), 'Adaptation or Change? The Social Purposes of Continuing Education', *New Zealand Journal of Adult Learning,* vol. 14, no. 1, pp. 47–66.

Squires, G. (1993), 'Education for Adults', in Thorpe, M., Edwards, R. and Hanson, A. (eds), *Culture and Processes of Adult Learning*, London: Routledge and Open University Press.

Sutch, W.B. (1966), *The Quest for Security in New Zealand 1840–1966,* Wellington: Oxford University Press.

Thompson, A.B. (1945), *Adult Education in New Zealand*, Wellington: New Zealand Council for Educational Research.

Tobias, R. (1990), *Adult Education in Aotearoa/New Zealand: A Critical Analysis of Policy Changes, 1984–1990*, Christchurch: Centre for Continuing Education, University of Canterbury.

Tobias, R. (May 1992), 'Defining Non-formal and Community Education', *New Zealand Journal of Adult Learning,* vol. 20. no. 1, pp. 77–92.

Tobias, R. (1993), 'Summaries of key documents in the 1980s', in *Information Kit: Adult Education Policy Project*, New Zealand Association for Community and Continuing Education.

Tobias, R. (August, 1993), *The Politics of Meeting Learner Needs,* Paper presented at the Annual Conference of the New Zealand Association for Community and Continuing Education, Christchurch.

UNESCO (1972), *Third International Conference on Adult Education: Final Report*, Paris: UNESCO.

UNESCO (1976), *Recommendations on the Development of Adult Education*, Nairobi: UNESCO.

Walker R.J. (1980), 'Maori Adult Education', in Boshier, R. (ed.), *Towards a Learning Society – New Zealand Adult Education in Transition*, Learning Press, Vancouver.

Walker, R.J. (1982), 'Development from Below: Institutional Transformation in a Plural Society', in Shirley, I. (ed.), *Development Tracks*, Palmerston North: Dunmore Press.

Walker R.J. (1990), *Ka Whawhai Tonu Matou/Struggle Without End*, Auckland: Penguin.

Welton, M. (1987) 'Vivisecting the Nightingale: Reflections on Adult Education as an Object of Study', *Studies in the Education of Adults,* vol. 19, no. 1, pp. 46–68.

Welton, M. (1993), 'Social Revolutionary Learning: The New Social Movements as Learning Sites', *Adult Education Quarterly*, vol. 43, no. 3, pp. 152–164.

Williams, B.M. (1978), *Structures and Attitudes in New Zealand Adult Education, 1945–75,* Wellington: New Zealand Council For Educational Research.

Wilson, A.L (1993), 'The Common Concern: Controlling the Professionalization of Adult Education', *Adult Education Quarterly*, vol. 44, no. 1, pp. 1–16.

3

Mapping the Field in the 1990s

Jennie Harré Hindmarsh

Introduction

The 'field' of adult and community education is like a kaleidoscope – its patterns of activities are forever changing and endlessly diverse. The meanings of these patterns are described and interpreted differently by different peoples in different contexts. Therefore, mapping the field of adult and community education in the 1990s in Aotearoa/New Zealand is a daunting task. However, that is the objective of this chapter – to provide an outline of the sector as it is at this moment in the 1990s. This map is drawn from a Pakeha woman's perspective and concentrates on the Pakeha dimensions of the field, on the understanding that Maori contributors to this book will provide their own map of the field as it relates to them.

This chapter is in two parts. First, adult and community education is mapped in relation to the range of sites through which learning opportunities are provided – local community groups and voluntary organisations, national community organisations, schools, tertiary institutions and places of paid employment. At the same time, some comments are provided on the patterns of participation in and sources of funding for learning opportunities offered through these sites. Attention is then turned to outline the key policy and funding issues which currently preoccupy the fourth sector in Aotearoa/New Zealand.

Like all landscape maps, this one is embedded in the mapper's context. In this chapter the template I use and the features I choose to highlight, reflect my perspectives on the scene from where I stand in the field. The map presents my way of ordering and making sense of the diversity, within the boundaries and purposes set by this book's editors' definition of the field and their delineation of the chapters within which it is to be embedded. It is not presented as a definitive map representative of everyone's realities.

Diversity of Provision

Law (1987: 63-64) groups learning opportunities in the fourth sector of education into three categories – community education, institutional education and labour market education. Community education commonly refers to learning opportunities offered by community groups and voluntary organisations, including marae. It also includes some forms of community-oriented education offered by institutions. Institutional education includes 'second-chance' formal education undertaken by adults in schools and tertiary institutions, as well as non-certificated programmes offered by these institutions. Labour market education refers to professional or vocational education, including trade union education and programmes aimed at increasing the skills of unemployed persons, e.g. current Training Opportunities Programmes (TOP) offered by groups now able to register as private training establishments (PTE). This range of learning opportunities is most commonly provided by and through small local community groups, nationally linked community organisations, school community education, tertiary institutions (most universities and polytechnics and some colleges of education), private training establishments and paid employment settings. Thus, diversity is a key feature of the fourth sector – diversity of purpose, location, structures and processes of provision and of sources of funding and other resources.

Local Community Groups and Voluntary Organisations

The multitude of small local community groups offering learning opportunities is characterised by their responsiveness and relative autonomy. Often such groups do not regard themselves, first and foremost, as providers of community education – but rather as providers of health, welfare, justice, cultural or other forms of service. Whilst the funding for such programmes is typically drawn from diverse national, local and government sources, the bulk of the work of small local community organisations is educational. In addition, such groups apply for Vote Education funds made available through Community Learning Aotearoa/New Zealand (CLANZ) and school-based community education funding. CLANZ is a committee established to promote and foster non-formal and community learning as result of the *He Tangata* Report (Shallcrass, 1987). Initially it had both a role to provide policy advice to the Minister of Education as well as to distribute grants. In 1991 its policy advice role was removed and funding was cut by 61 per cent.

Small local community organisations provide opportunities to develop skills, attitudes and knowledge for personal and group development and in relation to social issues such as unemployment, cultural maintenance, intercultural understanding, social justice and parenting. Such learning occurs in a huge range of venues – on marae, in community halls and centres, in homes, women's centres, health centres, Pacific Islands and Multicultural Resource Centres, churches and so on. The flexibility, responsiveness and autonomy of local community groups and the lack of research information about them make it difficult to provide a detailed analysis of the part they play in educational opportunities. However, it is safe to propose that the activities of these groups are significant to us as individuals, families, whanau/hapu/iwi, communities of interest and nationally (Gunn, 1993; Harré Hindmarsh with Bell, Addison, Gunn and McGray, 1994: 298–299).

National Community Organisations

Currently the nationally linked community organisations, whose primary functions are to provide adult and community education learning opportunities, include the Adult Reading and Learning Assistance Association (ARLA), Parents Centres New Zealand Inc., the Rural Education Activities Programmes (REAP), the New Zealand Federation of Workers Education Associations (WEA), Te Ataarangi and Project/Network Waitangi. The Country Women's Co-ordinating Committee does not provide learning opportunities directly, but rather it encourages such provision through rural women's organisations such as the Country Women's Institutes and the Women's Division of Federated Farmers.

Until 1991 each of these national organisations, except Te Ataarangi and Project/Network Waitangi, had received some direct line Vote Education funding on a regular basis. They supplement this direct line Vote funding with funding from a range of other sources – including grants, sponsorships, fees and indirect Vote funding through schools, CLANZ and tertiary institutions. No Maori-based organisation has ever received such direct line funding. As a result of the 1991 Budget the WEAs' and Country Women's Co-ordinating Committee's Vote Education funding was withdrawn. In the period of 1985–1992 all community organisations have experienced a Vote Education budget cut, with ARLA the least affected (Harré Hindmarsh and Davies, 1993).

The ARLA Federation, established in 1982, is made up of approximately 73 literacy schemes which offer free adult basic education in small group and one-to-one tuition. ARLA is a Treaty of Waitangi-based organisation working towards allocating 50 per cent of its resources to Maori. As an expression of this commitment, in 1990 it established Te Whiri Kaupapa Ako, a Maori Development Committee, which fosters services for Maori, by Maori and in te reo as well as English (Harré Hindmarsh and Davies, 1993: 30–37; NZACCE, 1993). As learners, men have traditionally outnumbered women by two-to-one in ARLA schemes, excluding Te Whiri Kaupapa Ako. In recent years participation has moved closer to a 50:50 ratio (Benseman and Sutton, 1994: 6). In 1991 Maori accounted for 14 per cent of the learners and almost four per cent identified as 'Pacific Islander'. Two-thirds of learners are under 30 years and 23 per cent between 30 and 40 years. A high proportion are beneficiaries and in low socioeconomic occupations. ARLA schemes rely mainly on trained volunteers as tutors, although some schemes do obtain some funding to pay tutors and/or co-ordinators. The majority of tutors are female and on average, older than the learners and from higher socioeconomic groups. Maori and Pacific Islands people are less well represented amongst tutors than students, although their representation as tutors has increased in the last four years (Benseman and Sutton, 1994; Harré Hindmarsh and Davies, 1993: 35–36).

In 1993 there were 60 Parents Centres affiliated to Parents Centres New Zealand Inc. with a combined membership of 9,295. These centres provide courses and seminars especially in birth and parent education; facilitate support groups such as mothers' support groups, playgroups and Caesarean support groups; and teach others about their work. In 1991, almost 16,000 people participated in their courses. Birth education courses are about equally attended by men and women and women outnumber men in parenting courses. In 1991, some six per cent of participants in antenatal and antenatal refresher classes were Maori and less than one per cent from Pacific Islands groups. Most participants are in their 20s or 30s (Harré Hindmarsh and Davies, 1993: 46–50).

Thirteen REAPs were established between 1979 and 1982 – in the far North, Eastern Bay of Plenty, Central Plateau, Central King Country, Tairawhiti, Taihape-Ruapehu, Southern Hawke's Bay, Wairarapa, Marlborough, Buller, Westland, Central Otago and Southland. The purpose of REAPs is to provide services to the 'whole' rural community: to promote as well as to provide learning opportunities across the whole spectrum of life and all education sectors – from early childhood, through schooling to adulthood – which will enhance, promote and provide lifelong learning opportunities, community development and personal development (REAP Handbook, 1991: 2). Locally, variable emphasis is placed on these functions, but all REAPs include adult and community education development, brokerage, networking and some course provision in their activities. At present there is little hard data available regarding the profiles of those using and providing REAP adult and community education programmes, although it is commonly noted that the trend is to increase Maori participation and that participation by gender, age and socioeconomic status (SES) varies with the diversity of provision (Harré Hindmarsh and Davies, 1993: 54–55).

Te Ataarangi emerged from the work of the Maori Advisory Committee of the now disestablished National Council of Adult Education (NCAE), the late Ngoi Pewhairangi and Katerina Mataira in the 1970s and grew rapidly in the 1980s. Its primary goal is to promote and foster te reo Maori – especially through teaching that uses the rakau method, encouraging Maori language groups and research into Maori language learning and by training te reo tutors. This prime function has expanded to include the teaching of life skills, parenting, health, environmental issues, literacy, language research and adult learning. Its services are almost exclusively provided by volunteers. Whilst Te Ataarangi do not keep statistics, they estimate that women and men are both well represented amongst learners and that women outnumber men as tutors. Maori predominate as learners with an estimated 20 per cent being non-Maori. Tutors are mainly Maori. A wide range of age groups participate.

The Workers' Educational Assocation (WEA) was established in this country in 1915. Its historical roots lie in the labour movement of England (Shuker, 1984). Today the WEAs operate as a federation of 11 independent organisations offering a range of learning programmes to a wide range of people – short courses, public forums on economic, political and social issues, book discussion schemes, summer schools, interest groups and support for local adult education and community development groups. No data are available on current participation patterns nationally. However, Shuker (1984) provides a discussion of historical patterns and Coleman (1992) of course provision offered by the Canterbury WEA.

Project Waitangi was established by Pakeha as one of several initiatives to develop community education programmes regarding Te Tiriti o Waitangi, anti-racism and related issues. From 1985 to 1990 Vote Justice funding, amongst other sources, was used to fund the core group for this education project. Since then Network Waitangi has continued to co-ordinate and promote such education programmes without direct line funding.

Other national organisations provide adult and community education as part of their activities – for example, the Young Women's Christian Association (YWCA), Young Men's Christian Association (YMCA), Maori Women's Welfare League, New Zealand Marriage Guidance, Aotearoa/New Zealand Community Workers Association, Women's Studies Association, National Collective of Women's Refuges, Men for Non-Violence, and Combined Trade

Unions to name but a few – all funded from a wide range of sources and never through any Vote Education direct line funds (NZACCE, 1993).

School Community Education

At present, 254 schools provide Vote Education-funded community education programmes in this country. The Ministry of Education's new School Community Education Instructions which took effect in 1993 require that school programmes using government funding fall within the categories of adult basic education, training of volunteer community workers, parent education, programmes to meet a defined local community need or personal development. Schools are also to appoint community advisory committees and to make available to community groups at least 15 per cent of the school's Vote Education funding (Ministry of Education, 1992; Harré Hindmarsh, 1993: 193–195).

Information from an unrepresentative 24 per cent of schools providing community education, suggests that personal development programmes, especially those to develop work-related skills or skills for further education and training are most predominant in their programmes today, followed by adult basic education, then parent education, volunteer training and programmes to meet a defined local community need. Some schools are also beginning to offer self-funding and profit-making contract courses and NZQA-recognised programmes. From the same information it appears that Pakeha women predominate as learners, with an increasing number of Maori groups obtaining funding for their programmes through the allocation required to community groups. Pakeha women also predominate as tutors, organisers and community advisory group members (Harré Hindmarsh *et al.*, 1994: 308–309).

Tertiary Institutions

Adult and community education is provided through polytechnics, universities and colleges of education in the form of courses to encourage a return to formal learning, labour market education opportunities (often in-service) in conjunction with employers and professional associations and short courses designed to meet a range of community interests and needs. Since the implementation of 'Learning for Life' funding policy, some adult and community education programmes in tertiary institutions are partially funded through the Equivalent Full-Time Student system, the system used to allocate bulk Vote Education funds to tertiary institutions. An increasing percentage are developed on a full-cost-recovery basis through user-pays policies such as student fees or contracts.

Most tertiary institution based programmes are not assessed, nor do they carry credit value towards a formal qualification. However, there is a trend to offer more courses for credit through the 'community' or 'continuing education' sections of these institutions.

Again, detailed data on current patterns of participation in the fourth sector of tertiary institutions are not available. Information which is available suggests that in general women, especially Pakeha women, dominate as participants, organisers and tutors – slightly less so for universities than for polytechnics and colleges of education. However, in some institutions (e.g. Lincoln University) men outnumber women, reflecting that the majority of programmes meet the needs of traditionally male occupations. Whilst Maori participation and that of ethnic minority groups is increasing in some institutions, their participation is still underrepresented. Studies in the 1970s also indicated that it is more likely that those participating are from higher socioeconomic groups and have higher than average education qualifications (Boshier 1970, 1971; Waghorne, 1975). Up-to-date studies are required to map trends in the 1990s.

Employment-based Education

As in all other contexts, adult and community education in the context of paid employment is diverse. This sub-sector includes a decreasing trade union education sector. It also includes an increasing on- and off-the-job in-service professional and vocational development in a multitude of forms and settings (Todd *et al.*, 1994). Funding typically comes from private and government sector human resource development budgets, learners' pockets and sponsorship. There is an increasing emphasis on the development of workplace skills type programmes and the need for employees to become more highly qualified – what some have termed 'creeping credentialism' (Stalker, 1992). In 1992 the Trade Union Education Authority was disestablished and paid union education leave (introduced by a Labour government in 1986) was abolished by the new National government, in line with the 'new labour market' ushered in by the Employment Contracts Act in 1991 (Harré Hindmarsh, 1993: 198).

Policy Trends and Issues in the 1990s

Government policies relating to the provision of adult and community education between 1985 and 1993 have increasingly placed priority on labour market-related adult and community education. At the same time, government funding to the sector has decreased, especially that to community organisations. During this period the fourth sector, like all sectors in education, also has been preoccupied with struggles between the competing interests of those who promote social justice dimensions of adult and community education and those promoting such education for economic and vocational development. By the mid-1980s, liberal and radical forces promoting equity, the honouring of Te Tiriti o Waitangi and greater recognition of community education for social justice purposes were losing ground to increasing dominance of neo-liberal New Right proponents, within and outside the state. New Right proponents promote managerialism and technicist ideologies and education for vocational skills development. These forces have struggled to influence policies in recent years (Harré Hindmarsh, 1993; Harré Hindmarsh *et al.*, 1994; Tobias, 1991; 1993b). The struggles have revolved around the following key issues: legitimation and recognition of education offered by the fourth sector – especially through improved funding and accountability mechanisms and the recognition of learners' non-certificated learning, recognition of prior learning (RPL) in relation to qualifications; the implementation of tino rangatiratanga as promised in Te Tiriti o Waitangi; the implementation of equity principles; the lack of consultation by governments with the sector; lack of co-ordination within the sector; and the need for increased research and professional development opportunities for those developing programmes.

Recognition and Legitimation through Funding and Recognition of Prior Learning (RPL)

Trying to find adequate funding and resources is the constant preoccupation of those involved in the fourth sector in Aotearoa/New Zealand. It is also a difficult task to track and analyse the distribution of funding to this field. Such research has been hindered by a dearth of research funding and personnel and by the lack of consistent and regular collection of data by the Ministry of Education and organisations. In addition, as discussed above, adult and community education is like a kaleidoscope – what constitutes the field and ways to divide it up for the purposes of funding allocation, recording and analyses continually changes (Harré Hindmarsh and Davies, 1993: 18–19).

The *Learning for Life* policies (Minister of Education, 1989: 12) triggered a series of policy and associated funding changes in post-compulsory education in our country. Whilst these policy documents made statements such as,

> ... education at a university, training at a polytechnic, on-the-job training at the workplace and non-formal education at a rural location are of equal value in their personal, social and economic worth ...

and raised hopes for more legitimation, recognition and funding for the fourth sector, the reality has been that since 1990 there have been significant decreases in Vote Education funding for all quarters of the fourth sector and increased learner fees. This has occurred in a context where polytechnics and universities as a whole have received a relative increase in government funding (Harré Hindmarsh and Davies, 1993: 24). In addition, the Vote dollars have been redistributed within the sector to further advantage school and tertiary institution provision of adult and community education. For example, in the 1991–1992 budget non-EFTS community education Vote funding was cut by 78.7 per cent (Lenniston, 1991). Community organisations receiving government funding had been receiving 11.5 per cent of Vote Education dollars to the fourth sector. This allocation was reduced to 9.7 per cent of Vote funding to the sector in 1991. At the same time, within the sector the proportion of Vote Education funding increased to tertiary institutions, until then receiving approximately 50.5 per cent of Vote allocation to the sector, and to school providers, receiving approximately 38 per cent (Harré Hindmarsh, 1993: 25). Within institutions and schools more pressure is being applied for adult and community education to be self-funding, to return a profit and to be labour market and qualification oriented (Harré Hindmarsh, 1993; Harré Hindmarsh *et al.*, 1994).

In the 1990s there has been a trend in institutions and by the New Zealand Qualifications Authority to begin to develop recognition of prior learning policies and programmes – a mechanism to recognise learning achievements people have obtained through the fourth sector and informally, through life and work experience, in relation to more formal programmes and qualifications. On the one hand, this development can be interpreted as legitimation of the learning through the fourth sector. On the other, it can be interpreted as meaning that legitimation is conditional on the learning fitting and being approved by the qualifications framework or tertiary institutions (Harré Hindmarsh *et al.*, 1994: 296–297).

Tino Rangatiratanga and Equity

Around the mid-1980s, equity took over from equality of opportunity as a key concept and issue to be addressed in policy papers. For example, in the name of equity it was argued in a National Council of Adult Education paper in 1985 that priority be given to the educational interests of those who are economically and socially vulnerable, both as learners and contributors to learning (Harré Hindmarsh, 1992b; Tobias, 1993a). In the 1989 Report of the Learning for Life Working Party on Non-formal and Community Education, it was argued that those experiencing inequalities be given a disproportionate share of the resources to enable them to achieve more equitable outcomes.

Concepts of biculturalism first appeared in the 1986 Report of the Interim Advisory Group on Non-formal Education. The Learning for Life Working Party (1989) took this further and argued for principles of partnership, protection and participation as embodied in the Treaty of Waitangi as a key principle for policy development. In these contexts it was argued that Maori have special rights as tangata whenua under the Treaty of Waitangi as well as on the basis of equity for a larger share of the resources and for rangatiratanga (loosely translated as self-determination) in the development of programmes by Maori for Maori. Both rangatiratanga and equity remain key policy issues given the inequitable allocation of resources and participation and that there are still few Maori-controlled programmes.

Consultation and Co-ordination

Since 1989 there has been increasing concern in the fourth sector about the trend for public servants and the Minister to decrease consultation with the 'field' when developing policy. During the same period, the trend has been to require providers to consult more widely with their communities of interest when devising their policies and priorities, especially with Maori and with underrepresented groups (Harré Hindmarsh, 1993: 197–198).

Another issue has been the fragmentation of this diverse sector and the need to co-ordinate locally, in relation to the provision of learning opportunities and nationally, with respect to policy and provision. The New Zealand Association for Community and Continuing Education (NZACCE) (now known as Adult and Community Education Aotearoa/New Zealand) provides an important vehicle for such co-ordination. This is illustrated by the NZACCE initiative in 1991 to apply to the New Zealand National Commission for UNESCO for funding to develop a coherent policy statement from the sector, a focus of which was to benefit marginalised groups. This application was successful and in 1993–1994 a consultative process was developed in order to write this policy (NZACCE, 1993; Harré Hindmarsh *et al.*, 1994: 288–291). CLANZ, until its policy advice role was cut by the Minister in 1991, also had an important role to play as a voice for community-based providers direct to the Minister. The 'Learning for Life' policy suggested that local structures, i.e. community education networks, be developed to enhance co-ordination of the sector. However, this, along with many other recommendations which were accepted, has not been implemented.

Research and Professional Development

Within the fourth sector there is an increasing demand for research-based information to provide a basis for advocacy for the field and to document how such learning opportunities are used by adults. Both the National Resource Centre and NZACCE have actively promoted discussions of research priorities and encouraged those with access to research funds and skills to become more proactive (Benseman, 1992; Harré Hindmarsh, 1992a; NZACCE, 1993). In addition, the increasing pressure to 'be qualified' (partly fuelled by the new qualifications framework) and the instability of the labour market have increased both the demand for and availability of courses for the professional development of those working in this sector – in paid and unpaid capacities.

Conclusion

The 1990s have heralded a significant period of change for adult and community education in Aotearoa/New Zealand. At the same time, the key issues and struggles remain constant. Whether involved in learning through marae, local or national community groups or voluntary organisations, schools, tertiary institutions or private training establishments or in the context of the paid workplace adult educators continue to be preoccupied both with gaining greater recognition and resourcing for the contribution of the sector to the development of communities, the nation and individuals and with issues of inequities in provision and access. Like the kaleidoscope, the specifics of the patterns keep changing but the basic colours stay the same – the more things appear to change, the more they stay the same ...

References

Benseman, J. (1992), 'What Role for Research? A Few Thoughts on Possibilities', *Lifelong Learning in Aotearoa*, vol. 1, p. 5.

Benseman, J. and Sutton, A. (1994), *National Statistics of ARLA Member Schemes*, Wellington: ARLA.

Boshier, R. (Nov. 1970, Apr. 1971), 'The Participants: A Clientele Analysis of Three New Zealand Adult Education Institutions', *Australian Journal of Adult Education*, Part 1 (vol. X, no. 3) pp. 131–142; Part 2 (vol. XI, no. 1) pp. 20–44.

Coleman, B. (1992), 'Participation in Canterbury WEA', *New Zealand Journal of Adult Learning*, vol. 20, no. 1, pp. 21–30.

Gunn, C. (1993), 'Community Based Learning: Some Present Trends and Future Possibilities', *New Zealand Journal of Adult Learning*, vol. 21, no. 2, pp. 23–42.

Harré Hindmarsh, J. (1993), 'Community and Continuing Education in 1992: Trends and Issues', in Manson, H. (ed.), *New Zealand Annual Review of Education Te Arotake a Tau o Te Ao o Te Matauranga i Aotearoa*, Wellington: Te Tari Matauranga Whanui Faculty of Education, Victoria University of Wellington, pp. 179–204.

Harré Hindmarsh, J., Bell, A., Addison, A., Gunn, C. and McGray, D. (1994), 'Community and Continuing Education in 1993: Who is Deciding? Who is Benefiting?', in Manson, H. (ed.), *New Zealand Annual Review of Education Te Arotake a Tau o Te Ao o Te Matauranga i Aotearoa*, Wellington: Te Tari Matauranga Whanui Faculty of Education, Victoria University of Wellington, pp. 285–318.

Harré Hindmarsh, J. and Davies, L. (1993), *Vote Education Funding for Adult Education: Who Benefits? Phase One: Community Organisations*, Wellington: Ministry of Education.

Law, M. (1987), *Second Report of the Task Force on Trade Union Education*, Wellington: Department of Education.

Lenniston, M. (1991), *Adult Learner/Community Education Review: Funding Synopsis and Feasibility of Cost Effectiveness Survey*, Wellington: Ministry of Education.

Ministry of Education (1989), *Learning for Life: Two*, Wellington: Ministry of Education.

Ministry of Education (1992), REAP Handbook, Wellington: Ministry of Education.

NZACCE (1993), 'A Brief Outline of Adult and Community Education in New Zealand 1993', *Information Kit Policy Project*, Auckland: NZACCE.

REAP Handbook (1991), Wellington: Ministry of Education.

Shallcrass, J. (Chair) (1987), *He Tangata*, Wellington: Interim Advisory Group on Non-formal Education.

Shuker, R. (1984), *Educating the Workers? A History of the Workers' Educational Assocation in New Zealand*, Palmerston North: Dunmore Press.

Stalker, J. (1992), 'The Race for Credentials: A Challenge to the Field's Integrity', *Akina*, no. 40, pp. 21–25.

Tobias, R. (Nov. 1991), 'Lifelong Learning and the 1991 Budget: Summary', *Akina*, no. 36, pp. 25–29.

Tobias, R. (1993a), 'Summaries of Key Documents in the 1980s', in *Information Kit Policy Project*, Auckland: NZACCE.

Tobias, R. (Aug. 1993b), 'The Politics of Meeting Learner Needs', Draft paper presented to NZACCE Conference, Christchurch.

Todd, J. et al. (1994), *Funding Growth in Tertiary Education and Training: Report of the Ministerial Consultative Group*, Wellington: Ministry of Education.

Waghorne, M.(1975), *Adult Learning Activities in the City of Christchurch*, Christchurch: Department of Extension Studies.

WEA (1992), WEAs Making a Difference: publicity brochure, Wellington: Federation of WEAs.

Part 2

Te Kaupapa Akona no nga Iwi o Aotearoa

Introduction

Ko Kahuranaki te maunga
Ko Tukituki te awa
Ko Ngaati Kahungunuu te iwi
Ko Ngaati Te Whatuiaapiti te hapuu
Ko Keke Haunga te marae
Ko Renata te tangata.

E nga iwi o te motu, teenaa koutou.
E nga rangatira, teenaa koutou.
E nga kaumaatua, teenaa koutou.
E nga tangata katoa, teenaa koutou, teenaa koutou, teenaa koutou katoa.
He mihi nui teenei ki a koutou katoa.
Nau mai, haere mai ki te kaupapa mo teenei pukapuka.

We are very privileged to have people of iwi descent represented in this book. The toll on their already overly committed time and therefore very highly taxed energy levels is recognised with deep gratitude. E waahine toa, teenaa koutou. Kia ora koutou mo o mahi nui me o tautoko i te kaupapa nei.

It is seen by current writers and publishers that iwi representation is essential to the completeness of discussing an issue, either in written or verbal form. However, their representation must never be taken for granted. Why? The desire to be represented must come from the people themselves, not imposed upon them.

The kaupapa has to be seen as valuable in voicing and/or addressing their needs. After all there is a cost and that cost is time – time which could be spent on their mahi, rather than committing pen to paper for a book whose readership will be predominantly tauiwi.

In devising this section, it was important to show how for people of iwi descent, community education is located at the harakeke roots. Often it is not viewed as 'education' but rather as 'welfare' (Tapara and Weir, 1989). However, the necessity to recognise the very informal nature and basic situation of community learning amongst people of iwi descent, was a primary consideration. They are the people who are most consumed by their mahi and for whom, contributing to a book is very low on the list of priorities.

As you will see, the majority of the contributors in this section are from primary agencies and tertiary institutions. Again, it is the people who supposedly have access to more resources who are involved in these projects.

The contributors are all women. People may criticise this imbalance, but the reality is that women are primarily doing the mahi in this field and following the footsteps laid down by their tupuna, Papatuanuku.

Education is not just a process of learning, either in the pursuit of knowledge or for acquiring the skills to increase employment potential. It is also a means by which social norms and values are transmitted to succeeding generations. In this, competition and co-operation become dialectics argued by Maarie McCarthy, in the distinction between New Right philosophies and kaupapa Maori followed by whare wananga. The question of literacy is a political issue, for whose literacy are we referring to? This vexed question is discussed on a national level by Bronwyn Yates, te Apiha Kaiwhakahaere o te Motu of the Adult Reading and Learning Assistance Federation Aotearoa/New Zealand (ARLA). The macro issues are reflected to a degree at a micro level when Huhana Mete describes the translation of literacy to a local situation. The place of tauiwi in supporting nga take o nga iwi o Aotearoa cannot be denied, for their knowledge is invaluable in strategising the way through Pakeha organisational structures and this is reflected in the chapter by Christine Herzog.

There are glaring gaps in this section and these I acknowledge. There is a lack of discussion of the traditional view of learning as in whare wananga. Representation from Te Atarangi and other iwi and Maori based community learning facilities also needs to be addressed. However, for me, it is important to see this book as just the beginning. The first step has been made from which other steps will be taken, to explore the many different pathways which are essential elements to the overall picture of the fourth sector in Aotearoa/New Zealand.

No reira, kia kaha e nga kaiako raua ko nga kaimahi katoa i roto i teenei Ao Hurihuri. Ka aupakitia nga taonga oo taatou tuupuna. E nga rangatira, e nga kaumaatua, e nga tangata katoa, e nga mana, e nga reo, teenaa koutou, teenaa koutou, teenaa taatou katoa.

na Miriama R. Scott
Tamaki Makaurau

4

'He Hinaki Tukutuku: The Baited Trap'

Whare Wananga: Tensions and Contradictions in Relation to the State

Maarie McCarthy

Introduction

The movement by people to develop institutions outside the mainstream typifies what resistance theorists call the power of human agency, that is, the power of the people to negotiate and/or resist, whether it be in a passive or active form, as opposed to merely accepting and conforming to dominating forces (Giroux, 1983; Willis, 1977; Young, 1971).

The beginning of the 1980s is a significant period in Maori educational history, for it is the decade that marks the development of a number of Maori educational initiatives that reflect the power of Maori human agency. For instance, this is demonstrated in establishment by iwi and pan-tribal groups of contemporary forms of whare wananga, Kura Kaupapa Maori schooling and Te Kohanga Reo. The primary focus of this chapter is an examination of contemporary forms of whare wananga.

Remodelled from a traditional concept, these contemporary forms of higher education generally share in common a number of key features. First, they have usually been established in response to the traditionally poor participation rates of Maori within the higher educational arena (Davies and Nicholl, 1993). Second, they are institutions whose ideological base is either distinctly Maori or more specifically iwi-focused. Consequently, these organisations possess a strong Maori or iwi-specific ethos which permeates every facet of them. Last, and importantly, whare wananga generally sit within a wider iwi or pan-tribal plan as one of the many cogs which contribute to the attainment of the overarching goal of rangatiratanga.

Prior to the introduction of the Education Amendment Act 1990, all whare wananga were developed, nurtured and operated under the full authority of the Maori tribal or pan-tribal groups responsible for their establishment. Operating in this mode has become for whare wananga a rewarding but burdensome process. This can be attributed in the main to the increasing difficulties both iwi and pan-tribal groups have endured in locating sufficient funding. Further, this struggle has been intensified because these institutions have relied financially upon their own people, who in the main occupy the lower socioeconomic sector of this society. A major consequence of whare wananga being economically marginalised by the state is that their legitimate status is continually queried.

The opportunity for whare wananga to have their financial struggles relieved occurred when under the Education Amendment Act 1990 provisions were officially made to include these institutions under the auspices of the state and as such, qualify to be state funded. Given that Maori sit ideologically in opposition to the current New Right theory which informs government policy and practices, the state option becomes problematic at a number of levels. This chapter seeks to examine this by drawing from a comprehensive study of three whare wananga (McCarthy, 1994). Several of the key findings from this study are introduced here. First, a brief comparative analysis of New Right dogma and key Maori concepts will highlight ideological conflict between the two. Second, the various views raised by the whare wananga of the impact of a New Right state will be highlighted. This section specifically focuses on funding, curriculum and research.

Ideological Conflict

To ignore the interplay between educational institutions and the wider social, economic and political forums is to make the false assumption that educational institutions are islands. Within the New Zealand context since the 1984 elections there has been a shift in the relationship between the state, the economy and civil society. This change of relationship can be attributed to the adoption by the government of policies that are informed by New Right theory.

Individual versus Collective Perspectives

Central to New Right logic is the view of the possessive individual. It is claimed that the individual is a possessive being who egotistically pursues wealth, power and status (Lauder, 1991). Subsequently, collectivity of any form is believed to be comprised of a set of completely separate individuals whose actions seek to protect their own interests (Codd, 1990).

In contrast to this concept is the Maori notion of collectivism as found in whanau, hapu and iwi. In traditional Maori society the basic social unit was that of the whanau, the lowest level of a three-tiered sociopolitical system. The whanau operated as a self-sufficient domestic unit. Membership was generally through descent, consisting of approximately three to four generations. Each whanau was tied genealogically to the hapu and iwi which gave overall organisation to its way of life (Buck, 1982; Firth, 1972).

In contemporary New Zealand society whanau groups based on descent are still intact. However, what has also emerged is a form of whanau whose unifying element has extended beyond the boundaries of descent to include whanau groups who unite under the aegis of a common cause. This is illustrated in the formation of whanau groups attached to many Te Kohanga Reo, Kura Kaupapa Maori schooling and Whare Kura. Given the pan-tribal nature of these institutions, it is likely that the key unifying factor of the whanau becomes the common interest each member shares in the kaupapa of the institutions. This is not to say that whanau groups unite solely by descent or cause. It is also common to have groups comprised of people from both categories. More importantly, however, is the point that despite the changing face of the whanau system, what has remained unchanged is its core operational components, that is, the underlying philosophical base which determines the terms of operation has remained constant. For example, some of these components are notions of group responsibility, obligation, support, reciprocity, aroha and manaakitanga.

In order to highlight the collective nature of Maori society, the notion of group responsibility, as one of the core operational components of the whanau will be discussed in relation to mana.

Group Responsibility

The Maori view of who an individual is extends beyond the individual to include both horizontal and vertical lines of that person's genealogy. That is, the substance of who you are relates to your ancestors, from both the past and present worlds. You are a result of your genealogy. This view extends beyond the domain of the genetic pool to include the intangible sphere of mana.

> I te oroko putanga mai o te tamariki i roto i tona whaea, no reira ano
> i timata mai ai te mana, otira no mua iho no nga tupuna.

> In the very coming of the child into his [sic] mother, from there indeed, his [sic] mana began, but it comes from right back, from his [sic] ancestors.
>
> (Grey, 1845: 126)

Mahuika (1975: 73), discussing the deeds of Tuwhakairiora, also illustrates this point:

> It was Ruataupare, though, who was the acknowledged leader ... it wasn't until Tuwhakairiora proved himself as such an outstanding leader in war that he was able to usurp her authority. His mana was such that he was able to pass it on to his children and his line is still one of the most prestigious in Ngati Porou.

The conferring of mana not only operates according to the actions of those from the past, but also it is a concept that is active within the present. It is a concept that is all important to Maori. The actions of an individual, whether honourable or not, reflect always on the mana of that individual's whanau groups. In other words, the enhancement of an individual is viewed as the enhancement of a group, as is the debasement of an individual the debasement of those groups. At stake always is the mana of the individual and the wider whanau groups. It is this element that an individual as a member of the unit seeks to protect and enhance. As Pere states (1982: 33):

> Mana permeates the ethos of Maori life in subtle ways and is associated with aroha and utu (reciprocity). An individual or group will reciprocate anything they receive, whether good or bad, because of the challenge such an act represents to the concept of mana. While members of a whanau may quarrel and bicker amongst themselves, uniting together to keep their mana intact in dealing with people outside their kinship group is of paramount importance.

Pere (1982) elaborates on this issue asserting that the importance whanau members associate with upholding the mana of the group, is also illustrated in the way members make personal sacrifices, particularly by returning the hospitality that the group or individual whanau members may have received. Equally however, the same fervour applies if the whanau feels that they have been insulted or attacked by people outside the group. The appropriate steps will be taken to confront offenders and their kinship group or the implementation of more subtle forms of meting out a just and appropriate settlement will be adhered to.

In discussing the concept of mana, what the above illustrates is that Maori as individuals are embraced within the wider group. In this way, the individual's concerns are focused at a group level as opposed to a personal one.

Co-operation versus Competition

Coupled with the view of the collective is the co-operative way in which the collective operates. As the focus of the individual is on the wellbeing of the collective, each individual works together with others. This is, for example, illustrated in the co-operative mode in which a group works at a hui (Pere, 1991; Salmond, 1975).

Additionally, the notion of co-operation is also demonstrated in well-known proverbs:

> Nau te rourou, naku te rourou, ka ora te manuhiri,
> Nau te rakau, naku te rakau, ka mate te hoariri.

> Your food basket and my food basket will satisfy the guests,
> Your weapon and my weapon will dispose of the enemy.

> Ma te pango, ma te whero, ka oti te mahi.
> By black and by red the work is done.

> Ko koe ki tena, ko ahau ki tenei kiwai o te kete.
> You at that and I at this handle of the basket.

This is distinct from the New Right ideology which, because of its focus on the possessive individual, exalts competition.

In summary, New Right ideology neglects to take into account any culture that is not synonymous with the competitive forces of the marketplace in its analysis of society. Rather, what has resulted is a blanket policy that operates on the assumption that everyone is homogeneous. In particular, New Right ideologues argue that the individual is the central focus and second, that competition is the accepted and natural mode within which to operate.

The collective as a unit and co-operation the resulting mode of operation are fundamental principles of Maori society. Ideologically, then, it could be argued that New Right dogma sits in opposition to Maori philosophy. In this way the aims of the New Right, whether intentionally or not, seek to undermine and dismantle the cultural base from which being Maori is sourced.

This has implications for contemporary whare wananga which seek to actively contribute towards the advancement of a rangatiratanga status. For rangatiratanga is not only about being in control of the destiny of one's people, but also it is about advancing, retaining, relearning and accepting the knowledge, systems and institutions of Maori. For the further loss by Maori of their cultural base will essentially be the final blows of assimilation policies as first advanced in the 1800s.

The withdrawal by Maori from the mainstream in the development of whare wananga is viewed by Maori as a catalyst for the advancement of rangatiratanga. A concern that arises, however, is the ability and power of the state to require institutions to adapt and conform to the rules and regulations that are consistent with its own ideological base. The question that comes to the fore is, what are the consequences for whare wananga given the ideological conflict?

Whare Wananga and the State

He Hinaki Tukutuku: The Baited Trap

Royal's (1993) use of the analogy of the hinaki is an interesting one; it captures the essence of the relationship Maori share with the state. A hinaki tukutuku is a baited eel weir that is highly effective. Laid at the bottom of a river or creek, the eels swim into the hinaki to feed on the delicacies provided. More importantly, however, is the fact that once the eels enter the hinaki it is difficult for them to escape. The question that these eels fail to ask is 'Who will really be doing the eating?' Beyond their own bellies being satisfied, whose bellies will they eventually satisfy? Is it possible to escape?

Maori establishing whare wananga under the state, mirror the relationship of the eels and the hinaki. As it was openly acclaimed by the whare wananga studied, the need for economic sustenance is the primary reason for becoming formally affiliated with the state. One whare wananga in particular clearly stated that without state funding their institution would not have been established at all. Importantly, the point to be made is that the option of receiving fiscal support has been fundamental to the survival of the whare wananga.

Bowles and Gintis (1977) outline the relationship between the power of financial capital and the education arena. They argue that capital serves as a key determinant for the provision of skills, knowledge, values and attitudes of students from different classes, ethnicities and gender. The difficult position Maori face in the establishment of whare wananga supports the claim of Bowles and Gintis. Maori are disadvantaged in the development of higher educational institutions by the fact that as occupants of the lower economic stratum of society they do not have the capital to provide their communities with higher educational institutions. In this way whare wananga are in fact forced, in most instances, to pursue the state option.

As the case studies acknowledged and stressed, while being in receipt of state funding relieved their institutions of a considerable amount of stress and pressure, it was on the other hand an option that was conditional in nature. That is, there are guidelines, restrictions and criteria that are integral components of the state package.

The following section will discuss some of the issues, as highlighted by whare wananga, that impact on their institutions in ways that conflict with their underlying philosophical base.

Funding Issues

Prior to 1990 all newly established educational institutions which were positioned under the state were provided with substantial establishment grants. These grants primarily served as a means by which new institutions could quickly establish without being hindered by the initial extra costs incurred as a new institution. One such cost, for example, is the accreditation fee, resources, buildings and equipment.

The decision by the state in 1990 to abolish the establishment grant system has in effect constructed an unfair barricade for whare wananga. The inequities of this decision are significant at a number levels. First, the option for whare wananga to be included under the auspices of the state has only been an option since 1990. Given that the establishment grant policy was also changed in 1990, this essentially means that no whare wananga has ever had the luxury of receiving this grant. Therefore, this leaves Maori higher educational institutions placed in a position of disadvantage in comparison to the many mainstream institutions that were established prior to 1990.

Second, the logistics of not being in receipt of the establishment grant has meant that whare wananga seeking accreditation need to have sufficient monies to cover the New Zealand Qualifications Authority fee. As claimed by one whare wananga, it is a 'Catch 22' situation – the accreditation authority requires payment before accreditation status is granted; the state is reluctant to release any funding until accreditation is attained and the whare wananga has no money.

Such a system serves to perpetuate and preserve the inequalities that exist within society for Maori. Whare wananga are institutions that have in the main been developed by those who occupy the lower stratum of society. The likelihood of institutions of this nature having access to or possessing the necessary funds in order to be accredited are limited in comparison to institutions developed by more economically affluent groups. Paradoxically, the primary reason whare wananga seek state support is for financial security and yet, as the above example illustrates, it is this very factor that serves as a hindrance to counteract their existing financial instability.

Equivalent Full-Time Students (EFTS)

In a simplified form, funding allocations for tertiary institutions in New Zealand are distributed according to their EFTS. That is, funding is allocated according to the number of enrolments that a particular institution has captured. This method of monetary distribution is problematic for whare wananga on a number of counts. First, unlike bigger tertiary institutions, whare wananga in their initial stages do not have a large stable population base. Consequently, as smaller, newly established institutions, they are constantly left in a position of uncertainty. The uncertainty, in part, impacts upon their legitimacy.

Second, the EFTS system is a means of promoting competition amongst higher educational institutions, which is central to the New Right logic of creating more choice for the consumer. This raises a number of issues. In the first instance, there exists an assumption that through the accumulation of credentials one will gain employment. Consequently, the student population tend to monitor the labour market in order to pursue those qualifications which are seen to most likely enhance their employment opportunities. In this sense, whare wananga become caught in and affected by the forces of the free market. In order to maintain and increase their student population there is a need to cater for the demands of the students. Student choices, however, are fashioned by the marketplace, which is strongly informed by New Right dogma and subsequently shapes one's perception of what counts as knowledge. Whare wananga then, become entangled in the web which supports and perpetuates New Right ideology through the accommodation of courses that sustain the marketplace.

Third, given the insecure financial position new whare wananga operate from, as institutions that lack a strong, established student population base, it becomes absolutely essential to cater for the marketplace in order to survive within the EFTS system. This raises concern given cultural interests in the low-status category under New Right dogma. At the extreme, whare wananga could as a result of market forces be forced to offer courses that are no different from that in the mainstream.

The antithesis of the above situation lies in the tremendous demand from the Maori community for the development of courses in Maori language and culture. Maori people have, despite the dynamism of the New Right, not relinquished their desire to learn their language and culture. From Maori the demand for Maori language and cultural courses constitutes a form of resistance that stands in opposition to New Right theory. Additionally, from the New Right court, the accommodation of whare wananga as an institution for the maintenance, dissemination and advancement of Maori language and culture is surely a contradiction unto itself. As Giroux (1983: 285) asserts, methods of reproduction are never complete, they are always faced with elements of opposition:

> [R]esistance theory assigns an active role to human agency and experience ... there is recognition that different spheres or cultural sites ... are governed by complex ideological properties that often generate contradictions both within and among themselves.

The subtlety of state domination is illuminated in its skilfulness in fashioning, shaping and moulding institutions such as whare wananga under the guise that these organisations are relatively autonomous. In other words, the state would claim that whare wananga have acted under the jurisdiction of their own power in their choice of courses offered. However, a failure by these organisations to sustain student enrolments translates as a loss of state financial support. In this way, whare wananga unintentionally and paradoxically contribute to the maintenance and perpetuation of the dominant group's power and consequently their own subjugation.

Curriculum

> Control of consciousness is as much or more an area of political struggle as control of the forces of production.
> (Gramsci, 1971: 165)

The curriculum, as the above discussion has demonstrated, is inextricably linked to the funding process. This is captured in the above statement by Gramsci who points to bourgeois development being carried out not only through the forces of production, but also through dominance in the area of consciousness. The curriculum can be a major source of the individual's consciousness. While whare wananga have *relative autonomy* over curriculum development, the following discussion illuminates the mechanisms of the state which deliberately serve to fashion and shape curriculum. This is illustrated in the requirements of NZQA to have all institutions provide details of the specific learning outcomes of each course. Maori learning, as will be emphasised, cannot be readily reduced to statements of competency. In essence, Maori institutions are being required to fit into a Pakeha framework in order to be accredited.

Such requirements strongly reflect the New Right shift towards commodification. Smith (1993: 12) defines this notion as follows:

> Commodification emphasises the market value of things including such items as knowledge, values and rights. Within the New Right economic view everything is regarded as having a price and therefore considered to be goods which can be bought and sold within the open marketplace. Through subsidiary policies such as user pays, these commodified properties are potentially able to be fully commercially exploited.

Knowledge packaged into reductionist and neatly defined sets of this nature, makes it susceptible to market forces, as its value becomes increasingly associated with economics as opposed to culture. In this way, the value of culture becomes determined by its economic worth within the marketplace. Given the conflict that exists between the views of the New Right and Maori, the value appropriated to Maori culture and language will be low in status. This will have a direct bearing on whare wananga in terms of the amount of support they will receive from the state.

Further, commodification of knowledge supports the facilitation of principles such as individuality and competition as promoted in the free market (Smith, 1992). In this way, Maori knowledge, culture and language become packaged and compartmentalised as goods. This ironically supports concepts that occupy oppositional positions to that of their own culture.

Mead (1993) raises the point that the organisation of knowledge in this manner is inconsistent with Maori. Pere (1982) supports this claim, advancing first that Maori did not compartmentalise knowledge into reduced, finite sets nor was it organised in a multi-level structure. Rather, it is claimed, Maori have a more holistic view of knowledge. She further advances that knowledge was disseminated according to the judgement of the teacher and the collective. The emphasis was based on appropriate ways of knowing according to the collective's assessment of the responsibilities and experiences the recipient should encounter.

Commodification of knowledge, it can therefore be claimed, not only clashes with Maori culturally, but also serves to shift the power to define from Maori to Pakeha on two levels – first, the power to define what this knowledge might mean and second, the value of such knowledge.

The effects of Pakeha controlling the thought and reality of Maori has been well documented by Maori researchers (Jackson, 1992; Smith, G., 1989; Smith,

L., 1986; Walker, 1991). Control in this form has been a crucial means through which Pakeha have been able to maintain their dominance over Maori. As Linda Smith (1986: 4) asserts:

> ... Maori culture has been defined, evaluated and packaged to suit the reality of the Pakeha. From the Studies of Elsdon Best to *The Beginners Guide to the Marae* (1984), from the blatantly offensive cartoons of newspapers in the 1920s and 1930s, to the neatly defined and delineated concepts in Taha Maori curriculum plans, what being Maori should be, has been well prescribed.

Commodification as a mechanism of control over Maori knowledge should sound loudly the alarm bells of caution for Maori. For as Graham Smith (1993: 9) succinctly states, '... commodification equates with assimilation'.

Research

The ability of a whare wananga to engage in research is central to the successful running of these tertiary institutions. Research forms the basis for informed teaching. Furthermore, it functions as a means by which knowledge can be preserved and advanced. Under the Education Amendment Act 1990 whare wananga are charged with the expectation that they will contribute to:

> ... teaching and research that maintains, advances and disseminates knowledge and develops intellectual independence and assists the application of knowledge regarding ahuatanga Maori (Maori tradition) according to tikanga Maori (Maori custom).

Engaging in research is problematic for whare wananga. In order to contribute on any significant basis to the dearth of Maori research, there is a need for funding. Notwithstanding the efforts of some whare wananga to win research grants, research that primarily contributes to the advancement of Maori knowledge stands in opposition to what is seen as priority research needs by the dominant culture. As a consequence, being in a position to be able to engage in research becomes extremely difficult.

Shor (Shor and Freire, 1987: 9) maintains that knowledge is controlled by the dominant group through the power they have over funding. This notion, in Shor's terms, is referred to as the political hierarchy of knowledge. A hierarchy of knowledge is formed through substantial funding allocated to certain areas and forms of knowledge at the expense of others. Shor (Shor and Freire, 1987: 9) adds that capital power of the dominant culture is also utilised to manipulate less valued knowledge into conforming to the shape, form and criteria as they define it.

> ... the problem is the political hierarchy of knowledge. Some knowledge is given more value than other [knowledge]. Some knowledge can't get recognised for its value unless it takes a traditional shape in one discipline or another. For example ... pro-corporate research is handsomely funded, while peace studies or feminist research or socialist scholarship are marginalised.

Shor's analysis reflects the situation whare wananga confront within the curriculum field and also in their efforts to undertake research. The blocks these institutions face in winning research grants essentially means that they are unable to fulfil the state's expectation to engage in research. The question that becomes obvious for the future is whether or not the state will penalise whare wananga for not fulfilling this condition or whether funding will be made for Maori-determined research priorities?

Unfortunately for Maori, not being able to capture research funding serves to hinder the advancement and preservation of Maori knowledge. This is of significant importance to Maori people given that there are many older Maori people who are prepared to share their knowledge, skills and experiences with the appropriate people. A lack of resources to engage in the process of researching and recording such information could mean the loss of these treasures. In this respect, the state as the major contributor of funding has relative control over Maori research – whether it be the shape, form or content area the research project should adhere to, or just simply whether or not it will be funded.

Ko Tangaroa Ara Rau

Conclusions

The compromises whare wananga must make as a consequence of being under the auspices of the state should be critically viewed. While the veneer has taken on a new form, the underlying agenda of assimilation still exists for the state. The participation by whare wananga in a conditional funding arrangement places these institutions in a position of having to carefully strike a balance between compromising in order to be funded and jeopardising the integrity and impetus of the institution. As outlined, the state has a significant influence on the shape the institution takes. In this sense, whare wananga serve as agents of the Crown, since they assist in the maintenance and enhancement of the

Crown's domination. Paradoxically, as a result of this, they also contribute to their own oppression.

In terms of rangatiratanga, the relative autonomy whare wananga have is severely curbed. On the other hand, however, whare wananga to some extent do have their needs catered for in that they are provided with the funding in order to develop their own higher educational institutions. While such institutions are making tremendous inroads in terms of higher education for Maori, the prevailing question is 'For whose state are Maori being educated?' The power of the state to redefine whare wananga to suit state ideology impacts in a way that has the effect of dismantling the underlying philosophical base of Maoridom and which sets such an institution aside from the mainstream.

The ideal solution for whare wananga would be to operate from a self-generated economic base capable of supporting the institution and, at a wider level, the iwi or pan-tribal groups. However, realistically, for many Maori, operating under the state system will be the only option for a long while. Those who pursue the state option as a means of attaining absolute rangatiratanga, are likely to be disappointed. As the eels within the hinaki remind us, the hand that feeds is the hand that rules. Therefore, while Maori may dine on the delicacies provided, they need to ensure that they develop many ways and means of managing and negotiating the tensions that arise so that they can protect this sphere. A complacent eel will undoubtedly be consumed.

References

Bowles, S. and Gintis, H. (1977), *Schooling in Capitalist America*, New York: Basic Books.

Buck, P. (1982), *The Coming of the Maori*, Wellington: Maori Purposes Fund Board.

Codd, J. (1990), 'Policy Documents and the Official Discourse of the state', in Codd. J., Harker, R. and Nash, R. (eds), *Political Issues in New Zealand Education*, Palmerston North: Dunmore Press.

Davies, L. and Nicholl, K. (1993), *Te Maori I Roto I Nga Mahi Whakaakoranga: Maori in Education*, Wellington: Data Management and Analysis Section, Ministry of Education.

Firth, R. (1972), *Economics of the New Zealand Maori*, Wellington: Government Print.

Giroux, H. (1983), Theories of Reproduction and Resistance in the New Sociology of Education: A Critical Analysis, *Harvard Educational Review*, vol. 53, no. 3, August, pp. 257–293.

Gramsci, A. (1971), *Selections from Prison Notebooks*, New York: International Publishers.

Grey, G. (1845–1854), George Grey Collection of Maori Manuscripts, Auckland Public Library, Catalogue Number GNZMMSS 28.

Jackson, M. (1992), 'The Colonisation of Maori Philosophy', in Oddie, G and Perrett, R. (eds), *Justice, Ethics and New Zealand Society*, Auckland: Oxford University Press.

Lauder, H. (1991), 'Notes Towards a New Agenda', in *New Zealand Annual Review of Education: Te Arotake a Tau o te Ao o te Matauranga i Aotearoa*, Education Department, Victoria University, Wellington.

Mahuika, A. (1975), 'Leadership Inherited and Achieved', in King, M. (ed.), *Te Ao Hurihuri: The World Moves On*, Hicks Smith/Methuen, New Zealand.

Mead, H. (1993), Interview Material, 22 September, Wellington.

McCarthy, M. (1994), 'He Hinaki Tukutuku: Rangatiratanga, Whare Wananga and the state', MEd thesis, Victoria University.

Pere, R. (1982), 'Ako: Concepts and Learning in the Maori Tradition', Working Paper No. 17, Department of Sociology, Waikato University, New Zealand.

Pere, R. (1991), *Te Wheke: A Celebration of Infinite Wisdom*, Ao Ako Global Learning NZ Ltd, Gisborne.

Royal, T. (1993), Interview Material, 20 August, Wellington.

Salmond, A. (1975), *Hui: A Study of Maori Ceremonial Gathering*, Wellington: Heinemann Reed.

Shor, I. and Freire, P. (1987), 'A Pedagogy For Liberation: Dialogues on Transformation Education', New York: Bergin and Garvey.

Smith, G. (1989), *Kura Kaupapa Maori: Contesting and Reclaiming Education in Aotearoa*, Education Department, Auckland University.

Smith, G. (1992), 'Tane-Nui-A-Rangi's Legacy... Propping Up the Sky, Kaupapa Maori as Resistance and Intervention', Paper presented at NZARE/AARE Joint Conference, Deakin University, Australia.

Smith, G. (1993), 'For Sale: Indigenous Language, Knowledge and Culture', Paper presented at the World Indigenous Education Conference, Wollongong, Australia.

Smith, L. (1986), 'Seeing Through the Magic: Maori Strategies of Resistance', in *Delta*, Palmerston North: Massey University, vol. 37.

Walker, R. (1990), *Ka Whawhai Tonu Matou: Struggle Without End*, Auckland: Penguin.

Walker, R. (1991), 'Liberating Maori from Educational Subjection', Paper presented at Matawhanui Hui-a-tau, University of Canterbury, New Zealand.

Willis, P. (1977), *Learning to Labour*, Farnborough: Saxon House.

Young, M. (ed.) (1971), *Knowledge and Control: New Directions for the Sociology of Education*, London: Collier McMillan.

5

Striving for Tino Rangatiratanga

Bronwyn Yates

Whakarongo ake au, ki te tangi a te manu, i runga i te rangi e
E karanga mai ana, 'No hea to mana, e te iwi Maori e?'
E koe, e manu, i runga i te rangi, tenei whakarongo mai!
Ko te mana i ahau, no oku tupuna, no tua-whakarere!
Kei runga, kei raro e auahi ana ...

As educationalists, we may understand the relevance of information and education as a way of accessing opportunity, achievement and power. We may also be aware that in determining what is relevant to whom, without critical reflection as to who benefits by the form and scope of information and education provided, we can condone restrictions to access and the perpetuation of structural inequities that act to the detriment of particular sectors of society within Aotearoa.

I present this korero in the hope that as educationalists, those who read this article may begin or continue the challenge to examine their practices, beliefs and attitudes with the understanding that the history of colonisation in this country has had a major impact on the full and rightful participation of Maori within Aotearoa in every aspect of society's functions. The solution to addressing the negative impact of colonisation can only lie in re-establishment of Maori rights as tangata whenua, with rightful access to and implementation of tino rangatiratanga. A process for change lies within the construction of educational systems and curricula that give expression to critical knowledge, analysis and understanding within culturally affirmative practices and systems.

My korero as follows are my impressions at this time. It is said knowing that I am part of a network of Maori literacy workers and educationalists who work hard to create opportunities to inform and advance Maori aspirations. Especially to those with whom I have worked and networked, what I say is open for challenge.

Providing a Framework

If there is one thing I am growing to understand in my work in the development of Maori literacy provision, it is that it is full of contradictions and stresses. Determining the kaupapa, establishing provision, maintaining quality and responding to requests for support and advice based within the reality of *immediate* needs of te iwi Maori necessitates much patience and commitment. Some of us, the 'privileged few', sustain our work within an employed, supported environment. For most, no financial recompense is available for the massive outputs of energy, time, brain drain and incessant demands made, due in part to the lack of funding and Maori personnel within the field. This is one more facet of the multitude of social, economic and political circumstances that as Maori we face and work to change. We are part of a vast number of networks of Maori working hard on the field of literacy because this is where we have identified that we can make our contribution to addressing the impact of colonisation on te iwi Maori. This then becomes our contribution to working for the attainment of tino rangatiratanga. In clarifying what the unifying feature of our work is, it may be necessary to provide an explanation to those who are unfamiliar with the term *tino rangatiratanga*.

Tino Rangatiratanga, 13 May 1995, is a discussion paper presented to the Maori Congress Executive Meeting, Muru Raupatu Marae, with the purpose of providing a background framework for a discussion on tino rangatiratanga. Section 3 of 'Defining Tino Rangatiratanga', discusses the term as follows:

> 3.1 – Although there is general understanding and acceptance that tino rangatiratanga is about the constitutional rights expressed in the 1835 Declaration of Independence and guaranteed to Maori in Article 2 of the Treaty of Waitangi, the English translation of the words and perhaps more importantly their meaning in today's terms, does not have universal agreement.
>
> 3.2 – In the Orakei Report (1987) the Waitangi Tribunal discussed the meaning of tino rangatiratanga, concluding that it equated with

full authority and that to Maori it conveyed a meaning similar to mana.

3.3 – Among Maori there is some debate as to whether tino rangatiratanga is applicable only when referring to the position of tribes in respect of their properties and human resources or whether it is about Maori people generally, being able to assert control and management over their resources, their future development and their own policies.

3.4 – There is also a view that tino rangatiratanga means Maori control over all policies and resources in the country whether they are owned by Maori or not.

3.5 – A number of English words have been used to describe tino rangatiratanga: Maori sovereignty, Maori nationhood, Iwi nationhood, full chiefly authority, Maori autonomy, tribal autonomy and full power and control.

3.6 – The differing shades of meaning are significant, but what is particularly important to this discussion is the recurring theme of *self-determination.*

3.7 – As an equivalent to tino rangatiratanga, self-determination captures a sense of Maori ownership and active control over the future and avoids a semantic debate often of academic rather than practical interest. Moreover, self-determination is a term which can be applied at iwi and hapu levels as well as to all Maori people collectively.

It is at least with this understanding of the concepts embodied within the term tino rangatiratanga that we work within a wider context of Maori movements whose goal is to achieve a quality of life and power for ourselves that restores our cultural, social, political and economic wholeness by working with and re-establishing our methods, practices, processes and beliefs. We strive to regain Maori control and direction of issues and practices that impact on Maori, in a way that gives legitimate and rightful recognition of Maori values, beliefs and aspirations. We feel privileged by being part of a form of liberation that is fulfilling, all-consuming and exhausting. At the same time, we experience pain in knowing that this work has to be successful in uplifting te iwi Maori as a whole to be of any benefit at all.

In saying all of this, I acknowledge the constant challenge to examine the implications and benefits of the work of literacy development to te iwi Maori. The challenge has now manifested itself into re-establishing the priorities, buying out of the colonial ideal and facing the fact that by not pushing the issues, at times I have been unhelpful to those I strive to work with and for.

From this I am coming to fully comprehend the difficulties in trying to implement Maori literacy developments as part of the solution to the issues and needs faced by te iwi Maori without significant changes to structures, systems and values that operate within New Zealand society. To be effective, the development of Maori literacy must operate as a framework that provides expression to the concepts embodied within tino rangatiratanga. To truly address the literacy needs of te iwi Maori it is necessary to position these needs within the social, economic, cultural and political contexts of te iwi Maori. Maori literacy development cannot be seen separately from other aspects of life in Aotearoa, but rather as integral to the ability to participate and determine one's destiny within the activities and dynamics operating in today's society and that of the future. Maori literacy development is set within the multitude of layers and strands of factors external and internal to Maori dynamics. The factors exist to enhance and hinder Maori development.

Te iwi Maori struggle with the impact of being unconscionably and systematically denied our unique rights as tangata whenua of this land and through the 1835 Declaration of Independence, rightful sovereigns of Aotearoa. The joys of times like Christmas are countered by the realities faced by our people of sickness, death at too young an age, violence, imprisonment, injustice, obesity, smoking-related health problems, oppression – and hearty humour is required to cope with it all.

A Snapshot of an Indigenous Reality

The indigenous status of particular cultures throughout the world and their relative needs are not highlighted nor dealt with as a specific form of powerlessness and oppression by non-indigenous peoples. The situation of indigenous peoples becomes invisible within the overall social and economic statistics of the general population. This in turn disguises the impact of colonisation on indigenous peoples.

Common features of indigenous peoples throughout the world are that:

- they are the original inhabitants of their country
- they maintain a special relationship with the land – as being created from that land and as protector and caretaker of that land
- they are the unrecognised legitimate and [yet] dispossessed inheritors of the land
- they have experienced colonisation by imperialist powers, which has created an economic, political and social structure of which they are the subordinate group

- they struggle to regain and maintain sovereignty and self-determination of their people
- their access to decision-making, power-sharing and resource allocation is marginalised by the dominant group
- the preservation of their ethnic identity, language and culture has been the target of colonist policies of assimilation and/or annihilation
- they hold separate status to other ethnic groups/immigrants
- they experience problems of land dispossession, urbanisation, high infant mortality, economic marginalisation, environmental poisoning, high rates of imprisonment, alcohol and drug abuse, mental illness, physical abuse, unemployment and the impact of immigration
- their continued assertion for acknowledgement of status and needs are seen as separatist and unfair to other ethnic groups.

(Smith and Yates, 1993)

A Second Snapshot: Te Tiriti o Waitangi

The Treaty of Waitangi was signed in 1840 between two sovereign nations. It consists of two texts, one in Maori, the other in English. The two texts can be differentiated as: the Maori version – Te Tiriti o Waitangi; the English version – the Treaty of Waitangi. There are several inconsistencies between the two texts. According to international law, any ambiguity of meaning between texts will be resolved by the Contra Preferentum principle, i.e. that the indigenous language texts take precedence (Project Waitangi, no date). Without recognition of this, New Zealand Governments have exercised their power of definition by redefining the terms and clauses of the Treaty and in 1975, further exacerbated the issue with the introduction of the Doctrine of Balancing. This act provided equal weight to both versions and called for interpretation of the texts to be balanced alongside the interests of the majority as opposed to the interests of the minority. Effectively this allows for decisions to be made in favour of Pakeha, the majority population, and therefore against Maori.

> In the context of this country's past, present and future, sovereignty is about the Treaty of Waitangi. In its Maori version, the Treaty attempts to set forth a 'Common-wealth by Institution' describing the manner in which two races might live together in amity in these islands. It has never been honoured. In the hands of the colonists who took over the governance of New Zealand in 1852, the Treaty was transformed into a charter for 'Commonwealth by Acquisition'. In true Hobbesian style, they arrogated to themselves all the attributes of sovereignty: the ability to make laws and enforce them and the

power to declare treasonous any attempt to challenge the legitimacy of their regime.

(Trotter, 1995: 4a)

For Maori, marginalisation and domination have developed from the open rejection of the Treaty of Waitangi, illustrated by a series of laws and legal rulings made during the past 156 years. The National government's 'Fiscal Envelope' – which has precipitated the recent troubles – is just the latest attempt by the New Zealand state to legitimise the dispossession of the weaker by the stronger, a process which has characterised the relationship of Maori and Pakeha for the past 155 years (Trotter, 1995: 16–28b).

Other examples of this rejection are clearly evident in laws passed during the late 1800s and early 1900s: the Tohunga Suppression Act 1907 – the spiritual and educational role of the tohunga in the preservation of traditional Maori society was seen as a threat to amalgamation and was outlawed (Project Waitangi, no date); The Validation of the Invalid Land Sales Act 1894 – by this piece of legislation, unjust deals were able to be made, by a stroke of pen, valid and therefore legal. The effect was to legitimise past misdealings by Pakeha (Project Waitangi, no date); Judge Prendergast's ruling in 1877 in the case of *Wi Parata v Bishop of Wellington* was made on the basis that rights were exclusive to those deemed to be 'civilised'. Maori were not 'civilised' and therefore had no rights. Because Maori were not 'civilised' they could not therefore be a sovereign nation and as such 'the Treaty was a simple nullity'. 'Prendergast's judgement in 1877 ... more or less determined official and non-official responses to the Treaty' (Hackshaw, cited in Durie, 1995: 31–47). More recent examples include the restriction to powers of recommendation only of the Waitangi Tribunal and the 1995 Government Fiscal Cap on Land Claims.

Dr Pita Sharples (1995) in an address for the Foundation of Peace Studies outlines the effects of the Tohunga Suppression Act and 1867 Native Schools Act as two of the major tools of colonialism that served to negate Maori knowledge, beliefs and values and to drive them underground or to be lost. Moreover, these Acts also served to promote the view, which is still widely held today, that Maori culture and Maori language have no measurable value for New Zealand society. It is a position that he states te iwi Maori do not support and he goes further to challenge all citizens of Aotearoa to accept this fact. By not doing so, Sharples believes 'we all become accomplices to the [oppressive] acts of parliament, by not accepting some responsibility to repair the cultural destruction meted out to the Maori people by our forebears'.

And so, irrespective of such continued government resistance and manipulation of the rights attributed to the Crown under Te Tiriti o Waitangi, Maori have consistently sought ratification of the Treaty, which has been documented and more recently sensationalised by the media with little serious attempt at balanced reporting. The Decade of Maori Development of 1984–1994 (Durie, 1995) highlighted the continued Maori struggle for recognition of the Treaty and with the emergence of the theme of biculturalism during this period, the flow-on effect has resulted in motivating certain sectors of New Zealand to question and review the values, structures and practices within their organisations. An intention of review has been to 'sensitise' systems and operations to cater more appropriately to Maori requirements. Concepts of power-sharing and cultural inclusivity aim to bring about change, but often are limited in effectiveness due to the lack of resources targeted to achieve change and commitment by executive management to holistically implement such a shift. These concepts are then viewed as superficial, within a newly disguised form of assimilation and ethnocentricity. Moana Jackson describes a similar situation within the context of constitutional reform. 'The term constitutional reform implies that things are okay as they are, they just need tutuing [sic] around with. What is really needed is constitutional change' (Davies, 1993: 4).

A Pedagogical Imperative

According to Bourdieu, the cultural capital of some social groups leads to adverse educational outcomes of other groups (Corson, 1992). This can be seen to be the case in Aotearoa where the state educational system has operated at an ethnocentric, monocultural level, by introducing policies of assimilation.

'In undertaking the colonisation of New Zealand, Her Majesty's Government has recognised the duty of endeavouring by all practicable means to avert the like disasters from the Native people of these Islands, which object may be best attained by assimilating as speedily as possible the habits and usages of the European population' (Tamahori, 1991).

As part of the colonising and assimilation processes, Maori culture and language have been treated as if deficient in all aspects. The teachings of Maori by the missionaries required the rejection of Maori spirituality in favour of Christian beliefs and practices. The inherent belief of the superiority of Christian values entailed the inferiority of Maori cultural values (Jenkins, 1991). The denial of the validity of Maori cultural values has led to the disempowerment of the Maori population by removing the structures and mechanisms that influence and affirm the practices of te iwi Maori. An example can be seen in the introduction of the Native Schools Act 1867, when despite the apparent inappropriateness of English as the language of education for Maori, English was proclaimed as the sole medium of instruction in Native Schools (Jenkins, 1991). The subsequent difficulties experienced by Maori in acquiring either spoken or written English skills contrasted with the ease with which Maori had become literate in te reo Maori, prior to the introduction of this Act.

The effects of this Act continue to disenfranchise Maori from both traditional Maori learning and state educational opportunities. 'Maori school leavers who left school in 1991 with no formal qualifications was 36.9 per cent in comparison with 11.9 per cent for non-Maori school leavers. Although Maori students are more likely than ever to leave school with a formal qualification, they remain three times as likely as their non-Maori peers to leave school with no formal qualifications' (Davies and Nicholl, 1993: 47). The impact that such policies and attitudes have had on Maori culture has created a situation whereby the future of te reo Maori continues to face a serious threat, and the gap between Maori and Pakeha educational achievement within the traditional state system continues to widen.

Ngata, often cited for his support of the English language as the medium of teaching, is not often enough acknowledged for his conclusion that there was nothing worse than a person with the physical identity of a Maori but who could not speak his [sic] own language (Walker, date unknown).

Dr Pita Sharples discussed the need to redress the impact of this Act:

> In the knowledge that the Maori people want the Maori language to live on in this country (the only country to which it belongs) – and in the knowledge of world-wide linguistic evidence that without extreme promotion the Maori language will soon die as a spoken language, then you and I both must accept the responsibility for those post suppressive Acts and the impending death of the Maori language and its loss to the world unless:
>
> - we acknowledge the Maori language loss to most tribal areas caused by the **ban** on spoken Maori
> - we acknowledge that **ban** as the most single most contributing factor to a prevailing attitude that Maori language is not important
> - we acknowledge that the contemporary New Zealand society, which we have constructed, currently provides few avenues or opportunities for encouraging Maori language to be spoken as a living language

- we become proactive in establishing conditions suitable to the growth and spread of Maori language in our society.

(Sharples, 1995)

Sharples further states that the past destruction of spoken Maori cannot be healed without positive, proactive initiatives of support by both the government of the day, the Maori people and, equally important, New Zealand society as whole.

Proactive initiatives of support require dramatic changes to current government educational policy and implementation. Maori concepts, delivery and practices of learning differ greatly to the models prevalent within New Zealand schools, and Maori have continued to highlight the racial inequality and cultural inappropriateness of the traditional state education system. Maori regard learning as a lifelong process, holistic in nature and thereby encompassing the spiritual, physical and intellectual dimensions and relationships that exist within the framework of people as part of the environment. Learning is an integral part of life, all areas of growth having equal value and requiring equal emphasis. The education of the individual is seen to be a matter of relevance that includes the whanau and hapu. Participation and achievement relate not only to the individual but to the group as a whole.

A Context for Development

Much of the literature I have read confirms the need for culturally affirmative provision, content and delivery of education. Smith (1990) states that it is critical that the validity and legitimacy of Maori knowledge is acknowledged. Maori educational initiatives aim to regain and ensure the survival and development of the cultural values and practices suppressed by assimilationist educational policies.

To ensure education is meaningful and effective for tangata whenua, Maori are adamant that there must be greater participation of Maori in all structures and processes of Maori education (Hirsh, 1990). Improved participation and attainment can be best achieved with hapu and whanau involvement, and direction that focuses on an alternative delivery system that is controlled by Maori people. With kaupapa Maori-based educational agencies, there remains a continued need to maintain design and control of both the organisational operations and provision of curricula-based activities. Within educational agencies, including those that are kaupapa Maori-based, it is vital that effective support is given to increase Maori participation and decision-making at all levels to redress the monocultural nature of the educational administration and provision.

Freire (1972) states:

> The pedagogy of the oppressed ... is the pedagogy of men [sic] engaged in the fight for their own liberation. And those who recognise, or begin to recognise, themselves as oppressed must be among the developers of this pedagogy. No pedagogy which is truly liberating can remain distant from the oppressed by treating them as unfortunates and by presenting for their emulation models from among the oppressors. The oppressed must be their own example in the struggle for their redemption.

In this, Freire identifies that it is the role of the oppressed to free themselves and in doing so will free the oppressors.

Meaningful education requires that skills and content are relevant to and determined by Maori learners, integrated across several learning areas to bring together a broad range of knowledge and perspectives. Meaningful education enhances the learners' awareness of the influences of structures and institutions of their social environments, thus creating critical analyses of factors that impact on their lives. In doing so, learning considers the power and potential of literacy [and therefore education] as both a tool of domination and resistance (Lankshear and Lawler, 1987).

Jenkins (1991) states: 'It is important to re-establish Maori language literacy in order that Maori recreate and achieve the cultural basis of their political, social and cultural existence. It is imperative that the new learning of Maori language literacy be directed by a critical approach to learning'.

An important consideration not to be left aside in the Maori struggle for critical or 'proper' literacy, is the need to struggle for knowledge and understanding of the language and practices of the coloniser.

The strength of one's literacy is then left open to the challenge of knowing how to maintain one's cultural roots within the dual relationship and working out a strategy of resistance to any attempts by one of the groups to undermine or corrupt the other. Within the struggle of working out political and social relationships, it is crucial to Maori power and control that their critical literacy is at a level that will cope with the pressure of any challenge from colonising forces (Jenkins, 1991).

There are many definitions of literacy, distinguishable by the extent to which they incorporate the global characteristics that literacy entails. Of those developed overseas, I believe the definition most similar to that espoused by Maori pedagogies would be the Freirean model which argues that, to become more fully human, is to become ever more critically aware of one's world and be in creative control of it (Lankshear and Lawler, 1987). At the end of the day the priority, and ultimately the focus, that literacy takes rests with those who wield the power to define it. The form of literacy and therefore the understanding of what literacy is, are crucial to the ways in which literacy skills are transmitted and acquired.

Freire (1972) works from the premise that all languages are valid, systematic, rule-governed systems with some aspects of language use and development specific to particular cultures. At the point where different cultures interact, there is a need to understand culturally different practices and behaviour. This would include both verbal and non-verbal behaviour. Freire talks about language as being the terrain of domination and the field of possibility (Jenkins, 1991: 89). The notion of one language and its practices being superior over another, Freire continues, is a social phenomenon. Gramsci asserts that language is both hegemonic and counter-hegemonic – instrumental in both silencing the voices of the oppressed and in legitimating oppressive social relations (cited in Jenkins, 1991: 89). Given that literacy is a tool of language, it follows that language and literacy have the potential to oppress and/or liberate both individuals and groups of people.

In considering literacy, it is necessary to establish what role oracy has in any of the discussions. For te iwi Maori, the values of the colonisers have defined the form that literacy has taken in ensuing years. The perception of the colonisers has been that tangata whenua were without valid methods for recording and transmitting information. The subsequent emphasis placed on the written word has contributed to a lack of recognition of oracy and other cultural forms of literacy as legitimate forms of communication.

The provision of literacies for Maori by Maori, needs to ensure that the use of models of behaviour, content and delivery actively affirm and promote Maori concepts of knowledge and learning. For Maori this requires literacy provision in te reo Maori and English that reinforces Maori learning and enables critical participation within the worlds of Maori and Pakeha.

The ARLA Federation – A First Step

The Adult Reading and Learning Assistance Federation (ARLA) was established in 1982 and comprises a national body with approximately 100 literacy providers associated with the organisation (see Hill, 1990). Its mission statement is to develop accessible quality literacy provision that ensures people of Aotearoa are critically literate.

The Federation first began to look at Te Tiriti o Waitangi following the 1988 ARLA Conference Biennial General Meeting held in Palmerston North. Due to a number of events at the conference and its occurrence at a time when some Pakeha were becoming more cognisant of continued Maori struggle for recognition of the Treaty, a remit was passed that called ARLA to address issues of biculturalism and multiculturalism. In looking to see how this remit would be fulfilled, the National Committee attended a Project Waitangi course and from there, the work began to establish the Treaty as fundamental to the process of development for the organisation (Smith, 1990).

The Federation has made considerable effort in trying to fulfil its obligation under Te Tiriti o Waitangi and since 1989 has looked at how Maori participation within the organisation could be increased. The first step was co-opting Maori members to participate at the National Committee level and then at the staff level. With Maori participation in national projects and development, changes have been made. Constitutionally, the ARLA Federation includes within its objects a commitment to honour Te Tiriti o Waitangi and requires that the National Committee and Executive Officers be equally represented by Maori and tauiwi. The Maori Development Committee, Te Whiri Kaupapa Ako, has the responsibility of maintaining tino rangatiratanga o te iwi Maori throughout the organisation. Through its voting practices, a Maori roll and tauiwi roll aggregate to become one vote each, regardless of the number of constituents on each roll. The policy document incorporates principles that promote Te Tiriti o Waitangi throughout its philosophy and practices and by the expression of tino rangatiratanga through the development of Maori literacy initiatives by Maori for Maori.

In 1989, the ARLA Federation agreed to move towards sharing the government grants to the national organisations equally between the Maori and tauiwi partners for Maori and tauiwi literary development and co-ordination. The funding does not include those grants allocated to local schemes through other government funding sources and therefore, to date, Maori literacy provision at the local level remains largely unfunded and reliant on local funding sources. Despite the lack of funding at the local level, the number of Maori students has increased significantly over the past five years, particularly from 16.9 per cent of all students in 1993 to 25.96 per cent in 1994 (Sutton and Benseman, 1995) and opportunity for literacy learning within a whanau context has developed, increasing opportunity for learners to have a choice of provision. Within the Federation, avenues now exist where working with and valuing Maori tikanga and practices are part of the everyday working and learning environments.

Day after day for six years has been hard work for all those involved, Maori and tauiwi, grappling with concepts, frustrations, anxiety and anger. Set against a history of systematic loss of language, cultural practices and rights as tangata whenua, the achievements to date and the progress made can only be seen as a beginning and require review at the implementation level.

A Time for Critical Reflection

In terms of working within a treaty partnership, I believe that the one underpinning and ultimately undermining factor is the difference of perspectives. *Underpinning* because that is the reality of a partnership between two cultures; *undermining* because ultimately in a non-equitable, unequal relationship where one partner is working to reclaim tino rangatiratanga and where the other partner is working to understand and implement the actions required to share resources and more importantly, power at the crucial decision-making levels, the perspective of the second partner is seen to be the traditional norm in its setting and is therefore validated. In any point of contention between the two partners, anything different from that perspective has to be justified and its validity endorsed. Immediately this sets up an unequal power relationship. To further complicate matters, there is not a universal 'right' answer and given any particular context, set of circumstances, personalities, constraints, and so on, one solution that seems appropriate at the time, may be inappropriate in another.

Partnership based on the Maori text of Te Tiriti o Waitangi within an organisation which already exists with structures and systems operated by Pakeha, automatically creates an unbalanced relationship between partners – that of one partner (Pakeha) having profile, experience and knowledge on one's own turf, as opposed to the other (Maori) coming into that existing framework to be part of creating a partnership relationship. Acceptance that things will change may be understood from the outset but once again in hindsight, I wonder whether at the outset of such a brave move, it may have been better to recreate and restructure an organisation in the initial stages to enable participation that is equal from the beginning.

I have come to the conclusion that separate development is a natural eventual outcome of any treaty-based relationship, although it is often seen as an outcome to accommodate the work of Maori. What is not understood is that prior to Maori involvement within an organisation, separate development is continually reflected in the traditional Pakeha methods of operation. This is evident from figures that show Maori are underrepresented in areas of educational achievement, health statistics, and overall equitable social representation. The figures show that systems work best for one (Pakeha) group of people to the detriment of the other (Maori). An example can be seen in the 1995 statistics that the government cites as demonstrating a recovery of the economic situation of the country. There is evidence that this recovery tends to be true for only certain sectors of the New Zealand population. The recent decrease to six per cent overall of unemployed workers within this country is not a universal reality for all ethnic groups. Proportionately, 16 per cent of Maori and Pacific Island groups are registered unemployed in comparison to Pakeha at four per cent.

Despite this evident continuation of differential treatment and receipt of government economic benefits to Maori, Maori are criticised for being overt and transparent in the outright claim that first and foremost our concern is to support and service the needs of te iwi Maori. We are often denied funding because we are overt in who our target client group is, and because this focus is deemed to be racist, separatist and of minimal benefit to the overall population, we are forced to consider watering down the kaupapa of our various areas of work to create a more favourable and flavourable picture to those who hold the purse strings. The work and funding that is essential for the basic requirements of Maori survival is thus compromised. Maori applications for funds are judged against those of groups who say they are there for everyone and who have an open-door policy. The reality of these apparently fair, non-racist policies is that representation of workers, client groups and decision-makers is dominated by Pakeha. Thus, while the intention may be to have an open-door policy, the reality shows that either the door is only open to certain sectors of the community or that the door is only visible to certain sectors of the community. Either way, the difference is that one group (Maori) is overt and acknowledges its focus, the other (Pakeha) proclaims to do what it is not culturally capable of doing. Maori continue to struggle to have their position understood and to justify the necessity for kaupapa Maori educational initiatives.

The situation is compounded by the meaningless amount of money granted to adult literacy in the overall allocation of funds to the educational sector – 0.013 per cent of the 1991 Vote Education was allocated to the national body of the ARLA Federation (Harré Hindmarsh and Davies, 1993). The reality is that the literacy field as a whole is vastly under-resourced and will continue to be so while there is a general lack of recognition of the literacy issues as they exist within Aotearoa/New Zealand. For Maori more specific attention to the arena of Maori literacy development is needed; the educational statistics indicate that the need for Maori literacy initiatives is proportionally greater and is by the under-resourcing evident in all Maori educational activities. The Maori educational movement that is thus trying to establish itself within a field that lacks adequate funding to meet even the minimum need, despite Lockwood Smith's praise of Maori educational initiatives as recorded in the Educational Gazette (early 1995). A key example is the slashing of access to funds available to Te Kohanga Reo whanau. A Ministry of Education report documented the success of movements such as Te Kohanga Reo to open access to education for those whose needs were not being catered for by mainstream initiatives (Davies, 1993.) The slashing of access to childcare subsidies for parents who are not in employment or training meant that the door was closed to the same group of children who had previously not accessed childcare in its mainstream set-up. The changes to criteria made this group no longer eligible to apply.

Creating change within a Pakeha context requires Maori to identify and justify the change without the mutual identification and justification of the validity of what already exists. The assumption appears to be that control must be rendered as a partnership, or from a Pakeha base, assuming that control from a Maori base cannot be as beneficial to all participants. A fear lurks that Maori sovereignty means no rights of participation for non-Maori and highlights the lack of trust of transference of power to tangata whenua.

In 1995 my belief is that 'treaty partnership' will only be a farcical phrase unless the reality of the partnership is based on a relationship of Maori sovereignty. Awatere (1984) explains Maori sovereignty as our ability to determine our own destiny and to do so from the basis of control of our land, our fisheries, our tikanga, our language, our people. It changes the paradigm from which biculturalism and partnership are developed.

The development of Maori literacy cannot be modelled on traditional tauiwi systems that continue to perpetuate tauiwi structures and practices. As it is, the development of Maori literacy provision has to first respect the mana of iwi a rohe and within their established framework, the needs of Taurahere and the requirements of legislation. It needs to grapple with the issues surrounding mana whenua and accountability to tangata whenua, whilst being available for pan-tribal Maori organisations and authorities.

With its limitations being played out within state control, the development of partnership with Te Tiriti o Waitangi as the framework remains difficult. Real power will not be passed over. Meanwhile there is a need for tangata whenua to protect and conserve resources for the needs of tangata whenua. In the end Maori must demand the most from tauiwi and settle for nothing less.

The pain and struggle towards Maori inclusion and further on towards tino rangatiratanga mo te iwi Maori have been shared by those Pakeha who have dared to effect change and share power and resources. They remain a limited but significant few, who ride above the discomfort and intimidation of reaction to raising Te Tiriti o Waitangi as an issue of relevance in training, practice and power. Paulo Freire says that to remain neutral is to side with the oppressor.

Ta Hemi Henare, in his speech to Labour Members of Parliament, 9 September 1988, said:

> The principles of the Treaty of Waitangi are many and I suggest the real way to deal with them is to stand by them when they are unpopular as well as when they are popular, knowing that their truth will one day manifest itself.

The work of Maori literacy is driven by a relentless energy and vision. Considerable commitment and sacrifice are evident in the non-paid work of the many tangata whenua who are involved in the work of whanau literacy. Kua tae mai te wa.

References

Awatere, D. (1984), 'The Impact of Maori Sovereignty', *Broadsheet*, 124.

Corson, D.J. (1992) 'Minority Cultural Values and Discourse Norms in Majority Culture Classrooms', *The Canadian Modern Language Review*, vol. 48, no. 3.

Davies, J. (1993) 'Constitutional Reform – Some Options', *Treaty Time*, December, p. 4.

Davies, L. and Nicholl, K (1993), *Te Maori i roto i nga Mahi Whakaakoranga, Maori in Education: A Statistical Profile of the Position of Maori Across the New Zealand Education System*, Wellington: Ministry of Education.

Durie, M.H. (1995), 'Beyond 1852, Maori, the State and a New Zealand Constitution', *Sites*, 30, pp. 31–47.

Freire, P. (1972), *Pedagogy of the Oppressed*, Harmondsworth: Penguin.

Green, W. (ed.) (1993), *The Insistence of the Letter: Literacy Studies and Curriculum Theorising*, London: Falmer Press.

Harré Hindmarsh, J. and Davies, L. (1993), *Funding for Adult Education: Who Benefits?*, Wellington: Ministry of Education.

Henare, T.H. (1988), Speech to Labour Members of Parliament.

Hill, K. (1990), *From this Fragile Web*, Wellington: NZCER.

Hirsh, W. (1990), *A Report on the Issues and Factors Relating to Maori Achievement in the Education System*, Wellington: Ministry of Education.

Holt, L. (1992), 'Aboriginal Justice, Democracy and Adult Education', *Convergence*, vol. 25, no. 1, pp. 18–22.

Jackson, M. (date unknown), *Te Tiriti o Waitangi*.

Jenkins, K. (1991), *Te Ihi, te Mana, te Wehi o te Ao Tuhi*, MA thesis, University of Auckland.

Kelsey, J. (1990), *A Question of Honour? Labour and the Treaty 1984–1989*. Sydney: Allen and Unwin.

Kohere, R. and Smith, C. (1992), *He Ringa Raupa*, March.

Lankshear, C. (1993), 'Curriculum as Literacy: Reading and Writing in "New Times" ', in Green, W. (ed.), *The Insistence of the Letter: Literacy Studies and Curriculum Theorising*, London: Falmer Press.

Lankshear, C. and Lawler, M. (1987), *Literacy, Schooling and Revolution*, Lewes: Falmer Press.

Lauder, H. and Wylie, C. (eds) (1990), *Towards Successful Schooling*, Lewes: Falmer Press.
Project Waitangi (no date), *Te Tiriti o Waitangi*. Pamphlet published by Project Waitangi, Wellington.
Sharples, P. (1995), Public address to the Foundation for Peace Studies, Auckland.
Smith, C. and Yates, B. (1993), 'An Indigenous Discourse', unpublished paper.
Smith, G. (1990), 'The Politics of Reforming Maori Education: The Transforming Potential of Kura Kaupapa Maori', in Lauder, H. and Wylie, C. (eds.), *Towards Successful Schooling*, Lewes: Falmer Press.
Sutton, A. and Benseman, J. (1995), *National Statistics of ARLA Member Schemes*, Wellington: Adult Reading and Learning Assistance Federation.
Tamahori, M.J. (1991), *Research into Literacy and Numeracy Needs of Maori ACCESS Trainees in South Auckland*.
Te Whakakotahitanga o Nga Iwi o Aotearoa (1995), *Summary of Maori Congress Policy*, 13 May 1995.
Trotter, C. (1995a), 'Editorial', *NZ Political Review*, April–May.
Trotter, C. (1995b), 'The Struggle for Sovereignty', *NZ Political Review*, April–May.
Walker, R. (1984), 'The Maori Response to Education in New Zealand', Proceedings in a Maori Education Conference.

6

Maori Literacy — The Local Reality

Huhana Mete

He mihi whakamaharatanga, he mihi oranga ngakau, he mihi aroha pumau tenei ki te Huarahi Education Trust mai ki te rohe o Otepoti. Anei ra etahi korero tino whakahirahira mona. Me ki penei au, ko tenei te whare aroha e manaaki nei i te tini, i te mano, ahakoa ko wai te iwi, ko wai te tangata, ka maanakitia ratou i te whanau o te Huarahi. Ko tenei te whare poutokomanawa, hei tuara whakamarumaru whakaruru hau, he marae turangawaewae hoki mo matou e whaiwhai nei nga tikanga Maori katoa. Ara nga waihotanga a kui a koro ma ratou kua rupeketia i te tua ote arai. Kua tutuki ia matou nga kaupapa ataahua nga mahinga e waka ritea mo nga akonga. Kua ea etahi o nga wawata, nga moemoea a nga kai mahi, nga kai arahi o te reo Maori me ona tikanga, na te mea kua hou te matauranga, te mahana me te wairua Maori ki roto i nga akonga ko te tumanako ka ora tonu mai to tatou reo rangatira mo ake tonu atu. Kia tu tangata hoki a tatou rangatahi, mokopuna kia tu pakari ai ratou i roto i nga ahuatanga katoa e pa ana kia tatou, kia noho ai ratou hei tauira kai arahi mo to tatou iwi Maori ma te wa e whakaatu. Ma te wa e whakaatu. A tatou mahi kia u kia maia kia kaha kia manawanui.

Waiho me te tapapa i te po e rongoa kua puta te maramatanga ki enei uri o nga maata waka huri noa i te motu. Mai i tenei ao hurihuri he Maori au, mai i te rangi, titi ki te whenua, Mauri tu, Mauri ora, Mauri noho, Mauri mate. Na Nanny Bella Ihipera Morrell Neha. No Ngati Porou me Ngati Kahungunu.

Introduction

What is literacy? What is Maori literacy? Who is it designed for? What are effective delivery systems? In the development of tino rangatiratanga, Te Huarahi Education Trust established a 'whare ako' in which to plant a definition of Maori literacy, by gathering our people from the community together to find out what was needed and how it could be achieved.

Te Huarahi Education Trust began its work in November 1991 and until 1995 ran the following programmes:

- remedial adult literacy 1:1
- volunteer tutor training for adult literacy
- homework support tutor training
- parenting skills
- waiata
- te reo me ona tikanga (beginners, intermediate, fluent)
- tutor hui on whanau learning management
- Treaty workshops
- homework support for rangatahi
- tautoko – learning skills intervention programme for rangatahi contracted to schools
- Maori literacy contracts for Maori Private Training Establishments (PTEs)
- small business management for Maori women
- Learning Enterprise including: module 1: Marketing; module 2: Business and computer skills; module 3: Catering
- consultation hui for NZQA Whakaruruhau for Maori
- adult education and training.

During our operation we also housed two kohanga reo temporarily – one for six months while their whare was restored from fire, and the other for one year while they waited for the construction of their new whare. Parent support groups from local schools, Whanau AA, Iwi Whanau Waiata, Maori Womens Welfare League and kura kaupapa initial support groups were among others who utilised our whare. Just over four years later the trust closed because of insufficient funding. How could a trust that was established for community development of iwi Maori close when the education achievement, employment figures and crime statistics are still crying out for immediate and long-term Maori solutions? The irony of the closure was that it happened in the 'Year of the Whanau', the same year in which it was claimed that Aotearoa/New Zealand had the highest rate of youth suicide and family violence per capita amongst Western nations.

Establishing a Whare Ako

The local reality of establishing a Whare Ako for Maori was a test for iwi Maori within the Otago community to establish and contribute to a centre which had the possibility to become a self-sufficient education trust. The long-term vision of the trust was to train and contract Maori literacy tutors into schools, government agencies and TOP courses and to provide programmes which would contribute to individuals' educational growth, their whanau's wellbeing and consequently, aid the development of the wider community. It was also a test of the effectiveness of literacy programmes including their methods of delivery. Lastly, we wanted to find ways to operate a client-driven operation for Maori which did not necessarily have to react to current funding limitations. Our challenge was to find ways in which to gain government and community funding which we knew had been mainstreamed into a Pakeha delivery system, and still retain autonomy as a delivery system for Maori.

The name *Huarahi* was given by Koro Hori Mete with the explanation that there were ways to uplift iwi Maori in their spiritual, emotional, social, educational and employment standing in the community. The trust never saw itself as the only entity for an individual's learning. It was established as a support mechanism for iwi Maori in both Pakeha and Maori systems of education. It saw itself as a place for iwi Maori to find their way in their personal identity, to recognise and develop the talents and gifts that they were given and to establish ways to utilise these skills for their own and their whanau's development. Part of this process was also to realise how many of our skills had been abused by the traditional education system and the colonised society in which we now live.

The concept of *whanau* emphasised the way that individuals could learn in a supportive and safe environment in accord with lifelong learning. Mistakes were never seen as mistakes, but were discovered to be the best ways to learn wherein achievements were shared and celebrated. The whanau allowed individuals to find their cultural heritage and respect for one another's differences as well as their similarities. The development of personal growth entailed the development of whanau, hapu and iwi and most importantly, the respect of individuals within the whanau. Therefore the acknowledgement of kaumatua, matua, rangatahi, tamariki and pepe and the spiritual, physical and mental wellbeing of learning was paramount to our operation.

When the Whanau Literacy Project of Te Huarahi Education Trust opened its doors on 4 June 1992, it did so with the definition of whanau literacy having originated from an initial feasibility study. This study had been conducted with kohanga, primary, secondary and adult education organisations. Local runanga and Maori community organisations had also been consulted. The needs were diverse, with school-aged tamariki and rangatahi requiring assistance with basic reading, comprehension, spelling, writing, maths confidence and exam techniques. TOP students wished to have programmes which would support further education qualifications, such as School Certificate Maths and English and in some cases, University Entrance subjects. They were prepared to work within their TOP programme and outside these hours if evening and late afternoon classes were run. Some adults wanted remedial literacy classes, but stressed the need to be able to assist preschool and school-aged tamariki with their learning. Some matua wanted skills that could be utilised for the development of kohanga reo and other Maori organisations they belonged to. Local runanga and kohanga reo started the development of te reo within the kaupapa and opened the doors to the development of waiata, raranga and te reo me ona tikanga.

It was imperative to be seen as a community trust open to everyone's contribution. The constitution and the responsibilities of executive members and whanau had established this in November 1991. Because our centre was to be broad-based but with literacy and education as its primary focus, our initial funding thrust had been primarily for Ministry of Education funding and to Te Puni Kokiri for policy advice. Second, we targeted community funding sources. The pathway of operation began a week after opening, with ratification of the kaupapa and its development plan by local kaumatua. A funding proposal for a three-year participant-driven research project was to provide funding of resources and a part salary for the tumuaki, as the researcher. Te Puni Kokiri was to assist with salaries in the first year.

Issues

The reality we faced within the first six months, was that even though we had been assured by educational experts within the local area and also by talks with the then Group Manager Maori for the Ministry of Education, that our centre did cater for the 10-point plan (the priorities of Ministry funding for Maori), we did not fit ministerial policy criteria. Iwi Maori learning support programmes were not part of preschool, primary, intermediate, secondary or university education structures. We did receive rental assistance for Te Whare Ako, because at the time of opening, the building we wanted had been empty, but was part of the Ministry's targets for asset sales. Ministry of Education and Te Puni Kokori funding was imperative if we were to be able to sustain the development plan for the first three years. The original research proposals were to investigate: the consultation and recruitment process of students and professional volunteers for a community-based learning centre, i.e. Te Whare Ako; the development of programmes relevant to supporting Maori educational achievement; and development of appropriate assessment procedures and methodologies of teaching utilised in Te Whare Ako.

Participant-driven research meant that the trust could provide documentation of a whanau based educational intervention support mechanism to aid and support current Maori educational initiatives, as well as iwi Maori individuals housed within the Pakeha system. Once established, Huarahi could be a model that could then be established in other regions. The possibility of incorporating a nationally accredited tutor training programme with a Maori perspective and national certification for many of our programmes became a reality when we became part of the advisory group for the development of NZQA unit standards for Maori Adult Education and Training. Representation on an advisory group for accreditation of Adult Literacy for ARLA enabled us in the long term to provide our people with qualifications for employment in the Maori literacy field.

The Tautoko programme and Homework Support Programme aimed at picking up rangatahi Maori who were floundering in the education system waiting for the day they could leave or be asked to leave school. The idea of utilising accelerated learning skills taha Maori style, created the possibility of cultural enrichment and educational success for those who had missed out on kohanga reo, kura kaupapa and learning achievement within today's schools' traditional learning environment.

When the Maori Foundation put out a press release in 1993 concerning educational statistics which confirmed the underachievement of Maori in formal 5th Form Certificate and stated they were considering paying parents to ensure their tamariki did their homework, we believed that we might have been able to access their support. But once again we seemed to be knocking on the wrong door. Maori Education funding from the Ministry of Education and Te Puni Kokiri seemed to focus on those Maori initiatives which replicated the public system (i.e. kohanga – preschool, kura kaupapa – primary, intermediate and secondary, and whare waananga – university). A whanau based intervention system which could have offered remedial support to those adults who missed schooling opportunities (which may affect the development, retention and achievement of their own children's educational learning) was not seen to be a priority. Neither was it a priority to devise more Maori traditional methods of learning for Maori.

The introduction of the registration of Private Training Establishments (PTEs) within former MACCESS and ACCESS programmes and the pull of ETSA funding has resulted in the concentration on Pakeha methods of teaching and content instead of Maori ways of learning being upheld and developed. In some cases during the MACCESS years, removal altogether of kaupapa Maori programmes from the funding arena pressurised many Maori providers to continue the assimilation process in education that we have been under for the last 150 years. There has been some hope instilled in our people by the establishment of the Whanau Unit of NZQA. However, while the establishment of Maori advisory groups to write practical and theoretical content for learning unit standards for the NZQA framework offers the possibility for implementation of Maori content and delivery systems, it is still a slow process. This strategy will only work if Maori PTEs overcome their nervousness of competitive funding rounds and can go past mainstream methodologies of teaching and formulate programmes which draw upon our own cultural richness. The current reality is that many Maori PTEs are being closed down as ETSA providers, because they do not have enough programmes to sustain the expensive quality management systems that NZQA and ETSA both require. The fear of contestable processes has also meant that many Maori PTEs have become less trustful of one another.

Teaching Styles

Although literacy work is imperative to a TOP course, the literacy skill content within Maori programmes still focuses on Pakeha teaching styles. With the introduction of accelerated learning techniques such as 'braingym', 'whanau-based learning', has sunk away. Until Maori PTEs realise the effectiveness of employing their own people utilising culturally safe methods of delivery in both Maori and Pakeha languages, they will always be part of a Treaty that has denied our rights instead of working together for tino rangatiratanga. When any Maori community-based organisation is established, the interest and support is always there, but in education (and especially in a literacy support centre which is whanau based and houses functional programmes) it becomes difficult for the community at large to ascertain the kaupapa. Without training and knowledge of the kaupapa, developments such as Huarahi are thwarted from the beginning.

Huarahi's development in the first six months primarily involved finding cost-efficient ways to begin the kaupapa and finding funding sources. Although we had two literacy workshops within the first six months and had established about 20 tutors for adult literacy and homework support, many of the volunteers were unable to satisfy the needs of their students with one hour a week voluntary time and some tutors therefore had to take three or four students. At holiday time the tutors were always transient, mainly because it was younger, educated, students who did tutor training, rather than older adults, who lacked confidence in their own skills. However, a TOP tutor training hui on whanau learning management systems (funded by a Maori works collective) did attract a successful wananga at a local marae and for some there was cultural enlightenment into better ways to work with their students. Another learning management hui for kohanga reo staff and volunteers was also given acclaim by the participants.

Te reo classes began with small numbers but their methodology of teaching enabled both Maori and Pakeha achievement and we managed to train kohanga whanau, university student teachers and individuals from the wider community. Through various tutor training and whanau hui to attract Ministry of Education support, Friday kai was firmly established as part of a drawcard for empathetic people to look around, meet each other and share. This strategy was conceived in 1993 and welcomed kaumatua to korero, developed a realistic environment for waiata and mihi; it was also a marketing tool for the programmes.

Work with Schools

When contract work with schools began, we had very few guidelines and our work was misinterpreted because some groups thought we wanted to take over the valuable work of local runanga. However, over time we formulated clear strategies for the development of the Tautoko programme and it incorporated both intermediate and secondary school contracts. Its ultimate success was due to the consultation process, an ability to work with parents in their own homes and also to provide the Parenting Skills Course. In 1994 it seemed that this programme could have entailed a research project which Te Puni Kokiri would have taken up – however, this opportunity came too late for the Trust.

Because we were a Maori, community-based organisation, we were open to community impressions of our kaupapa. Some people thought that just having Maori tutors for Homework Support was enough and there was no need for training in whanau-based learning. The aim of our Homework Support tutor training was to share Maori-based accelerated learning techniques among university and teachers college students. While successful, these people were still constrained by their own exam stress and competitive learning situations.

Our principle of 'safe learning' meant that we had to ensure that any student who came to Te Whare Ako was going to be taught the philosophy that the student and tutor were partners in the learning process and that the students be given credit for the wealth of knowledge they already possessed (despite the fact they may have reading skill needs).

Finance

Some members of management suggested that we did not need to train in the kaupapa nor in whanau-based learning methods. Nor did they see the need to have a comprehensive funding budget in order to ensure that experienced and professional staff develop the quality management systems required. The voluntary commitment of many of our unemployed Maori in other community organisations meant that some felt that Te Huarahi's budget was not necessary. It is this writer's view that to initiate an organisation without planning, management and staff training on the kaupapa of Maori literacy and whanau-based learning is a mistake. Ultimately, it is a weakness of the kaupapa not to have the support that the whanau should have.

The premise on which Huarahi was based (i.e. to support other Maori organisations), was also thwarted by this lack of training and acknowledgement of the kaupapa. We became yet another Maori organisation competing against others for community funding. Ironically, instead of the worthwhile developments of the Trust being discussed in the community, we were often open to personal criticisms and management frictions, mainly caused by disorganisation through not enough funding and burnt-out volunteer workers.

Because of our failed funding requests in the first year, the trust was soon in debt and some initial developers left and requests for closing down were voiced. The most obvious plan, apart from closing down, was to look at established funding and we began our first MACCESS Programme of 'Introduction to Small Business for Maori Women'. This course had been devised with the help of a Whakapakari (Maori Women's Business Enterprise Project) trainee and was an intensive confidence, self-awareness and enterprise-orientated course that aimed to provide a broad range of functional literacy skills for business. Its skill base involved a te reo me ona tikanga component, but it also taught communication, negotiating skills, computer, cooking and sewing skills as well as essay writing, accounting and office management. After six months, a second-level course for three graduates from the initial course was developed to foster abilities in tutoring in selected skill areas and this led on to the introduction of business goals. This programme utilised whanau-based learning techniques aimed at students' independence in learning and promoted goal setting, evaluation and design of individualised learning pathways within the confines of the programme objectives. As with all other programmes the emphasis was on the concept of *'ako'* (i.e. the balance of *taha wairua, taha hinengaro me taha tinana*). The outcomes of 'Learning Enterprise' and other courses have been highly successful if one looks around the community and sees ex-students now setting up small businesses, being successfully employed, possessing the confidence to continue to study and further develop and contribute to Maori community organisations and Maori education initiatives.

The Role of Community Support

However, the local community was not always supportive. Once we began to operate literacy programmes which were funded by MACCESS and ETSA, we had to become a competitor in the ETSA round of funding and some of the community objected to this, because that was not how they saw the provision of Maori literacy programmes.

With the introduction and development of a Maori literacy organisation (especially one which embraces other kaupapa), there needs to be a consultation and marketing plan which continually feeds the community with knowledge of its developments. Any Maori literacy organisation must facilitate this, because of the necessity for community group participation and the meeting of needs of our whanau. Although Huarahi did involve the community, it was not done consistently. Therefore the community at large could make assumptions about what they thought was happening and the question of personalities within the organisation easily overrode the developments of the kaupapa. When competition is rife among Maori groups for the funding dollar, this uneasy situation can grow out of proportion. It also means that a few, strategically situated people in local Maori politics can dictate what succeeds in the community and what does not. The sadness of the situation is that it is not the groups themselves or the individuals who are promoting this dissension, but the national policies and criteria for government and community funding.

Nationally, the change from MACCESS to TOP funding took place in 1993. This meant that there were no contestable rounds for funding, when Huarahi most needed to open the way for 18 students who fulfilled ETSA criteria and were involved full-time with the Learning Enterprise course. With the changeover, however, we were also reduced to six places when we had previously had nine. The difficulty we had was convincing people at a local level that there can be many Maori PTEs who have the right to run generic skills programmes and introductory small business or enterprise programmes which hold a Maori perspective. Our entire programme was literacy-based, utilising both Maori and English languages. Because there were also two other Maori PTEs engaged with similar content, it appeared that we were not needed. Nor did many understand the literacy focus. Although we were part of the establishment of the Association of Maori PTEs, we never really saw Huarahi achieve what it was set up for – to work together to gain as much funding as we could for Maori, instead of competing against one another for the scraps.

If one looks at how many courses are run in the English language currently, there is room for thousands of courses with Maori language as basic content. Unfortunately in that time of change, when the NZQA unit standards were only just being written for courses like Learning Enterprise, we had no hard facts on which to base our korero.

The rationale behind the Learning Enterprise course was that apart from full-time students, it had the flexibility to take part-time adult literacy students for components of the course. We believed in the right of every individual to have the opportunity to learn; few people were turned away, regardless of funding. Unfortunately when an organisation takes this stance, funders do not appreciate the ability to be flexible. It is often difficult to convince authorities that whanau are necessary for the support of a programme when ETSA still retain learning as an individualised affair. For Domestic Purposes Benefit (DPB) mothers, we were able to find other funding, but it was difficult for those on Independent Youth or the Unemployment Benefits to contribute towards fees. When we sought other funding through the Lottery Grants Board in 1994 to address this deficit we were unsuccessful because of what the Board said was a 'lack of organisational management and community support'.

With our registration as a Private Training Establishment in 1994 effective administration, management and organisation of all programmes became the major aims. Funding plans were strategically developed and the budget incorporated realistic figures to provide well-equipped professional programmes. We finally had a plan to show the community what the Whanau Literacy Project was all about. However, some of the past executive members objected to the budget. They had no understanding of the needs to be met or of the quality systems and resources required for a project which had the potential to enhance academic success, cultural wellbeing and employment to lift our people out of the co-dependent state that our education and government systems have put us in.

The budget formulated in 1994 was based on realistic figures for programmes that we thought had been trialled and evaluated. Developments for effective administration and assessment relevant to whanau learning methodology would become a reality. By the time our first National Lottery Application in 1994 had gone through and we were told we were unsuccessful because of lack of community support (despite hundreds of letters to say otherwise), we came to realise that liaison officers from funding organisations, who had no understanding of kaupapa Maori, were part of the problem. They seemed to only want to talk to people in the community who had little to do with our operation and not those individuals or organisations who were utilising the Trust's services.

We could never understand why our national body of Te Whiri Kaupapa Ako (TWKA) had not been consulted when Maori literacy was our kaupapa.

The misuse of funds by a few Maori organisations from the past seemed to have made funders hesitant to provide sufficient funding. They needed to realise that if resources were made available, then more effective administration and organisation is possible.

Staffing and Management

Although staff were dedicated, we lacked funding for outside training and sometimes this affected the confidence of workers. The need to calculate and keep effective records of outcomes became prominent at this time. Lack of calculation of the thousands of voluntary hours that had been put into the Trust over its three-year operation was something that was rectified too late. This documentation must be in place at the beginning. However, the implementation of the initial Ministry of Education research would have ensured that these processes would have been in place.

The 'Catch 22' is that without sufficient funding, it is impossible to employ experienced personnel who may have been able to implement the systems we desperately required sooner. In terms of staffing, many Maori professionals had expressed their willingness to work within the kaupapa of Te Huarahi on a full-time basis but were unable to, because of the salaries they were able to get working within formal education institutions. Without this type of expertise, the management, major training, funding, programme development, contracts and so on were left in the hands of the tumuaki who was paid for 20 of the 36 months that the Trust operated and who generally worked 20 hours overtime a week. I do not provide this last statement as a need to be acknowledged, but more as a point that this working pattern leads to even more ineffectual organisation of a kaupapa. All workers were sorely underpaid in terms of their job descriptions. They were all trained in some way on the premises, but it was difficult to give them the support they deserved. There was also a need to continually fight for funding and they were required to do too many tasks.

Our management committee was difficult to co-ordinate because they were insufficiently experienced in the educational management practices we were striving for. Without training in the kaupapa, it is difficult to make the decisions that are relevant for the Trust's development when knowledge is housed within a few people. The application of tikanga versus sound business practices constituted a problem, which was not assisted by the broad and intangible definition of Maori literacy. Somehow for kaupapa Maori, anything is sufficient to initiate community support, but for a kaupapa such as Maori literacy, which is still in its infancy, the trend has been more towards 'wait and see'. A lack of confidence in establishing Maori educational initiatives is a reality when many iwi Maori have suffered under education kaupapa in the mainstream.

Active local support needs to be strategically planned. The combination of lack of training and little knowledge of the kaupapa meant it was easy for community organisations to use the Trust according to their own agendas and forget its kaupapa. Inevitably, when any disorganisation occurred within the Trust's Whare Ako, the result was more negative than positive developments.

We decided to face our criticism and made a whanau presentation to the Maori Council (Runanga and Matawaka representatives) to plead for support. We made strategic and dynamic changes within all our operations and then we went as far as to seek a quality audit from ETSA head office, assisted by the ETSA Maori Unit. Within the outcomes of the review report, it was requested that the local ETSA give us time to implement what they had suggested, but local ETSA staff decided not to take this advice. When it was discovered that ETSA had already let the Lottery Grants Board know that we would not be funded by them (before we ourselves knew), the funding Committee of Lottery Welfare had no option but to turn down our grant because of financial instability.

The Lottery Grants Board had originally turned us down in February 1994, but commented they would look at us again in October. By this time we had been exhausted by eight months of no funding, apart from ETSA's six places and Taskforce Green projects for workers who were expected to carry out highly professional tasks. Most workers were now doing massive hours or voluntary work and training and were suffering from burnout.

When the local ETSA and other funders decided to withdraw (we had no grounds on which to renegotiate our 18 places with ETSA without other funding), the decision to close, with a debt to Inland Revenue, was an easy one to make. We were totally worn out by our three-year process of chasing funding and working with only hope and love in our hearts, the memories, the good times and the not-so-good times. It was only with sheer love, determination and courage that both students and staff ran their last farewell kai for the community in early December and completed the commitments of the ETSA Learning Enterprise Programme and the Year of the Family-funded Parenting Skills Programme on 16 December 1994.

Achievements

On reflection, the irony is that when the doors closed and we looked back, we realised that we had accomplished most of what we had set out to do. There were systems by which whanau-based teaching methodologies had been trialled, refined and developed. We had also developed programmes that had grown from the needs of the community and had an opportunity to develop these and put in place strategies for their ultimate success. Our academic assessment procedures were still at a developmental stage, but we knew that every individual had in some way benefited in terms of our original aims.

The definition of Maori literacy derived from the experiences of Te Huarahi Whanau Literacy Project is the development of programmes which develop thinking, listening, speaking, writing and problem solving and enable the practice of communication skills relevant to Maori development today. The most productive ways for implementing literacy needs of Maori are throughout the whole of whanau and can be integrated into the kaupapa of all Maori organisations. Parenting skills, homework support, tautoko for schools and Learning Enterprise are programmes which can easily be transferred to organisations anywhere in the country. One-to-one literacy in both te reo and English can be provided as well.

The concept of *whare ako* may be too early for the kind of change that we are experiencing in Maori education today. I am sure, however, that the taonga that was laid at Huarahi will continue in the local area for many years to come. A kuia of the Trust said to me in 1993 that Huarahi's kaupapa was '150 years too late and 10 years too early'.

The first National Conference of Maori Literacy Workers, held at Te Puea Marae in Mangere in 1994 by Te Whiri Kaupapa Ako (ARLA), allowed Huarahi an opportunity to recognise its accomplishments within Maori literacy and provided the opportunity for these to flourish within other organisations.

The most positive support Huarahi Whanau Literacy Project received in the time of its operations was from Te Whiri Kaupapa Ako (ARLA Federation). They nominated Huarahi to work with a Pacific National Conference on Youth and Literacy, held in Fiji in 1992, to work with other Pacific Nations and to jointly sponsor with the New Zealand Association for Community and Continuing Education (NZACCE) our nomination to a UNESCO Conference held in Thailand for Adult Educators from Pacific and Asian Nations in 1993. Both these workshops occurred at the national and international level and were unanimous in their promotion of indigenous concepts of literacy and the development of national and international funding and delivery systems.

Our first Parenting Skills Pilot introduced in 1993 was funded by **TWKA** and became a pilot project for other literacy organisations. The course's uniqueness was that it reintroduced taha Maori into parenting and explored ways for spiritual, physical and mental growth of a whanau. In keeping with the kaupapa of literacy, it introduced concepts of *mana wahine* and *mana tane* through the oral stories of kaumatua and mythology and assisted parents to support their own children's literacy skills.

At the 1995 Maori Literacy Development Conference held at Ihumatao Marae in Mangere the number of newly formed Maori literacy organisations had increased to 30 throughout the country. Maybe some or all of the programmes devised by the three-year unfunded, participant-driven research project of Te Huarahi will now have a place to fly. I say 'fly' because the programmes can be based in Maori literacy organisations that can learn from the achievements and mistakes of Te Huarahi's Whanau Literacy project.

Lessons Learned

From our study, we believe that literacy concepts need to be instilled in every Maori community organisation and it is with more flexible and resource-efficient strategies that Maori literacy organisations will flourish. Maori literacy organisations ought to have the facilities to train volunteer tutors who represent Maori community organisations, be able to train individuals willing to work in their own homes and provide more comprehensive training to those who wish to gain employment. These organisations need to concentrate on developing literacy skills within a certain kaupapa which are relevant to individuals. They need to develop, support and offer resources and programmes, which will hopefully bring Maori community groups together in order to strategise literacy provision to iwi Maori in a community. Advisors can assist and train the management committee. Tutors need to have regular support hui and both students and tutors need to attend frequent gatherings.

The opportunity for iwi Maori to develop their own personal, family and community's literacy resources must be the basis on which any Maori literacy organisation is run. Maori literacy organisations, especially ones which embrace other kaupapa, need a consultation and marketing plan which continually feeds the community with knowledge of its developments. When a Maori literacy organisation incorporates other community organisations (it has a natural facility to do this) and when competition is rife for the funding dollar, it needs a mechanism to alleviate this competition. Programmes will be initiated by the individual organisations themselves and it is presumed that they will differ from one group to another. However, national Maori literacy organisations will need to provide support at a local level. The development plan of the Maori literacy organisation will allow other Maori organisations to take responsibility for literacy skills of their members and fast-track the provision of Maori literacy skills nation-wide.

The kaupapa of Huarahi in its short lifespan was perhaps just as Koro Hori Mete described, 'a garden in which to grow seeds of hope' for the infancy of Maori literacy. It achieved that. Its 'Whare Ako' was a small step in gaining knowledge of the Maori system of literacy based on tino rangatiratanga. Its journey was one which developed Maori literacy skills for today. Huarahi's biggest downfall was that its expectations of whakawhanaungatanga principles within which it operated were not replicated by the community locally, due to current funding and political policies. For Maori literacy to succeed, it must achieve wider acceptance. At the national level, co-operation and co-ordination of strategies for Maori literacy need to gain effective levels of funding which will continue the pathway of delivering Maori literacy methodologies to uplift the spiritual, emotional, social, educational and employment standing of iwi Maori in the community.

It is only with co-operation both at local and national levels that Maori may challenge mainstream funding criteria to be available for literacy programmes which reflect tino rangatiratanga and not Pakehatanga programmes run by Maori.

He korero whakamutunga

He korero whakamutunga maku i tenei wa, kua whakatohia te kakano. E pono ana ki te kaupapa o te whanau Akoranga i roto i te Huarahi Education Trust.

Ahakoa kua katia tenei whare ako, kua kitea te puawaitanga o nga hua papai e puta mai ana te paenga i roto i tenei tu momo ahuatanga o te whanau Akoranga.

Ahakoa nga piki, nga heke, nga uauatanga o nga tau tohetohe e toru kua hipa ake, na te piri pono tahi o nga whanau mana huhua nga kaiako, kaiawhina, kaitautoko, kaitiaki, te kaitakawaenga me nga kaumatua hoki, e tutuki ai te kaupapa o Te Huarahi Education Trust. E taea e matou te whakato te wairua Maori o nga tipuna, me nga ahuatanga katoa e pa ana. Ki to tatou mana Maori manamotuhake.

Ko te tino mahana, me te ataahua hoki o te mahi tahi a nga whanau o Te Huarahi, e awhi nei a tatou rangatahi, me nga akonga pakeke. Ara ka kitea te pumau tuturu o te aroha, tetahi ki tetahi te whakawhanaungatanga o te hohunutanga o tenei kaupapa o te whanau akoranga.

Otira na te aroha me te whakapono i roto i te tumanako, kua tutuki kua ea etahi o matou wa wata, o matou moemoea.

Ka tu tangata te huinga o nga akonga i puta mai ana waho o tenei whare akoranga Te Huarahi. Kei roto i o ratou ringaringa e pupuri ana te mana mauri o to tatou ao Maori mo nga ra e heke mai nei.

Na Nanny Bella Ihipera Morrell Neha. No Ngati Porou me Ngati Kahungunu.

7

Toward a Sustainable Relationship:

Pakeha and Tangata Whenua
in Adult and Community Education

Christine Herzog

Ko te kairapu, ko ia te kite   S/he who seeks will find

Introduction

This essay is a summary of my current thinking about working as a Pakeha with tangata whenua in the fourth sector. Although Te Tiriti o Waitangi provides the foundation for my own work, I have based this essay on a broader premise – that however our concepts of Te Tiriti may vary, we all agree that a sustainable relationship between tangata whenua and Pakeha is desirable. It is written primarily for those Pakeha who share my concerns about the status of tangata whenua in traditional fourth sector organisations and activities; therefore, it does not include the argument as to why this issue is important.

The concept of 'sustainable relationship' is derived from the current emphasis on sustainable management of resources, which has been prompted by the Resource Management Act. Unfortunately, the Act specifically restricts itself only to consideration of 'natural and physical resources'; I would suggest that one of the most important resources in this country is the tangata whenua – Pakeha relationship. Since 1840 the government has not managed this resource in a sustainable way; the belated recognition that resources disappear forever if there is a constant taking and no putting back must be applied urgently to the social environment as well. I believe that the fourth sector can play a major role in this by exploring alternatives.

In the first part of the essay some models of possible relationships between Pakeha and tangata whenua[1] are outlined. Then I briefly discuss how they relate to educational policy in Aotearoa/New Zealand. Finally, a case is made for the self-determination model, as at least an intermediate objective in establishing a sustainable relationship.

Some Possible Bicultural Relationships

The following diagram is a simple representation of some possible relationships between Pakeha and tangata whenua in the institutions of our society. My world-view tends to be conflict theorist;[2] therefore, I am inclined to focus on the power[3] balance. The models can be, and more frequently are, considered in terms of culture. Although there is considerable overlap between the power and the cultural components in a relationship, the models are not necessarily the same in both areas (examples below).

Some Possible Relationships Between Tangata Whenua and Pakeha

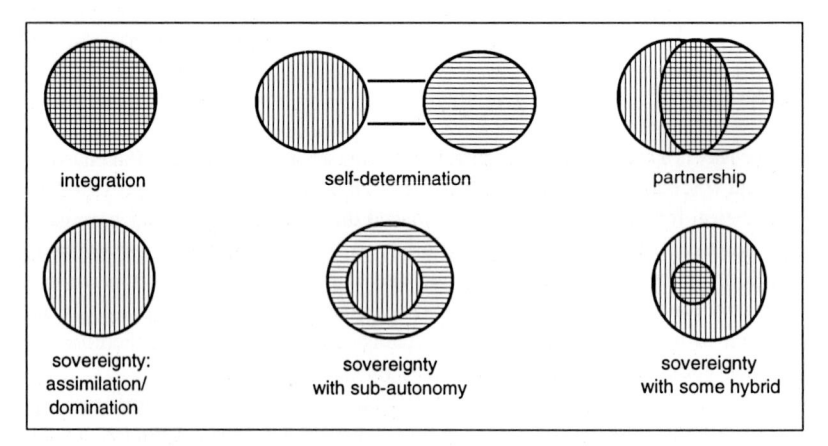

integration

self-determination

partnership

sovereignty: assimilation/ domination

sovereignty with sub-autonomy

sovereignty with some hybrid

Integration is when two distinct components are brought together to create a different whole. In terms of power, it means both parties are involved in all aspects of institutional decision-making. In terms of the cultures, the outcome is mono-cultural, but the underlying value base is a hybrid of the two different groups' cultures – it has aspects of each but is not the same as either. This option would reduce the stress that often arises from working cross-culturally but would not allow for much diversity. In theory, it is appealing to all those who feel that we are 'one people' first and that the cultural differences are relatively minor. In my experience, though, these proponents are those who expect others to become more like themselves but are not willing to share power or fundamentally change their own ways of doing things in order to create a hybrid (i.e. they really want assimilation with their own group dominant).

Self-determination, sometimes referred to as separatism,[4] is when each group has authority over its own group, but not over any other group. It is possible for a group which is dominant politically to leave space for at least some cultural self-determination for other groups, but for a group to be fully self-determining culturally it must have political self-determination as well. Some people consider political and cultural self-determination to have been the expectation of tangata whenua who signed Te Tiriti, but many Pakeha are uncomfortable with the notion that tangata whenua would want to be separate.

Partnership is a combination of some integration and some self-determination; for many people, this model seems to capture the best of both worlds. Negotiation is usually involved in deciding which aspects of the relationship will be integrated and which will be autonomous. Partnership may apply in the political and/or cultural arenas. When it includes sharing power, it is usually assumed to be in the ratio of 50:50, but this is not inherent in the definition. Te Tiriti is often described as a contract for partnership, though no comparable word is in the document. In many respects, there are parallels with business and domestic partnerships.

Sovereignty, in this essay, means having ultimate power in relation to other groups.[5] Its exercise may or may not accommodate difference; the latter includes domination and/or assimilation. Domination is when the dominant group holds power over another group. Assimilation is the monocultural outcome when one group's culture disappears as its members adopt the culture of the dominant group; this may occur voluntarily (e.g. with some immigrant groups) or be imposed by the dominant group (as in the case of educational policy in New Zealand – see below). In both domination and assimilation, the value base underlying institutional decision-making is that of the dominant group.

Where difference is tolerated by the group with sovereignty, there may be areas of sub-autonomy by the other group and/or hybrid situations. Sub-autonomy is delegation of specified power and/or allocation of space within which another culture may operate. Hybrid situations are comparable to having integration on a small scale. Neither situation alters the fundamental structure of power in which the dominant group is still in control of deciding what and how much to do and can rescind its decisions. Tangata whenua sovereignty is a total reversal of the current situation, but it can be read as the literal interpretation of Article 2 of the Maori text of Te Tiriti.

Of course, there are several models which I have not included and even more variations on the ones I have. For example, in partnership, the area of overlap could be substantially larger or smaller. In self-determination, there could be a third circle for those who choose not to affiliate with either tangata whenua or Pakeha. The integration model could have two small circles within it in which each group could retain some of its distinctive character.

The Models in Practice in Education

The tangata whenua sovereignty with sub-autonomy model best represents the period between 1816 (when the first mission school was set up) and 1840, both in terms of power and of culture. It appears to have been very successful, particularly from a fourth sector perspective. Not only was there a rapid spread of literacy amongst tangata whenua but also they taught each other and set up their own schools to do so. Biggs (1968: 73) has concluded that 'it seems possible, indeed likely, that by the middle of the 19th century a higher proportion of the Maori than of the settlers were literate in their own language'.

Shortly after 1840, the assimilation model was put forward as a way of protecting tangata whenua from the effects of contact with Europeans:

> ... And whereas great disasters have fallen upon uncivilised nations on being brought into contact with Colonists from the nations of Europe and in undertaking the colonisation of New Zealand Her Majesty's Government have recognised the duty of endeavouring by all practicable means to avert the like disasters from the Native people of these Islands, which object may best be attained by assimilating as speedily as possible the habits and usages of the Native to those of the European population.
> (Preamble, Native Trust Ordinance, 1844)

In the 1860s and 1870s the Pakeha government was in a position to begin exercising sovereignty over tangata whenua; tangata whenua responded with self-determination initiatives.[6] It was not until the early 1920s that domination in education was complete: by that time, the government had succeeded in having virtually all Maori children enrolled in Native Schools.

There were some examples of (cultural) integration in the Maori schools in the 1930s and 1940s (that is, of including some taha Maori – see Waitangi Consultancy, 1992: 81), but the official policy of assimilation was still in effect in 1960 when the Hunn Report was published. It promoted the concept of (cultural) integration, which was eventually defined as:

> ... a dynamic process by which Maori and Pakeha are being drawn closer together, in the physical sense of the mingling of the two populations, as well as in the mental and cultural senses, where differences are gradually diminishing. Remembering that the dictionary meaning of the verb 'to integrate' is to 'make whole', we regard the integration of Maori and Pakeha as the making of a whole new culture.
> (Booth and Hunn, quoted in Metge, 1990: 22)

It was another 10 years before it was realised that integration would require change by the education system to meet the needs of tangata whenua and that this would involve re-educating Pakeha teachers and introducing taha Maori to non-Maori (Metge, 1990: 24).

In the 1980s tangata whenua were abandoning efforts at integration (which were not resulting in shared power) in favour of creating space for autonomy within the system and even outside it (self-determination):

1984: Maori Education Development Conference recommended that Maori people have the right to 25% of vote education ...
1985: Hui Taumata (Maori Economic Summit) recommended that one of the existing teachers' training colleges should be turned into a Maori Community College with a kaupapa Maori.
1986: 416 kohanga reo operating ...
1988: Hui held to plan for an independent Maori Education Authority as a fully funded autonomous statutory body.
(Waitangi Consultancy, 1992: 82)

Further impetus was added by the 1986 Waitangi Tribunal finding that:

> ... it is a classic example of British understatement to say as the [Education Department] report does 'The record to date is mixed'. We think the record to date is quite unmixed. It is a dismal failure and no amount of delicate phrasing can mask that fact.
> (Waitangi Consultancy, 1992: 82)

On the other hand, the Ministry of Education policy in 1991 was still focused on cultural integration but sub-autonomy was being considered (see *Education Gazette*, 15 March 1991).

What is the situation in the fourth sector? By definition, we are outside the mainstream of government educational policy, though the negative outcomes for tangata whenua appear to be comparable to those in the tertiary sector.

> In the 1990 review of REAP prepared for the Minister of Education, the report concluded (p. 83) 'They (Maori people) did not, however, enjoy an equitable share of the REAP resource'. The authors criticise the low level of Maori participation in REAP decision-making, management and delivery areas (p. 92). ... Although there has not been much analysis of the participation patterns in these [university extension or continuing education] programmes for some time, the research done to date has been very consistent. Maori are among the most under-represented groups in these programmes' clientele... . Again, a similar picture [is seen in high school night class programmes].
>
> (Benseman, 1992: 28)

My own experience in education in Auckland, both inside and outside the fourth sector, would indicate that the fourth sector is trying to do more than others, with fewer resources, to address the issues.

Groups seem to begin with strategies to increase bicultural[7] awareness, bicultural sensitivity and/or bicultural safety[8]; then questions arise about more fundamental changes as it becomes clear that these may be essential but are not sufficient for a long-term resolution of the problems. Partly because of my planning background and partly because of the structural analysis models, I strongly recommend that individuals and groups at this point must consider what their visions are for the future (the models above were designed to help people with this activity). Then the factors which are obstructing achievement of the vision(s) may be identified, which in turn indicates what would be other appropriate strategies.

The Case for Self-determination

My personal experience in doing vision ⇒ blocks ⇒ strategies ⇒ action ⇒ review over the past 10 years has led me to the conclusion that self-determination is an inevitable step if we wish to achieve a sustainable relationship between Pakeha and tangata whenua.

In some Pakeha community groups we have tried adapting both the culture and the decision-making to incorporate tangata whenua. We have researched why tangata whenua were not involved, analysed what we could do to change that, contacted key informants, allocated resources. Implementation has been slow and laborious. Eventually we realised that those tangata whenua who had become involved were doing so more to meet our needs than their own; furthermore, our attempts to become more relevant to tangata whenua often compromised what had worked well for Pakeha. Instead of becoming effective for both groups, we were increasingly effective for neither.

In a community education department in which I worked, we tried very hard to develop sub-autonomy for tangata whenua: affirmative action in employment so there would be tangata whenua to make the decisions, allocation of 25 per cent of the resources exclusively for tangata whenua initiatives, etc; this was in addition to trying to make the other 75 per cent of the programme more culturally appropriate. After three years of hard work, we had to admit that the programme still was not meeting tangata whenua needs. The underlying vulnerability of this type of approach was emphasised when a few staff changes of key decision-makers meant that the strategies were abandoned.

Finally, after 10 years of trying to decide what a group should do to improve its relationship with tangata whenua, it belatedly occurred to me that it was not a decision Pakeha could or should make on our own. Community development theory makes it clear that decision-making between parties with unequal power does not meet the needs of both partners equally and therefore will not be stable.[9] By then, several of us had seen the National Council of Churches model which suggested that self-determination was essential if both parties were to be in a position to negotiate a future which would meet the needs of both (and thus be sustainable).

About the same time, the Auckland Workers Educational Assocation (WEA) was reconsidering its Treaty strategies; so we decided to try the self-determination model – instead of trying to fundamentally change the WEA we would begin to prepare ourselves for a future negotiation (e.g. what is our vision for the future, what is important to us about how we operate and what are we willing to change, what can we offer to attract tangata whenua to be in a relationship with us, what do we expect to get out of the relationship). Painfully aware of the history of Aotearoa/New Zealand and its consequences for tangata whenua, we realised that we had to do something to support tangata whenua in becoming self-determining and particularly in having power comparable to our own. Somewhat arbitrarily we decided to address the financial component of power and, after much soul-searching, committed ourselves to raising a six-figure amount and handing it over to a tangata whenua group[10] with no strings attached. Imagine our surprise (and relief), when the group turned the offer down; instead they wanted us to enter into an ongoing relationship (hence the horizontal connecting lines in the self-determination model). We have been jointly involved in several projects over the subsequent years and, for myself at least, this was the first time that I felt the relationship was sustainable. I get at least as much out of it as I put in; the tangata whenua group not only says it works for them but seems to demonstrate it by initiating activities with us.

I certainly cannot guarantee that what worked for the WEA would work for other groups, or even that it was directly a result of trying the self-determination model. What I would suggest is that the model is worth trying, not only because it worked once but also because it is congruent with the kaupapa of the fourth sector. Most of this essay has not been peculiarly relevant to the fourth sector, but I believe the conclusion is. The fourth sector is in a potentially strong position to explore this option because surely self-determination is what we're all about.

If we're not part of the solution, we're part of the problem.

Notes

1. I have restricted myself to the Pakeha:tangata whenua relationship because of the shortness of the essay and because this is the basis of most of my experience. I do feel, however, that other tauiwi will need to explore their own relationships with tangata whenua; hopefully, some points in this essay will be useful.
2. In simplistic terms, conflict theory believes that the powerful in any group, structure the group and its institutions so that they retain power, at the expense of others; social problems are structural and thus fundamental change is needed to achieve social justice/equity.
3. By 'power', I mean 'control of choices' – in one's own life and in the lives of others.
4. Some people mistakenly confuse this with apartheid, but in that situation, the dominant group retains power and imposes cultural separation.
5. I am using the term 'self-determination' for the situation where a group has ultimate authority over itself only; sometimes 'sovereignty' is used by others to refer to what I have called 'self-determination'.
6. The Crown thought it had acquired sovereignty in Article 1 of the English version of the Treaty, but more tangata whenua had signed the Maori text which only gave the Crown the right to govern, not sovereignty, and thus they opposed the government's presumption of ultimate authority. Self-determination initiatives included Kingitanga establishing its own schools, and Rua Kenana discouraging his followers from sending their children to the Native Schools so they would not be socialised as Pakeha.

7. That is, by Pakeha of tangata whenua; the reverse is already required of most tangata whenua in order for them to survive in a society in which Pakeha institutions dominate.
8. Which means doing whatever is necessary to ensure that members of non-dominant cultural group(s) are not disadvantaged because of being culturally different.
9. The fisheries 'agreement' is a good example.
10. We were well aware from the 'Pay the Rent' campaign that even the power we had, to choose which the group would be, was a privilege and a burden.

References

Benseman, J. (1992), *Whare Wananga*, Wellington: Research and Statistics Division, Ministry of Education.

Booth, J.M. and Hunn, J.K. (1962), *Integration of Maori and Pakeha*, Wellington: Government Printer.

Biggs, B. (1968), 'The Maori Language Past and Present', in Schwimmer, E. (ed.), *The Maori People in the Nineteen-sixties*, Auckland: Blackwood and Janet Paul, pp. 65–84.

Education Gazette (1991), 'Ten Point Plan for Maori Education', 15 March.

Metge, J. (1990), *Te Kohao o te Ngira: Culture and Learning*, Wellington: Learning Media, Ministry of Education.

Schwimmer, E. (1968), *The Maori People in the Nineteen-sixties*, Auckland: Blackwood and Janet Paul.

Waitangi Consultancy (1992), 'Maori Language and the Education System', in *Cultural Identity: Whakamana Tangata*, Wellington: Quest Rapuara.

8

So, Whose Logic is it Anyway?

The Dilemma of Working as a Person of Iwi Descent in a Tertiary Educational Institution

Miriama Scott

Introduction

Do we use Aristotelian logic or mauri (life principle)? Equality of opportunity or oppression? 'We are all one people' or do we mean tino rangatiratanga (sovereignty)? Is the preservation of the status quo at the expense of cultural safety? These questions symbolise the dilemma of working cross-culturally, both on a macro level of the wider society and on the micro level of the person, who is placed in this situation. At stake, is the identity of the person concerned and in this respect, cultural safety is indeed an issue.

If logic is the 'science of reasoning', then whose logic prevails when a person of iwi descent is employed as a facilitator of learning by a tauiwi tertiary educational institution? In order to answer this vexed question, the following discussion will examine the notions of 'the self', 'identity' and 'cultural safety' within the context of learning.

The Question of Identity

The thesis of Herbert Mead presents the distinction between the 'I' and the 'me' as composites of the 'self'. The 'I' is the unique part of a person and the 'me' reflects that part, which is socialised by the wider society and therefore acts as a moderating force over the 'I'.

> The unity and structure of the complete self reflects the unity and structure of the social process as a whole; and each of the elementary selves of which it is composed reflects the unity and structure of one of the various aspects of that process in which the individual is implicated ... the structure of the complete self is thus a reflection of the complete social process.
> (Mead, 1970: 45)

But what if the complete self is in conflict with the complete social process because of two systems of reasoning, which are antithetical to each other? In the context of this discussion, education is a social process, of which an aspect is working cross-culturally. Both the educational process and cross-cultural encounters have the potential to impact on the identity of the person to bring cultural safety into question.

> If the given human individual is to develop a self in the fullest sense, it is not sufficient for him merely to take the attitudes of other human individuals toward himself and toward one another within the human social process and to bring that social process as a whole into his individual experience merely in these terms. He must also, in the same way that he takes the attitudes of other individuals toward himself and toward one another, take their attitudes toward the various phases or aspects of the common social activity or set of social undertakings in which, as members of an organised society or social group, they are all engaged. And he must then, by generalising these individual attitudes of that organised society or social group itself, as a whole, act toward different social projects which at any given time it is carrying out, or toward the various larger phases of the general social process which constitutes its life and of which these projects are specific manifestations.
> (Mead, 1970: 45–46)

We are primarily social beings, interacting with one another and creating the very social processes that set the context for our interaction. But the values inherent in this interaction, it is suggested, are based on certain forms of logic which can be both inclusive and exclusive.

To re-examine the interplay between individual and social environment,

... the essential basis and prerequisite of the fullest development of that individual's self: only in so far as he takes the attitudes of the organised social group to which he belongs toward the organised, co-operative social activity or set of such activities in which that group as such is engaged, does he develop a complete self or possess the sort of complete self he has developed ... and only through the taking by individuals of the attitude or attitudes of the generalised other toward themselves is the existence of a universe of discourse, as that system of common or social meaning which thinking presupposes as its context, rendered possible.

(Mead, 1970: 46)

If the thesis of the 'self' and the resulting logic is followed, then it is suggested the 'I', which may be considered the essence of 'self', has just as much potential to moderate the impact of the 'me', the part that is influenced by the 'generalised other'. But if the 'I' is pervasive in the logic of whakakotahitanga (the process of making one), then the 'self' is the 'generalised other' as is the 'generalised other' the 'self'. Identity is then as much a response to social phenomena as is social phenomena a response to identity.

Identity and Cultural Safety

The situation to which both forms of logic are applied is as a person of iwi and Pakeha descent, working in a tauiwi tertiary educational institution. Here the dialectic between 'servant' and 'expert' is apparent.

It can be argued that identity is affirmed by the 'generalised other' according to iwi membership and ascribed by the wider tauiwi society. There are in this context, two 'generalised other', both of whom carry their own set of expectations, their own set of reasonings and both seek to influence the person of iwi descent. This duality has the potential to result in conflict and the question of 'Please tell me who I am' indeed becomes an issue. It is therefore suggested that 'identity' is preserved and nurtured *only* within the boundaries of a social environment that is culturally safe.

How do the 'self', 'identity' and 'cultural safety' translate into the everyday existence of a person of iwi descent working within a tertiary educational institution? It is suggested here that the translation involves three areas: the structure of the institution itself, the expectation placed on the person of iwi descent by the institution (in that ethnic membership is seen to equate to 'expert'); and how the source of this expertise (that is 'identity') is maintained by the person of iwi descent under these conditions.

The structure of the institution has its own 'identity', its own set of values and expectations, its own reasoning which culminate in the 'generalised other'. The process of education, it is argued, originates from a perception of learning which in Aotearoa/New Zealand is largely British in origin but in these current times, overlaid by North American ideals. The context therefore has a distinctive ethnic and cultural bias.

Curricula are influenced by perceived demand, which tends to be based on an economic system imported into Aotearoa/New Zealand from distant lands. The aspect of 'user pays' typifies the New Right ideals of economic reform and this has been and is continuing to be inculcated into tertiary educational institutions. Educational wares are now marketable commodities being sold in the open marketplace. But who is going to buy? Only those who can afford to buy. These people, it is suggested, espouse a commonality of social meaning which is derived within the context of Western European values. It is therefore argued that tauiwi tertiary educational institutions merely serve to preserve the status quo.

Honouring Te Tiriti o Waitangi

Confusion prevails when iwi and tauiwi honour Te Tiriti o Waitangi in the quest for equality: recognising ethnocentrism (ethnic bias) and striving for the understanding of cultural difference, become primary objectives. Into this arena steps the person of iwi descent, whose employment within the tertiary educational institution is seen as essential to fulfilling these sociocultural objectives. But the essential question to be raised is 'will the structure really change' or is the perceived change merely 'window dressing'? If the structure does not change overall, then the identity of the person of iwi descent runs a very high risk of being abused. The very uniqueness of tangata whenua in terms of ethnicity and status within Aotearoa/New Zealand is now being determined, in accordance with utilitarian value, by a structure which is primarily, culturally unsafe. The practice of understanding cultural difference is now at the discretion of the dominant 'generalised other'.

The abuse can be seen in terms of tauiwi expectation. For a person of iwi descent is expected to be an instant 'expert', always presenting and preserving the tikanga of iwi, while often having to challenge the very basis from which the expectation has arisen. In this aspect cultural awareness goes hand in hand with cultural safety. They are not necessarily compatible either, because awareness does not always bring about safety.

The person of iwi descent is frequently caught between the commitment of a tauiwi tertiary educational institution to facilitate the learning of nga take o nga iwi o Aotearoa in honouring Te Tiriti o Waitangi and yet the structure of such an institution is a manifestation of a social process (namely, education), which reflects the inherent values or identity of tauiwi.

The consequence of this dichotomy is an apparent duality of expectation. On the one hand, tauiwi tertiary educational institutions expect people of iwi descent to meet the obligations of Te Tiriti o Waitangi, while the person of iwi descent often has to exert an expectation, reflected by iwi, to ensure the information being shared is protected by a realm of cultural safety. In this respect who is bicultural now?

> By virtue or by default Maaori are inherently bicultural. It is what has been conditioned in their here and now. It is what a Maaori is because of his or her encounter with tauiwi experience. It is what one has to be to survive. Biculturalism cannot be taught. Thinking, behaving and doing are all part and parcel of creating life and one's experience. It has to be lived and experienced, ...
> (Mataira, 1995: 10)

Whether intentionally or not, the person of iwi descent is expected by tauiwi to bring about awareness of nga take o nga iwi o Aotearoa, while the tauiwi tertiary educational institution does not necessarily guarantee the fulfilment of the expectation by iwi, that the information shared will be treated within a safe environment. In this way, the commitment to cultural awareness, cultural safety and ultimately biculturalism is only carried by the person of iwi descent. The one-way street scenario is obvious, with a potentially very serious consequence of who is going to change whom?

But honouring Te Tiriti o Waitangi is not just looking at the issues of iwi – the place of tauiwi within these issues also has to be examined. Why? Tauiwi are the other half of the equation, the instigators of social processes and structures, who are seen to dictate expectation and influence identity. But this is a journey that many tauiwi find difficult, because it does require a scrutiny of tauiwi identity and recognition of the influences of social processes and structures that often do not take cognisance of iwi values. In this instance, biculturalism is perceived by some tauiwi as an unnecessary struggle, thereby supporting the prevalence of one form of reasoning.

The place of tauiwi in the debate surrounding cultural safety is clearly delineated within the nursing profession. In particular, it is identified in an article by Ramsden and Spoonley:

> Therefore cultural safety is an educational process. It involves teaching nurses to recognise themselves as bearers of their own

culture and to understand how that culture impacts upon other people. Cultural risk in nursing occurs when people from one culture believe they are demeaned and disempowered by the actions and delivery systems of people from another culture. Cultural safety assumes that all nursing interactions are bicultural regardless of the number of people or the number of cultural frameworks through which messages are filtered between the giver of the message and the receiver of that message.

(Ramsden and Spoonley, 1993: 164)

The wider society is therefore implicated and the prevailing attitudes are scrutinised as the debate about cultural safety has moved from the preserve of nursing and health professionals and out into the public domain, it has highlighted the generic issues and obstacles for any form of service delivery which seeks to be culturally sensitive. ... It highlights the obstacles to consideration of options that might be post-colonial, that is, structures and practices which try to neutralise the inequities of a colonial past ... the substantial opposition to any move towards tino rangatiratanga and raises central questions about what is guaranteed by way of citizenship rights in Aotearoa.

(Ramsden and Spoonley, 1993: 171)

The traditional values of the 'generalised other' inherent in the context of social processes and structures are now being challenged as impeding the attainment of a bicultural society.

If Aotearoa/New Zealand is to become expansive in its adherence to biculturalism, then tauiwi have to accept responsibility for change, to enable iwi to achieve full and equitable citizenship within this country. One of the terms of reference for the Royal Commission on Social Policy (1987: 4) stated, 'Acceptance of the identity and cultures of different peoples within the community and understanding and respect for cultural diversity'.

This standard recognises that the people of New Zealand come from many different cultures. It sees cultural diversity as desirable – something to be supported and encouraged. 'It reflects our commitment to the International Covenant on Civil and Political Rights. Article 27 states that those belonging to ethnic and linguistic minorities shall not be denied the right to enjoy their own culture and to use their own language' (Royal Commission on Social Policy, 1987: 4). One can only ponder the logic of this statement and the ramifications for practical implementation.

In the context of this discussion, the very reason that a person of iwi descent was selected for employment by the tauiwi tertiary educational institution is because of the uniqueness of ethnic membership – 'identity' or the essence of 'self', the mauri. The affirmation of identity is an integral part to the sustenance of the person of iwi descent.

> My being Maori is absolutely dependent on my history as a Tuhoe person as against being a Maori person. It seems to me there is no such thing as Maoritanga because Maoritanga is an all-inclusive term which embraces all Maoris. And there are so many different aspects about every tribal person. Each tribe has its own history. And it's not a history that can be shared among others.
> (Rangihau, 1977: 174)

The affirmation and maintenance of identity also carries an expectation by iwi of iwi that whakahiihii (to make vain) will not prevail. The label of 'expert' ascribed by the tauiwi tertiary educational institution is offset by the iwi itself, which invests the person of iwi descent with the responsibility to represent iwi and therefore remain located within the group, not to step outside to assume the mantle of 'expert'. In this the roles of 'expert' and 'servant' become enmeshed in the 'self', the 'generalised other' and a social process which supposedly gives meaning and context to a social environment. But how does the person of iwi descent in a tauiwi tertiary educational institution marry these two disparate forms of reasoning? With extreme difficulty, it is suggested.

The person of iwi descent can both 'champion' issues pertaining to iwi and ensure the cultural safety of students of iwi descent is recognised. But as well, this person is engaged in 'educating' the tauiwi tertiary educational institution in culturally sensitive processes, while being subject to the reasoning of the overall educational structure as a staff member. Being 'between a rock and a hard place' seems to be a rather apt description.

The person of iwi descent is therefore spanning two sets of expectations, which inherently reflect two sets of value systems and as a consequence, imply the existence of two forms of logic. The role of the person of iwi descent can be perceived as being both 'intellectual' and 'radical', but at stake, it is argued, is the preservation of 'identity', the mauri, the 'self' in its entirety. Conflict or compromise can entail a very bitter personal battle.

What is the resolution of such a potentially divisive experience? It is in the rectifying of imbalance by establishing an equitable relationship between the 'self', the 'generalised other' (both iwi and tauiwi) and the social processes, which are the consequences of this interaction. The dilemma of 'who I am' is no longer an issue, because the question is no longer relevant, as the 'I' and the 'me' have undergone whakakotahitanga within a supportive social environment, within which preservation of identity is a right.

The co-existence of two forms of logic is acknowledged and the paramountcy of one over the other is no longer adhered to, because citizenship in Aotearoa/New Zealand is viewed as both manifesting self-determination and tino rangatiratanga. We can therefore look at the future.

I finish with two quotes from very different traditions:

Ideals for the Year 2000

The Ideal Maori:
The ideal Maori of the year 2000 is a person whose mauri or spiritual essence is strong, who is comfortable in both worlds, Maori and Pakeha, who is educated to his or her full potential, who is visionary in the sense of being able to think on a broad scale and positively, who is committed to being Maori and who has a strong commitment to the Treaty of Waitangi.

The Ideal Pakeha:
The ideal Pakeha of the year 2000 is a person who is supportive of the ideal Maori, who speaks and understands the Maori language, who is comfortable in Maori cultural situations, who is visionary in the same sense as described for the ideal Maori, who is committed to Aotearoa and to the Treaty of Waitangi.

The Ideal Iwi:
As a social, political and economic unit, the ideal iwi of the year 2000 is strong, its members are committed to belonging to the unit, its integrity as an iwi is secure, its economic wellbeing is evenly distributed among its constituent hapu and it has a progressive development plan for the future.

Ideal Environment:
- Te Tiriti o Waitangi is properly honoured as a covenant between two peoples
- reflects the values of both partners
- equal justice for all under the Treaty of Waitangi
- by the terms of the Treaty of Waitangi, the Maori partner's rights to a fair share of assets is guaranteed
- the natural environment and national assets are protected

- no alienation of land to foreign powers without the consent of both partners
- being Maori is no longer an issue
- tino rangatiratanga is achieved.

(Ngaa Tuaraa, 1990: 3)

After all:

> Who is it that says most? which can say more,
> Than this rich praise, that you alone are you?
> In whose confine immured is the store
> Which should example where your equal grew.
> Lean penury within that pen doth dwell
> That to his subject lends not some small glory;
> But he that writes of you, if he can tell
> That you are you, so dignifies his story.
> Let him but copy what in you is writ,
> Not making worse what nature made so clear,
> And such a counterpart shall fame his wit,
> Making his style admired everywhere.
>   You to your beauteous blessings add a curse,
>   Being fond on praise, which makes your praises worse.

(William Shakespeare, Sonnet 84)

> You are unique
> You cannot be replaced or duplicated,
> Your value is not in what you do or become
> Your value comes simply from being you.
> You alone are you!

References

Mead, G.H. (1970), 'The Self', in Worsley, P. (ed.), *Modern Sociology,* Middlesex: Penguin Books Limited.

Mataira, P. (1995), 'Bicultural Wisdom: Navigating the Bicultural Seas', in *Te Komako: Social Work Review,* vol. vii, no. 1, January.

Ngaa Tuaraa (1990), *He Taahuhu mo te Tau Ruamano: Discussion Paper for the Year 2000,* Wellington: Te Tira Ahu Iwi.

Ramsden, I. and Spoonley, P. (1993), 'The Cultural Safety Debate in Nursing Education in Aotearoa', in *New Zealand Annual Review of Education*, Number 3, Wellington: Education Department, Victoria University.

Rangihau, J. (1977), 'Being Maori', in King, M. (ed.) *Te Ao Hurihuri: World Moves On: Aspects of Maoritanga*, Hicks Smith and Sons/Methuen New Zealand Limited.

Tapara, T. and Weir, T. (1990), Unpublished survey on community education in Tamaki Makaurau, Auckland.

The Royal Commission on Social Policy (1987), *A Fair and Just Society: A Guide to the Terms and References of the Royal Commission on Social Policy,* Wellington.

Part 3
Learning Contexts

9

Learning in the Community:

Non-formal and Informal Education

Colin Gunn

Introduction

For the purposes of this chapter it has been assumed that the term 'learning in the community' refers to that learning which takes place *outside* classrooms or formal settings. This assumption excludes areas long considered part of community education, namely those adult programmes offered by schools, the continuing education centres of universities and their community education equivalents in polytechnics. It also excludes courses run by private training establishments and work-based learning. With the exception of private training establishments, all of these are covered elsewhere in this book.

When limited in this way, the term adult education in the community covers two principal forms of learning. First, that learning provided by community organisations for their membership/clientele (e.g. people with asthma) or for the public at large (e.g. an anti-smoking campaign). This type of learning is sometimes called 'non-formal learning' (see page 153). Second, that learning undertaken by individuals independent of formal and non-formal educational providers, whether they are state, private or community-based. This latter form of learning may involve family, whanau, friends or workmates and is sometimes called 'informal independent learning' (also see page 155).

This chapter concentrates substantially on the learning provided by community organisations, looking first at some common characteristics, trends and problems and then outlines some of the diversity found within this broad spectrum of learning. It concludes with a brief discussion on aspects of informal independent learning.

Learning Provided by Community Organisations – Characteristics

Autonomy is a key feature of these organisations. They appoint their own leaders and largely direct their own fate. While most groups have a formally elected management committee or board, they are often run in an informal way and make decisions by consensus rather than by formal motions and votes. Traditionally, many have had no legal status, although in recent years this has been changing as many funding providers now require this (e.g. incorporated society or charitable trust). Common groupings include health, welfare, justice, sport and recreation, church, arts and crafts, cultural/ethnic and trade unions. While a few have an explicit educational base – for example, Workers Educational Association (WEA), Te Ataarangi and Adult Reading and Learning Association (ARLA) – many do not immediately define their prime purpose as being educational, for example Birthright, arts centres. In practice, however, educational elements, either for the direct users of their services or the public at large, are considerable. It is difficult to assess the extent of learning experienced in this manner, but as it covers a great deal of adult learning in areas as diverse as health, parenting, hobby, craft, recreation and sport, ethnic/cultural, spiritual, social attitudes and many others, it is undoubtedly considerable.[1]

Similarly, it is difficult to document the total number of adults involved in these activities, although it is unquestionably large. In the Nelson region for example, one local directory of community organisations contains some 1,200 organisations[2] for a total population of approximately 77,000 which equates to one community organisation for every 64 adults. While some adults may not be involved in any such community group, given the wide range of activities (from hobbies and sport through to cultural and church groups), it might be assumed that the great majority are participating in one or more groups.

In an educational as well as in a social service sense, these community organisations can be very innovative. Learning often has a very practical and immediate purpose as learners look to make changes in their personal lives and/or in society. Learner-centred activities were central to this form of learning long before it became a buzz word in formal education and techniques such as brainstorming and the use of action methods have strong roots in community organisations. Many te reo and adult literacy and numeracy movements had their origins in this sector and have only slowly been incorporated into the formal sector. The same may be true of developments in women's studies, Maori studies, prison education, distance education and seniors' learning.

Common Trends

The community sector used to be called the voluntary sector, but the last 10 years has seen increasing difficulty in recruiting and retaining volunteers and there has been a significant increase in the number of paid workers in voluntary organisations. Regrettably, however, this paid employment is usually part-time, low-paid and of limited tenure, reflecting both the difficulty of raising money and the social value attributed to work once done voluntarily and predominantly by women workers (see Gunn, 1995).

Financial pressures have demanded fresh approaches. Membership fees and fundraising activities (the proverbial raffles and cake stalls) have been the traditional funding mechanisms, but in the last 15 years there have been significant increases in grants from government, the New Zealand Lottery Grants Board and philanthropic trusts. Recently, contracting for service and the development of an entrepreneurial or trading arm have emerged as new possibilities.[3]

In the past decade there has been a strong push towards increased professionalism with many community organisations voluntarily developing training programmes, codes of practice and ethics, business plans, systems of worker supervision, systems of assessment and organisation review. There has also been a move (in part promoted by funders) to prove the need for services, to document effective outputs and to account for expenditures, so that many in effect now operate as small businesses.

An increased demand for services has been fed by hard times and the government policy to devolve former public services. These factors, together with the increased professionalism of workers, have meant some increase in status in some areas (e.g. counselling). Community work has provided an important vocational training ground and I believe it has played a huge, if largely undocumented, role in building or re-establishing confidence in those out of the work force, especially women.

Over the past five or six years, there has been a significant increase in formal training opportunities for community workers. At the same time, some community organisations with national links (e.g. ARLA and Women's Refuge) have national input into their training and have moved to standardise their training. Some groups even issue their own 'qualifications' (such as certificates), although they are likely to increasingly look toward the National Qualifications Framework for this function. In the 1990s, mechanisms to recognise prior learning should also assist community workers to translate some of this non-formal learning into formal academic credit. Ironically, the trend towards increased training may threaten one of the key characteristics of community organisations – autonomy – at least when it comes to deciding on training needs, competency levels and registration requirements. Increasingly, institutional providers are becoming active in the training field. For example, Nelson Polytechnic currently has, or is developing, certificate programmes in community work, basic counselling, youth work, outdoor education, leadership, early childhood education, the performing arts and others – all areas where, traditionally training has been provided by community groups.

Interestingly, there has also been some movement the other way. For a variety of reasons, including funding, some community organisations have begun to provide formal learning (such as TOP courses). In most cases these are programmes funded by government departments in response to high unemployment levels and the need to raise skill levels. Again, with the development of the New Zealand Qualifications Authority National Framework, it is possible that more groups will expand provision into this area.

Very little of Vote Education is allocated to this sector. The Interim Advisory Committee on Non-formal Education (IAGNE 1987) calculated this sector's allocation to be 0.01 per cent of the total Vote Education budget. As Harré Hindmarsh (1992 and 1993) has noted, this condition has not improved in more recent years. Yet without doubt, there are large sums of money available from other sources. In an analysis of community organisations that I worked with in 1992, in excess of $700,000 was raised through grant applications and contracts in the area of health, welfare, justice, etc. and less than one per cent of this total came from Vote Education.

Problems and Prospects

Some problems have been alluded to above. They include financial insecurity, threats to autonomy that come indirectly or directly through funder requirements, the difficulty of getting and keeping both volunteers and paid workers, externally imposed certification requirements and the huge increase in the resulting volume and nature of the work, as New Zealand experiences difficult economic times and widespread structural change.

Other problems faced by community organisations include administrative difficulties (e.g. worker and management relations, filling key positions such as treasurer and chairperson), increased competition (and therefore less co-operation) between community organisations and from private sector organisations (e.g. in the provision of childcare and the servicing of the needs of people in community care). A fuller coverage of both trends, problems and prospects may be found in Gunn (1993).

The Diversity of Learning Provided by Community Organisations

The common features outlined above are substantially administrative and structural in nature. When it comes to a discussion of the intent and content of learning then diversity is also apparent. Given the space constraints of this chapter it is convenient to group this diversity into three broad types. In doing this, however, it is acknowledged that there is a range within each type, that blurring occurs at the boundaries and that many groups provide learning services in more than one type.

Type 1:   Learning with High Elements of Educator Ownership and Control

Here the educator plays a significant role in determining the content of the learning, initiating the process and evaluating outcomes. The learner is seen as a student or 'customer' who may choose to enrol or 'buy' a learning package from an expert provider. The service is provided for members (e.g. those hard of hearing) or for 'the public'. This type of learning has strong similarities to formal learning as outlined by Coombs *et al.* (1973) and further developed by others (including Gunn, 1986). It is also typical of what has been called the community service approach to community work (for a brief overview see Gunn, 1992), where groups provide services especially to those who are seen as 'disadvantaged'. Implicit in this approach is the belief that neglect or injustice can be corrected and people can 'catch up', given adequate knowledge skills and support.

Type 2:   Learning with High Elements of Learner Ownership and Control

Here the learner (either individually or collectively through a group process) has considerable control over the learning process. The learning is deliberate and purposeful, with learners deciding what they will learn, how best to achieve this and who (if anyone), will be asked to lead the instruction. Self-control and self-help are strong elements. In educational terms, this type of learning is often described as 'non-formal learning' (see Coombs *et al.*, 1973 and Gunn, 1986). In community work terms, it may also include the concept of 'community development', where the intent is to empower members or users by giving them the confidence, skills, knowledge or attitudes to make decisions for themselves. Unlike community service, where the educator's emphasis is doing things *for others*, community development stresses a process where the educator encourages or empowers the learner to do things *for themselves*.

*Type 3:   Learning with High Elements of Educator Control Over the Content
and Delivery of Learning but Not Over its Reception*

This type of learning includes the work done by community activists and by community organisations using the media for public education campaigns. Here the educator, not the learner, identifies the learning needs and strategies and delivers the message to an audience not always directly known to them and who may or may not be receptive to the message in terms of its content, learning styles, time or place. Learners can and often do, choose not to hear, see or read the messages or to act upon them if they do. The target of learning may be decision-makers, opinion makers (such as community leaders and the media) or the public at large.

This type of learning includes two forms of learning described by Gunn (1986) – 'action-based learning' and 'informal, independent media learning'. Both contain elements of formal learning in that the 'educator' sets the content and methods. When decision-makers are targeted, the 'learner' may have considerably more power than the 'educator' – an interesting reversal of the formal learning scene. In community work, this type of endeavour is increasingly called 'community action' (see Gunn, 1992 for a brief overview). An example in my region is Health Action, a small autonomous trust that aims to address issues of alcohol abuse and smoking (among others). They do so by making submissions on public policy at the local and national levels, monitoring policy implementation and by using the media to 'educate' public opinion. The Maruia Society is an example of a national organisation operating in the environmental field.

In community action, specialist knowledge and strategies are required. For example, to lobby effectively, educators need to understand the political and/or decision-making processes well and be able to judge accurately the most appropriate position between co-operation and confrontation. They have to know how to build coalitions of support, how to make an effective submission, how to seek compromises and many other things. If their aim is to enlist public support, a different range of skills and knowledge will also be required, such as identifying their prime audiences and deciding how, where and when to approach their 'learners', understanding what might motivate them to learn and so forth.

Community organisations operating in the preventive area often come under this category and one of the educational challenges they face is to find practical and economical ways of monitoring progress and evaluating success. If the desired learning outcome is a change in policy ultimately, their effectiveness might be easy to judge (i.e. the policy was or was not changed). The ability to monitor or adjust throughout a campaign, however, may not be so easy. Similarly, the impact a media message has on individual learners is normally unknown – except in broad sense (e.g. x number people wrote a letter, y attended a meeting). Little is usually known about why people react to these strategies in the way they do and why it works for some and not for others. Evaluation methods such as polling may be used to try to answer these questions, but this in itself is a special skill and it is not yet widely used by community organisations. Much community action and media learning is aimed at changing people's attitudes and consequential behaviour, but this is often a long-term goal over years, if not decades. Also, a number of forces may be acting at the same time and it may be difficult to calculate the particular contribution of a single programme.

Educators in this area of learning need to be as skilled in their trade as any. While they may face a high proportion of reluctant learners, they also face the prospect of having widespread influence, as it is possible to simultaneously address thousands of potential learners.

Cost may be the critical factor in determining the form of media education. National organisations such as the Cancer Society, the IHC and the AIDS Foundation mount national promotions which are often as much linked to fundraising as they are to public education. For small autonomous community groups, low- or no-cost campaigns are the norm. This usually involves a planned sequence such as short 'info' clips (say, 10–15 seconds on local radio), talkbacks and interviews, news releases, news stories, feature articles and letters to the editor. If carefully negotiated, week-long or month-long campaigns can be conducted at no cost to the group.

Technological advances in the communications industry are likely to transform this type of learning. Multi television channels (including eTV – educational television), interactive programmes, access to Internet, computer-based bulletin boards and databases are already developing (see Benseman and Stewart, 1995). For the learner, media learning already involves costs (including newspaper subscriptions, hardware, TV sets, etc.) and this cost may disadvantage social groups with poor financial resources.[4] Modern technology is also likely to continue to internationalise knowledge. As New Zealanders get easy access to overseas programmes and processes, it will be important that a New Zealand component is protected and that minority and local ethnic interests are not swamped.

Informal Independent Learning

This is probably, in quantitative terms, the principal form of adult learning, although only a brief overview is possible here. As noted above, Tough (1978) estimated self-planned learning to account for approximately 70 per cent of all adult learning. Because it is largely undocumented and 'occurs anyway', it gets little direct support from the state or from people who consider themselves community educators. Rather, support comes from whanau, friends and family, public libraries, community learning exchanges and informal media learning sources.

There is also a paucity of recent research into the type and nature of this learning – Tough (1978) for instance, only considered *deliberate* learning that exceeded seven hours per learning project. He found, in his study covering Canada, U.S.A., Ghana and New Zealand that the average person conducted eight such projects and spent a minimum 700 hours (the equivalent of 88 eight-hour days) on them. When *non-deliberate* or *incidental* learning (which may include changing attitudes, some parenting skills) are considered, the sum total of this type of learning is likely to be even more impressive. As computer and communication technology continues apace, changes to independent learning are even more likely and this will lead to the need to explore and define this type of learning further.

Two important characteristics of informal, independent learning are the wide range of locations in which it occurs (home, work, recreation) and the source of inspiration (whether personal and/or supported by family, friends and workmates). In some cases (e.g. attitudinal change, parenting) the learning and/or sources may not be immediately acknowledged by the learner. The motivation for the new learning may simply be the desire to do something different because of boredom, the need to try something which is more effective, or the desire for self-satisfaction (see Gunn, work in progress).

Conclusion

It is highly likely that informal independent learning will remain the single most important source of learning for adults and that advances in information and communication technology (providing cost is not a dominant factor) will bring new and fruitful learning opportunities to the population at large.

Learning provided by autonomous community organisations, as discussed above, looks set to remain the 'Cinderella' of the fourth sector and of the education sector as a whole. Such agencies receive little recognition in terms of Vote Education funding and are substantially overlooked in educational research. The introduction of the New Zealand Qualifications Authority's National Framework, with its emphasis on formal learning, may further divert funds away from this form of learning. In the past, relative neglect has had an advantage in that it has protected community organisations' autonomy, but recently however, increased demands for services (many resulting from the devolution of government services), the difficulty in raising funds, problems in recruiting volunteers and the increasing sophistication of skills required have all conspired to impose new stresses on their traditional autonomy and to test their ability to keep up with the demands. This said however, learning provided by community organisations is not diminishing. New groups emerge every year and the level of professionalism continues to grow. Undoubtedly adults personally benefit by contributing to community groups and, where these individual needs are matched to community ones, it is not unrealistic to predict both a secure role for this form of adult learning and in the mid to longer term, a growing recognition of its value and power.

Notes

1. There is a lack of accurate, recent research on the extent of learning in non-formal and informal contexts, but a study in 1979 by Tough estimated that 70 per cent of all adult learning is of an informal, independent nature. Of the 30 per cent remainder, I estimate most would be non-formal, with formal learning accounting for only some 5–10 per cent.
2. This total is conservative as it does not cover all organisations or list multiple sub-branches of groups such as Plunket.
3. Examples of this approach are found at Te Whanau o Waipareira and the People's Centre in Auckland.
4. Although to date there appears to be no sign of any slowing of the pace of either the decrease in the price or the increase of the capacity of the communication technology involved. The rule of greater capacity at a cheaper price should continue for some time yet.

References

Benseman, J. and Stewart, L. (1995), *Evaluation of an Electronic Bulletin Board Service for Alcohol Health Promotion Workers*, Auckland: Alcohol and Public Health Research Unit.
Coombs, P.H. *et al.* (1973), *New Paths to Learning* – prepared for UNICEF by the International Council for Educational Development, New York.
Gunn, C. (Oct. 1986), 'Redefining Types of Adult Learning', *New Zealand Journal of Adult Learning*, vol. 18, no. 2, pp. 31–47.
Gunn, C. (1–3 July 1992), 'Public Bodies, Community Development and Economy: Maximising the Effectiveness of Health Promotion Services in Investing in Health: The Economics of Health Promotion', Papers from the Health Promotion Forum Second National Conference, Auckland: Health Promotion Forum of New Zealand.
Gunn, C. (Oct. 1993), 'Community-based Learning: Some Past Trends and Future Possibilities', *New Zealand Journal of Adult Learning*, vol. 21, no. 2, pp. 23–41.

Gunn, C. (1995), *What is Happening to Community Education?*, Nelson: Nelson Polytechnic.

Gunn, C. (work in progress), 'The Community Educator and the Enhancement of Informal Independent Learning'.

Harré Hindmarsh, J. (1992), 'Community and Continuing Education in 1992: Trends and Issues', *New Zealand Annual Review of Education 2*, Wellington, pp. 179–204.

Harré Hindmarsh, J. (1993), 'Vote Education Funding for Adult Education: Who Benefits? Part One: Community Organisations', Wellington: Ministry of Education and Victoria University.

IAGNE (1987), 'Interim Advisory Group on Non-formal Education Report to the Minister of Education', Wellington: Ministry of Education.

Tough, A.M. (1978), 'Major Learning Efforts: Recent Research and Future Directions', *Adult Education*, vol. xxvii, no. 4, pp. 250–263.

10

Workers' Education and Training in a New Environment

Michael Law

Introduction

The economic and social restructuring that began in New Zealand in the early 1980s has changed fundamentally the relationship between working people and education. For much of this century that relationship was underpinned by the social democratic assumptions and practices we associate with the welfare state. Now, in line with 'neo-liberal' (New Right) ideology, educational opportunities have been firmly located within the framework of 'voluntarist' labour market policies that emphasise 'human capital development' as the key to improved economic performance. Two important legislative initiatives in 1992 confirmed this general trend: the abolition of the Trade Union Education Authority (TUEA) and the adoption of the Industry Training Act (ITA).

The purpose of this chapter is to trace and analyse recent developments in workers' education and training. It examines those changes in an historical and theoretical context that has regard to both domestic and international influences and the interaction between them. The central theme of the chapter is that the 'ideology of the market' has squeezed the democratic dimension out of workers' education and training and that this has important implications for the field of adult education. The analysis is presented in three sections. The first introduces some theoretical ideas and highlights some major characteristics of the welfare state era; the second briefly describes and evaluates the TUEA experiment; the third examines developments in the 1990s. The chapter ends with a set of formative conclusions.

Workers' Education, Training and the Welfare State

Origins and Traditions: A Theoretical Note

The welfare state was a compromise that began to take shape in the late nineteenth century as working people started to secure industrial and political rights. By the middle of this century welfare capitalism was consolidated throughout the 'Western' world. In New Zealand, key landmarks were the election of the Liberal government in 1890 and of the first Labour government in 1935 (Sinclair, 1969; Sutch, 1966). The essence of this compromise was that those who did not own the means of production accepted private ownership while those who owned capital stock accepted a political system that permitted 'other groups to effectively press their claims to the allocation of resources and the distribution of output' (Przeworski and Wallerstein, 1986: 207).

The inherently democratic idea that access to public education was a *social right* was an important element in this compromise (King, 1987). In general, two sets of pressures led to the coming together of a complex alliance in favour of public education. The first was the general democratic movement, of which the growing labour and socialist movement was an important element; the second was the economic and industrial imperative: the need to train and retrain the expanding work force (Williams, 1961/1980). In most countries, including New Zealand, the second of these imperatives was the more influential. Much of the story of education, including adult education, from the 1870s through to the present, can be viewed as a series of 'settlements' that attempted to resolve the tension between these two sets of pressures. These settlements were never final, with shifts in economic and political circumstances often leading to adjustments.

Workers' education contributed significantly to the making and development of the welfare state compromise. This education was both critical and instrumental. Originating within the long struggle for social justice, workers' education had as its central purpose the economic, political and social advancement of working people. In keeping with twentieth-century working-class politics, this tradition's ideology and strategy were largely social democratic. But in New Zealand, as in other countries, radical perspectives were active, even if as a minority current. This proved important during the first half of this century. For as an intellectual as well as practical force within the political Left, workers' education played a key role in creating a constituency for the extension of a much richer vision of public education, including adult education, than industrial capitalism required and would have willingly conceded.

That vision incorporated a view of *training* that implied much more than the narrow acquisition and renewal of workplace skills to which it is at present being reduced. Artisans most obviously, but beyond them a wide range of skilled and semi-skilled workers, have long valued the cultivation of talents and understandings that not only enabled them to earn a living but also to achieve an element of autonomy and an enriched quality of life. This can be illustrated by innumerable experiments in adult education from the first mechanics' institutes and worker libraries through to recent experiences with TUEA. Unfortunately, this vision has often been at odds with the dynamics of industrial capitalism, especially its tendency to break down and fragment holistic crafts and skills.

Tripartism: A Co-operative Approach to Economic Growth

A core characteristic of welfare state compromises was a legislated industrial relations system that recognised workers' collective rights and which attempted to balance their interests with those of employers. The usual corollary was a tripartite strategy whereby the government worked with employers and unions, as *social partners*, in the formulating and implementing of economic and social policies designed to achieve the central goals of welfare capitalism: economic growth, full employment, a steady rise in the standard of living and the moderate reformation of work in order to humanise, within limits, production. In education, these goals implied policies that:

- integrated working people as citizens in the modern state
- satisfied their educational expectations for themselves and their children
- accommodated employers' desire to have the state bear the cost of training and retraining the work force.

In the 1960s and 1970s a complicated mix of economic and social pressures led New Zealand to adopt a more systematic approach to locating training within a comprehensive labour market strategy (Williams, 1980). Post-secondary education was expanded; later, regional community colleges (now polytechnics) were created and, as unemployment emerged, special training schemes were introduced. A sense of order was brought to training with the enactment of the Vocational Training Act in 1968. This established a Vocational Training Council (VTC) and a network of industry training boards and regional training offices

(Pearce and Stuart, 1978). In 1969, the National Development Conference (NDC) identified enhanced training as vital to economic and social development. A significant feature of these measures was the cementing in, structurally, of tripartism with unions and employers well represented on the VTC and its boards, the NDC and its various working groups and the governing bodies of technical institutes and community colleges.

'Lifelong Learning': A Democratic Initiative

By the late 1960s, however, the upsurge in radical politics and the early signs of economic strains prompted a dramatic rethinking internationally of educational policies. The United Nations Educational Scientific and Cultural Organisation (UNESCO) formulated and actively promoted the concept of 'lifelong learning' (Fauré, 1972). This explicitly democratic vision attracted widespread support because of its 'potential to respond to the new challenges caused by rapid and unprecedented change by continuing the process of renewal of knowledge, skills and values throughout life' (Rubenson, 1994: 13). Similarly, the International Labour Office (ILO) advanced a concept of workers' education that went well beyond vocational and industrial relations training and which strongly affirmed workers' right to paid educational leave (PEL). The Organisation for Economic Co-operation and Development (OECD) also appeared to endorse UNESCO's vision. But while its rhetoric was similar, the OECD concept of 'recurrent education' placed priority on economic growth, the rights of capital and managerial prerogative.

In New Zealand, the publication of a report on lifelong education (Simmonds, 1972) coincided with the election of the third Labour government, which had policy commitments to the extension of educational opportunities at all levels. These were endorsed by the Educational Development Conference and steadily introduced over the rest of the decade. Thus for a period it seemed that New Zealand had, on a bipartisan political basis, 'embarked on a systematic attempt to create a learning society founded on principles of lifelong education' (Boshier, 1980: 1).

Developments in Workers' Education

The Labour government (1972–1975) made modest, although not insignificant, efforts to breathe new life into workers' education. Restoration of the grant for the Workers' Educational Association (WEA) undoubtedly benefited a proportion of working people and their children, as citizens (Shuker, 1984). But there was very little recognition of their learning needs as workers, apart from labour market training.

The exception was the establishment in 1974 of a Trade Union Training Board (TUTB) under the auspices of the VTC. This tentative initiative was always doomed to produce limited results. The TUTB was hampered by inherent structural and resource weaknesses, a narrow concept of trade union training, an absence of paid educational leave and problems of credibility in the eyes of many unionists. Nevertheless, it did enable trade union education to begin to gather some traction. Between 1978 and 1985, TUTB-sponsored programmes rose from 119 to 303; over the same period participation increased from approximately 2,000 to 4,461, peaking at 5,183 in 1984 (Law, 1985). Much of this education was, at least at one level, instrumental, with over 85 per cent of the programmes for job delegates or union officials; most of the remainder (seven per cent) were concerned with health and safety. Two small, but important, exceptions were seminars for women unionists (approximately two per cent) and seminars for education officers (two per cent) (Law, 1985).

Undoubtedly the great achievement of the TUTB was the focus it gave union education. Its regular seminars for union educators led to a far-sighted policy statement from the Federation of Labour (FOL) that, for the first time, outlined a planned approach to trade union education within the wider context of lifelong learning. The policy aspired to improve 'the broad knowledge and understanding of rank-and-file members, so that they are empowered to act in promoting their collective interests' (NZ FOL, 1981). Although its starting point was unionists as workers, the policy consistently underlined their rights and responsibilities as citizens. It also stressed the importance of union control over trade union education and insisted on the need for state funding and legislation providing for paid educational leave. This maturation in the trade union movement's understanding of the nature and purposes of trade union education and its (reluctant) acceptance of a statist approach to securing resources and PEL provided the basis for the eventual establishment of the Trade Union Education Authority in 1986.

The Unravelling of the Compromise

A welfare state government has 'two contradictory imperatives': the provision of welfare expenditure and the securing of 'the conditions of capital accumulation necessary for capitalist development' (Plant, 1985: 5). By the early 1970s it was becoming evident that welfare capitalism was struggling to reconcile this contradiction. On the Left, critics focused on the inability of social democracy to deliver on its promise to reform society in the interests of working people; education was one sphere that attracted considerable critique (see Whitty, 1985). However, as the crisis of welfare capitalism deepened, other, relatively dormant, critiques were repolished and reformulated as 'New

Right' ideology (Barry, 1987). These included, but were by no means limited to, concerns about welfare capitalism's inability to secure conditions of capital accumulation.

Western governments concluded that enterprises had to become more profitable and the public sector had to become more productive. Initially, they tried to effect change through greater intervention in the economy while remaining within the broad parameters of the welfare state compromise and the framework of tripartism. This strategy often included new initiatives in vocational education and training with special attention devoted to youth unemployment. In New Zealand, unions were represented on a plethora of local, regional and national bodies concerned with the 'transition from school to work' and, as unemployment became more endemic, training and retraining. Meanwhile unions employed workers' education to popularise the outline of a more aggressive, nationalist, economic policy. Essentially Keynesian, this policy advocated full employment, an incomes policy, an industrial development strategy and some redistribution of income and wealth (Campbell and Kirk, 1983). However, this approach lost momentum in the year preceding the 1984 election as the deepening economic crisis and the abolition of compulsory union membership put the union movement into something of a tailspin.

The Labour Market Debate

By the time Labour took office in mid-1984, the 'labour market' was already being subjected to increasing scrutiny. This debate or, more accurately, complexity of debates has had a profound impact on current developments in workers' education and training. Very briefly, the 1980s saw quite widespread acceptance internationally that significant changes were occurring in workplace relations and work organisation (Littler, 1991). Much of this centred on new production concepts and a qualitative shift from 'Fordism' to 'flexible specialisation' (Piore and Sabel, 1984). These, it has been claimed, imply a move from 'industrial relations which are confrontational at a collective level' towards an approach involving 'increased participation' (ibid.: 41).

As the flexible specialisation view gained wider recognition, so too did the accompanying argument that a regular upgrading of skills would become the principal trend (Littler, 1991). Yet it was not until the mid-1980s, it seems, that concern about a 'skills gap' became more urgent. In 1988, an OECD conference on education stressed the 'interaction between education and the economy' (OECD, 1990: 64). With respect to education of adults, it held that 'the private sector in particular must assume primary responsibility for the provision of training and retraining opportunities' (ibid.: 64).

Two related strands of New Right thinking have influenced the general direction of the labour market debate. The first, which is more philosophical, focuses on 'individual freedom'. It advocates an individually-based, contractual employment relations system that is located within the common law rather than discrete or specialist legislation (Brook, 1990). The second, which emphasises the economic, argues 'that liberal institutions of free markets and limited government will maximise' best the aims of prosperity and liberty (Barry, 1987: 26).

The three main parties in industrial relations responded by staking out different positions (Wood, 1989). Governments, urged on by powerful agencies such as the OECD (1990), focused on deregulating the labour market in order to reduce rigidities, including pay rigidities and to encourage greater overall flexibility. Employers focused on job flexibility, multi-skilling and on increasing their ability to hire and fire. Trade unionists and parties of the Left tried to emphasise the value of employee involvement, the need to develop career paths and to link skill recognition with bargaining and the desirability of retaining the outline of a tripartite industrial relations framework while accommodating pressures for more flexible bargaining.

Ambiguous Restructuring: Labour's Strategy 1984–1990

Labour faced the same paradox that other similar governments confronted in the 1980s of how to reconcile social democratic beliefs and values with rapidly globalising market economies (Mishra, 1990). The result was policies that were riddled with ambiguities. With respect to the labour market, Labour introduced new industrial legislation, the Labour Relations Act 1987 (LRA), made concessions to New Right ideology and confirmed the earlier (late 1984) removal of compulsory arbitration. But the LRA retained the essence of the tripartite, welfare state industrial relations framework. Labour also took an initiative to explore the idea of industrial democracy. However, its failure to subscribe fully to New Right ideology quickly earned the condemnation of employers and the New Zealand Business Round Table (Brook, 1990).

Labour accepted the emphasis placed internationally on the centrality of education and training, as a unified concept, in economic strategies. In the mid-1980s, it facilitated a tripartite study of developments in Australia and began moves to establish a national qualifications framework. Although conceived within a neo-liberal context and indebted to British initiatives, Labour's model retained residual social democratic values and elements. In part this reflected Labour's schizophrenic relationship with neo-liberalism; but in part it also reflected the extent to which the new framework was derived more immediately from similar developments in Australia and thus was shaped, albeit indirectly, by the corporatist logic of the 'Accords': a series of negotiated agreements between the Australian Labor government and the Australian Council of Trade Unions (Alexander and Lewer, 1994).

Although driven substantially by labour market considerations, the original idea of the qualifications framework did not abandon education's democratic heritage. It incorporated a recognition of the importance of a general education for all, placed some emphasis on equity consideration and afforded recognition of Maori language, culture and knowledge. Also significant was the intention to structure the framework and its associated qualifications authority along corporatist lines: tripartism, an emphasis on the training needs of industries, rather than enterprises, an assumption of industry-based, nationally co-ordinated, development strategies, and a skills regime that was implicitly linked to wages. It also offered working people the opportunity to gain portable, recognised qualifications and provided enhanced opportunities for women, Maori and Pacific Islanders to break through traditional qualification barriers. Not surprisingly, therefore, it attracted strong union endorsement.

The TUEA Experiment

A 'Lifelong Learning' Initiative

Labour's Union Representatives Educational Leave Act (UREL) was a milestone in adult education in New Zealand. In many respects the most progressive piece of legislation of its kind in the world, the Act established a publicly funded Trade Union Education Authority (TUEA) and provided a measure of paid educational leave (PEL), as a union right, for trade union education. The National government repealed the legislation with effect from August 1992.

The general philosophy underpinning TUEA drew explicitly on UNESCO's democratic concept of lifelong learning. In sketching the scope of union education, the Task Force on Trade Union Education (Law, 1985; 1987) stressed the importance of social partnership in a modern economy, the need for competency in industrial relations and in the area of occupational health and safety. But the Task Force also placed considerable emphasis on social equity considerations and the broader educational rights of working people, as citizens. The UREL defined union education as that which assisted union representatives to become well informed about industrial relations and able to participate in an active and well-informed manner both in the affairs of any union to which they belong and in their employment. TUEA's statutory functions were also far reaching. They included provision for it to make recommendations to the government, government departments, education agencies and other bodies on matters relating to:

- union education for union members
- education about unions
- adult education affecting union members
- education of workers generally.

This mandate enabled TUEA to introduce a democratic perspective into a wide range of educational activities.

TUEA's Practice of Workers' Education

As a provider, stimulator and co-ordinator of trade union education, TUEA's accomplishments in six short years were quite remarkable. In excess of 150,000 participant days of approved education took place over that period. Like its predecessor, the TUTB, much of TUEA's work was instrumental: providing union representatives with basic skills. In this respect it broke considerable new ground by developing systematic programmes for Maori unionists, Pacific Island unionists, women unionists and courses on working with other cultures.

TUEA also took advantage of a more comprehensive, organising concept of union education, more flexible functions and better resourcing in order to rekindle the critical dimension of workers' education. To some extent this was implicit in its work in special interest areas. But it also was necessitated by the union movement's need to come to terms with a rapidly changing economic and social context that was at odds with its social democratic heritage and ethos. Thus TUEA's role in assisting unions educationally to work effectively in the new environment assumed increasing importance as that environment became more difficult.

Once it had managed to establish its own education programme, TUEA turned its attention to other providers of education. Its strategy was to encourage, goad and push tertiary institutions to meet their responsibilities as outlined in the second report of the Task Force on Trade Union Education (Law, 1987). TUEA was directly involved in establishing the Centre for Labour and Trade Union Studies at the University of Waikato and in facilitating less ambitious developments at Auckland and Massey universities. It also tried, within the limits of its resources, to provide better support for union representatives on the councils of tertiary bodies and on other educational committees. And it became a major voice in the wider educational and training community.

TUEA and the Changing Workplace

Inevitably, TUEA played a central role in facilitating some of the major labour market transitions that took place under Labour; this in turn generated some criticism, usually muted, from the political Left. After the change of government at the end of 1990, TUEA was also required to assist the transition to the Employment Contracts Act (ECA) regime.

TUEA promoted education about the restructuring and reform of work very actively. This reflected a changing mood within the union movement in response to the growing dominance of New Right ideology. In late 1990, TUEA's Deputy Director, Dick Lowe, captured an emerging view that unions needed to rethink radically many of their traditional attitudes and strategies. Lowe claimed that unions and employers needed 'to foster a more co-operative approach to ensure survival in a highly competitive environment' (Lowe, 1990: 71). Traditionally, he noted, union concerns related to wealth distribution while those of employers related to wealth creation. Lowe suggested that issues such as job security, standard of living, participation and consultation and career paths could link together successfully these clusters to the benefit of all. This required, he argued, an evolutionary reframing of workers' education in line with notions of a co-operative economy. Fully aware of the new ground TUEA and the New Zealand Council of Trade Unions (NZCTU) were attempting to break, Lowe observed that some unionists might view this approach as 'advocating collaboration with the ruling classes. However, in my view the interests of workers must be furthered by using every means at our disposal' (ibid.: 71).

TUEA's Achievements

Much of TUEA's work focused on cultural, economic and social change, public sector restructuring, union reorganisation and amalgamation, changes to industrial relations and wider issues concerning the education of working people and their children. This helped shift unions' attitudes to educational activity. TUEA demonstrated how an active education policy could enhance the quality of participation in union affairs and could serve as an effective means of involving those who had previously been marginalised. It also stimulated a resurgence in publications designed to meet the intellectual and practical needs of working people.

Had TUEA survived, it undoubtedly would have made a significant contribution in the changing workplace. Instead that role has been left almost exclusively to the Workplace New Zealand project which TUEA helped establish. However, the demise of TUEA and weakening of the trade union movement in the ECA environment has altered significantly the balance between employer and union input into that project. TUEA's most visible legacies are the centres and programmes in tertiary institutions, and there is a very positive sense in which they continue to sustain the democratic dimension of the workers' education tradition. However, in retrospect, its most important contribution educationally may prove to be the ripple effect of its work on Treaty of Waitangi issues.

Workers' Education and Training in a New Environment

The Triumph of Ideology

Notwithstanding the frequency of glib references to 'choice', for working people the present environment for education and training is inherently undemocratic. As Ruth Richardson (1995) has now made very clear, National went into the 1990 election determined to complete the transition from welfare capitalism to a neo-liberal market economy by restructuring the labour market. National's permissive approach is 'deceptively clean of overly harsh and oppressive measures' (Harris, 1993: 6). It purportedly allows employers and workers to do what they like. It assumes the primacy of individual property rights ('labour services' are a property right) and that employers, as the owners of jobs, should have full control of workplaces. It rejects tripartism and eschews any substantial role for government, other than that of facilitating the employment relationship.

The ECA purports to offer two basic 'freedoms': freedom to associate and freedom to contract. However, workers' ability to exercise these freedoms are limited in practice by the difficulties experienced by unions. The Act treats unions as third parties or bargaining agents. It places no obligation on employers to bargain in good faith, provides no recourse to arbitration and, by omission, makes it difficult for unions to organise. These problems are compounded, of course, by a hostile economic environment and widespread unemployment, with the result that the whole balance in workplace relations has been shifted heavily in favour of the employer (see Haworth and Hughes, 1995).

The New Training Regime

National retained Labour's qualifications and training regime but redefined it along lines that are much more consistent with New Right ideology. In this respect, there has been a drift in policy in favour of elements of the British model. There, observes Desmond King (1993: 222), the skills and training debate has been influenced by 'four New Right based objectives': (1)

undermining apprenticeships, (2) individual and labour market disincentives, (3) enhancing the market and the employers, and (4) minimising government interventions. These policies represent 'a decisive rejection of legislative backing for training and for any notions of social partnership and tripartite control of training design and delivery' (Keep and Rainbird, 1995: 537). Instead, 'the main thrust of policy has been to pursue sweeping institutional reform in the belief that the creation of a market-based, employer-led training system can, of itself, deliver a fundamental change in the quantity and quality of training' (p. 538).

Faith in the private sector is now the cornerstone of training policies in New Zealand. The Industry Training Act (ITA) adopts a permissive approach that is consistent with the ECA and other labour market legislation. Its underlying premise is the view that training must be 'industry-led' through narrow, self-defined Industry Training Organisations (ITOs) that set skills standards, arrange for the delivery of training and arrange for the monitoring of training and the assessment of trainees (New Zealand Government, 1991). The legislation effectively abandons the tripartite approach to training. Membership of ITOs is not prescribed, although there is a vague requirement for the Education and Training Support Agency (ETSA) to ensure employee involvement.

New Right logic also applies to funding. The ITA provides for some government assistance, but the system assumes that 'industry as the owner of its ITO and the programmes it develops will be the major funder' (Education and Training Support Agency, 1992: 7). Initially the government contemplated making provision for training levies but under pressure from employers it retreated to a voluntary approach whereby members of an industry 'would contribute to the cost of the training only if they saw the value in doing so' (New Zealand Government, 1991: 24).

From Key Players to Spectators? The Role of Unions

In the late 1980s New Zealand unions saw themselves as key players in a workers' education and training regime that promised positive economic, industrial and social outcomes. Today, they are struggling to avoid being sidelined. In the view of the present National government, most employers and, it seems many workers, the very idea of union involvement has outlived its usefulness.

Like their Australian counterparts, most New Zealand unions support a 'high skills/high wage strategy' to economic recovery. The influential Engineers' Union, for example, accepts that unions operate in the market and that 'integration into the global marketplace means that New Zealand manufacturers, services and workers are required to produce to equivalent standards of quality, flexibility, speed of response, variety and cost as the best producers in the world (Smith, 1991: 4). Smith suggests that there are four elements to manufacturing for a global market: new technology, upskilling, new work design and changed industrial relations. This implies 'co-operative procedures, consultative committees, professional negotiation and dispute resolution all work to maximise production and minimise disruption to the mutual benefit of workers and employers' (ibid.: 5). Education and training, he argues, 'provides the common core to all these developments. Training is not only required for upskilling, but a good base education will be required to make the best use of new technology' (p. 5).

The New Zealand Council of Trade Unions (NZCTU) (1993; 1995) has developed a well-thought through, integrated education and training strategy. It offers strong support for workplace reform, advocates a 'quality future' by proposing a co-operative growth strategy, stresses the need for a quality public education system from early childhood through to tertiary level and promotes an industry training plan that emphasises the development of skills. However, by the time this policy was finalised, the complexity of difficulties presented by National's labour market strategy had already reduced organised labour's capacity to influence the direction of education and training policies.

Union support for training reform assumed organisational strength, including the high levels of union membership, the continuation of TUEA and access to PEL, the retention of a tripartite framework and a continuing commitment by the government to general education. National's almost overnight removal of compulsory union membership and access to collective bargaining structures quickly undermined many unions' membership base, especially in industries with high staff turnover and an increasingly casualised labour force. By the mid-1990s, union density had dropped from around 60 per cent of the labour force in the 1980s to an estimated 30 per cent. In addition, the widespread devolution of bargaining to the enterprise level, coupled with the enormous task of servicing members employed on individual contracts, has meant that union staff, already reduced in number because of declining membership, are now spread so thinly that immediate 'firefighting' is often their main priority.

TUEA too was an early casualty of the new order. A non-prescriptive, free-market approach to economic management left little room nor any need for the state to support workers' education legislatively or financially. National, supported by employers and the Business Roundtable, regarded TUEA and paid educational leave as ideologically and structurally inconsistent with a view of employment relationships based on a libertarian philosophy of individual rights, a facilitative legislative environment and the primacy of contractual arrangements. The government did, however, wait before it disestablished TUEA. In 1991 the government set up a review, but continued to fund TUEA for a further 12 months. The principal reason seems to have been to facilitate, through TUEA-sponsored education, the transition to the new ECA environment. In the end, however, notwithstanding a very favourable review (Trotman and Jackson, 1991), TUEA was abolished with effect from August 1992.

In order to mitigate some of the fallout, the government created a contestable Employment Related Education Fund. The first grants were not made until 1993. Some unions and the NZCTU were successful in receiving project funding from this source. However, the announcement of the 1995/96 allocations resulted in claims from the NZCTU that political considerations had influenced decisions on applications (Douglas, 12 June 1995). Of just under $1 million allocated, about one-third went to projects that explicitly involved unions (Kidd, 7 June 1995). The scheme is to be discontinued.

The combined effect of the ECA and the ITA has been a patchy pattern of union participation in the 50 or so ITOs recognised by ETSA. In effect, unions only participate if employers see some advantage in having them involved. On a positive note, many do. In some industries, especially those where unions and employers have long co-operated, employers either recognise or have come to recognise that unions have established expertise, can facilitate worker confidence in training programmes and even may be willing to contribute financially. In some industries, however, employers have shown determined hostility to union membership on the ITO and have managed to shut them out. In other industries, union willingness to contribute has been frustrated by the inability of employers to organise an effective ITO.

The case of the dairy industry illustrates the problems unions now face. Following the enactment of the ITA, dairy industry employers abandoned an established national training committee on which the union was represented and quickly constituted an ITO comprising employers only. The Dairy Workers Union objected vigorously and made strong representations to ETSA. In response, employers effectively argued that the ITA rendered inoperative the previously negotiated arrangement and that they were not required to invite union participation on the ITO. ETSA subsequently recognised the ITO as constituted by the employers (Law, 1995).

Towards 2001: Some Formative Conclusions

Three considerations may force a responsible government in the future to rethink the folly of an ideologically driven, permissive approach to training. First, New Zealand faces a serious skills crisis. This was recognised by the New Zealand Employers' Federation (NZEF) as early as 1990 and is now the subject of widespread employer concern (e.g. *Waikato Times*, 4 August 1994). British research suggests that voluntarist frameworks do not deliver either the quantity or quality of training required (Keep and Rainbird, 1995). This view is supported by informed educators in this country (e.g. Willyams, 1995). Second, there is the 'free-loader' problem. Employers who do train are becoming frustrated with those who contribute nothing and then poach trained staff. This frustration is even being reflected in the NZEF's own surveys. Third, there is the possibility that New Zealand's voluntarist approach may complicate or even undermine the harmonising of the Australian and New Zealand qualifications frameworks. However, the recent change of government in Australia is likely to soften that possibility.

While 'to participate or not to participate?' in ITOs and other aspects of the training regime is a real question for unions, it is not the central issue. Even more critical is organised labour's response to the total situation in which it finds itself. Notwithstanding a minority tradition of militancy and, within that, resistance to statism, New Zealand unions have largely been creatures of legislation mediated by prevailing norms and values. In other words, the majority of unions have defined themselves or allowed themselves to be defined within a framework of acceptability or tolerance that has been prescribed by the government and employers.

In practice, of course, unions can only operate within the boundaries of possibility that prevail in particular circumstances. But there is growing evidence that a debilitated union movement, ineluctably rather than willingly, is already reconstituting itself on the New Right's terms. This is reflected not only in the widespread acceptance of market forces as the key driver of economic society, but also in an implied acceptance of the pre-eminence of the individual worker's property rights as the basis of the employment relationship. Thus there is an inclination within the union movement to adopt the mantle of third party status conferred on it by the ECA. This is not to deny attempts to remain trade unions, in an historical sense and to draw on residual values and aspirations in order to organise collectively and to educate members to bring about political change. Ironically, however, this approach, which for the moment hinges on the results of electoral reform, leads to the advocacy of the very statist strategy that many on the Left previously eschewed.

Adult educators often under-recognise and under-value the extent to which the field itself is a product of the social democratic environment workers' education, as an inherently democratic and collective undertaking, played such a critical role in creating. Thus while this chapter has focused on workers' education and training, it also has attempted to provide the basis for extending the analysis to the field as a whole. For there is a powerful sense in which many providers are abandoning core values and redefining themselves ideologically as private training enterprises in order to conform to the market model.

Less than two decades ago, Roger Boshier (1980: 1) believed that New Zealand had 'embarked on a systematic attempt to create a learning society founded on the principles of lifelong learning'. This chapter has shown how that voyage has now run aground. One of the distinguishing characteristics of the 'second generation of lifelong learning', Kjell Rubenson (1994: 13) ruefully observes, is 'that the concept has lost its utopian origin and has been reduced to a narrow definition centred on meeting the needs of the economy by equipping the work force with the necessary skills and competencies'. The challenge for those who believe that adult education has a social purpose is to find new ways to revitalise a practical utopian vision.

References

Alexander, R. and Lewer, J. (1994), *Understanding Australian Industrial Relations*, Sydney: Harcourt Brace.
Barry, N.P. (1987), *The New Right*, London: Croom Helm.
Boshier, R. (1980), *Towards a Learning Society*, Vancouver: LearningPress.
Brook, P. (1990), *Freedom at Work,* Oxford: Oxford University Press.
Campbell, R. and Kirk, A. (1983), *After the Freeze,* Wellington: Port Nicholson Press.
Douglas, K.G. (12 June 1995), Press Statement, Wellington: New Zealand Council of Trade Unions.
Education and Training Support Agency (1992), *A Guide to the Industry Training Act,* Wellington: ETSA.
Fauré, E. (1972), *Learning to Be: The World of Education Today and Tomorrow,* Paris: UNESCO.
Harris, P. (1993), 'Labour Market Deregulation in New Zealand' (A background paper prepared for Swedish trade unionists), Wellington: New Zealand Council of Trade Unions.
Haworth, N. and Hughes, S. (1995), *New Zealand and the ILO* (Research Report), Auckland: University of Auckland.
Keep, E. and Rainbird, H. (1995), 'Training', in Edwards P. (ed.), *Industrial Relations: Theory and Practice in Britain,* Oxford: Blackwell.
Kelly, T. (1970), *A History of Adult Education in Great Britain,* Liverpool: Liverpool University Press.
Kidd, D. (7 June 1995), Press Statement, Wellington: Office of Minister of Labour.
King, D.S. (1987), *The New Right: Politics, Markets and Citizenship*, London: Macmillan.
King, D.S. (1993), 'The Conservatives and Training Policy 1979–1992: From a Tripartite to a Neoliberal Regime', *Political Studies,* XLI (2), pp. 214–235.

Law, M.G. (Chair) (1985), *First Report of the Task Force on Trade Union Education*, Wellington: Government Print.

Law, M.G. (Chair) (1987), *Trade Union and Worker Education: Directions for Change (The Second Report of the Task Force on Trade Union Education)*, Wellington: Government Print.

Law, M.G. (1993), 'The Changing World of Worker Education: An Historical Perspective', *New Zealand Journal of Adult Learning*, vol. 21, no. 1, pp. 7–33.

Law, M.G. (1996), 'Workers' Education and Training in a Voluntarist Environment: What Role for Unions?', in Olesen, H.S. (ed.), *Adult Education and the Labour Market II*, pp. 117–133. Roskilde and Strubl Adult Education Research Group, University of Roskilde and Bundesinstitüt für Erwachsenenbildung St Wolfgang for ESREA.

Littler, C.R. (1991), *Technology and the Organisation of Work*, Geelong: Deakin University Press.

Lowe, D. (1990), 'The Role of Trade Union Education in Empowering Workers and their Unions', in *Union-Tertiary Research Conference*, vol. 4, Wellington: Trade Union Education Authority.

Mishra, R. (1990), *The Welfare State in Capitalist Society*, Hertfordshire (U.K.): Harvester Wheatsheaf.

National Development Conference (1969), *Recommendations Approved*, Wellington: NDC.

New Zealand Council of Trade Unions (1993), *Building Better Skills*, Wellington: Author.

New Zealand Council of Trade Unions (1995), *Building Better Skills: Unions and Skill New Zealand*, Wellington: Author.

New Zealand Government (1991), *Industrial Skills Training Strategy*, Wellington: Education and Training Support Agency.

New Zealand Employers' Federation (1990), *Industry Training Bill: Submission by the New Zealand Employers' Federation* (Draft), Wellington: Author.

New Zealand Federation of Labour (1981), *Policy Statement on Trade Union Education*, Wellington: Author.

New Zealand Government (1991), *Industrial Skills Training Strategy*, Wellington: Education and Training Support Agency.

Organisation for Economic Co-operation and Development (1990), *Labour Market Policies for the 1990s*, Paris: OECD.

Organisation for Economic Co-operation and Development (1993), *OECD Economic Surveys 1992–1993: New Zealand*, Paris: OECD.

Pearce, L.A. and Stuart, R.C. (1978), *Impact of the Vocational Training Council and Industry Training Boards on New Zealand Industry*, Wellington: Vocational Training Council.

Piore, M.J. and Sabel, C.F. (1984), *The Second Industrial Divide,*. New York: Basic Books.
Plant, R. (1985), 'The Very Idea of a Welfare State', in Bean, P. *et al.* (eds), *In Defence of Welfare,* London: Tavistock.
Przeworski, A. and Wallerstein M. (1986), 'Democratic Capitalism at the Crossroads', in Przeworski, A., *Capitalism and Social Democracy,* Cambridge: Cambridge University Press.
Richardson, R. (1995), *Making a Difference,* Christchurch: Shoal Bay Press.
Rubenson, K. (1994), 'Popular Adult Education and Social Mobilisation: Reflections in Connection with the Swedish Committee on Power', in Tesse, S. *et al.* (eds), *Social Change and Adult Education Research,* Trondheim: The Norwegian Institute of Adult Education.
Shuker, R. (1984), *Educating the Workers?,* Palmerston North: Dunmore Press.
Simmonds, E.J. (Chair) (1972), *Lifelong Education,* Wellington: New Zealand National Commission for UNESCO.
Sinclair, K. (1969), *A History of New Zealand,* Harmondsworth: Penguin.
Smith, M. (1991), 'Manufacturing Skills for the Global Economy', in *Curriculum – Core or Corset? Community and Business Views,* Wellington: New Zealand Planning Council.
Sutch, W.B. (1966), *The Quest for Security in New Zealand,* Wellington: Oxford University Press.
Trotman, I.G. and Jackson, G.L. (1991), *Review of the Trade Union Education Authority,* Wellington: Department of Labour.
Whitty, G. (1985), *Sociology and School Knowledge,* London: Methuen.
Williams, A. (1980), 'Trade Union Adult Education', in Boshier, R. (ed.), *Towards a Learning Society,* Vancouver: Learning Press.
Williams, R. (1961/1980), *The Long Revolution,* Harmondsworth: Penguin.
Willyams, R. (1995), 'Reform Threatens Polytechnic Learning', *New Zealand Herald,* 18 September, p. 1:6.
Wood, S. (1989), 'The Transformation of Work?', in Wood S. (ed.), *The Transformation of Work? Skill, Flexibility and the Labour Process,* London: Unwin Hyman.

11

Workplace Literacy:

Issues and Trends in Aotearoa/New Zealand

Liz Moore

The historical development of adult literacy and basic education in Aotearoa/New Zealand has been fairly well documented (see Hill, 1990). With its origins in volunteer effort, a community rather than institutional focus and its association with access and equity issues for learners, adult literacy has played a major role in the adult and continuing education sector of this country.

The relatively new domain of workplace literacy education, however, is likely to be less familiar territory. This chapter aims to introduce readers to this developing arena of literacy practice, by exploring the context which gave rise to its existence and by reflecting on some of the issues its existence has highlighted.

Changes in the Relationship between Education and the Economy

It could be argued that until recently the relationship between the world of work and the world of education has been a reasonably clear one. Put very simply, formal schooling was intended to develop general thinking processes, outside of a vocational context, so that the thinking process developed could be used universally across all contexts (Bruner, 1960). Post-compulsory educational institutions met industry skill needs by educating groups of novices in the skills and practices which would be demanded of them at work either through pre-employment training programmes or through the apprenticeship system. Education was what you did before you went to work. Ongoing education and training once in the world of work was very much the domain of management or senior technical staff. Novices became experts at work through watching others and practice.

It was possible to see education and work as two distinct chronological components of an individual's life, while the economy was stable and technological development was progressing slowly.

In a stable economy with plenty of jobs, there was no imperative to consider the ongoing educational needs of adults in the work force. The influence of Ford and then Taylor, on work organisation meant that jobs consisted of discrete components, with workers responsible for different parts of a process. Quality control was usually the responsibility of one person. Taylor's scientific management approach emphasised specialisation and standardisation in the belief that this contributed to greater efficiency (Pugh and Hickson, 1989). In manufacturing, work on the shop floor was organised around the production line, with a layer of supervisors to handle the paperwork and decision-making. Many jobs existed where reading and writing skills were not demanded or used.

In this climate, the literacy skills of a nation were important, but not crucial and the importance of literacy usually emphasised the right of an individual to participate in civic and community life.

> A person is literate when he [sic] has acquired the essential knowledge and skills which enable him to engage in all those activities in which literacy is required for effective functioning in his group or community and whose attainment in reading, writing and arithmetic make it possible for him to use these skills towards his own and the community's development and for active participation in the life of his country.
>
> (UNESCO, 1962)

For a long time literacy was considered to be predominantly an issue for developing countries, not one for developed and industrialised nations. The introduction of mass literacy campaigns in developing countries was the response of governments who could clearly see the connection between literate populations, social justice and economic prosperity. Policy development in literacy in OECD countries on the other hand, has been slow and lacked political imperatives.

Literacy campaigns for example, in New Zealand and the United Kingdom, had their origins in community based initiatives. Both campaigns relied heavily on the drafting of volunteers from the local community. Government involvement and funding was minimal and improving the literacy skills of adults was clearly not an urgent priority.

However, during the 1980s the relationship between education and the economy in developed countries began to change dramatically and one outcome of this change has been the shifting of literacy from the wings to centre stage in debates about economic performance.

Workplace Change and the Focus on Skill Development

Increasingly, national economies have begun to operate in an international context. The globalisation of markets meant that economic competition increased and the development of new technology underpinned the race for 'the competitive edge'. The emphasis on customer service and quality has contributed to the reorganisation of work in individual enterprises and across industries.

Workplace reform initiatives and the growth of interest in the workplace as a 'learning organisation' (see Senge, 1993), encouraging employee participation in continuous learning, have contributed to the changing face of the workplace.

So what has all this change actually meant for the worker? For a start, many unskilled jobs have disappeared, often as a result of technological development. New management approaches have placed greater emphasis on workers being trouble shooters for quality; spotting problems before they come up and solving those that exist. Workers are now required to perform a variety of tasks within their job, often working with others in teams and being responsible for whole processes rather than part processes. Multi-skilling has meant that groups of workers can be moved from one task to another as production responds to customer orders. Traditional demarcations have been eroded.

International Standards Organisation (ISO) accreditation, which many companies pursue as a hallmark of quality, has led to more and more documentation in the workplace as policies and procedures are written down, often for the first time. Workers are expected to be able to read and act on written information contained in ISO manuals, and workplaces are subject to audits which check workers' knowledge and practice of quality procedures. The reorganisation of many workplaces into self-managed work teams has led to a reduction in the supervisory and middle management layer which had previously provided a buffer between reading and writing responsibilities at work.

Increasingly, countries involved in industrial change began to ask whether the work force had the skills to enable industry to operate successfully within this new international scene. Suddenly there is a skills crisis; it is linked to a nation's economic performance and the lines between education and work are redrawn. The concept of lifelong learning re-emerges, this time within a vocational context.

The massive education and training job that many countries saw in front of them in order to meet the skills demands of the future, led governments to act along more interventionist lines. School curricula have been revised with a view to producing potential workers equipped with the 'essential' skills their country needs (Ministry of Education, 1993). In Aotearoa/New Zealand the National Qualifications Framework and new arrangements for the delivery of training enable schools to provide programmes with a greater vocational focus, an important shift from the previously pre-vocational secondary education sector. Increasingly, large-scale work force training strategies like the government's 'Skill New Zealand' have been developed, which encourage initiatives designed to train and re-train people currently in the work force, as well as those preparing to enter it.

Alongside this has been the growth of competency-based assessment in education which provides for the clear articulation and mapping of skills and knowledge and which emphasises the learner's ability to apply their newly learned skills, usually within a vocational context.

All these policies and programmes are aimed at tying education and training more closely to economic needs, placing industry and the needs of industry to the fore. The prominence of the discourse of business in national education strategy has occurred rapidly and been underpinned in Aotearoa/New Zealand by legislation such as the Industry Training Act (1992). We have seen little *public* debate about the direction or effectiveness of these policies and practices, however; they have largely been accepted as necessary steps in the development and growth of the economy.

The Literacy Platform Begins to Shift

We need to look at what has happened to adult literacy within this whole debate, how definitions have changed and who has now become interested in it. In the context described above, literacy has increased in importance in the sense that it has become an economic issue. Literacy is now viewed in many OECD countries as being 'critically linked to competitiveness' (Benton and Noyelle, 1992). Workers are faced with an increasing print load at work, need to be able to communicate clearly both orally and in writing and need to be able to tackle the literacy and language demands of new training. The ability of workers to interact with the range of texts which appear in the workplace and handle the new workplace environment is seen as crucial to a company's ability to compete.

We are told that the results of successful competition contribute to the capacity of the country to provide a good standard of living for all its citizens. Described in this way, it is in everybody's interest to be concerned about literacy in the population. However, the shift away from literacy as important for community and civic participation, towards an emphasis on literacy for work and economic performance, has brought with it a wide range of issues which demand examination. Before we begin to explore some of these, it might be helpful to look at the responses of the key players in Aotearoa/New Zealand to the emerging importance of literacy in a work-oriented context.

Education and Training Providers

In the early 1990s, a key thrust for promoting literacy learning opportunities for those in work originated with education and training providers.

The Adult Reading and Learning Assistance Federation (ARLA) Aotearoa/ New Zealand Inc. established a national project, Workbase, from funds received from government during International Literacy Year (1990). Since 1991, Workbase has operated as the Federation's national workplace literacy resource unit with a brief to develop literacy and language projects in collaboration with workplaces, train and support providers and undertake work which informs development of the field.

During the period that Workbase has been active in the field, other providers have emerged – including private training consultancies, polytechnics, union providers and local ARLA schemes. A variety of practice has developed and a range of philosophies about the purposes of literacy and language drive workplace literacy provision.

Currently, there are few opportunities for debate amongst literacy providers about theoretical or practical issues and few opportunities for contact between providers for professional development and collaboration. Lack of funding for this purpose and the competition which arises from providers pitted against each other in the pursuit of contracts in industry all contribute to the current fragmentation in the field.

Government and its Agents

Historically, adult literacy in Aotearoa/New Zealand has received little government attention and few resources. The field has developed in the cracks between policy and resourcing of other education sectors and initiatives with no coherent national message about what is and what is not government responsibility in respect to literacy development for adults in Aotearoa/New Zealand (Sutton 1994).

The New Zealand Government's directions for industry training are spelled out in the Industry Training Act (1992). The legislation provides for the establishment of Industry Training Organisations (ITOs); bodies which can prove they represent the interests of their industry. Priorities for training within industries are set by the ITOs. There is currently very little information available about how much of a priority literacy and language training is within individual ITOs, how needs are being assessed and what strategies are being used to meet them.

Sections 11(d) and 13(b) of the Industry Training Act make provision for those people who have been traditionally underrepresented in industry training and education to get access to new training opportunities. Currently, the description of this category centres around women, Maori, and Pacific Island people. It will be interesting to see what specific initiatives ITOs develop in response to those sections of the Act and to what extent literacy and language training will feature in the strategies which are implemented.

In contrast, the British and Australian governments have made literacy development a key priority. The Australian Literacy and Language Policy launched in 1990 has had a tremendous impact on resource allocation and policy development for adult literacy and language. The British Basic Skills at Work Initiative managed through the Adult Literacy and Basic Skills Unit (ALBSU) and the Australian Government's Workplace English Literacy and Language Project (WELL) and a range of other initiatives, have all provided resources to develop workplace literacy learning opportunities and encourage research to inform practice.

In Aotearoa/New Zealand we have various claims as to the importance of literacy, language and numeracy skills. The Education and Training Support Agency (ETSA) has indicated the priority of 'capability skills' which includes literacy, numeracy and communication skills, for the nation and workforce (Education and Training Support Agency, 1993) and in the Ministry of Education's document on *The New Zealand Curriculum Framework* literacy and numeracy are perceived to be essential skills, also critical for effective participation at work.

What is not yet in existence is a government policy to set priorities and targets and thereby provide impetus in an area which on the one hand is spoken of as being crucial to the nation's development and on the other hand left to develop piecemeal and without a clear strategy.

Workplace Literacy

Employers and Employer Organisations

As ITOs are in a fairly early stage of development and have as yet generated few directions for workplace literacy education and training, individual enterprises have taken responsibility for identifying and providing literacy learning opportunities at work.

The introduction of the national unit standards in Communication Skills (which include reading and writing) into the New Zealand Qualifications Framework will undoubtedly provide many workplaces with a recognisable benchmark to assess their employees' skills. However, there is considerable diversity of practice in the assessment arena, including 'home grown' and 'borrowed' literacy and numeracy tests administered as a pre-employment screen or in-house assessment. Employers do not have a reliable method of critiquing these tools and evaluating them against each other.

As yet, no publicly available data exist to provide information on which types of companies have implemented literacy programmes at work, how the programmes have been organised, what the curriculum looks like or what the effects of this training have been. Moreover, little is known about how individual companies define literacy and which skills to what level are perceived to be falling within the literacy training brief. Documentation and dissemination of practice has been limited and there is a role for national employer groups to engage in the dissemination of key lessons.

Employees and Employee Organisations

Some individual unions have been active in supporting literacy and language projects in individual enterprises; they have participated in promoting programmes to the work force and in committees established to monitor programmes.

The New Zealand Council for Trade Unions (NZCTU) advocates training which gives high priority to basic skills and literacy and points to a role for ITOs: 'ITOs should be required to set up tripartite programmes to promote literacy in the workplace in terms of improving productivity, health and safety, workplace relations and morale' (New Zealand Council for Trade Unions, 1992: 19).

As for employees themselves, it is easy to be glib about what receivers of literacy training at work have made of it. Project and course evaluations usually provide opportunities for feedback from learners. However, this is only a snapshot impression and as yet, there is no in-depth study in Aotearoa/New Zealand which provides a voice for literacy learners in the workplace to speak out about their experience.

The Incidence of Literacy Difficulties in the New Zealand Workplace: What do we know about it and what do we need to discover?

Much of the rhetoric which exists in the promotion of literacy learning opportunities in the workplace revolves around the potential hazards, inefficiencies and problems which are the result of having a workforce with an inadequate level of literacy and numeracy. There is a direct implication that once workers' literacy difficulties are 'fixed up' there will no longer be damage to expensive machinery or workplace accidents because workers cannot read or communicate in English. Whilst these arguments have been used by workplace literacy providers to convince employers of the need to see literacy and language as a workplace issue, they can also serve to reinforce the idea that people who need to improve their literacy and language skills are in some way feckless and a liability within their workplace. Critical educators from Australia such as O'Connor (1993) and from the United States such as Arnove and Graff (1987) remind us to examine whose interests workplace literacy training is serving and to look critically at the ideologies which are played out in the workplace literacy field.

These same issues, then, are inherent in any attempt to assess the incidence of literacy difficulties at work. Some attempts have been made to provide evidence of the costs to industries and therefore countries, of inadequate literacy in the workplace. Figures from Australia (Singh, 1989) indicate that it costs A$3.2 billion annually in additional communication time needed at work as a result of instructions not understood, etc. Recent research in the United Kingdom indicates the total cost to industry in value terms is £UK4.8 billion (ALBSU, 1993). This research (based primarily on employer surveys) helped to make literacy a priority in these countries and opened up debate about how needs could be met.

The first documented evidence of the incidence of literacy difficulties in the New Zealand workplace was a study undertaken by ARLA Workbase involving some 300 respondents (Moore and Benseman, 1993). Managers, supervisors and workers were interviewed. Supervisors indicated that one in six of the workers they supervise have significant reading difficulties and one in four have significant writing problems.

This study, although only claiming to be exploratory, raises some important questions for follow-up research. Further work is needed on the needs of particular industries and cultural groups within those industries. Whilst there is some research data available on the education achievement and performance of Maori, there is very little known about the learning needs of Maori in the workplace.

In addition data is required on the degree to which new industry qualifications are accessible to those employees with reading and writing skill development needs; and, importantly, there is a need to trace and document successful models of workplace literacy delivery to provide direction for those engaged in the field.

The Question of Responsibility

All the above, of course, begs the question of whose responsibility it is to take an active role in the research and development of workplace literacy and language education in Aotearoa/New Zealand? We have seen that government has placed responsibility in the hands of industry for industry training. The current ideology operates on the basis that priorities will emerge from industry involvement in the training arena and will be met in the way that industry sees fit. First, this approach leaves government free from taking action on adult literacy education in terms of policy development and from seeing adult literacy as part of an overall education strategy. Second, it leaves industry and particularly ITOs, with little assistance to either recognise and analyse needs or resource literacy and language provision.

Part of how this issue of responsibility resolves itself, will depend on just how big an issue adult literacy becomes in Aotearoa/New Zealand during the next five or so years. How it gets to be an issue will depend in large part on who speaks for it and, for literacy providers concerned with literacy promotion, this will involve them in dilemmas about which arguments to choose and which definitions to pursue.

There is a role here for academics and theoreticians in Aotearoa/New Zealand. Without the theoretical frameworks to inform the understanding of literacy practitioners, industry personnel and learners themselves, there are real limitations on this country's ability to develop a literacy strategy for those currently in the workplace which is both theoretically sound and practically achievable within our particular cultural and economic context.

Workplace Literacy: Some Features of an Emergent Domain

For readers relatively new to workplace literacy in Aotearoa/New Zealand, and in the context of this book on the wider adult and community education field, the following section provides a brief overview of the domain. It also attempts to point up some of the theoretical issues which practitioners need to give consideration to as they engage in workplace literacy and language practice.

Literacy in the Marketplace

Although general adult learning principles form the philosophy of those providers who have emerged from the adult and continuing education sector, the arena in which workplace literacy is being played out and developed is a different one and increasingly involves providers from a variety of backgrounds and conceptual starting points.

Providers of workplace literacy operate in a marketplace context where the provision of literacy is a service or product which is 'for sale'. Whilst it is not new for many vocational training providers to operate in a context where success or failure to provide their service depends on convincing management of the benefits of what they can deliver, it is a new scenario for adult literacy, which has a history of being driven by learner needs and access and equity issues. Access and equity, perhaps two of the strongest principles underpinning adult literacy and basic education philosophy, can often be difficult to promote when company management are talking about the effects of training on the bottom line.

Workplace literacy providers package and shape their product in a variety of ways to 'win' contracts with industry. In the marketplace, literacy is a 'training good' to be purchased by companies seeking to improve work force skills. The language that surrounds literacy and literacy learning in this context and how this positions literacy is revealing. As such a good, literacy is frequently interpreted simply as a set of basic skills or competencies in reading and writing, often derived from the need that one group has of another group to cope or function in a particular context. Difficulties with concepts of functional literacy have been identified by Benton and Noyelle (1992):

> The term 'functional illiteracy' suggests a high value placed on conformity to specific functional contexts. Each context crystallises a set of social, political and power relationships and simply exhorting participants to function better entails encouraging conformity to its structure .... In the realm of national or local politics, in contrast, fully functional citizens have analytical and critical abilities that allow them to question the very framework and language in which political issues are presented and discussed.

Critical literacy educators who understand literacy to be about learning to 'read the world' as well as learning to 'read the word' (after Paulo Freire) work with a curriculum which engages learners in exploring how language is used to construct meanings that serve particular purposes. Some of these purposes are designed to protect the status quo and some of these purposes can be to challenge the status quo.

The notion of literacy as a set of basic skills which is required for functional competence in the workplace and the notion of literacy as construction or reflection of social and political realities are based on different understandings about the nature and role of literacy and language and derive from different discourses. For literacy practitioners concerned with developing critical readers and writers, taking literacy learning into the workplace can involve doing business with a discourse based on different values and concerned with different things. In simple terms, the language which describes literacy as a set of basic skills required for work, places all the responsibility for change on the learner. The language describing literacy in the context of social and political realities, also places the need for change on those structures which restrict the access of individuals and groups to information and power.

A Variety of Stakeholders

The proximity of interested parties other than the learners to the setting up and implementation of learning provision is a distinguishing feature of literacy work taking place in a workplace.

The fact that there are different stakeholders in workplace literacy sets the field at some distance from many other forms of adult and continuing education. In adult and continuing education, defining learning needs and making decisions about how to meet these directly involve the learner and the tutor. However, it is often a human resource manager or trainer who in broad terms defines literacy learning needs in a workplace and then calls in a literacy provider to see if there is a 'problem' and how to proceed if there is. A workplace literacy tutor needs to balance the expectations of management who, after all, allocate funds for literacy training, with the learning needs and expectations of learners.

The Role of a Workplace Tutor

The delivery of literacy learning in the workplace is not a straightforward matter. Practical difficulties such as complicated shift patterns which require innovative solutions so that learning can actually take place, noisy surroundings, production crises which take priority over learning are all regular features of workplace literacy projects and present issues which the workplace literacy and language tutor needs to engage and workplace personnel need to work patiently to resolve.

The role of a workplace literacy tutor can be seen from a number of perspectives, including as an instrument of management control brought in as a top-down approach to fix up literacy and language problems or as an advocate for access and equity of opportunity for workers. The role is not a neutral one, simply being there to teach a predetermined programme. The perspective and understandings the tutor brings on the nature and role of literacy and language are highly influential agents in workplace literacy implementation. For example, if learners in a workplace literacy programme reveal they cannot read and understand their employment contracts, the workplace literacy tutor is immediately faced with some decisions about what action to take and what role to play. A great deal of the time in workplace literacy, practitioners are engaged in a process of working through apparent conflicting interests and perspectives.

The Role of Literacy and Language in Creating and Maintaining Climates of Communication

Employers are not looking for an outstanding learning experience whose benefits remain within the confines of the classroom. They are seeking evidence of newly applied skills and knowledge back on the job and in the workplace in general. Most workplace literacy curricula therefore are tied very closely to the context of the workplace and the literacy and language perceived to be required to participate in that context. However, learning to write reports, read manuals and develop successful communicative practices for meetings in the classroom, may not necessarily mean that people will actually perform any differently when faced with those texts or occasions in the workplace. Ultimately, individuals are the final decision-makers on whether they use the skills they possess.

Many workplace literacy and language programmes are introduced with a view to increasing employee participation in a reorganised work environment. Companies are often looking for workers to speak out, share their ideas, offer solutions to workplace problems and take on more responsibility within their job and team. These needs are reflected in the objectives of workplace literacy curricula. However, if employees do not feel safe or are not provided with opportunities to participate, then the language and literacy strategies they have developed in the classroom are not likely to be demonstrated in the workplace. The language used in workplace written and verbal communications, between peers and between management and workers helps to form an organisation's communication climate. Language is one of a number of semiotic systems which exist in the workplace. How people think and feel about each other and about the activities occurring within a workplace can be understood by analysing the language that people choose to use with each other. Lack of verbal participation in team meetings, may not necessarily mean that individuals do not possess the required oral language skills. It might mean that they choose not to use these skills. Perhaps there is no history of the organisation listening to their viewpoint; perhaps the language they hear being used at work excludes or marginalises them, placing them in a position of powerlessness. It is too easy to assume that people need literacy and language training just because they are not participating in the way that management expect, or that providing literacy skill development opportunities will automatically result in improved participation in workplace activities.

> Literacy should not be defined only as a facility with different communication channels or linguistic needs. Rather, the acts of speaking, listening, reading and writing, should be seen as ways of participating in social life. Communication is not simply sending messages to each other, but ways of engaging with one another to build aspects of meaning in social life.
> (ABEAF, 1992: vol. 2; 2).

This approach to literacy involves an awareness that texts are '... written by persons, with particular dispositions or orientations to the information. We are arguing therefore for the necessary status of a role for the reader that involves conscious awareness of the language and the ideas systems that are brought into play when a text is used' (Freebody and Luke, 1990: 13).

These views lead us towards a definitional stance of literacy which places as much focus on the role of the 'crafter' of written or spoken material as it does on the reader or listener and encourages curriculum which examines how language is used to achieve particular ends. It also requires that literacy learners understand the roles of particular people and how they use written and spoken language to make or break relationships in the workplace.

There are examples where supervisors express as a learning need for others, the written and verbal skills required for taking on greater responsibility at work, yet are themselves unable to delegate these new responsibilities because of fear of losing their position of power in the workplace. There are managers who institute team meetings as a means of encouraging input from operators, but whose language and cultural practice during those meetings excludes the language and cultural practices of those from whom they wish to hear.

The conceptualisation of literacy which sees some people as deficient in basic skills with training being the way of bringing them 'up to scratch' is too narrow a description to apply to a complex and diverse workplace context. Learning to read and write and use language competently is more than just being able to complete a shift report accurately or understand the health and safety manual. Effective users of language are able to critically reflect on the language used by others in written and spoken texts and choose from a wide range of language resources to express opinions, create solutions and challenge positions.

Any organisation which is serious about improving literacy and language at work will need to include learning opportunities for supervisors and management so they can recognise and support new communicative behaviours learned in literacy and language programmes. They will need to learn how to write clear workplace documentation and training material, to understand that there are diverse cultural and language practices in the workplace and that literacy is inextricably linked to ways of behaving, thinking and being.

Literacy then is relevant to every person within an organisation and every person has ongoing language awareness and language development needs, not simply the group of persons deemed to have minimal written or spoken language skills. Literacy is as much about organisational communicative practices and processes as it is about the skill levels of particular individuals.

Developing Our Own Voice

It is important to be aware of the attempts which are currently being undertaken to determine how literacy will feature in industry training initiatives. Industry training organisations in Aotearoa/New Zealand, in common with comparable bodies in Australia and the U.K., are aiming to establish a minimum set of literacy and language skills needed by workers in order to cope with the literacy and language demands in the industry and within new industry qualifications. With the increasing pressure to pin training programmes at clearly definable levels of literacy, it is easy to lose sight of some of the theoretical questions about literacy and language. It is critical to have a clear conceptual framework about what literacy is and what literacy training in the workplace is trying to achieve. Such a framework is a benchmark on which to measure the various practical and political interpretations which exist about literacy. In particular, curriculum which is developed to ensure competencies are achieved needs to be informed by theoretical considerations. The challenge for workplace literacy providers in Aotearoa/New Zealand will be to develop curricula which places literacy in the wider context of social interaction rather than simply as a prescribed set of generic decoding skills required for functional competence.

The emergence of literacy as an economic issue and the resulting attempts to improve literacy and language skills in industrialised nations has generated new interest in definitions and descriptions of literacy. There is a new focus internationally on research into literacy needs and increased documentation about ways of meeting needs. There are new resources going into workplace literacy.

In Aotearoa/New Zealand the domain of workplace literacy is at an early stage of development. It is already at some distance from traditional community-based adult literacy provision and involves many different providers grappling with different delivery issues. What it needs is a resourcing mechanism which recognises the responsibilities of government and industry in meeting the literacy and language needs of those in the work force, the entrance of critical adult educators into the debate and to provide theoretical input into the work of practitioners. Importantly, we need research and evaluation to enable future development to be based on a clear understanding of where we have come from. The next stage of development must see the emergence of a clear voice or voices in Aotearoa/New Zealand which can express workplace literacy in terms of our unique language and cultural context.

References

ALBSU (1993), *The Costs to Industry: Basic Skills and the U.K. Workforce*, London: ALBSU.
Arnove, R. and Graff, H. (1987), *National Literacy Campaigns*, New York: Plenum Press.
Benton, L. and Noyelle, T. (1992), *Adult Literacy and Economic Performance*, Paris: OECD.
Bruner, J.S. (1960), *The Process of Education*, Harvard University Press.
Division of Further Education, Ministry of Employment Australia (1992), *Adult Basic Education Accreditation Framework*, Victoria: Department of Further Education, vol. 2, no. 2.
Education and Training Support Agency (1993), *Future 2000*, Wellington: ETSA.
Freebody, P. and Luke, A. (1990), ' "Literacies" Programmes – Debate and Demand in Cultural Context', *Prospect*, vol. 5, no. 3, pp. 35–42.
Hill, K. (1990), *This Fragile Web: the Adult Literacy Movement in New Zealand – its Rise and Development*, Wellington: NZCER.
Ministry of Education (1992), *The New Zealand Curriculum Framework*, Wellington, Ministry of Education.
Ministry of Education (1993), *Education for the 21st Century*, Wellington: Learning Media Ltd.
Moore, L. and Benseman, J. (1993), *Literacy at Work: an Exploratory Survey of Literacy and Basic Education Needs in the Workplace*, Auckland: ARLA Workbase.

New Zealand Council of Trade Unions (1992), *Building Better Skills, Industry Skills Formation to Take New Zealand into the 21st Century as a High Skill, High Wage Economy,* Wellington: NZCTU.

O'Connor, P. (1993), 'Negotiating Out of Neutral in Workers' Literacy', *Critical Forum,* vol. 2, no. 3, pp. 71–87.

Pugh, D.S. and Hickson, D.J. (1989), *Writers on Organisations,* London: Penguin.

Senge, P. (1993), *The Fifth Discipline: the Art and Practice of the Learning Organisation,* London: Century Business.

Singh, S. (2 June 1989), 'The Hidden Costs of Literacy', *Business Review Weekly,* p. 6.

Sutton, A. (1994), 'Adult Basic Education Policy in New Zealand', Unpublished MA paper, Massey University.

UNESCO (1962), *Statement of the International Committee of Experts on Literacy,* Paris: UNESCO.

| 12 |

Adult and Community Education in the Universities

Brian Findsen and Jennie Harré Hindmarsh

Introduction

Adult and community education in the universities of Aotearoa/New Zealand is commonly thought of as comprising those learning and teaching activities offered through their centres for continuing education or extension departments. But adult and community education opportunities are offered on a much wider front in and through the universities. For example, such learning opportunities are developed through many faculties and departments, through the university, professional and community activities of staff members, through students' associations, university clubs, the alumni associations, research activities and media reports and so on. However, while acknowledging this range of fourth sector activities in and through university communities, in this chapter we particularly focus on adult and community education through contemporary centres for continuing education or departments of extension. This concentration relates to these units being the primary public face of the universities for adult and community education and their more overt agendas to fulfil missions in this sector.

In this chapter we initially trace the development of centres for continuing education nationally from an historical perspective and then endeavour to identify their current characters. Next, within the context of prevailing political, economic and social forces, we examine contemporary developments with special reference to models which have emerged for delivery of university adult and community education and issues of mainstreaming or marginalisation, existing curricula and participation.

Historical Development

From the very early beginnings of Pakeha adult and community education in this country the universities have played a significant part in provision, especially in the urban areas in which they are located. While initially universities began in this country as colleges of the University of New Zealand, as each of the current seven universities acquired its administrative autonomy, it was faced with the question of provision for adult education for those not part of the mainstream degree programmes. Historically, the university colleges had fostered adult education via their long-standing relationship with the Workers Educational Association (WEA), particularly in the more established city centres and through voluntary leadership in selected adult education organisations (Dakin, 1992). Each university developed its own pathway and ethos, though heavily influenced by the dominant model of extramural studies transplanted from Britain. In the four main centres, where universities were established earlier, the universities without exception adopted the British university extramural model, but the newer universities (e.g. the University of Waikato) opted for the more organisational basis of a centre for continuing education.

The differences between 'university extension' and 'centre for continuing education' are more than semantic. The notion of university extension, as the name suggests, emanated from the university (e.g. Oxford in Britain) taking its academic staff to the people in public lectures and the like. Over time this evolved into a specialist unit within the university where staff were employed as tutors/organisers to take their discipline to the general public as part of the university's service to the community (Fordham, 1983; McIlroy and Spencer, 1988; Taylor, Rockhill and Fieldhouse, 1985). Once transplanted to New Zealand, this pattern of provision persisted wherein academic staff related to communities from a subject specialism background.

Over the past two decades, the Universities of Auckland, Waikato, Canterbury, Victoria University of Wellington and Lincoln University have established and remodelled centres for continuing education; the University of Otago has allowed its extension department to wind down after dabbling with distance education through teleconferencing; and Massey University has disestablished its university extension to focus on developing its distance credit courses through an extramural department. As a consequence, a diversity of formats for and underlying philosophies about the nature of fourth sector education most appropriately delivered from universities has developed in the university sector – with some common features.

Hence, centres for continuing education are much more recent suborganisations within universities. Essentially, these units, in their pure form, entail programme planners working with the university's diverse publics to develop continuing education programmes relevant to communities' learning needs and interests while using the resources of the university. This organisational form was principally borrowed from the North American equivalents (see Bagnall, 1978, for an extended discussion) where the ethos was one of entrepreneurism in education. In the New Zealand context, staff have been appointed as continuing education officers whose tasks have been to plan and develop appropriate programmes for adults in a university context.

The Current Macro Environment

The development of adult and community education within universities in this country has been dramatically affected by the larger socioeconomic political scene, including how the universities themselves have responded to these forces. While there have been the expected regional variations, currently all the centres for continuing education have been pressured to 'manage change' as part of their everyday strategy for survival and growth.

In the last decade, there have been massive economic, political and educational changes which have occurred as New Zealand has attempted to balance the books after years of purported overspending in the public sector. This country has undoubtedly been influenced by international trends as social commentators have observed (Naisbitt, 1984), but it has also retained a considerable degree of idiosyncracy (Snook, 1989). So what are these changes? What have been their effects on adult education in New Zealand universities?

Historically, this country has remained a two-party political system for many decades, veering between the progressive welfarism of Labour governments and the more conservative liberalism of National governments. In effect, substantive social change in recent years, until the advent of the fourth Labour government in 1984, had been minimal as there was a period of sustained prosperity (at least for some). Under the six years of the Labour government's policy of 'Rogernomics', its practices were heavily weighted to the New Right ideology of the 'mimimal state' (Snook, 1989). Under 'Rogernomics' (and subsequently by the existing National government) there has been streamlining of government-owned enterprises, and the sale of assets to the private sector and to international conglomerates. 'Inefficient' bureaucracies have been privatised to make them work better and to return a profit. Snook (1989: 3) sums up the New Right position as follows:

Economic growth is promoted by liberating free enterprise, reducing social expenditure and restructuring taxes to shift the burden from those who save (the rich) to those who consume (the poor).

Education, including adult and community education, has been a small pawn in this economic-political chess game. Massive restructuring has occurred in all sectors of the system: early childhood education; primary and secondary schooling; tertiary and adult and community education (see Harré Hindmarsh, 1993). Snook's analysis of recent trends reveals some patterns which are particularly noticeable in the state-provided education system (which are also pertinent to the fourth sector because much of its funding comes either directly or indirectly from government, particularly in the case of the universities):

- the education system has become part of the market where 'choice' determines quality. Just as parents are 'free' to choose schools to best fit the needs of their children, adults too can choose which adult education opportunities match their 'learning needs'
- accountability or responsibility is located at the local 'face-to-face' level with decision-making devolved to local groups. While continuing to control and monitor, the state washes its hands of direct responsibility for outcomes
- post-compulsory education is perceived as a privilege, not a right. Since education benefits the individual it should be paid for, in part at least, by the individual. The substantial increase in fees to tertiary students during 1989, the implementation of 'Study Right'[1] in 1992 and the loan system to tertiary students exemplify this rationale in action
- control and responsibility are to be more cogent than freedom and self-evaluation. Charters have been incorporated into every educational institution across all levels.

Juxtaposed to these political and economic imperatives of the New Right, Snook (1989) points to New Zealanders having retained the following unique features to their lives:

- a long-standing commitment to equality; even though New Zealand is not a classless society, many hold firm to the ideal of egalitarianism
- a tradition of a strong central state which has been manifest in social welfare and education. It may be difficult to overthrow the centralism of the past
- the co-existence of the Maori (as tangata whenua) with the Pakeha and a deep-seated belief that 'we are one people' living harmoniously. Importantly,

the Treaty of Waitangi acts as a founding document as one basis to promote Maori sovereignty and to redress inequities (e.g. land confiscations).

Given the above scenario, what has been the impact on adult and community education within universities? The same 'macro' factors have affected provision throughout the field, though the already marginalised agencies were especially targeted in the 1991 Budget (Harré Hindmarsh and Davies, 1993; Law, 1991). The most obvious manifestation of economic retrenchment within universities has been an increasing drive towards user pays and people's heightened interest in credentials as the job market shrinks. While these problems are hardly new – O'Rourke (1980) wrote about external factors in the Otago community affecting provision some 16 years ago – the renewed force of these external factors is hard to combat.

Paradoxically, at the same time as the Labour government promoted market liberalism, it also fostered equity in education. Previously, New Zealand educators had believed in and acted upon the imperative of equality of educational opportunity (based on the notion of equalising access to learning opportunities and resources, regardless of personal circumstances). Through social equity, the fourth Labour government had sought to redress inequalities, especially those based on grievances derived from the Treaty of Waitangi, by acknowledging that groups or sectors of society had been disenfranchised from access and use of resources (education included). Hence, the solution was to direct resources to those most disenfranchised to try to equalise outcomes. For many adult educators, including those working in a university context, this has been a time of reconciling the contradiction of market forces and social equity goals.

The Contemporary University Context

It should not be assumed that each centre for continuing education is the same. There are marked differences between them based on many factors, including: the parent institution's character and structures; the perceived importance of adult/continuing education as a function of a university; the geographical location of the centre and its political location within the structures of the university (i.e. mainstreamed or marginalised); the leadership of respective directors (a few but not many of whom received specialised professional education in the field); and the degree to which the university has developed networks within its communities. While in the instance of the University of Waikato, the Centre for Continuing Education evolved out of the Registry to become a fully fledged organisational unit, in other sites (e.g. Victoria University at Wellington, Canterbury, Auckland) centres were developed from the older university extension model. Indeed, it is only very recently that these changes have occurred in the main centres, triggered in part by internal reviews, but also by a realisation by the university system as a whole that new structures are required to meet the demands of the 1990s.

Staffing

It should be remembered that the central purposes of universities are to undertake teaching, research and community service. The position of centres for continuing education within universities have traditionally been uneasy because they have not been considered to engage in the 'real' tasks of a university. For example, the academics appointed under the former system of extension tended to be expected to undertake a wider range of duties than academics within other mainstream departments and were frequently disparaged by colleagues as 'second-class' academics (Fordham, 1983). As they were not usually engaged in teaching degree courses and undertook less research, they struggled to retain credibility. On the other hand, those appointed as continuing education officers have been even more marginalised. Not appointed on an academic basis, these adult educators have struggled to capture and maintain credibility with academic staff and have been engaged in tasks which did not allow for any research capacity and only very limited teaching. Typically, those employed as adult educators in a university setting (unless appointed as an academic with no programme development responsibilities) struggle for status within these élitist institutions. They are expected to behave as representatives of the university but also to be effective adult educators, in which case there are numerous often competing expectations from the community to meet learning needs.

Some centres for continuing education have a mix of staff rather than a straight continuing education officer or academic portfolio. From the experiences of the authors these structural features have tended to create tensions in the workplace. Often academic staff are perceived as parasitic on the organisation (quite typically now, centres are expected to generate a high proportion of their income) whose work conditions are 'freer' than those for non-academics; continuing education officers are employed as programme developers who sometimes feel constrained in their roles. The tension is especially felt by those academics who are employed to carry out multiple roles – programme supervision; teaching and research. Recent reviews at both Canterbury and Victoria have resulted in a much more entrepreneurial and managerial function for these centres; the academic staff in general have.been moved sideways into mainstream departments related to their subject specialty. This move raises the question of the value placed on the continued academic study of adult education and the support given to such staff, whether based in centres for continuing education or education departments. Counterbalancing this trend, as a result of the Review of the Centre for Continuing Education at the University of Auckland (Marshall, 1995), it was decided to retain academic adult education specialists.

Curriculum and Provision

The range of continuing education structures and curriculum provision remain broad in the university sector. Even within a centre, there can be considerable controversy as to what constitutes appropriate curricula (programme provision). This fact was highlighted by Alcorn (1987: 27), not long after she had assumed the director's position at Auckland:

> ... we have been aware of continuing contradictions and tensions not only between our practice and our intent but between competing ideologies and theories, between the demands of community groups and University expectations, between programme areas that claim priority status.

There are real difficulties involved in determining adult learners' needs (Benseman, 1980), what constitutes appropriate resource provision and the relative merits of different programme areas (e.g. general studies, professional courses).

Across the system of centres in this country, it is possible to discern the following activities (not all of which are present in any one centre):

1. general liberal adult education – a range of diverse seminars/courses designed for 'the general public'
2. continuing professional education
3. enrolment of adult or mature age students into undergraduate (or certificate or qualification) programmes
4. vocational continuing education and role training (e.g. training of counsellors; teachers)
5. preparatory and bridging courses to provide access for adults to degree programmes (e.g. New Start)
6. academic teaching and research in the field of adult and community education
7. professional training of adult and community educators
8. community issues forum (programmes based around contemporary events/ issues)
9. community education initiatives/community development – more localised programmes

10. education for older adults (Elderhostel and New Zealand College for Seniors programmes)
11. Maori adult education (e.g. non-credit hui; Certificate in Maori Studies)
12. summer or Easter Schools (e.g. in the arts)
13. educational travel (tours to other countries)
14. public lectures, performances, exhibitions which contribute to the cultural life of New Zealanders
15. distance education in a variety of forms (e.g. teleconferences)
16. continuing professional education programmes for university staff.

To many people, there is little apparent coherence in this extensive list of potential programmes. This apparent incoherence may reflect a range of philosophical positions which are held simultaneously even within the one centre; it may reflect the reality of a consumer-driven field where the most articulate get the most from the system. In this respect, the challenge of critics (Apple, 1981; Findsen, 1992; Giroux, 1979) that (adult) education serves to reproduce inequalities in New Zealand society is yet to be adequately addressed.

In the final analysis, the control of curriculum is increasingly in the hands of continuing education staff themselves, mediated by the pervading socioeconomic circumstances of which centres are a part, and the power élite of the universities. For example, whether a director can choose to cross-subsidise access programmes or community development (examples of highly socially desirable goals but requiring intensive labour) by traditionally profit-making enterprises (e.g. continuing professional education or Elderhostel) may not be entirely in that person's control. If the university requires that the centre for continuing education be an income generating organisation based on a user-pays regime, it is unlikely that there is much freedom to move without jeopardising staff jobs. On the other hand, if the university itself acknowledges the importance of these programmes under its social equity policy, it should fund these socially desirable initiatives and not expect a centre to be burdened unnecessarily.

Mainstreaming or Marginalisation?

The contemporary organisation of university continuing education in Aotearoa/New Zealand, as elsewhere (UCACE, 1992), is characterised by debates regarding the extent to which adult community education provision is or should be marginal to, loosely connected to, integrated with or fundamental to learning opportunities offered by universities. Is such provision an optional extra, a luxury for well-heeled, white middle-class matrons, a way to do a bit of equity work, a way to serve the community (however, defined), a way to serve business, government, industry and professional interests, a way to more widely disseminate lecturers' research and knowledge, a public relations exercise? Or is it an essential part of the lifelong learning university (Duke, 1992)?

Underlying these questions are differing ideas about the primary purposes of university adult and community education and its relationship to the purposes of university education in general – what should be delivered, how, by whom, who should pay and on what basis? These differing ideas are reflected in the implementation of contemporary policies and reviews of centres and departments in the context of the changing faces of university education in the New Right-influenced 1990s. They are reflected, for example, in the different structural and physical locations of continuing education within universities; in the different staffing composition of centres/departments; in the differing sources, conduits and amounts of funding and resources allocated, including different ratios of institutional government funding to user pays and cost recovery; in differing statements in charters and strategic plans; in differing profiles of curriculum provision and learner participation; and in differing relationships with the range of communities of learners it serves and with other providers.

In this section, we analyse current trends in the provision of continuing education in Aotearoa/New Zealand universities in relation to the matrix outlined in Figure 13.1 (page 202). The matrix, like all such analyses, oversimplifies distinctions. However, it does provide a way to tease out the emergent variations in university adult and community education in the 1990s. The matrix is based on two intersecting axes. On the vertical 'marginal to central control' axis, we can locate the delivery of adult and community education in relation to the extent to which it is controlled by the university – is it loosely connected with or integrated into the policies, structure, functions, administrative systems and physical environment of the university? On the horizontal 'low to high dollar support' axis we plot patterns of provision in relation to the extent to which the university funds adult and community education through its allocation of funding (high support) relative to user-pays fees (low support).

Four models emerge from the possible combinations of the extreme points on each of these two axes. These are the mainstream, traditional extension, entrepreneurial and separate business unit models.

The *mainstream model* represents situations where continuing education is embedded in a 'learning university', a university which is a lifelong learning resource centre (Duke, 1992). At the extreme points of this section of the matrix, adult and community education is considered to be an integral and essential part of government-funded university services. In its purest sense, it is when mainstreamed adult and community education is an integral and funded part of the roles of all departments, faculties and academic staff – part of the

Figure 13.1: University Continuing Education Alternative Models

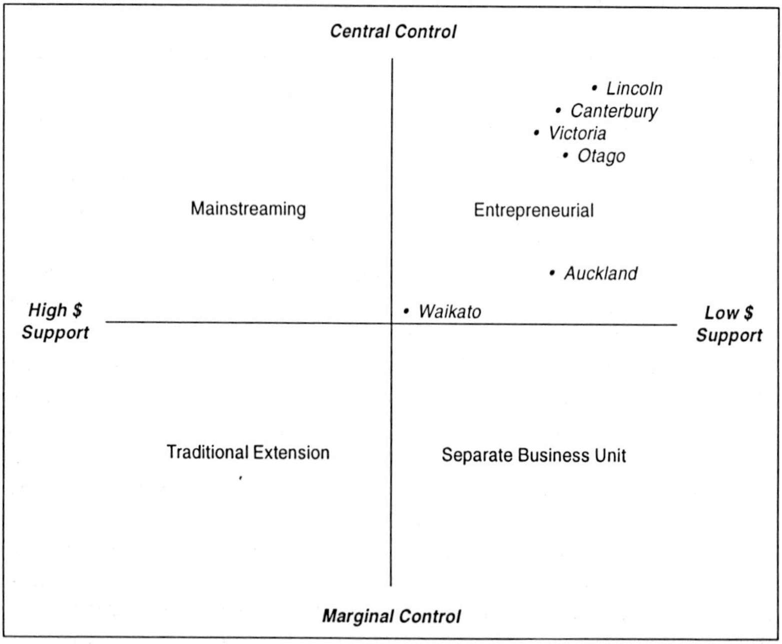

```
                        Central Control
                              |
                              |         • Lincoln
                              |         • Canterbury
                              |         • Victoria
                              |         • Otago
                              |
         Mainstreaming        |       Entrepreneurial
                              |
                              |          • Auckland
  High $                      | • Waikato                Low $
  Support  _____|_____      Support
                              |
                              |
                              |
      Traditional Extension   |    Separate Business Unit
                              |
                              |
                              |
                        Marginal Control
```

(Developed by Jennie Harré Hindmarsh, from UCACE April 1992 and discussions with Chris Duke 1993)

teaching, research, administration and community service elements of their job description.

The *traditional extension model,* in contrast, is characterised by a high level of central funding but allocated to a separate department, often on the outskirts of campus – the 'old' British liberal tradition upon which university extension in this country and elsewhere was originally modelled, as noted earlier.

The *entrepreneurial model* represents a centrally controlled (in terms of policy and general programme priorities) entrepreneurial unit or centre which is expected to be increasingly self-funding, with minimal support from the university (government-funded) coffers. University support is mainly for programmes and services which assist the university to meet its equity commitments as stated in the charter.

Finally, the *separate business unit model* represents potential situations where provision is through an off-campus, profit-making business unit of the university, with little central support or policy input – other than requirements to cover expenses and overheads and to return at least a small profit within generally stated terms of reference.

In Aotearoa/New Zealand over the past one-and-a-half decades, the trend has been to move away from the traditional extension model. This had been evident at all universities except Lincoln, where mainstreaming was in operation. Before 1970, Lincoln (Agricultural College as it was then) allocated its Vote Education continuing education funds direct to departments whose academic staff were involved in community education as part of their jobs (e.g. farm management advisory services). A diversity of models has emerged during the 1980s and 1990s. More recently, at the Universities of Auckland, Canterbury, Otago, and Victoria University of Wellington the trend has been to move increasingly towards the entrepreneurial centre model. That is, there has been a decrease in central university (Vote Education) funding, especially since the introduction of Equivalent Full-Time Students (EFTS) funding post 'Learning for Life' policies in the early 1990s; an increased requirement to obtain funding from users of the services; and a trend to increase central control and oversight of policies and programmes. The same trend is evident at Lincoln, which moved from a mainstream model to a user-pays approach in the 1970s and which has reached the highest level of user-pays funding to date. Lincoln's emphasis on user pays has been related to its emphasis on vocational and professional development programmes rather than general and community studies. Auckland was the second centre to activate this funding trend in the 1980s, a trend which has developed more recently in the other centres as a result of their reviews in the late 1980s and early 1990s.

Within this broad trend, there is diversity in relation to where in the entrepreneurial quadrant of the matrix each centre is located given its university's position on the central to marginal axis. Central control is increased by making the director position non-academic and by introducing a Board to oversee policies and programmes – an early move at Waikato and more latterly at Otago, Canterbury then Victoria. Victoria's centre also has just been relocated off-campus to a city block (in advance of the relocation of the Law Faculty to the Lambton Quay end of the city) and academic staff have been relocated to other university departments. At the same time, there is an attempt to increase central control of mainstream activities through the new Board of Continuing Education which advises the Vice-Chancellor on all continuing education policy campus-wide and approves the centre's strategic plan and programmes. Victoria may yet move along the continuum to mix the entrepreneurial centre with features of a mainstream model. Otago has been reviewed and indications are that it will continue to move further into this model. Throughout this period, Waikato has remained predominantly funded by the central university with a relatively minor level of funding required from user-pays sources. This centre has retained more control of those EFTS dollars in that the university passes through it control of all EFTSs related to the community education non-credit courses and those generated by the credit course, the Certificate in Continuing Education. Thus, Waikato appears to be located most centrally on the matrix – somewhere on the continuum between the extension and mainstream model, a mix of some features of both, with a bit of entrepreneurialism added in. This is reflected in its curriculum content, more weighted to community or general studies and less to professional development programmes than any other centre – possibly reflecting the fact that the university has traditionally not had large professional schools and that some faculties (e.g. Management) have developed their own (mainstream) programmes.

The trend to more entrepreneurial activities raises questions with regard to which particular programmes ought to be fully user pays and which subsidised and then subsidised by whom – the centre or the university (government)? These questions are constantly negotiated in centres. At present, they are 'resolved' in two ways. There is strong agreement that all continuing education vocational/professional education should be largely, if not totally, self-funding but disagreement about how to define that. Some courses may appear non-vocational but are used by people for both vocational and non-vocational purposes. There also appear to be some common assumptions that programmes designed to address Treaty of Waitangi and equity commitments and those to bridge potential mature students back to study, ought to be heavily subsidised: but through what avenues – special grants, the centre's profit-making courses, the central university, government-tagged funding?

Centres in the 1980s and early 1990s have had a significant role in initiating and implementing new developments – a university community development role where they have been 'at the cutting edge in higher education – a Trojan horse, perhaps to smuggle in change' (Duke, 1992: xii). For example, at Victoria University of Wellington, the Centre for Industrial Relations grew out of courses developed through the Centre for Continuing Education; the University's Link programmes arose from the Centre for Continuing Education as did, in part, the current developments in relation to the Recognition of Prior Learning (RPL); and Maori Studies Outreach and Liaison developments have been assisted through the activities of the Maori Community Education Officer. Similarly, at Waikato, Women's Studies and the Centre for Trade Union and Labour Studies grew from continuing education and at Auckland, Women's Studies has been introduced to the university via a Centre for Continuing Education certificate and parallel developments in the degree programme.

In addition, most centres have developed the facility to offer some programmes for university credit in the move away from the extension model. This practice is also under review, the outcome of which will provide another indication of where centres lie on the axis between entrepreneurialism and mainstreaming and away from a business unit-entrepreneurial axis. It remains to be seen whether the trend for centres to become more entrepreneurial will curb these university community development and credit roles or enhance them – indicating a mainstream-entrepreneur mix rather than an entrepreneur-business unit mix.

Participation Trends

Who participates in university adult and community education programmes in the 1990s? Who defines programme priorities, organises and hosts the learning opportunities? We lack definitive and up-to-date research to answer these questions, especially with regard to all but the first question. In the 1970s, four of five New Zealand studies of participation in adult and community education analysed participation in the university programmes. All indicated that participants (as with those in other adult and community education settings) were a fairly homogeneous group of white, middle-class and relatively well-educated people – with women tending to dominate in non-vocational areas (Benseman, 1992: 11–13). In 1992 and 1993 the Ministry of Education collected statistics of those enrolled in courses offered through centres for continuing education in one particular week at the end of July. These data suggest that overall, women slightly outnumber men in university programmes, with more men relative to women participating in university programmes than in school and polytechnic programmes. They also suggest that men predominate amongst the under 20-year-old participants. A similar gender pattern of participation is evident in polytechnic enrolments (Ministry of Education, 1993; Davies and Harré Hindmarsh, 1993). However, these data must be treated with caution as course offerings vary week by week, the data from polytechnics apply to full-year programmes and the definitions of adult and community education between institutions vary (Harré Hindmarsh, 1992; Harré Hindmarsh and Davies, 1993).

Given this lack of information, in the preparation of this chapter Jennie Harré Hindmarsh conducted a simple survey of all centres for their most recent learner participation figures. These data revealed that in all but the Lincoln centre (25 per cent women/75 per cent men), women outnumbered men as enrollees – by approximately 27 per cent men/73 per cent women at Waikato; 32 per cent/68 per cent at Victoria University of Wellington; 35 per cent/65 per cent at the University of Canterbury; 39 per cent/61 per cent at Otago; and 43 per cent/57 per cent at Auckland. It could be suggested that Lincoln's predominance of males reflects the predominance of user-pays professional development programmes in traditionally male (agricultural) occupations; and

Waikato's highest percentage of women reflects their higher percentage of community or general studies-type programmes and more highly (university/ government) subsidised programmes. The data from the University of Canterbury also provided information on the variable pattern of gender participation across types of courses. In 1993, men significantly outnumbered women in continuing professional education and community development/University of the Third Age programmes, and women outnumbered men in general studies, New Start and inbound study tours – suggesting that the above interpretation of the gender ratios is accurate.

Only Lincoln, and Victoria had ethnicity data on participants, both of which indicate that Maori and Pacific Islands participation is not representative of their presence in the population. For example, at Victoria only four per cent of participants identified as Maori in 1993–1994, three per cent as Pacific Islanders and three per cent as from other non-Pakeha groups. At Lincoln, two per cent were Maori, the remainder Pakeha. These figures suggest that continuing education is lagging behind the trend to increase Maori and Pacific Islands people's participation in degree programmes. The Todd Taskforce (Ministerial Consultative Group 1994: 52), for example, reports that Maori made up eight per cent of university students in formal programmes in 1993. However, in continuing education programmes specifically designed with, by and for Maori and delivered in Maori contexts, their participation increases significantly (e.g. Auckland's 1993 New Start organised in conjunction with Waipareira Trust in West Auckland attracted 45 per cent Maori participants).[2]

Figures regarding the age of participants indicate national variability, again reflecting variability in curriculum emphases and user-pays policies. For example, 70 per cent of Lincoln's participants are in their 30s and 26 per cent over 40, whereas at Waikato 56 per cent are over 40 and all others (except for 4.6 per cent) between 20 and 40. Waikato's figures are influenced by the fact that they now offer regionally fifteen 60+ group programmes, many of which were meeting in the week in July from which the Ministry of Education data were collected. In contrast yet again, at Victoria 30 per cent are over 45, with the rest of the participants spread evenly over the 15 to 44 age group. There is a slight tendency for Otago's participants to be under 20 or over 60 with an even spread between. In Auckland, participants are predominantly 20–50 years.

Variability is also the theme of national staffing patterns. Pakeha dominate beyond their prevalence in the general population. At the time of the survey (late 1994) only 2.5 of 26 permanent Continuing Education Officer positions (programme planning staff) are Maori and they are at two of the six centres (Victoria, 0.5 and Waikato, two). There are no Maori academic staff and of 31.5 administration staff, two are Maori. The gender of programme planning staff varies across centres. For example, women predominate at Waikato and Auckland, men and women are evenly spread at Victoria (now with the only female director) and men are predominant at Canterbury and Otago. Of the 5.2 academic positions (Auckland 4.2 and Canterbury 1.0), 1.2 are female. All but two general staff are female.

More detailed research is required to collect more rigorous data and analyse the patterns suggested by these figures in relation to population and participation patterns in post-compulsory education and across occupations. Overall, the provision of university continuing education continues to reflect patterns of inequity common nation-wide and across professions. Maori and Pacific Islands people are underrepresented in continuing education as participants and providers, women are generally underrepresented in professional programmes and men in New Start and general studies. In recognition of cultural biases, Waikato and Victoria recently have proactively employed Maori staff to develop programmes for Maori, and Victoria employed a Pacific Islands staff member part-time to run a contract course for Pacific Islands managers until the demise of that contract course. If university adult and community education is to live up to Te Tiriti o Waitangi and equity objectives then much change is required – in curriculum, staffing delivery and funding patterns.

Conclusion

This paper has demonstrated the complexity and variety of forms of adult and community education in the university context within Aotearoa/New Zealand. The issues canvassed – staffing, curriculum, alternative models, participation – are necessarily related to the distinctive national history of centres for continuing education, but also they reflect regional emphases. Currently, the New Right has a direct impact on the shape of provision in every centre and some centres are resisting this influence more than others. There is a direct challenge to all centres, in the light of data collected to this point about patterns of provision, adult student participation and staff profiles, to address more proactively the distortions revealed by our analysis. For centres to more readily reflect the communities in which they are based, there is a clear message for more active engagement with them in spreading university educational resources, developing relevant programmes and upholding the notion of lifelong learning for all people.

Notes

1. Under 'Study Right', the Government provided a higher rate of subsidy towards the tuition costs of school leavers in comparison with students over the age of 25.

2. The Maori proportion of the population is about 12–14 per cent (depending on the definition of 'Maori').

References

Alcorn, N. (May/Oct. 1987), 'Determining Continuing Education Priorities in a University: Theories, Demands, Constraints', *New Zealand Journal of Adult Learning*, vol. 19, nos 1 and 2, pp. 27–42.

Apple, M.W. (1981), 'Reproduction, Contestation and Curriculum: An Essay in Self-Criticism', *Interchange*, vol. 12, nos. 2–3, pp. 27–47.

Bagnall, R.G. (Oct. 1978), 'University Extension in North America: Some Patterns and Issues with Implications for New Zealand Practice', *Continuing Education in New Zealand*, vol. 10, no. 2, pp. 19–43.

Benseman, J. (1980), *The Assessment and Meeting of Needs in Continuing Education*, Stockholm Institute of Education, Lärerhögskolan Department of Educational Research.

Benseman, J. (1992), 'Participation Revisited: Who Gets to Adult/Community Education 1970–1990?', *New Zealand Journal of Adult Learning*, vol. 20, no. 1, pp. 11–19.

Dakin, J. (Oct. 1992), 'Derivative and Innovative Modes in New Zealand Adult Education', *New Zealand Journal of Adult Learning*, vol. 20, no. 2, pp. 29–49.

Davies, L. and Harré Hindmarsh, J. (1993), Tables presented at the New Zealand Association for Continuing and Community Education Conference, Christchurch.

Duke, C. (1992), *The Learning University: Towards a New Paradigm?*, Buckingham, England: The Society for Research into Higher Education and Open University Press.

Findsen, B. (May 1992), 'What Really Counts as Knowledge? A Sociological Approach to the Certificate in Maori Studies at the University of Waikato', *New Zealand Journal of Adult Learning*, vol. 20, no, 1, pp. 51–64.

Fordham, P. (1983), 'A View from the Wall: Commitment and Purposes in University Adult Education', *International Journal of Lifelong Education*, vol. 2, no. 4, pp. 341–354.

Giroux, H.A. (Dec. 1979), 'Toward a New Sociology of the Curriculum', *Educational Leadership*, pp. 248–253.

Harré Hindmarsh, J. (Nov. 1992), 'Vote Education Funding for Adult Education: The New Zealand Experience', Paper presented to NZARE/AARE Conference, Deakin University, Australia, pp. 26–27.

Harré Hindmarsh, J. (1993), 'Community and Continuing Education in 1992: Trends and Issues', *New Zealand Annual Review of Education*, vol. 2, pp. 179–204.

Harré Hindmarsh, J. and Davies, L. (1993), *Vote Education Funding for Adult Education: Who Benefits? Part One: Community Organisations*, Wellington: Ministry of Education.

Law, M. (Aug. 1991), 'The Budget: Implications for Adult Education and Community Development', Paper presented to a Community Education Forum, University of Waikato.

McIlroy, J. and Spencer, B. (1988), *University Adult Education in Crisis*, University of Leeds, Department of Adult and Continuing Education.

Marshall, J. (1995), 'Report of the Committee Established to Review the Centre for Continuing Education', University of Auckland.

Ministerial Consultative Group (1994), *Funding Growth in Tertiary Education and Training*, Wellington: Ministry of Education.

Ministry of Education (1993), Data from Statistics Section, personal communication to Jennie Harré Hindmarsh.

Naisbitt, J. (1984), *Megatrends*, New York: Warner Books

O'Rourke, B. (Oct. 1980), 'The Role of the University of Otago in Continuing Education in the Region', *Continuing Education in New Zealand*, vol. 12, no. 2, pp. 4–14.

Snook, I. (1989), 'Educational Reform in New Zealand: What is Going On?', Paper presented at the New Zealand Association for Research in Education, Trentham.

Taylor, R., Rockhill, K. and Fieldhouse, R. (1985), *University Adult Education in England and the U.S.A.*, Beckenham, Kent: Croom Helm Ltd.

UCACE (1992), *Good Practice in Continuing Vocational Education: The Internal Organisation of Continuing Education*, University Council for Adult and Continuing Education, Occasional Paper no. 9, by Chris Duke, University of Warwick.

13

The Role of Polytechnics in Community Education

Nick Zepke

Introduction

Polytechnics, a fractious family of 25 institutions, have very different approaches to adult and community education. This chapter sketches briefly how such differences emerged. In greater detail, it examines the impacts on adult and community education of the great post-compulsory education reformation of 1989. Discussion then turns to the various guises of adult and community education. The Wairarapa Community Polytechnic is used as a case study to explain why some withered and others prospered. Finally, the chapter turns to the future; a future in which polytechnics only have a small role in adult and community education.

Beginnings of a Problematic Relationship

Twenty-five providers of post-compulsory education belong to Aotearoa/New Zealand's polytechnic family.[1] But just like 25 people sharing the name 'Smith', each is very different. In fact the family name 'polytechnic' is relatively new and even now three family members spurn the common label by calling themselves 'Institutes of Technology'. Soon, no doubt, there will be a University of Technology or two.

Polytechnics were born in different eras for different purposes. The first were split off from Technical Colleges in the early 1960s to provide technical and vocational training in the main centres. Appropriately perhaps, they were called 'Technical Institutes'. 'Community Colleges' emerged during the late 1970s. In addition to vocational subjects, they had the mission of providing non-vocational adult and community education to people in larger secondary centres. The same mission was given to a third group of 'Community Polytechnics' which were started largely in rural centres with small and dispersed populations in the late 1980s.

No wonder that the orientation of polytechnics towards adult and community education has varied. Some of the larger urban vocational institutions never developed a community education focus at all. Wellington Polytechnic and the Central Institute of Technology were two of these. The former left the field to the neighbouring Community Institute at Wellington High School. The latter, according to Bateman and Munro (1985: 51) was founded to provide 'specialised vocational courses at an advanced level'. And that is just what CIT did until the 1990s. Other polytechnics operated Community Education Departments but these often taught vocational-type courses which would not fit easily elsewhere.

In provincial centres, however, attempts were made by Community Colleges to meet non-vocational community learning needs. Harrison (1981), Northland Polytechnic's foundation principal, listed an impressive list of activities. After only three years in 1981, close contacts had been established with small communities in Northland through good communications networks which included newsletters and an innovative partnership with Radio New Zealand as well as shared programmes with local providers and normal outreach programmes. Support had been given to the adult literacy movement, Maori language teaching had been introduced, parent education started. This pattern of outreach was repeated in Rotorua, Hawke's Bay, Gisborne, Wanganui, Southland and Nelson among others. As a result, growth in one facet of adult and community education, short courses, was considerable between 1976 and 1987. Participation in short courses grew from 15,456 to 81,918, a growth of 427 per cent (Department of Statistics, 1990: 35). Yet, the provision of adult and community education even by community colleges was always problematic. Harrison (1981: 20) quotes a research report written by David James:

> Several people ... deeply committed to community education, were openly questioning whether a community college, at least as national policies and regulations stand, is a possible base for community education.

James seemed deeply pessimistic that technical institutes and community colleges as 'closed' institutions would be able to embrace the 'openness' required by adult and community education. While community colleges were meant to be open, they 'have never been allowed to be on any large scale and are gradually being more restricted still' (Harrison, 1981: 20).

Effects of the 1989 Reforms: The Hegemony of the New Right

The reformation of post-compulsory education began in 1989. If the provision of open adult and community education was problematic before 1990, it became near impossible thereafter. Among the reasons: the reforms were effected in an intellectual climate unfavourable to adult and community education; they encouraged polytechnics to pursue missions poisonous to non-vocational programmes and created a funding regime which made adult and community education deeply unprofitable to run.

The prevailing intellectual climate of the late 1980s and early 1990s has discounted the value of adult and community education. A complex set of propositions, often loosely labelled as 'New Right' thinking is responsible. New Right thinking projects a very narrow view of human motivation and social purpose. According to Jenson *et al.* (1988), an economic dimension emphasises the competition of individuals in the marketplace, which alone decides the merit of ideas and actions. The state must not interfere in the operations of the marketplace. It should, though, help its sovereignty by enforcing a supportive unity of social values and actions through targeting and accountability mechanisms. Education's narrow task is to provide human resources for the marketplace and ensure that social values conform with this purpose.

Jenson *et al.* (1988) argue that New Right influence is now so great that Antonio Gramsci's concept of hegemony applies. Hegemony occurs when an already dominant social group, like big business or the bureaucracy, totally establishes the authority of its ideas with other groups and thereby gains their popular acceptance, even support. In the post-compulsory education sector especially, learning has been bound by the hegemony of the New Right. Numerous official reports,[2] media campaigns and conference appearances by business and government leaders have created an intellectual climate restricting adult and community education.

Learning for Life: Two, the government's 1989 blueprint for post-school education set the scene. It ensured that learning in polytechnics would have a vocational focus by expecting them to contribute directly to economic development. Polytechnics:

> ... are viewed as important instruments of national policy for vocational education and training, labour market adjustment programmes (including retraining), second-chance education and the transition of young people to adult life.
>
> (*Learning for Life: Two*, 1989: 40)

While polytechnics were allowed to offer community education programmes, 'the main focus and predominant role will continue to be vocational education and training' (*Learning for Life: Two*, p. 40). To facilitate this focus, they were given the right to offer degrees.

The ideas in *Learning for Life: Two* were enshrined in the Education Amendment Act (1990) and were further supported and published by reports produced by 'New Right' think tanks. The influential Porter Report (1991), for example, slammed New Zealand education as not having 'adequately prepared many New Zealanders to contribute to their own and the nation's economic wellbeing'. To change this, it wanted a greater vocational and practical focus and emphasis on technical, scientific and management skills.

The New Zealand Qualifications Authority (NZQA) enforces this growing hegemony of vocational learning. It has been unable to withstand the business sector's demands for control of national certification and qualifications. Its learning units-based qualifications framework with its tightly defined, competency-based learning outcomes tends to exclude the type of learning usually provided by open-ended adult and community education.

Seeking a Place in the Academic Sun

Many polytechnics have found this new climate congenial. Long before 1989 they sought escape from the academic shadow cast by universities. During the 1980s, amusing escape stories abounded. One positioned the principal of a well-known upwardly mobile institute before his office mirror trying on a vice-chancellor's gown, ready for the day when .... Many institutes ran graduation ceremonies closely modelled on those of universities. Some even recorded their ambitions on paper. CIT's council for example, in 1981 approved a vision:

> The primary function of CIT is to provide study towards defined vocational opportunities generally at the higher levels of the applied sciences and technologies.
>
> (Bateman and Munro, 1985: 54)

This vision was explicitly based on the Australian and United Kingdom models where non-university institutions could offer degrees. *Learning for Life: Two* finally gave polytechnics the opportunity to bask in the academic sun.

So a vigorous pursuit of degree approval and accreditation began. Most polytechnics at least planned degree developments. Even those like Wairarapa Community Polytechnic, which had no chance of mounting a degree of its own, sought strategic partnerships so it could offer first-year subjects for degrees granted by larger and richer polytechnics. The polytechnics' drive for degree status was powered further by traditional groups of polytechnic customers. Health professions such as Nursing, Occupational Therapy and Physiotherapy for example, pressured polytechnics for degree programmes. The chase for degrees had a profound effect on the way adult and community education was perceived by polytechnics. It did not fit with the new academic profile. Sandals did not live as happily with trencher as they had with cloth cap or lab coat. But much more importantly, degree accreditation changes the very culture of polytechnics. It requires huge resources, commitment and energy to mount degrees. Academic processes are transformed by NZQA requirements. The 'open' institution envisaged by Harrison and James as necessary for the provision of adult and community education is difficult to achieve in 'formal' cultures dominated by academic boards and quality assurance measures.

But it was not only by choice that polytechnics downgraded or even abandoned their involvement in adult and community education. In some instances they were forced into 'higher education'. *Learning for Life: Two* signalled a whole new class of private educational establishments. These had the same opportunities to bid for government funding to run programmes as had polytechnics. In the main they focused on delivering lower-level programmes particularly those for the long-term unemployed. In this area they were very successful in winning from polytechnics large chunks of their Training Opportunities Programme (TOPs) funding. One polytechnic lost about one-fifth of its total programmes to private providers. This led to redundancies, restructuring and conflict. To survive, such polytechnics had to reposition their programmes. Inevitably, they found survival positions higher up the programme tree in advanced full-time, multi-year programmes. Again, the resources, processes and energy needed to reach a safe position mitigated against adult and community education.

The Funding Problem

The reformation also created a funding system unsympathetic to adult and community education. Prior to 1989, its peculiar funding needs were met by a formula-based system. Some services attracted funding according to the student hours they produced. Adult and community education classes earned student hours and therefore funding. But non-teaching activities could also attract resourcing. So co-ordination, an absolutely vital ingredient in community development, for example, was specifically funded. At times, such co-ordination staffing was a major component in a community polytechnic's funding. At its birth in 1988, for example, Wairarapa Community Polytechnic received about 15 per cent of its setting-up staffing for co-ordinating work.

Formula funding ended with the introduction of the new funding regime on 1 January 1991. Now funding is based on a transparent count of Equivalent Full-Time Students (EFTS) enrolled at an institution. Each EFTS is equivalent to a typical year of full-time study. Institutions are funded a year in advance on the basis of an approved EFTS level within set cost categories abated by the government's current subsidy policy. A polytechnic's income from adult and community education can only be low. It sits in the lowest cost category and many enrolments usually make only a few EFTS. Since 1992, income has been further restricted by the government's Study Right subsidy. Most students in community education do not attract the Study Right subsidy, which further reduced income. The result: where some EFTS earn nearly $10,000, community education normally earns about half that amount. And there is no special recognition for co-ordination time.

True, something called a Notional EFTS was introduced with the new funding system. This was activated by community education programmes for which it was not practical to record formal enrolments. Initially greeted with great gratification by community educators, Notional EFTS were later restricted to such an extent that their impact on funding was truly notional.

If the income from adult and community education was small, costs were not. *Learning for Life: Two* introduced rigorous accountability requirements. These were the same for one-hour meetings or one-day workshops as for full-time, multi-year courses. This skyrocketed the overheads for adult and community education. Wairarapa Community Polytechnic, for example, enrolled some 3,000 students in 12 different locations for 16 EFTS in 1991. The accountability costs for these 16 EFTS far exceeded the costs of any 16 EFTS enrolled in a full-time course taught on the main campus. In addition, there were special accommodation and travel costs to cover the 11 temporary locations and one permanent outpost. Expensive co-ordination time had to be added. By the end of 1992, with Notional EFTS devalued, the costs of running adult and community programmes far exceeded income. As a result, community education programmes had to be pruned to those which recovered costs. This had major consequences for the balance of programmes offered. The story of programme balance will be taken up next.

Four Guises of Community Education

Adult and community education is notoriously difficult to define. Thankfully a rigorous definition is unnecessary for this chapter. Suffice to say that polytechnics have never been very hung up on definitions and that the use of the term 'community education' has been all inclusive – a many-guised dreamcoat to describe a vast range of educational activities: formal and non-formal; empowering both those with and without power. Using Wairarapa Community Polytechnic as a case study, this section now explores the nature and range of adult and community education offered by polytechnics, particularly since 1989.

Towards a Vision of Community Education

At Wairarapa Community Polytechnic two assumptions underpinned a very inclusive vision of community education. One stated that it could be both formal and non-formal. According to the report of the Interim Advisory Group on Non-formal Education *He Tangata* (1987: 6), 'The essential element which distinguishes non-formal from formal education is that non-formal groups control their own learning independently of imposed curricula, of outside professionals or of institutions'.

In formal education, decisions about curriculum and assessment are made by outside agents. Formal education therefore can be tightly focused, without any reference to the learner's personal world. Non-formal education cannot be so isolated from the learner's wider economic and social interests and experiences.

The other assumption held that adult and community education can achieve two quite opposing but legitimate outcomes. On the one hand, it can socialise learners so that they better fit into existing social and economic situations. The Club of Rome (Botkin *et al.*, 1979) dubbed the learning process which achieves this kind of outcome 'maintenance learning'. Such learning focuses on traditional processes and content such as is found in hobby classes. Learning is based on the ideas and solutions of established administrative and academic authorities. It preserves existing systems and therefore secures stability. On the other hand, community education can emancipate learners, empower them to work for change. Recently Peters and Marshall (1991) have spotlighted some problems with the concept of empowerment as an automatic cure for oppression. Nevertheless, community education can empower learners to think and act critically so that they effect changes in their own and their community's life (Giroux, 1988).

A two-dimensional matrix pictures these assumptions. The vertical line of the matrix divides empowering from maintenance learning. The horizontal line divides formal from non-formal activities.

Figure 14.1:

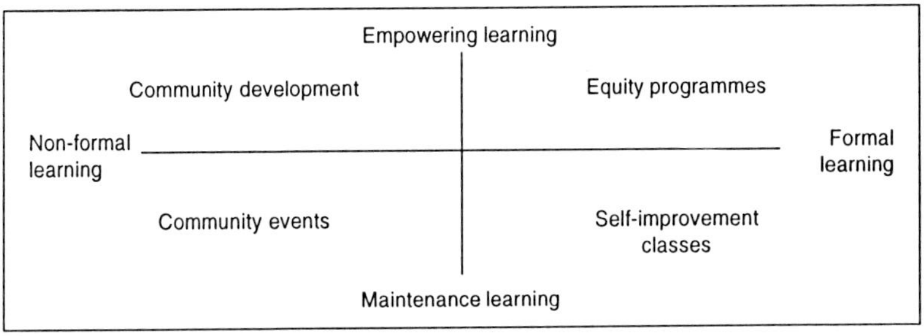

	Empowering learning	
Non-formal learning	Community development	Equity programmes
	Community events	Self-improvement classes
	Maintenance learning	

(Non-formal learning on the left; Formal learning on the right)

The matrix identifies four entirely different approaches to adult and community education. Community development probably best describes programmes which are both non-formal and empowering. Programmes which are formal yet empowering are often so-called equity programmes. Community events such as summer schools and special topic workshops usually involve non-formal maintenance learning. Hobby classes and self-improvement short courses leading to non-political outcomes usually involve formal maintenance learning.

To some degree polytechnics have used all four approaches to adult and community education. Empowering approaches, though, have always been marginal. It was about the survival of such learning experiences that James expressed his doubts in 1981. Freire (as quoted in the Lifelong Learning Taskforce, 1985: [i]) explains why:

> Those who hold power define education – what it is, its content, its methods. They will not tolerate an education system that works against them, so will not accept a true 'education for liberation'. Some reforms are tolerated, though only insofar as they do not threaten the existing power structure.

The 1989 post-compulsory education reformation further marginalised empowering community education in polytechnics. The hegemony of New Right ideas, aspirations for a place in the academic sun, financial restraints all contributed. The story of Wairarapa Community Polytechnic illustrates the point.

The Example of a Small Polytechnic

Between 1988 and 1992, Wairarapa Community Polytechnic (WCP) wanted to wear all four guises outlined above. Since 1993 only equity and self-improvement guises have been covered.

Non-formal/Empowering

The polytechnic's Interim Corporate Plan in 1990 set objectives to:

> ... achieve community development as a recognised and valued step in the learning staircase.
>
> (p. 11)

and

> ... actively involve WCP in political processes which advance community development goals.
>
> (p. 12)

It tried to attain these objectives by entering into strategic partnerships with community groups and networks. In exchange for auditable agreements, it helped fund such groups to run their own development programmes. Some examples: a short-course programme planned by women in a small coastal town was funded, as was a part-time development position in an autonomous community network. Two outposts largely run by local people were founded. A political pressure group to protest cuts to benefits was inspired and led by polytechnic staff. When a planned protest turned violent, the combined wrath of the establishment descended on the polytechnic. The National Party Member of Parliament and business leaders pressured Council and management, which lost heart for risky development activities. By the end of 1992, all community development was seen as risky and wound down. For financial reasons, the learning outposts closed also. By the end of 1992, no non-formal/empowering community education survived.

Formal/Empowering

The 1990 plan envisaged that the polytechnic would:

> ... mount 'catch up' adult basic education programmes targeted to educationally disadvantaged groups in the community ...
>
> (p. 9)

> ... establish a Maori Advisory Committee from Maori staff and council members and the Maori community to supervise the operation of Maori programmes, bicultural practices and the Te Waiora Marae.
>
> (p. 18)

An 'Open Learning Centre' was established. It ran a wide range of literacy programmes. All were student centred, giving learners some degree of control over their own learning. But the polytechnic retained control over administrative processes and, in the case of full-time programmes, formally documented the curriculum. While not perhaps strictly supervising Maori education, the Maori community exercised considerable power over appointments, programme decisions, marae operations and polytechnic ceremonial occasions. Maori suggested programmes, developed and taught them while the polytechnic funded and documented them. Scepticism within the wider community about 'pandering to minority groups' aired periodically in the local press. Nevertheless, both open learning and Maori programmes have done well recently. This may be because they have become good EFTS earners for the polytechnic rather than that they are empowering to the participants.

Non-formal/Maintaining

The 1990 Corporate Plan also established a 'Short Course Enterprise Unit' (p. 12) to plan and conduct special interest events. The programmes run by the Unit were all self-funding. Consequently, with one exception, they aimed at mainstream New Zealanders not striving for empowerment leading to change. The Unit ran a summer school featuring visual and dramatic arts, recreational topics and log building. Programme planning was tentative, giving participants considerable leeway to change things. A 'Garden Galaxy' weekend had a market-day feel, with hundreds of people from all over New Zealand feeding their very safe interests in plants. The Unit also organised study tours, mainly for people interested in geology. Many who attended the Unit's annual 'Every Woman's Show', however, felt empowered by an event aiming exclusively at the learning needs of women. The polytechnic also ran a computer bus. This trundled the Wairarapa's back roads giving rural folk the opportunity to upgrade their computer skills. In 1996, none of these programmes survive. They rest in the grave dug by the economic downturn.

Formal/Maintaining

The 1990 Interim Corporate Plan instructed the polytechnic to 'run community courses' (p. 13). Competition with local high schools, however, was prohibited. Its offerings in the usual hobby-type classes were therefore sparse. There were no foreign language, flower arranging or motorcar maintenance classes in its inventory. Instead, it developed programmes in computing and business related areas. It also ventured into the health field. Seminars, workshops and short courses instructing people how to develop healthy eating habits, how to apply alternative health remedies and how to be emotionally healthy were frequent. So too were seminars on child development and child rearing. The occasional theology series ran too. The polytechnic also offered vocational certificate courses in community work training and recreation management. In 1996, the polytechnic's inventory has been reduced; business and computing courses seem sovereign.

The Future

The polytechnic role in adult and community education has always been spotty. Since 1989, even the spots have all but disappeared due to social and economic factors. Will community education vanish altogether from the polytechnic portfolio in the future?

Very likely. Certainly the non-formal and empowering faces of adult and community education will have little place in the polytechnic of the future. It will continue to strive for a respected place in 'higher education'. And in the fairly likely event that government subsidy levels will be reduced further, polytechnics will increase student fees and up their drive for overseas customers. They may also develop partnerships with the corporate sector and wealthy community groups to provide designer qualifications. Such developments will so infuse their culture with academic protocols that they will not be able to accommodate the openness required by non-formal and empowering community education.

This is an optimistic prognosis. The doubts expressed by James in 1981 about the ability of community colleges to allow open learning have been confirmed for polytechnics; they should be allowed to get on with what they are good at – the provision of vocational education. This creates an opportunity to discover new models for adult and community education.

Notes

1. Aoraki Polytechnic, Auckland Institute of Technology, Bay of Plenty Polytechnic, Central Institute of Technology, Christchurch Polytechnic, Hawke's Bay Polytechnic, Hutt Valley Polytechnic, Manawatu Polytechnic, Manukau Institute of Technology, Nelson Polytechnic, Northland Polytechnic, Otago Polytechnic, Southland Polytechnic, Tai Poutini Polytechnic, Tairawhiti Polytechnic, Taranaki Polytechnic, Telford Rural Polytechnic, The Open Polytechnic, The Waikato Polytechnic, Unitech Institute of Technology, Waiariki Polytechnic, Wairarapa Community Polytechnic, Wanganui Regional Community Polytechnic, Wellington Polytechnic, Whitireia Community Polytechnic.
2. For example, reports on post-school education included: Probine, M. and Fargher, R. (March 1987), The Management, Funding and Organisation of Continuing Education and Training; Interim Advisory Group on Non-formal Education (September 1987), He Tangata; Hawke, G. (July 1988), Report on Post-compulsory Education and Training in New Zealand; New Zealand Government (1989), *Learning for Life: Two, Education and Training Beyond the Age of Fifteen.*

References

Bateman, J.A. (1981), 'Technical Institutes to the End of the Century', *TUTOR,* no. 23, pp. 10–17.

Bateman, J.A. and Munro, F. (1985), 'Happy 25th Birthday CIT!', *TUTOR,* no. 31, pp. 50–55.

Botkin, J., Elmandyra, M. and Malitza, M. (1979). *No Limits to Learning: Bridging the Human Gap,* Oxford: Pergamon.

Department of Statistics (1990), *New Zealand Social Trends: Education,* Wellington: Department of Statistics.

Giroux, H. (1988), 'The Hope of Radical Education: A Conversation with Henry Giroux', *Journal of Education,* vol. 170, no. 2, pp. 91–101.

Grocombe, G., Enright, M. and Porter, M. (1991), *Upgrading New Zealand's Competitive Advantage,* Auckland: Oxford University Press.

Harrison, N. (1981), 'Towards Equality for Community Education', *TUTOR,* no. 23, pp. 18–21.

Interim Advisory Group on Non-formal Education (1987), *He Tangata,* Wellington: mimeo.

Jenson, B., Ryan, A. and Spoonley, P. (1988), *Revival of the Right, New Zealand Politics in the 1980s,* Auckland: Heinemann Reid.

Lifelong Learning Task Force (1985), *Action for Learning and Equity: Opportunity for Change,* Wellington: NCAE.

New Zealand Government (1989), *Learning for Life Two: Education and Training Beyond the Age of Fifteen,* Wellington: Government Printer.

Peters, M. and Marshall, J.D. (1991), 'Education and Empowerment: Postmodernism and the Critique of Humanism', *Education and Society,* vol. 9, no. 2, pp. 123–134.

Wairarapa Community Polytechnic (1990), 'Interim Corporate Plan', Masterton: unpublished mimeo.

14

Community Development

Wendy Craig and Robyn Munford

Introduction

Community development sits on the boundary between adult education and social work. Located at times outside the conventional disciplines, community development struggles for formal recognition and relies heavily on the unpaid labour of predominantly women for its survival. Yet, paradoxically, this lack of connection with orthodoxy has been its source of vitality and innovation.

In this chapter, principles, models and case study material are presented with a view to acknowledging the diversity of opportunities for personal and community empowerment. The chapter draws on the research carried out for Wendy Craig's doctoral thesis on community work in Aotearoa/New Zealand which included in-depth interviews with 16 women community workers. It also utilises course material developed by us for social and community work students enrolled at Massey University. More importantly, it reflects our lengthy, ongoing learning experiences gained through working with women and oppressed groups in the community.

Adult Education and Community Development: A Necessary Relationship

Community development shares a close relationship with adult education in that they are both committed to the processes of empowerment of people and communities (Lovett, 1982; Rogers, 1992). Community adult educators frequently support the activities of people in the community, in their efforts to address issues affecting their daily lives. For many people already involved in community development, participation in adult education is viewed as an essential process in their struggles for change.

It is impossible to ignore the ways in which education underpins all community development activities. As Nyerere (1978: 27) claims, education is of fundamental importance in development:

> So development is for [people], by [people] and of [people]. The same is true of education. Its purpose is the liberation of [people] from the restraints and limitations of ignorance and dependency. Education has to increase [people's] physical and mental freedom – to increase their control over themselves, their own lives and the environment in which they live.

Freire (1972) also views education as a key to bringing about change and as a process whereby people not only acquire social skills but gain a wider consciousness of their role in an oppressed society and their ability to change it. Freire calls this process 'conscientisation'. The concept of conscientisation is widely used in community development work.

What is Community Development?

In Aotearoa/New Zealand the term community development is regularly interchanged with that of community work. Shirley (1979) points out that the term is somewhat ambiguous and that there are a number of perspectives from which it may be understood. He argues, however, that a recurrent theme in all perspectives is the notion of social change.

Traditionally, the focus of community development was on self-help and resident/client participation. The virtue of self-help in local problem-solving was (and still is) central to community development. This self-help concept is embodied in the United Nations definition (1955):

> Community development is a process designed to create conditions of economic and social progress for the whole community with its active participation.

Critical analyses of community development emphasise the conservatism and social control mechanisms contained within the practice of community development work (Craig, 1987, 1991). While we are aware of the possible shortcomings of community development, it is impossible to ignore the reality that this work has the potential for radical social and political transformation. We argue that community development in Aotearoa/New Zealand includes political education, empowerment, participation and resource (re)allocation. Community development workers frequently engage in social action and draw upon strategies and tactics used by community organisers, trade unionists, adult educators and other activists from diverse backgrounds.

Principles Underpinning Community Development

Craig (1991: 8) identifies a number of key principles underpinning community development work. While she is specifically referring to feminist community development work, these principles are derived from her experiences with a wide range of people in the community. The first principle is *self-determination*, which is closely related to the notion of *empowerment*. Self-determination embodies a belief that communities and people within them have an understanding of their needs and what has to be changed – the changes emerging from their own cultural history and aspirations. Community development workers actively try to empower people to take control of their own lives and determine their futures.

The second principle is that of *power*. Community development work focuses on understanding power relations in society and the ways in which power can be used to oppress people. Community development workers work alongside people to create ways to minimise power inequalities inherent in societal structures.

The third principle is that of *collectivity*. Although community development workers at times work with individuals, their aim is to work collectively with groups of people to bring about change. In working alongside groups, community development workers support people to identify resources and strategies for bringing about change.

Models of Community Development

A number of writers have identified a range of models for understanding community development work (Brookfield, 1983; Craig, 1987; Elsey, 1986; Lovett, 1982; Rogers, 1992; Wilkes, 1982). A common element present in the models is the way in which it is possible to categorise the ideological foundations underpinning community development work. These include conservative, liberal and critical perspectives. For the purposes of this chapter we will focus on models of practice arising out of the critical perspective.

Any critical model begins with the premise that society governs people's lives in such a way that benefits a few and oppresses the majority. Inequalities are the result of unequal relations of power where certain economic, cultural, social and political groups dominate. A critical model recognises that analysis and collective action is required to bring about change.

In order to cover the essential themes of culture, gender and class we briefly present three approaches to community development from the critical tradition. The first of these is based upon Maori development, the second on feminist ways of working and the third on working-class struggles for change.

Maori Community Development

Maori models of community development start with the recognition that the oppression of the Maori people is based on cultural invasion and political domination. This is linked to the alienation of their land and hence alienation from a major source of cultural identity (Walker, 1982: 72–73). This analysis provides the basis for community development work which seeks to transform the structures that maintain the oppression of the Maori people.

For many Maori community development workers, the necessity of self-determination and the reclaiming of one's identity is the key to social change. This is captured by Harata, a Maori community worker, in her comments about the goals of community development:

> Certainly for our own Maori people we have to take control of our own destiny. I don't believe that the partnership will work unless we're able to control our own. However, we've got to be careful that we take our people with us.
> (Craig, 1991: 262)

Indigenous writers identify a number of mechanisms through which change can be achieved by those engaged in Maori community development work. These include the provision for Maori language and culture within educational and political structures; the achievement of equal status for Maori culture and the opportunity for separatist development programmes. As Walker (1982: 87) states:

> ... for community development to succeed with the Maori people, it must draw its inspiration and power from the Maori community itself. It is not a gift to be conferred from outside.

Although the use of the term community development has not been explicitly used to describe Maori struggles for change, the Maori response to

Pakeha invasion and colonisation can be described as a process of 'transforming action' (Walker, 1982: 87), from oppression towards liberation and self-determination. This in itself typifies a critical approach to understanding of the goals of community development. The history of Maori responses includes 'warfare, guerilla [sic] activity, passive resistance and political participation' (Walker, 1982: 87). These events are richly portrayed in Walker's (1990) text which captures the past 150 years of Maori struggles for social justice, equality and self-determination. In her research, Craig (1991) argues that the process of transformation is evident in much of the grassroots Maori community development work throughout Aotearoa/New Zealand.

At the local level, Derrick (1993) provides us with a number of case studies based on his experiences with both Maori and Pakeha people involved in community development. Undoubtedly, Te Kohanga Reo movement is one of the best known examples of Maori involvement in community development.

Feminist Ways of Working

Feminists involved in community development begin with the premise that women are oppressed or discriminated against in society because of gender inequalities and that Maori, Pacific Island and working-class women experience the full impact of these inequalities (Horsfield, 1988). Community issues are of central importance to women, who often bear the brunt of economic and social hardship. As Craig (1987: 14) states:

> Day in, day out, women face the realities of what it is like to be poor. They experience the effects of unemployment if they and their husbands and children cannot find work. It is women who often pay the bills. Women get blamed for their children's poor health, poor diets and poor clothing or if their children stay away from school. It is women who have to suffer from male aggression when men lash out in protest.

A critical feature, then, of feminist community development work is to affirm and empower women by acknowledging their personal experiences and validating the diversity of these experiences. Any feminist model of community development work should also accommodate women's perceptions of what the world could be like if major social change took place. Craig (1991) emphasises that processes leading to social change must incorporate women's caring and nurturing ways of working. These in turn are linked to a specific goal of a more caring and just society.

As can be expected, women community development workers constantly balance the tension between their long-term objectives and that of providing immediate 'worthy' relief (Craig, 1991; Dominelli and McLeod, 1989). They approach caring at a wider level and even if they work with individuals this work is linked to the empowerment process. Rose, a feminist community development worker, highlights this:

> Community work is about social change, but it's connected to women as carers, women caring in the community and it's about actually moving from looking at things on an individual level, like me caring for my son and moving on to actually looking at – a recent example is that child care subsidies are tightening up and I just feel so passionate about that. So I'll be rallying people and encouraging people and getting them to actually sort of try and fight this, but I'll be building them up so that they've got the confidence and we will be working together.
> (Craig, 1991: 264)

For many women, involvement in community development work provides them with their first taste of further (adult) learning in that through their work they are able to recognise and validate their own experiences. Their activities provide the context to focus on issues such as childcare, education, housing, poverty and family violence and then the strength to make meaning out of the pain and anger that they and other women around them experience. This informal education process is often referred to by feminists as the 'personal is political' and is seen as the basis of consciousness-raising. Even when women choose to undertake more formal learning, at first this learning tends to be closely linked to the needs and issues arising out of their work (Craig, 1991).

We do not have to look very far to find examples of feminist ways of working. Women's refuges, rape crisis centres and women's health centres provide excellent examples. However, a large number of neighbourhood community development projects throughout Aotearoa/New Zealand have been set up based on feminist ways of working. Craig (1987: 44–48) describes one that she was involved with, whereby a group of predominantly solo mothers obtained a state house to use as a neighbourhood and health centre.

Working-class Struggles

Central to the working-class struggle is the premise that class-based inequalities are entrenched in the cultural, social, political and economic structures in society. The capitalist economic system is based on unequal relations of power and control and this gives rise to an unequal distribution of income, wealth and employment opportunities, with poverty and unemployment a natural consequence. Welfare policies are implemented to soften the extremes of harshness imposed by the economic system (Craig, 1987), although more recently these policies have demanded individual responsibility. Social problems are thus seen to be created by the exploitative relationships of capitalism.

The basis for community development work from this perspective is to work towards structural changes in the economic and political systems which 'dictate where people live and the conditions under which they live' (Craig, 1987: 13). This involves linking personal troubles to public issues; exposing capitalist ideologies and the development of a class consciousness through collective political community action. The latter is seen as critical for exponents of this perspective; political education plays an essential role in working towards change.

Here, organisations such as the Workers Educational Association (WEA) have provided a context for the development of certain educational programmes. For example, in Palmerston North while the negotiations over the sale of local authority energy supplies were taking place, WEA organised a series of seminars which examined the implications of the sale of local authority and state assets. This initiative not only led to further local community development action, but also created opportunities for making connections with other groups throughout Aotearoa/New Zealand.

This approach to community development tends to become very much focused on issues such as unemployment and poverty, with political education and action being seen as a mechanism for empowering the oppressed to 'become more aware of their common plight' (Elsey, 1986: 69). Greater consideration is given to working towards structural change and not simply towards meeting individual needs. A key strategy is to build alliances and develop networks between different sections of the working classes in terms of their common interests.

Working-class community development initiatives initially tended to focus on welfare and workers' rights issues (e.g. unemployment). Housing, health, recreation, peace and environmental concerns have become more prominent over recent years.

Women and Unpaid Work

Without a doubt, community development work is often undervalued, in part because it is seen as 'women's work' and this situation reflects in its substantially unpaid or underpaid status (Craig, 1991: 260). Yet its survival is totally dependent on the unpaid labour of women predominantly.

The state relies on women in the community to undertake numerous unpaid tasks, which, in the absence of such unpaid work, the state would have to fund. When the state does provide funding for an area which was previously confined to the unpaid sector, for example the funding of women's refuges, the amount provided is never enough to meet the whole costs of salaries involved in running the organisation (Craig, 1991: 120).

There is general agreement among feminist theorists that the institutions and practices of the welfare state have been organised around the assumption that women provide most of the caring and servicing work in society. This work which is primarily unpaid, contributes to women's oppression because it further restricts their opportunities for participating in paid work and in other areas of social life (Craig, 1992). Statistics collected from the 1990 Time Use Pilot Survey showed that women provided an average of five hours unpaid work in a 24-hour day. This does not include the indirect care of children which many women provide simultaneously (Statistics New Zealand, 1993: 100). As Munford (1992) points out in her research on women caregivers, there is an expectation that women should take on not only the caregiving work in the household but also the unpaid work in voluntary organisations.

Craig's (1991: 341–355), research on community work employment patterns revealed that women community workers provided many years of unpaid labour before they obtained paid employment as a community worker. The research also showed that of the 136 respondents surveyed, 23.5 per cent were welfare beneficiaries and received no other form of payment for their community work. The survey was conducted at a community workers' hui held in Gisborne in 1989. It must be acknowledged that as it is difficult for unpaid community workers to attend such hui, the numbers of women providing voluntary community work while on a benefit is likely to be significantly higher. Politicians seldom give recognition to this.

In her extended interviews with 16 women community development workers, Craig's (1991) research illustrated the fact that most of the women were not reimbursed for many of the expenses that they incurred in their unpaid community work. As Hira, a Maori woman, stated, 'eventually this gets to you':

> I've been told time and time again 'you people do it for nothing' and I don't want to go out there and say 'I do this and I do that'. But I get really pissed off when I see a so-called community social worker earning $49,000 for frig all. I don't mind doing the work, but the point is she's acting like she's doing it all. All I want to do is work for my people and I'm getting to the stage where I can't afford to.
> (Craig, 1991: 248–249)

Community Development: An Empowerment Process

The vitality of community development processes can be found in their capacity to empower people to identify their own resources and strengths and for them in turn to empower communities to work towards change. Through networking, people are able to find others to work with and thus can extend the basis of their struggle. Networking is seen as a key to obtaining a working knowledge of available resources and for information sharing, both of which are central to community development work. It also plays a necessary role in the provision of informal training and learning (Craig, 1991: 167).

Also critical to the community development process is the need to reflect on one's actions and, in part, the sharing of one's experiences exemplifies this essential task. Not only does this allow for sharing one's vision of change, but also it provides an ongoing opportunity to keep a check on whether the actions incorporate community work principles and processes.

Involvement in community development often has a profound effect on people. Craig (1991) found that all of the 16 women community development workers she interviewed believed that their involvement had changed them considerably. Community work gave them knowledge and confidence, but it also made them aware of the differences between them and some of the people they were close to. At times, this could be painful and several of them wondered 'if ignorance was bliss?'. Pare, for instance, claimed that:

> I can never go back to being that what I would call ignorant, a non-eventful woman that didn't dare challenge anything.
> (Craig, 1991: 276)

Although like the other women, and indeed many people with whom we have worked with in the community, Pare, at times, has 'paid a high price' for her involvement in community development, she recognised that she 'couldn't go backwards'. She went on to say:

> I sometimes think that there's no going back and that's being realistic because again it's life – if a tree's growing up, it doesn't go back into the ground, only in the area of reproduction does it go to ground as seed and that comes back to my reproduction.
> (Craig, 1991: 276)

It is, however, impossible to ignore the responsibility we take on when we become involved in people's lives. We need to provide ongoing support throughout the empowerment process. This will contribute to our own learning experiences.

Finally, laughter and celebration plays an important part in community development work and indeed should be included in the action/reflection process (Craig, 1987; Derrick, 1993). To stand back and look at even the smallest of achievements, contributes to the learning process and the celebration affirms and sustains people in their struggles.

References

Brookfield, S. (1983), *Adult Learners, Adult Education and the Community*, United Kingdom: Open University Press.
Craig, W. (1987), *A Community Work Perspective*, Palmerston North: Massey University.
Craig, W. (1991), 'From Rocking the Cradle to Rocking the System: Women, Community Work and Social Change in Aotearoa', Unpublished PhD thesis, Massey University.
Craig, W. (1992), 'The Politics of Caring', in Briar, C., Munford, R. and Nash, M. (eds), *Superwoman Where Are You? Social Policy and Women's Experience*, Palmerston North: Dunmore Press.
Derrick, E. (1993), *Community Development and Social Change*, Auckland: Auckland District Council of Social Services.
Dominelli, L. and McLeod, E. (1989), *Feminist Social Work*, London: McMillan.
Elsey, B. (1986), *Social Theory Perspectives on Adult Education*, United Kingdom: Department of Adult Education, University of Nottingham.
Freire, P. (1972), *Pedagogy of the Oppressed*, London: Sheed and Ward.
Horsfield, A. (1988), *Women in the Economy*, Wellington: Ministry of Women's Affairs.
Lovett, T. (1982), *Adult Education, Community Development and the Working Class*, U.K.: Department of Adult Education, University of Nottingham.
Munford, R. (1992), 'Caregiving: The Invisible Work of Women', in Briar, C., Munford, R. and Nash, M. (eds), *Superwoman Where Are You? Social Policy and Women's Experience*, Palmerston North: Dunmore Press.
Nyerere, J.K. (1978), ' "Development is for Man, by Man and of Man": The Declaration of Dar es Salaam', in Hall, B.L. and Kidd, J.R. (eds), *Adult Learning: A Design for Action*, Oxford: Pergamon Press.
Rogers, A. (1992), *Adults Learning for Development*, London: Cassell Educational Ltd.
Shirley, I. (1979), *Planning for Community*, Palmerston North: Dunmore Press.
Statistics New Zealand (1993), *All About Women in New Zealand*, Wellington: Publishing and Media Services Division of Statistics New Zealand.

Walker, R. (1982), 'Development from Below: Institutional Transformation in a Plural Society', in Shirley, I. (ed.), *Development Tracks: the Theory and Practice of Community Development*, Palmerston North: Dunmore Press.

Walker, R. (1990), *Ka Whawhai Tonu Matou/Struggle Without End*, Auckland: Penguin Books.

Wilkes, C. (1982), 'Development as Practice: the Instrument of Reason', in Shirley, I. (ed.), *Development Tracks: the Theory and Practice of Community Development*, Palmerston North: Dunmore Press.

15

Continuing Professional Education

John Benseman

Introduction

The acceptance of an initial professional education as being sufficient to provide the skills and knowledge for a professional's working life has gone. There is abundant evidence that virtually every professional group now takes lifelong education seriously as an essential requisite for achieving and maintaining desired levels of professional competence throughout a professional's working life. Over the past 20 years this change in attitude has led to a huge increase in the provision of continuing professional education (CPE) and has spawned a considerable educational expertise and professional literature of its own.

The justification for CPE varies from profession to profession, but usually includes:

- knowledge obsolescence where the 'half-life' of a profession's knowledge (the time after completion of formal professional education when half the body of knowledge covered in the curriculum is superseded by new advances and developments) is constantly decreasing.
- there are new and alternative roles to fill. Pharmacists were once primarily involved in the preparation of drugs and medicines – they now also fulfil much more of an advisory/information role. Houle (1980: 38) quotes the

American Council on Dental Education – 'Twenty-five or 30 years ago, dental practice was limited to relieving pain and treating lesions of the teeth, the gums and other tissues of the mouth. Today it is concerned with the comprehensive management of oral, facial and speech defects and with the oral structures and tissues as they relate to the total health of the individual'.
- how professionals acquire and utilise new knowledge and skills does not always readily relate to how they were taught in their undergraduate, or even postgraduate education (see for example Schön, 1987).
- there are increased demands for accountability and higher standards of care.
- legislative deregulation of many professions has meant that there is increased pressure for members to excel in their practice and thereby distinguish themselves from competing groups. For example, of a survey of 22 professional groups in New Zealand (Benseman and Morrison, 1992: 2), 10 of the groups operated under their own Act of Parliament and most of these were currently under review, or expected to be reviewed in the near future.
- there are new social and political demands made on professional groups. Advances in conception technology have demanded new ethical codes for obstetricians; recent educational reforms have radically altered the professional roles of school principals.
- no matter how comprehensive and competent professionals' initial education, the ongoing development of their working lives demand new levels of sophistication and breadth in their knowledge and skills. 'The student or apprentice starting out must gain a broad understanding of the various aspects of the process of architecture in order to then be able to select a preferred career niche; the practising architect then seeks further knowledge relevant to specific requirements in a particular area of practice' (New Zealand Institute of Architects, 1989, *Vision 2007*).

Models of CPE

Cervero (1989: 518) argues that the relationship between professional groups and society can be distilled into three fundamentally different conceptions and that these have important implications for the design and implementation of CPE programmes.

The *functionalist* viewpoint is based on a belief that professions are '... service- or community-oriented occupations applying a systematic body of knowledge to problems that are highly relevant to the central values of society'. With a strong emphasis on *expertise*, it is assumed that practice problems are well formed and that these problems are solved essentially by the application of scientific theory and technique. Continuing professional education within this model is largely concerned with keeping members up-to-date and correcting existing deficiencies in their practices.

The *conflict* viewpoint asserts that '... professions are in conflict with other groups in society for power, status and money'. Because *power* is seen as central to this viewpoint, continuing professional education is not concerned with competency, but with reducing the '... power of professionals so as to create a more equal relationship between clients and professionals' (Cervero, 1989: 519) and requires continuing educators to work in an adversarial role.

The *critical* viewpoint assumes that there is no consensus regarding professional quality and that there are conflicting value orientations among professionals as to what social ends they are seeking. Cervero (1989: 519) argues that 'practitioners are always in a dialectical relationship with situations that are characterised by uniqueness, uncertainty, or value conflict. Thus problem setting rather than problem solving is the key to professional practice'. CPE in this context is aimed at helping professionals critically analyse the technical and ethical choices they make in their work.

While it is difficult to identify any professional group in New Zealand that operates from a conflict viewpoint to any great degree,[1] and few professional groups fall exclusively into either of the other two categories, they nonetheless constitute a useful grid for analysing the intent and educational means used in CPE programmes.

Historically, most CPE programmes in their early stages of development have started out with a strong functionalist orientation. Courses are organised along traditional educational lines with a heavy reliance on didactic educational methods, and are predominantly geared to updating course participants in new developments in professional knowledge, technology or techniques and attract small to moderate numbers of members who are typically already very active within the profession and its groups. With this type of CPE provision, there are often problems with involving what are seen as reasonable numbers of professional members in programmes, challenges are made as to the adequacy of the programmes in meeting the needs of everyday issues and there are also challenges and criticisms about the educational methods generally. In some instances, CPE administrators attempt to remedy these issues by measures such as introducing mandatory participation, carrying out more sophisticated needs analyses and experimenting with a greater diversity of educational methods.

Other professional groups have sought to resolve these sorts of issues by reconceptualising them within more of a critical viewpoint. Recognising that practitioners work in different milieux and consequently face varying professional situations and issues, CPE in this framework utilises educational methods which start from the issues and realities of everyday practice and consider the ranges of options open to the practitioner, rather than overlaying ready-made solutions. The challenge is to provide opportunities for members to critically examine their practices and if necessary, look to solutions from colleagues' collective experience, or new sources of knowledge and skill if necessary. Problems of low participation are minimised by ensuring that the CPE content emanates from real issues, rather than having to find situations and issues to match the solutions given in a functional framework. The need to centre on members' practice and challenge them critically also leads to using non-didactic educational methods – small groups, practice audits, peer reviews and independent learning provision for example, rather than the traditional lectures by experts (whether face-to-face, travelling roadshows or via distance education media), producing textbooks or conferences.

While few CPE administrators and practitioners operate consciously in terms of any of the above approaches and the judgement of which is the most effective or appropriate is ultimately a political choice (albeit with important educational implications), all CPE programmes face a range of similar educational issues in their efforts to provide quality provision. The point is, that how the issues are perceived and resolved will largely reflect one of the overall approaches or viewpoints described above. The next section of this chapter reviews some of these issues and discusses their implications for CPE providers.

Needs Assessments and Curriculum Design

Away from the set curricula of undergraduate teaching, CPE organisers face the open questions of 'what should be taught' and 'how do we find out what should be taught?'. Answering these questions usually involves reference to the assessment of learners' needs, but despite what Wiltshire (1973: 30) calls their 'comforting air of scientific hard-headedness', needs assessments are by no means straightforward and warrant careful consideration (see Benseman, 1980). While working from people's expressed needs has the advantage of increasing the likelihood of ensuring their participation in programmes (people are more likely to attend a programme reflecting their stated needs), it is clear that learners' expressed needs do not necessarily coincide with their areas of deficiency – their real needs. If practitioners are proficient in a particular area of skill, they are likely to want to continue their educational involvement in that area (and therefore express needs related to that area); conversely, they are less likely to identify needs in areas that do not correspond to their interests or areas of expertise.

Self-reported needs are usually seen as an adequate reason for developing curricula within a functionalist framework. Surveys of professional members provide checklists of topics that can be simply added together to indicate the degree of need in the profession – and also the likelihood of members attending the programmes. 'The development of offerings within the continuing professional development programme was investigated by way of a needs assessment survey. This consisted of a questionnaire designed to find out the views of the participants in the industry as to what ideal competencies should be for effective and successful real estate personnel' (Locke and Gilray, 1990: 179). The problems of relying on this approach have been highlighted in a recent study by Tracey (1995) which clearly illustrated the discrepancy between expressed needs and needs measured by objective means with a group of GPs. The author concluded, 'One can only deduce from the results ... that general practitioners are very poor at self-assessment of knowledge' (Tracey, 1995: 18).

For the CPE organiser operating from a critical viewpoint, however, the challenge is to help practitioners to critically review their practices using methods that are more likely to identify areas of lesser competence or deficiency. Examples of these methods can be found in the Wellington School of Architecture's Post Occupancy Evaluation (POE) where architects have their buildings evaluated by a group of building users (see Baird and Kernohan, 1990) and the Goodfellow Unit at the Auckland School of Medicine's triad groups in their Continuing Medical Education for General Practitioners programme (see Thomson, Barham and Benseman, 1990).

Participation

The issue of who participates in CPE programmes and more importantly who does not participate, is one that has arisen with most professional groups at some time. See, for example, Norcini and Shea (1993), Mathews' article about the low CPE participation rates of New Zealand accountants (Mathews 1983) and *Vision 2007* (p. 17) on New Zealand architects: 'A major problem for CPD programmes is getting architects to attend – NZIA members' participation in past CPD programmes has been estimated to attract only 10–15 per cent of members'.

Houle (1980: 154) argues that any professional membership can be classified into five main groups according to their willingness to adopt new ideas and that these classifications transfer readily also to their rates of CPE participation. The 'innovators' and 'pacesetters' adopt new ideas readily and are also very active in most CPE programmes; the bulk of the profession (Houle suggests approximately two-thirds) are to be found in the 'early' and 'late' majority and a small group of 'laggards'. Concern over low rates of CPE participation is usually directed at the professions' 'laggards', who are seen as not only slow to adopt new innovations, but more seriously, are often also seen as professionally inadequate or even open to criminal prosecution for their incompetence. Talking about the option of making CPE for surveyors mandatory, Martin (1992: 110) says, 'Those who don't wish to be bound by such discipline (of compulsory CPE) – let them carry on and hopefully they will fall by the wayside, or be sued, or go out of business'.

While most professions have difficulties in involving their 'laggards', it is with the middle majority that there is most variation in CPE participation. With professions that are only involving 10–15 per cent of their membership, it is clear that few of this middle group, let alone the laggards, are active in CPE. In other professions there are much higher proportions of the middle majority involved. The CME programme for GPs at the Goodfellow Unit, University of Auckland shows that over one-third of all GPs in New Zealand and two-thirds of GPs in Auckland participate in at least one of its (largely Auckland-based) CME programme activities in any one year – a clear indication of involving the middle majority group.

The solution (especially within a functionalist framework) to involving the 'laggards' (and the less active end of the middle majority) is almost inevitably seen as introducing mandatory CPE participation, where members of a profession are required to accumulate a predetermined minimum of CPE 'points' in order to maintain their ongoing professional licences, or membership of the professional body. In brief, arguments (beyond those for justifying CPE generally) for making CPE mandatory include:

- no profession can afford to have any members not involved in CPE for the perceived good of the profession overall, if not for the individual concerned (there is an inbuilt assumption here that CPE automatically leads to improved performance as a professional)
- to avoid government intervention to introduce compulsion and greater regulation generally (assuming that government will not interfere with a profession that is seen to be actively managing its members' performance, which is increasingly unlikely with successive governments in New Zealand showing little interest in intervention strategies across the board)[2]
- expecting voluntary participation is simply unrealistic.

Overseas, most professions have tried this solution at some time, with varying degrees of success. In America, while many states which introduced mandatory CPE in the 1980s have since withdrawn the legislation following unsatisfactory results (see for example Phillips, 1987), an increasing number of states have required mandatory CPE for its professions (see Queeney and English, 1994). The withdrawal of mandatory CPE has largely been because administrators have realised the old adage that 'you can lead a horse to water, but you can't make it drink' – in other words, compulsory CPE attendance is no guarantee that the participants will necessarily learn effectively, let alone transfer the learning into their practice. Cervero (1988: 73) quotes a number of evaluations which showed that there was no difference in CPE participation for at least 70–75 per cent of professional members before and after the implementation of a compulsory CPE requirement.

There is also evidence that mandatory CPE leads to 'Claytons' provision, where participants gain more of a sunburn from commercially run courses in Hawaii than any challenges to their professional behaviour. Mandatory CPE may have appeal as having an immediate impact on the issue of low participation, but long term it is no panacea for solving this issue, let alone other complex and wide-ranging professional issues.

It is interesting to note that adult educators involved in CPE almost without exception oppose mandatory participation – it is largely promoted by professional associations. Nonetheless, while mandatory CPE for professions has become less of an issue overseas (see Cervero, 1989: 522), CPE administrators in this part of the world have increasingly adopted, or are currently considering adopting, mandatory CPE. In New Zealand, these professions include valuers, real estate, optometry, accountancy and architecture. The engineering profession introduced a mandatory system, but has since reversed this requirement.

From a critical viewpoint, the issue of low rates of participation is seen as a problem of relating CPE curricula to practitioners' issues. Getting this issue resolved will in turn lessen the difficulties of low participation because it is assumed that all practitioners will want to participate in CPE if it relates directly and effectively with their everyday issues.

Finally, writing on mandatory CPE, Brennan (1990a: 130) believes that the short-term use of mandatory CPE may be effective in initially increasing the participation rates within a profession, but that it has little justification as a long-term measure.

Effectiveness of CPE

Given the large-scale developments and increasing budgets in CPE over recent years, it is inevitable that the question – 'how effective is it?' – will be raised (see for example McGaghie, 1993). The question will be raised even more frequently as professions make CPE mandatory, as public controversies raise challenges about standards of professional conduct (for example the public outcry over lawyers' ethical behaviour in relation to the use of trust accounts), and private educational providers challenge traditional providers such as the universities.

The question of effectiveness in CPE can be answered at a number of levels, with varying levels of satisfaction. Consider the following:

- attendance/non-attendance at educational programmes
- assessment of learner satisfaction (cynically known as 'happiness indicators')
- assessment of knowledge outcomes (have the participants internalised the knowledge covered?)
- assessment of attitudinal outcomes (have their attitudes changed as a result of the programme?)
- assessment of behaviour outcomes (are they capable of carrying out new behaviours incorporating the new knowledge?)
- evaluation of behaviour performance (are the new behaviours transferred to the everyday routines of their practice and not just at the course?)
- impact evaluation of client outcomes (do the educational programmes have a positive impact on people's lives?).

Most CPE administrators would opt for the last of these levels as the ideal type of evaluation, as most would see impact on client outcomes as central to the aims of CPE and yet most evaluation carried out in CPE is centred on the first few levels. This is mainly because the evaluation methods needed to carry out the assessment of participation, knowledge, attitudes and even behaviour outcomes are much more straightforward and less expensive than evaluations of behaviour performance, let alone client outcomes. Assessing whether course participants can remember items of information about asthma, for example, is a much easier task than evaluating whether or not the information gained reduces patient asthma morbidity/mortality. There is also research evidence for example, to indicate that assessments of learner satisfaction are inaccurate indicators of whether learning has occurred, or transferred into practice (see Houle, 1980: 245) – in fact, rates of learning may well be higher in courses disliked by participants than in those they like.

On balance, however, and the limitations and difficulties of each type of evaluation notwithstanding, it can be argued that CPE evaluation ideally needs to cover all of these levels periodically, albeit not often in some cases. Each provides useful information for the CPE planner and should be used for specific purposes. For example, even though satisfaction indicators may be questionable in relation to cognitive gains, they are an important tool for feedback on programmes and thereby ensuring that programmes maintain reasonable levels of CPE participation in a profession. On the other hand, impact evaluations on professional practice while important, are unlikely to be undertaken on a regular basis because of the methodological difficulties and their cost.

Administration of CPE

The main institutional providers of CPE in New Zealand at present are professional associations, the universities (and increasingly, some polytechnics), employers and commercial groups, including commercial suppliers for the professions such as pharmaceutical companies. The extent of involvement of each of these providers varies considerably from profession to profession, but most CPE programmes would include at least some, if not all, of the above groups. Why CPE programmes are located where they are at present can be attributed to a mixture of historical, political and educational factors.

Professional associations are invariably involved in CPE, usually in conjunction with university professional schools and others. The associations have the advantages of being seen as representing the best interests of the profession, being able to readily access members' expertise (often at no, or little cost) and being able to integrate CPE into the activities of the profession. On the other hand, professional providers can find it difficult to isolate educational activities from political issues at critical times – which usually acts to the detriment of CPE, rather than professional politics – and there can be confusion over whether educational leadership should come from the voluntary educational committees or the CPE professional staff members.

Until a decade ago, universities were concerned almost solely with undergraduate and postgraduate education, but they are now all involved in some way in CPE. Some CPE programmes, such as law and veterinary science, are physically located in universities and even where CPE programmes are organised predominantly by the professional association, there are still very close links with the professions' university departments. In some cases, CPE programmes are being incorporated into professional postgraduate qualifications or the New Zealand Qualifications Authority (NZQA) Framework, but most provision is still non-credit.

University provision of CPE enjoys the advantages of being closely linked to the prime source of professional research and innovation, staff expertise (including other professions and in most cases, educational expertise) and resources such as libraries and are seen as credible and reasonably neutral institutions. Negative aspects of university provision include 'ivory tower' connotations of irrelevance to the realities of everyday issues, their 'poor cousin' status relative to under- and postgraduate education and in some cases, limited educational expertise.

While some professions, such as nursing, draw heavily on their employers as their provider of CPE, this form of provision is currently decreasing as government agencies increasingly withdraw from direct provision of services.

CPE provision from commercial groups is often overlooked or underrated by many analysts of the field and yet considerable 'CPE' budgets are spent by commercial interests on everything from unsolicited mail (see Benseman, 1985) to full-time residential courses and conferences. The main difficulty with this source of CPE provision is the widespread suspicion that its content is inevitably tainted by commercial interests. Why else would a pharmaceutical company pay for GPs and their families to stay a weekend at Queenstown, but for the purposes of selling more products in the long run?[3] Nonetheless, many professionals utilise commercial CPE programmes extensively and other providers such as universities and professional associations are increasingly offering joint programmes with commercial groups. In the case of the latter, there is often a fine balance for the university/professional association between utilising the commercial group's resources on the one hand and not being seen to have 'sold out' to commercial interests on the other, thereby losing their independent credibility.

CPE as a Profession

Finally, there is the issue of who should staff CPE programmes. Traditionally, CPE programmes have been planned and organised by volunteer committees or university staff who are primarily involved in under- and postgraduate education. As programmes have expanded and developed in sophistication, they have often taken on part or even full-time CPE staff. Initially these staff have been involved predominantly in the administrative aspects of CPE provision, but they have increasingly also become involved in developing the educational aspects of CPE.

With a few exceptions, these CPE staff have come from the profession concerned and generally with a limited background in education have had to 'learn on the hoof' or, in a few cases, have gained adult education qualifications. The exception to this pattern has been the employment of an adult education specialist working closely with either an advisory committee or another staff member from the profession. This type of arrangement has the advantage of ensuring that there are strong links to the profession itself with the availability of educational expertise relevant to planning and implementing CPE programmes. Overseas CPE literature (see Brennan, 1990b: 142) indicates that there is a strong case to be made for CPE provision to have input from adult educators, especially if it is to develop beyond conventional patterns.

CPE is often cited as the fastest-growing part of adult education over recent years. While there has certainly been considerable growth of CPE in most New Zealand professions, it is certain that this pattern will continue at an increasing pace for some time yet if the experiences overseas are any indication.

Notes

1. There are certainly groups working from a conflict viewpoint within professions, however, such as feminist and anti-racism groups.
2. See also Brennan (1992a), Morrison (1990) and Martin (1992) for fuller discussions on this issue.
3. A recent survey of 120 GPs (reported in *New Zealand Herald*, 15.7.94, p. 20) showed that only 17 per cent believed that drug company activities such as courses did not influence prescribing patterns.

References

Benseman, J. (1980), *The Assessment and Meeting of Needs in Continuing Education*, Stockholm: Stockholm Institute of Educational Research.

Benseman, J. (Autumn 1985), 'The Great Paper Waste: the Use of Unsolicited Medical Literature by General Practitioners', *New Zealand Family Physician*, vol. 12, no. 3, pp. 96–98.

Benseman, J. and Morrison, A.A. (1992), 'National Survey of New Zealand Continuing Professional Education', (unpublished paper).

Brennan, B. (ed.) (1990a), *Continuing Professional Education – Promise and Performance,* Hawthorn, Victoria: Australian Council for Educational Research.

Brennan, B. (1990b), 'Mandatory or Voluntary Continuing Professional Education: is there Really an Option for Professional Associations?', in McMorland, J. (ed.), *The Universities and the Professions: Partners in Enhancing Professional Practice – Proceedings of the Continuing Professional Education Conference*, University of Auckland, 11–14 October.

Curry, L. and Wergin, J. (eds) (1993), *Educating Professionals*, San Francisco: Jossey-Bass.

Cervero, R.M. (1988), *Effective Continuing Education for Professionals,* San Francisco: Jossey-Bass.

Cervero, R. (1989), 'Continuing Education in the Professions', in Merriam, S.B. and Cunningham, P.M. (eds), *Handbook of Adult and Continuing Education*, San Francisco: Jossey-Bass.

Dymock, D.R. (ed.) (1987), *Continuing Professional Education – Policy and*

Provision, Papers presented at a national conference at the University of New England, Armidale, 7–9 October.

Houle, C.O. (1980), *Continuing Learning in the Professions,* San Francisco: Jossey-Bass.

Locke, S. and Gilray, I. (1990), 'Continuing Professional Development in the Real Estate Industry', in McMorland, J. (ed.), *The Universities and the Professions: Partners in Enhancing Professional Practice – Proceedings of the Continuing Professional Education Conference,* University of Auckland, 11–14 October.

Martin, K. (1992), 'Continuing Education for the Professional: the Voluntary or Compulsory Options', in *'Distance Education: Quality and Equality',* 1992 DEANZ Conference, Dunedin, 22–24 May.

McGaghie, W.C. (1993), 'Evaluating Competence for Professional Practice', in Curry, L. and Wergin, J. (eds), *Educating Professionals: Responding to New Expectations for Competence and Accountability,* San Francisco: Jossey-Bass.

McMorland, J. (ed.) (1990), *The Universities and the Professions: Partners in Enhancing Professional Practice – Proceedings of the Continuing Professional Education Conference,* University of Auckland, 11–14 October.

Mathews, M. (1983), 'Continuing Education and the Modern Accountant', *New Zealand Journal of Adult Learning,* vol. 15, no. 2, October, pp. 16–25.

Morrison, A.A. (1990), 'Imprisoned in the Continuing Professional Education Classroom', in McMorland, J. (ed.), *The Universities and the Professions: Partners in Enhancing Professional Practice – Proceedings of the Continuing Professional Education Conference,* University of Auckland, 11–14 October.

New Zealand Herald (1994), 'Drug Companies War with Subsidiser', 15.7.94, Section 1, p. 20.

New Zealand Institute of Architects (1989), *Vision 2007,* Associated Group Media Ltd.

Norcini, J. and Shea, J. (1993), 'Increasing Pressures for Recertification and Relicensure', in Curry, L. and Wergin, J. (eds), *Educating Professionals: Responding to New Expectations for Competence and Accountability,* San Francisco: Jossey-Bass.

Ohliger, J., Nelson, J. and Farkas, M. (1987), 'Mandatory Continuing Education – Three Views', in Dymock, D.R. (ed.), *Continuing Professional Education – Policy and Provision,* Papers presented at a national conference at the University of New England, Armidale, 7–9 October.

Phillips L.E. (1987), 'Is Mandatory Continuing Education Working?', *MOBIUS,* vol. 7, pp. 57–64.

Queeney, D.S. and English, J.K. (1994), 'Mandatory Continuing Education: a Status Report', Columbus: ERIC Clearinghouse on Adult, Career and Vocational Education, Center on Education and Training for Employment, Ohio State University.

Schön, D. (1988), *Educating the Reflective Practitioner: Toward a New Design for Teaching and Learning in the Professions*, San Francisco: Jossey-Bass.

Thomson, A., Barham, P. and Benseman, J. (1990), 'The Triadic Approach to Professional Education', in McMorland, J. (ed.), *The Universities and the Professions: Partners in Enhancing Professional Practice – Proceedings of the Continuing Professional Education Conference*, University of Auckland, 11–14 October.

Tracey, J. (1995), 'Evaluation of the Validity of General Practitioners' Self-assessment of Knowledge', Unpublished paper, Goodfellow Unit, School of Medicine, University of Auckland.

Wiltshire, H. (1973), 'The Concepts of Learning and Need in Adult Education', *Studies in Adult Education*, vol. 5, no. 1, April, pp. 26–30.

16

Schooling Big Children?

School Based Community Education

Julie Barbour

Introduction

Schools have been described as 'little islands set apart from the mainland of life' (Herbert, 1986: 1), and institutions which teach students to 'adapt to rather than question the basic precepts of society' (Giroux, 1990: 4). However, to paint such a constraining picture of schools and especially their community[1] education activities does not fully recognise the efforts and actions of individuals and groups who may have significant social impact on their communities. As a practising adult educator based at Rutherford High School, I can see that individuals and groups have tried to resist the controlling interests of the state and its accompanying bureaucracy; some have developed their own educational alternatives.

In this account of school based community education in Aotearoa/New Zealand, I will first look at how history has influenced the variety and nature of activities encompassed in the field, then analyse two competing theoretical contexts in which they have developed. I argue specifically that the involvement of thousands of adults in these activities has contributed to improving social and political affairs in the wider society.

Community education in schools faces the contemporary issue of state control through the imposition of accreditation of learning. In the final section of this chapter, I question what this means for the school sector, especially how government's push towards credentialism might influence the potential that schools have to provide liberating pathways for adults.

The Development of School Based Community Education

Like working-class children, adults were originally excluded from schools. However, the first Labour government's Thomas Report in 1939 brought changes. Education Acts intended to reform schooling for children have had unintended positive consequences for adults too. The government aim outlined in the Thomas Report was to provide free education for all children. The resulting introduction of comprehensive schooling, together with the increased post-war birthrate, meant that extra schools were needed to cater for significantly increased numbers of children. This created a situation where many more adults became influenced by schools either as parents or simply because they lived close to one. Consequently, although the adult community did not often venture into the school gates, it was nevertheless being brought closer to schools. Hence, adult participation in schools was initially linked only to parents' concerns for their children rather than wanting their own learning needs met.

Curriculum changes triggered greater adult involvement. In this progressive era of the first Labour government, additional subjects were introduced into the liberal curriculum. Subjects such as home economics, art and physical education required specialist rooms, playing fields, gyms and equipment. In the rush to build extra school facilities, the local community was often roped in to subsidise and help build them, either by local body or direct community participation. As eminent educator Denny Garrett had advocated, new relationships were developing between schools and their local communities. Schools such as Rutherford High School encouraged the community to build their swimming pool. Te Atatu parents had dances, trading tables, bingo evenings and working bees towards the project. The local swimming club put their clubroom beside it as their base. The club used it for their meets while the school used it for their sports days. It is with justification that adults, whose taxes and labour were used to these ends, felt that they had a right of access to the facilities.

At the same time, this 'comprehensive' schooling created a dilemma. Parents who had not been schooled beyond basic levels of schooling became critical of their own lack of educational opportunity. As parents they found themselves in a frustrating position. While being urged to support and encourage their children's education, they were still unable to find avenues of learning of a kind that would help them to develop their own learning. 'New' mathematics was one example. It was common to hear parents complaining that they could not understand its language and methods. As groups of parents joined together, they found they were not alone. There were others experiencing the same frustrations. Many realised that education through a nightclass or attending school during the day with the children could be a way of not only overcoming these difficulties, but also of gaining their educational entitlement and influencing provision.

Influential Individuals

Enthusiastic enlightened individuals have been influential in leading resistance to traditional schooling practices that have excluded adults in the community. Among them was Denny Garrett who was the Department of Education first officer for Continuing Education and later the Assistant Secretary Tertiary. During the 1970s he promoted different approaches to learning – learning that would encompass both formal and informal methods. He supported local initiatives and helped educators to progress through the limiting regulations. Eric Clarke (Principal of Rutherford High School until 1984) and other school principals practised open defiance by enrolling adults from the community into day-school classes and for 20 years Charlie Herbert (1986; 1988), who also worked in the Department of Education, delivered his messages to the 'troops' (the developers of programmes for adults), of 'a new thrust forward'.

He advocated different approaches from following traditional structures in schools. For Charlie Herbert (1988: 1), education could occur 'in any suitable location, ... in groups of varying size, or on our own using resources close to home or at a distance'. He urged schools to 'meet the learning needs of people of all ages and to help learners towards independent learning, best achieved through involving the learners themselves in identifying their own specific needs'.

As we look back, his newsletters appear to be supportive of progressivism. He was promoting goals which extended beyond the school and its supposed primary task to educate children. This challenged the conventional structures and predominant existing relationships within teaching and learning. Schools such as Rutherford High in Auckland and Hagley High (now Hagley Community College) in Christchurch developed reputations as being vocal and visible sites of innovation and resistance, but this scenario has not been common to all parts of New Zealand.

The Effects of Progressivism

School based community education has developed in a range of contexts and forms subsequent to ideological support from the state. The rapid development of school based community education followed the 1974 Educational Development Conference which, in turn, was part of an international trend towards progressivism (Findsen and Lomas, 1993). The notion of a 'Community Learning Centre' (CLC) became popularised, some modelled off British prototypes (Lander, 1980). Government, perhaps in a bid to conserve resources, perceived schools, with their existing facilities and usually close links with communities, as appropriate sites for learning designed for adults as opposed to children.

In some schools, community education activities have been encouraged but their implementation has relied on the goodwill of the school administrators to provide adequate staffing and other resources for a programme. (Goodwill is a fickle quality often depending on personal philosophies and the ability of individuals to persuade others.) On the other hand, some schools have been fully stretched by finite resources in their education programmes for children so their community education activities have been given a low priority.

Urban centres have had the benefits of a larger adult population helping to create pressure on schools to respond and make appropriate resources and learning opportunities available. It is hardly coincidental that the first Community Learning Centres based in schools were located in metropolitan areas. Where communities are isolated or communication between the school and groups in the community is limited, adult education activities may have been further marginalised and more conservative in nature. Nevertheless, despite regional differences or times of financial depression, participation has continued to be extensive. It is not uncommon for adult enrolments in schools to exceed those of children by 3:1. For instance, Rutherford High School in 1993 had an adult roll of 3,146 students in school based community education courses while the day school roll was 1,050. Nationally, participation in one mid-winter week in 1993 (typically a non-peak time) showed that 49,681 adults were attending school based programmes (Ministry of Education, 1994). Thousands of other adults were also involved in the schools' supported informal programmes.

Contemporary Practice

School based community education currently falls into two levels of participation. First, there are the more visible activities: programmes which are planned, advertised and formally managed. Such programmes contain courses within categories such as 'second-chance education', 'personal development', 'home skills'. They take the form of seminars, short courses held both during the day and evening, weekend workshops and year-long, part-time certificate study. Adults might also attend training for volunteers, learning exchanges, support groups and sporting sessions. Crèches are often an extra facility. Activities are not always held on school campuses and many are organised by local community groups which are funded by government through schools.[2]

However, adult involvement and learning constitutes much more than organised classes. It is also the result of adults' informal relationships with the school as parents, members of sporting associations or as local residents. Often called 'community development' activities, schools encourage the use of the facilities by groups of all kinds. Some schools' community education activities extend to the administration of preschool facilities or the co-ordination of language or summer schools. With community education based in primary schools, there may be holiday and extramural programmes (for example, in music). Adults in the community come to rallies, parent evenings, speakers, films, discussion groups, public debates, open days, exhibitions and festivals. The variety of projects is endless but regardless of form, these endeavours are educative undertakings which have the potential to increase adult enquiry and insight.

Outside the institutions, school based community education contributes resources and administration to support situations where adults take responsibility for their own learning. This takes place in a variety of settings. For example, a new mothers group may meet in one of their homes to share experiences and learn from an invited local resource person; or keen badminton players discuss problems on the sideline in the school gymnasium during their weekly session. The learning at these encounters may not be intended by the group leader, nor able to be seen or measured until a considerable time later, yet it may be influential enough to play a 'substantial role in awakening the critical spirit' (Brookfield, 1993: 229). Such are the variety of practices. This is matched by a range of social theory perspectives which provide frameworks for why it is that way.

Theoretical Perspectives

Theories describing the philosophical context in which practice occurs depict adult education as ranging from conservative to radical in nature (Thomas and Harries-Jenkins, 1975). Towards the conservative end of the spectrum, are positivist and liberal views which stress efficiency towards achieving predetermined ends of an economic or social nature. In contrast, radical views such as the postmodern, conflictual outlook emphasise widely varying and changing perspectives, according to power relations and people's subjective positions. As I will elaborate later, this latter perspective allows us more optimism. But first to more traditional views.

Positivist and Liberal Views of the Field

Ewert (1991: 348) describes 'positivism' as the idea that problems may be dealt with by applying the 'right' actions. Through thoughtful, rational decision-making, schools can address the social problems in which they are inevitably engaged. This benign view is not shared by critics such as Freire (1987) and Kemmis (1986) who claim that institutions have selected and decided what knowledge and skills are to be transmitted to adults, and by what means. These adversaries to positivism also argue that by their restricted accessibility, institutions like schools have maintained control over resources and have succeeded in contributing to the reproduction of gendered, class and racial inequalities. In this logic, 'night-classes' (whether it be cooking classes or computer awareness) have only fostered the interests of the status quo. However, these approaches, in my view, are too deterministic: such a model of what schools do *for* adult students assumes that students, co-ordinators and tutors are merely 'puppets' – 'malign perpetrators of a repressive form of social engineering' (Bates, 1990: 52).

The liberal-humanist view promotes adult education as an activity which concentrates on bringing about worthwhile individual change for the betterment of society. For instance, according to Knowles (1980), the curriculum and learning in this field of education provide evidence of what people have needed in order to feel functionally useful and socially satisfied in society. A glance at course titles offered by school based providers and at government instructions to schools shows that state policy could be interpreted this way. It has been directed at individual improvement, social equity and vocationalism. For instance, government-funded community education programmes must be of 'social benefit to society and give opportunities for personal development'. Courses must fall into categories such as 'adult basic education, programmes for people on benefits ... or with low incomes to help towards self-reliance, or programmes to assist specific groups of the population' (Ministry of Education, 1992: 3). In this context, the provision of adult education has been maintained and tolerated within the State education budget as a cheap way of contributing to 'a better society'.

Seeing programmes as a way of allocating help for society's difficulties has popular support in the field too. It is a safe and personally gratifying stance, especially for co-ordinators whose jobs and status have been given importance under the guise of 'doing good'. Brookfield (1993: 229) perceptively suggests that as educators we prefer not to think of our actions as being ones which might be contributing to an oppressive status quo.

Adult students and co-ordinators have struggled to achieve their own meanings, often working outside regulations and, through these varied actions, schools have been put in the position of reform. Day school teachers comment on the difference to a class the inclusion of even one adult makes. More flexible administrative arrangements have been needed to accommodate adult learners (Cocklin, 1992). For instance, adults in schools necessitate wider considerations of uniform, discipline, timetable and personal factors (for example, childcare). Professional staff have needed to use more imaginative teaching methods for learners who are more experienced in life and usually more autonomous.

As a result of adults' formal and informal education in schools, there has been up to now a significant change in the responsiveness and determination of educational structures in Aotearoa/New Zealand. Community education has forced schools to cope with the tension between change and stability. Curriculum planning, based on old assumptions of the nature of the skills considered necessary for socialising children, has been broadened to incorporate adult values and differences. The traditional view that schools were for children has been replaced by the newer idea that schools are for adults as well. This view of schools as institutions of lifelong learning is gradually receiving wider acceptance. The terms 'cradle to grave' and 'seamless education' are more of an integral part of the contemporary language of education. On what basis has this change occurred?

An Alternative View

Theorists Habermas and Foucault (Ewert, 1991) promote the idea that how society *is* may be far more complex than the results of simple cause and effect. The way things seem are not 'natural' as is assumed in the positivist model nor is much achieved via liberal reformist strategies. Habermas (Ewert, 1991) maintains that all actions are struggles between competing rational, practical and personal self-interests.[3] Michel Foucault focuses on a circulation of power and how people perceive their reality within those struggles. He describes the outcomes of our activities as being fragmented and contradictory, multi-dimensional and changing. As adults, citizens, parents, teachers, bureaucrats we struggle to come to grips with what seems important to us. Our actions are constantly shaping and being shaped by the time we live in, political (power) relationships we have with others and our environmental conditions. Schools too have been enmeshed in the intricate 'web of power' which Foucault insists is everywhere. This dialectical approach to viewing relationships and processes points to schools as continually wrestling with the problems of serving multiple interests – those of children, their parents, adults in the community, the needs of industry and the state. Accordingly, just as there are wide variations in adult education practice, so there is within and between institutions, practitioners and students.

The attitudes taken by schools towards providing for adults are sometimes contradictory. Adults in school based programmes can be seen as a nuisance especially when they require additional administration or after-hours access to buildings. As fee payers, they can be perceived as a source of possible additional funding that the Trustees encourage for their financial advantage. Alternatively, in some schools adult education activities are an integral part of the philosophy, planning and consideration of the school's effectiveness. Charters and the policies are carefully worded to include objectives which encompass the gamut of adult activities. Such a school's mission statement might read '... College seeks to provide opportunities for lifelong learning to every adult in its community because further education is every person's right'.[4]

In addition, a student's learning itself may have contradictory outcomes. It may sometimes contribute to oppression and false hopes, as students with improved skills still find themselves unable to obtain work. At other times there can be the beginnings of new freedom. Learners may join together and gain insights into 'how things are' for them and then decide on what steps they might take to challenge the structures.

The practice of community education in schools is a reflection of these varied encounters. Therefore, I maintain that the consequences of adult and community education cannot be described in absolute terms. We cannot say with conviction that the state has succeeded in controlling school based adult education solely to achieve its predetermined economic or political ends. Nor can we say that 'autonomous' adults in schools have solved society's ills. We *can* say though that community education in schools has had the potential for a whole range of effects, including contributing to radical change. For instance, in some areas of health provision, justice and the schooling of Maori there have been changes in knowledge and power. People's resistance and defiance have resulted in law changes, as in the instance of *who* may attend schools. Community education in schools has introduced 'a means by which many women and men have dealt critically and creatively with their reality and discovered how to participate in the transformation of their worlds' (Freire, 1987: 14).

Examples? I point to Te Ataarangi, a movement established to maintain and enhance te reo for Maori. Adults being educated informally through the multitude of activities in schools have decided that school structures and curriculum were not contributing adequately towards the maintenance of their language and culture. This movement could best be described as a model of community education in action. It involves teaching using resources which are local (other native speakers) and is based on learners' needs wherever they are (in the workplace, in homes). Currently that movement and many other community initiatives are supported by school based community education either by incorporation into formal programmes on school sites or as non-formal community educational activity supported by tutor hour payments.

Such actions are political in that they have succeeded in widening the range of options and alternatives to state-controlled activities. The establishment of health collectives, Kohanga Reo and Maori wardens as alternatives to traditional policing are other initiatives which have germinated through the influence of the community being educated in schools. These activities are not only reactions to oppression but entail active and creative alternative constructions of liberation – in other words, critical pedagogy which contributes to the creation of wider social movements. This point is reinforced by Pita Sharples, in describing the origin of kura kaupapa schools, when he describes how '[we] have gone outside the system and there have been so many of us that they've had to recognise us' (1994: A5).

School based community education sets up the opportunity for adults to participate in education at low cost, in familiar surroundings, with like-minded people outside the whole gamut of 'regulated communications' which Foucault describes are part of other adult and higher education institutions. Typically, school based community education activities occur in a context in which tutors and learners are often indistinguishable. Dialogue between educators and participants is casual, supportive, non-threatening, flexible and constructive. Learners are generally able to decide for themselves what, when and how they learn, at what speed and to what level of achievement. It is the nature of these educational processes which has been its strength in New Zealand. That is until recently.

Contemporary Issues: The Challenge of State Control Through Credentialism

Within the framework of school based community education, there are many pressing issues. However, at a 'macro' level, the current ideological context wherein education is increasingly been packaged and sold as if a commodity, is a disturbing trend. Inevitably, schools as providers of (adult) education have had to cope with the marked trends towards vocationalism (with associated credentialism) and commercialisation. Influenced by global trends such as the emphasis on economic imperatives, quality standards and market forces, educational providers along with other institutions in New Zealand are being reformed within what Gibson (1986: 7) calls the confines of 'technocratic rationality'. In this final component of this chapter, I briefly explore some of the intricacies of the accreditation of adult and community education in schools.

Michael Apple (1982) believes there is an overt and subtle encroachment by big business on schools' curriculum, making functional efficiency rather than intellectual insight their most important aim. In New Zealand, Gerald

Grace (1990: 34) sees this as a move away from education as 'a public good', to a 'commodity in the marketplace' encompassing all areas of education, from early childhood through to higher education. Adult and community education in schools cannot remain untouched.

The reform framework of the New Zealand Qualifications Authority,[5] in line with economic patterns, has its own language of inputs, outputs, criteria and learning outcomes. The framework has created a new set of qualifications to be sought by learners. The organisation of curricula in the high school is progressively being restructured into modular standardised sets with measurable outcomes, pre-specified teacher actions and achievement-based responses.

At present, the fourth sector has managed to stand somewhat aloof from these developments because of its marginal position in the education system. However, the push towards credentials, the desire for learners to receive accredited learning and possible funding mechanisms linked to community education suggest that adult and community education will be entangled in this framework sooner rather than later. There are practical difficulties – there are problems of assessable skills being defined in the first place by people outside the situation, according to criteria seen as valuable to another context or time. Such prioritising and predicted learning may be quite unrelated to any one individual or group's needs. If adult learners *do* follow their preferred topics on a credited course and divert from the prespecified goals, this can be perceived by authorities as 'inefficient'. Such 'deviance' could jeopardise the expected outcomes and may make certification for that course impossible. Therefore, it is probable that flexibility for individual local and immediate needs and the dynamic interaction between adults as both teachers and learners (one of the basic characteristics of community education through schools) are likely to be jeopardised.

But, of current changes, it is the emphasis on 'outcomes' which most challenges the nature of community education activities. The problem of arranging education according to previously predicted outcomes is particularly problematic for adults. It is well documented by Merriam and Caffarella (1991: 108) that adult learning processes may be the result of a maze of factors, including their prior experience and personal goals. Community education activities are mostly short in duration and often in response to a significant local or personal life event, so that the same outcomes and the repetition of outcomes cannot be assumed. I believe that in the practice of adults learning through schools they are more often engaged in acts of insight and understanding than in the straight transferral of information. What is at stake here is the value of these educational processes. Knowledge is far more than what may be written down or demonstrated in accordance with gaining credits in a new system of qualifications. There are several emergent contradictions: of corporate versus community ideology; formal versus informal educational processes; measurable versus provisional outcomes; useful versus 'useless' learning; fundable versus ... ? In other words, undue emphasis on credit-able rather than credit-less learning.

Richard Bagnall (1994) writes of the desirability of 'client freedom' to choose to enter or withdraw from learning opportunities according to learning relevance. This may not be a choice for adult learners who typically seek their opportunities through schools. Some school based providers may not be able to afford to register programmes on the framework (except where the content is already part of the mainstream school curriculum).

In addition, if course fees are raised to cover accreditation costs, community learners may not be able to afford them. For the field as a whole, however, failure to join the establishment may be suicidal if future funding is to be determined by courses or programmes being accredited or part of the New Zealand Qualifications (NZQA) framework. It seems difficult to imagine how such an informal system could willingly embrace such a standardised and formalised structure.

Altogether, the technical demands of entering such frameworks may render the adult community learners and practitioners alike as outsiders. As the NZQA framework becomes part of education in Aotearoa/New Zealand, will the fourth sector (inclusive of school based community education) resist? Surely there are possibilities for new forms of enterprise within those constraints. Perhaps marginalised learners may draw attention to their informal learning by pressing for it to be formally recognised under Recognition for Prior Learning (RPL) procedures. Such learning needs to be valued alongside other more formal learning.

Conclusion

My argument here has been that historically, adult and community learning through schools has both created and been subjected to contradictions. Adults learning through schools have influenced changes in some of the main institutions of society such as schools, but also in upholding individual learning rights.

I have considered the potential impact of current moves to incorporate the philosophies and practices of the government-driven NZQA framework into the fourth sector with special reference to school based community education. Further, big business philosophy may threaten the local, affordable and flexible education opportunities for adults in schools. However, the history of school based community education in Aotearoa/New Zealand gives cause for optimism. Striving to overcome past barriers to people's learning paths has brought about a critical awareness in many learners. In turn, this has activated political responses which have included resistance and the creation of alternatives.

The often invisible adult learning which 'happens' in private homes, community houses, church halls, school classrooms or gymnasiums seems insignificant in relation to other learning in polytechnics and universities – a Cinderella.[6] Nevertheless, school based adult and community education has earned a reputation for effectiveness, innovation and resilience. Faced with change and competing pressures, I have no doubt that it will continue to play an important part in shaping and maintaining an active social and economic climate in our society of the future.

Notes

1. I use the titles adult and community interchangeably here.
2. Schools which operate community education programmes are allocated a finite number of 'tutor hour' payments through the Ministry of Education. In addition, according to the number of tutor hours a school administers, a responsibility allowance for the co-ordinator and administrative assistance is disbursed. These allowances are additional to the school's basic staffing. The schools are directed to administer at least 15 per cent of the tutor hour fund for community-based groups and organisations. Groups using this form of funding operated through school based community education include: The Workers' Educational Association, Te Ataarangi Society, Lifeline and community houses.
3. For an overview of Habermas's description of competing interests, see Ewert 1991: 345–378.
4. From 'A Guide to Co-ordinators for the Drafting of Charters', Auckland Community Educators Association, 1991.
5. This consists of learners being able to choose learning at their own level from a variety of providers in order to build their qualifications towards a National Certificate and Diploma.
6. The analogy is borrowed from *Come in Cinderella,* a report to the Australian Senate Committee on Employment Education and Training, November 1991.

References

Apple, M.W. (1982), *Education and Power*, Melbourne: Routledge and Kegan Paul.
Bagnall, R.G. (1994), 'Performance Indicators and Outcomes as Measures of Educational Quality: A Cautionary Critique', *International Journal of Lifelong Education*, vol. 13, no. 1, January–February, pp. 19–32.
Bates, R. (1990), 'Education Policy and the New Cult of Efficiency', in

Middleton, S. and Codd, J. et al. (eds), *New Zealand Education Policy Today: Critical Perspectives*, Wellington: Allen and Unwin.

Brookfield, S. (1993), 'Self-directed Learning, Political Clarity and the Critical Practice of Adult Education', *Adult Education Quarterly*, vol. 43, no. 4, September, pp. 227–242.

Cocklin, B. (1992), 'Adult Students at Secondary School: Recommendations for Policy and Practice', *Australian Journal of Adult and Community Education*, vol. 32, no. 2, pp. 73–83.

Ewert, G.D. (1991), 'Habermas and Education: A Comprehensive Overview of the Influence of Habermas in Educational Literature', *Review of Educational Research*, vol. 61, no. 3, Fall, pp. 345–378.

Findsen, B.C. and Lomas, G. (1993), 'Programming Issues in a Community Learning Centre: the Case of Rutherford High School', *New Zealand Journal of Adult Learning*, vol. 21, no. 2, pp. 43–73.

Freire, P. (1987), *Pedagogy of the Oppressed*, Auckland: Penguin.

Gibson, R. (1986), *Critical Theory and Education*, London: Hodder and Stoughton.

Giroux, H.A. (1990), *Curriculum Discourse as Postmodernist Critical Practice*, Victoria: Deakin University.

Grace, G. (1990), 'The New Zealand Treasury and the Commodification of Knowledge', in Middleton, S. and Codd, J. et al. (eds), *New Zealand Education Policy Today: Critical Perspectives*, Wellington: Allen and Unwin.

Herbert, C.M. (1986), 'Community Education Newsletter to Schools', no. 28, Wellington: Department of Education, July.

Herbert, C.M. (1988), 'Community Education Newsletter to Schools', no. 35, Wellington: Department of Education, June.

Kemmis, S. (1986), *Curriculum Theorising: Beyond Reproduction Theory*, Victoria: Deakin University.

Knowles M.S. (1980), *The Modern Practice of Adult Education* (rev. ed.), Chicago: Association Press.

Lander, J. (1980), 'The Emergence of School Based Community Education in New Zealand', *Continuing Education in New Zealand*, vol. 12, no. 3, pp. 40–52.

Paterson, A. (ed.) (1984), *Garrett on Education*, Wellington: Tutor Publications, New Zealand Technical Institutes.

Merriam, S.B. and Caffarella, R.S. (1991), *Learning in Adulthood*, San Francisco: Jossey-Bass.

Ministry of Education (1992), 'Programme Instructions', October.

Ministry of Education (1994), 'Statistics of New Zealand', March.

Sharples, P. (1994), 'Urgency Borne Out of "Loss and Wreckage" ', *Sunday Star-Times*, 24 April, p. A5.

Thomas, J.E. and Harries-Jenkins, G. (1975), 'Adult Education and Social Change', *Studies in Adult Education*, vol. 7, no. 1, pp. 1–15.

Part 4

Adult Learning Practices

17

Developing Educational Programmes for Adults

Brian Findsen

Introduction

'Curriculum' is often a neglected concept in most adult and community education settings. In others, it is treated with distaste possibly because of its formal education connotations. The preferred term 'programme' has a less imposing feel about it and suggests more neutrality on the part of the designer. Yet whatever term is used to denote that which counts as knowledge (*syllabus* or *content* are others), there is little real debate even amongst practitioners on how adult and community education content is selected and used in adult learning contexts. Most adult educators just do it![1]

Adult educators tend to want to dissociate themselves from connections with schooling, and curriculum is one of those words which smacks of heavy teacher-directedness and authority. Given that a prevalent ethos among fourth sector workers is the centrality of adult learners in the teaching-learning environment and their supposed greater autonomy and responsibility for the management of learning (Knowles, 1980), the notion of an 'expert-driven' curriculum is uncomfortable. Yet the development of curricula (in the compulsory education system) and the planning of programmes for or with adults are arguably closer together than most adult educators would care to admit. As will be demonstrated, much of what passes for orthodoxy in programme development for adults has been derived from child-centred learning or from a humanistic basis of planning which has serious conceptual flaws.

In this chapter I outline some common understandings of the term 'programme' before exploring conventional practice of programme development in New Zealand. Next, I explore models of programme development and evaluate their relative effectiveness. Issues of developing programmes will be investigated from the perspective of the sociology of knowledge in relation to current practice using examples from my own work. Finally, I point to a more radical paradigm for practice based on the work of Freire (1984) which may assist the more marginalised peoples of Aotearoa/New Zealand to have their voices heard.

The Programme Planning Process

Understanding Programming

The term 'programme' is used here to include all those adult learning events which exist in formal, non-formal or informal settings (Jarvis, 1986: 3). It ranges from micro level programmes such as a one-to-one tutoring in an adult literacy situation to macro level initiatives such as a regional public education programme for residents to conserve water. Programmes may be developed at a variety of levels – individual; group; organisational; community; regional; national; global. Given the enormous range of activities which fit under the adult and community education umbrella (see the Introduction to this book), the contexts for developing programmes are much broader than for any formally structured environment. Hence, the practice of 'developing programmes' can be fraught with philosophical diversity, conceptual confusion and practical tensions. Nevertheless, adult educators of most persuasions are expected to 'provide programmes' since most often it is such provision which the public or target groups see as the visible work. While the functions of adult educators are varied – instruction, counselling, programme development, administration (Darkenwald and Merriam, 1982: 16) – the role of programme planner or course organiser is considered by most organisations as fundamental to effective adult education provision.

Models of Programme Development

Underlying the up-front courses and seminars delivered by a vast range of providers in the fourth sector is a process of programme planning popularised in the New Zealand context by the work of Malcolm Knowles (1980; 1984; 1990). If practitioners are aware of a conscious mechanism of programme development, it is often his model which captures busy planners' attention. This is easy to understand because this model is based on humanistic principles which square comfortably with many liberal-progressives' ideologies and the procedures he invokes are seemingly based on common sense. I will return to this model soon. It is necessary to understand that Knowles' model is really an elaboration of an earlier version applied to the classroom context.

An early curriculum theorist from the United States who strongly influenced directions in schools was Ralph Tyler. In my own teaching related to 'Programme Planning' I often start with this seminal work to help students track through historically how and when models of programme development have come into vogue and to better comprehend both the strengths and limitations of such technically-oriented systems-approach models. Essentially Tyler (1949) argues for curriculum development being hinged on four essential questions:

1. What educational *purposes* should the school seek to attain?
2. How can learning experiences be selected which are likely to be useful in attaining these *objectives*?
3. How can learning experiences be *organised* for effective instruction?
4. How can the effectiveness of learning experiences be *evaluated*?

In each case the word which I have italicised is the key for action for the practitioner. Tyler expands on these four basic concepts as the basis for curriculum development in schools in his book *Basic Principles in Curriculum and Instruction* (1949).

Most readers will need no introduction to Knowles' major steps in the programme planning process. In brief, he explains them as follows (1980: 59):

1. the establishment of a *climate* conducive to adult learning
2. the creation of an organisational *structure* for participative planning
3. the diagnosis of *needs* for learning
4. the formulation of directions of learning (*objectives*)
5. the development of a *design* of activities
6. the *operation* of the activities
7. the rediagnosis of needs for learning (*evaluation*).

The italicised terms provide the focus for action. When the key terms are scanned, it is easy to identify the pattern previously established by Tyler (1949). So what Knowles presents as a very significant break from classroom pedagogy (in line with his four rather flimsy 'andragogical' assumptions about adult learners) is actually a veiled adaptation of mainstream school-based curricula.

Adult education has no shortage of programme development models. Others have elaborated on the basic core structure formulated by Knowles, in each case arguing for a new interpretation. Given that New Zealand adult educators have published minimally in this area, it is of no surprise that Boshier's (1978) model serves as a more indigenous source for discussion. Fundamentally, he demarcates programme development into three major subprocesses: programme planning (that which occurs prior to contact between teacher and students); management of instruction (including most of the steps which Knowles identified); and programme evaluation.

Figure 18.1: Programme Planning Model.

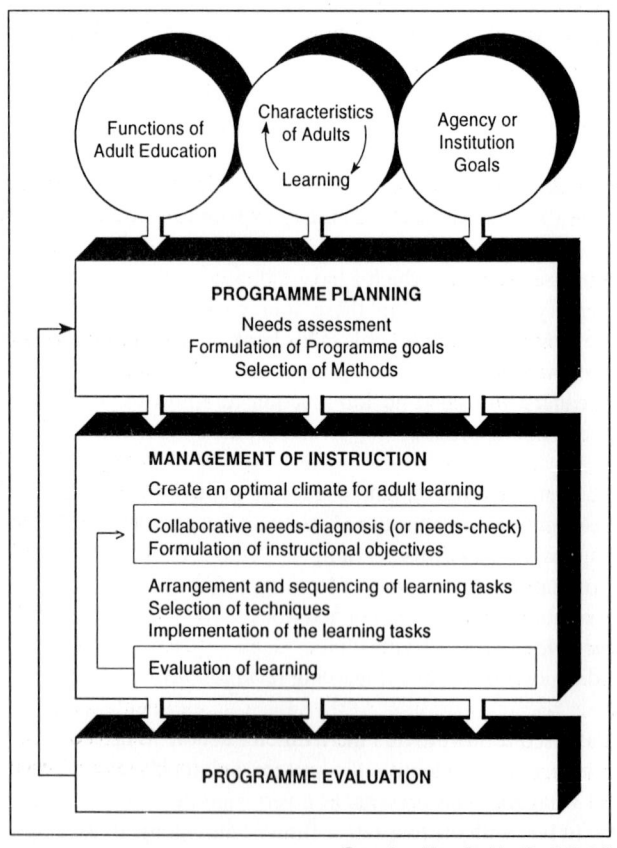

```
                Characteristics
  Functions of    of Adults      Agency or
  Adult Education               Institution
                  Learning       Goals

  ┌─────────────────────────────────────────┐
  │ PROGRAMME PLANNING                      │
  │   Needs assessment                      │
  │   Formulation of Programme goals        │
  │   Selection of Methods                  │
  ├─────────────────────────────────────────┤
  │ MANAGEMENT OF INSTRUCTION               │
  │   Create an optimal climate for adult   │
  │   learning                              │
  │   ┌───────────────────────────────────┐ │
  │   │ Collaborative needs-diagnosis     │ │
  │   │ (or needs-check)                  │ │
  │   │ Formulation of instructional      │ │
  │   │ objectives                        │ │
  │   └───────────────────────────────────┘ │
  │   Arrangement and sequencing of         │
  │   learning tasks                        │
  │   Selection of techniques               │
  │   Implementation of the learning tasks  │
  │   ┌───────────────────────────────────┐ │
  │   │ Evaluation of learning            │ │
  │   └───────────────────────────────────┘ │
  ├─────────────────────────────────────────┤
  │ PROGRAMME EVALUATION                    │
  └─────────────────────────────────────────┘
```

(Reproduced from Boshier, R., 1978: 34)

For me, as a teacher who occasionally uses this model (partly out of empathy for a New Zealand version), its real significance resides in the overriding macro factors which Boshier believes affect this somewhat linear decision-making progression. He identifies that any programme development cannot occur without planners' cognisance of the following:

- the functions of adult education
- characteristics of adults learning
- agency or institution goals.

In a similar vein Jarvis (1983), in his attempt to identify 'separate elements' which influence the dynamics of programme development, identifies philosophical factors, sociological factors and social policy factors as important features of the planning environment.

A Case Study

To illustrate the importance of an adult educator's wider vision for programme development (using significant factors from Boshier and Jarvis), I have identified a scenario of a co-ordinator in a school based community education centre who would need to have considered questions such as:

(a) In this agency, what is the central mission? What are my private views of what is important to achieve in this setting? (*functions of adult education; philosophical position*).
(b) What is known about the community this agency serves? What are the strengths and limitations of the people's learning potential in this community? How do they prefer to learn? (*characteristics of adult learners*)
(c) What are the aims of this centre and its parent institution (the school) and how do the values of both relate? What scope is there for experimentation and social change? (*agency/institution goals*)
(d) What is the prevailing culture of this centre and its community? What kinds of knowledge are relevant and who has access to them? (*sociological factors*)
(e) How do the new Ministry of Education requirements affect what can be achieved? What potential is there for cross-subsidisation of courses? What is the policy of the Advisory Committee and the Board of Trustees? (*social policy factors*).

In the daily practices of busy practitioners, such questions can easily be overlooked in favour of current exigencies.

The importance of social context in determining appropriate programme development strategies should not be underestimated. Both Boone (1985) and Boyle (1981) have emphasised this aspect in their models. Boone's version, primarily rooted in the context of co-operative (agricultural) extension, highlights the institutional context as paramount (the needs of the individual are secondary to the goals of the organisation); on the other hand, Boyle's developmental framework for programming allows for looser contexts where the presence or impact of an agency on learning may be less relevant. For each, the step of 'situational analysis' (i.e. a systematic critical examination of the most important elements in a given situation) is perceived as vital. Otherwise, there is great risk that the well-intentioned programme planners may actually exacerbate a problem which they supposedly want to relieve or solve. Stories abound (see Edward Spicer, 1952) of adult educators making cultural blunders because of a lack of sufficient analysis prior to entering a situation or community.

The models I have outlined above fit within the conventional framework of programme development. While they have their uses, they are limited by the ideological context in which they were established. The British and American contexts from which many of New Zealand's adult education concepts have been borrowed are heavily biased to (male) individualistic and organisational settings (Jarvis, 1983; Thompson, 1980). There is a strong call from minority status groups for their voices to be heard in the distribution of educational resources and knowledge and in their definition. We need alternative models which better reflect New Zealand realities, especially those of the marginalised.

Defining Learning Needs

Common to all models of adult learning programmes is the important step of needs analysis (see above models). This is seemingly a straightforward and practical exercise. However, as Benseman (1980) has pointed out and many analytical philosophers before him (particularly Paul Hirst, 1970 and R.S. Peters, 1967; 1970), the assessment of needs is very problematic. Apparently simply answered questions such as 'What are needs? Who should identify them? How should this process be carried out?' elicit inherently value-laden positions which are often disguised by planners in the name of 'neutral' decision-making. Adult educators are never neutral in the planning process (Freire, 1984) and very often the published programme reflects their unstated personal philosophies as much as it does the 'real needs' of the community. The community education services based in high schools loom as loci of decision-making which reflect the biases of co-ordinators as much as they do programmes based on in-depth situational analysis (see Findsen and Lomas, 1993, for the effects of changes of evening-class supervisors at one high school). These comments are likely to be applicable to many other contexts in which adult and community educators are expected to produce education provision on a regular cyclical basis.

I have signalled above the difficulties of assessing learning needs in the overall programming process but equally other major processes are similarly more problematic to enact than they appear. For example, at the other 'end' of the process, the issue of evaluation is not well conceptualised nor well implemented. The prevailing attitude of busy practitioners that 'if it's not broken, don't try to fix it' is not easy to counter. How do they know whether aspects of the programme need adjustment unless systematic evidence is collected and analysed? There is little training given and little sought to rigorously evaluate practices of programming; there is not much incentive for programme planners to improve their performance when conditions of work are unfavourable. For instance, remuneration is modest and positive initiatives or experimentation are usually given scant praise.

Whose Curriculum Is It Anyway?

A Sociological Framework

One framework I have previously found useful (see Findsen, 1992, for a sociological analysis of the Certificate in Maori Studies at the University of Waikato) is that suggested by the work of Michael Young (1971) and subsequently by Richard Bates (1978). The questions which they ask emerge from a critical tradition of what was previously the 'new' sociology of education. Essentially, in this approach 'taken for granted' or implicit aspects in (adult) education are subjected to fresh scrutiny based primarily on analysis of the systems or structures which help create inequalities or injustices for 'disadvantaged' adults. Rather than blaming individuals for 'failure' (the deficit model), writers from this tradition challenge those who create or have authority within the structures to review their practices and processes.

Translated into the curriculum context, the following questions were suggested (Bates, 1978; Young, 1971) as benchmarks for critical analysis of the creation, reproduction or transformation of knowledge. Sociologically, these questions allow marginalised or disenfranchised groups to fundamentally question the distribution of power, resources and knowledge in New Zealand society. The questions are as follows:

- What counts as knowledge and how is it produced?
- How is what counts as knowledge organised?
- How is what counts as knowledge transmitted?

- How is access to what counts as knowledge determined?
- What are the processes of control?
- What ideological appeals justify the system?

These questions challenge the legitimacy of dominant groups in society to define the curriculum for others. In a practical sense, the development of curriculum in continuing education settings (e.g. schools, universities, community houses) becomes problematic if the knowledge base represents only that of dominant groups. Based on the assumption that every group has equal rights to knowledge creation and dissemination (a basic principle of social equity), the uncritical regurgitation of set programmes from year to year (quite often the pattern of mass providers in the fourth sector) deserves close scrutiny. The voices of women, working people, Maori, Pacific Islanders, for example, are often not sufficiently heard (indeed not even sought) as the patterns of participation confirm (see Chapter 18). Instead of seeking a voice in the mainstream system, many marginalised groups opt for a substitutionist response where the control of knowledge is in their own hands. Not surprisingly, Maori people have asserted their rights for self-determination within many public spheres and overtly so in education. The success of kohanga reo, kura kaupapa Maori (and even whare wananga) testify to the validity of alternative curriculum development paths under the direction of Maori.

For mainstream providers there is a challenge to move beyond the traditional clientele or usual 'middle class capture'. No one denies the rights of the middle class to knowledge but they should not have a disproportionate slice of the fourth sector cake (see Harré Hindmarsh, 1993, for elaboration of this point). Programme planners need to work more creatively with communities to ascertain their learning aspirations and become more of a genuine part of community rather than act as a parachutist who occasionally descends for nourishment and disappears back to a desk to plan in isolation. While New Right practices of government make developmental work much more difficult than when resources were more plentiful, some organisations can still implement cross-subsidisation of finances to allow for more authentic needs assessment and community development to occur.

While the use of the above-mentioned programme models provides some guidance in alternative approaches to curriculum development, some adult educators have become familiar with Freirian philosophy and practice. Principles as espoused in *Pedagogy of the Oppressed* and Freire's subsequent writing provide a framework for action which promotes ownership of curriculum by groups as much as by providers. The Freirian approach presupposes a genuine desire by fourth sector agencies to engage in practices such as challenging orthodoxy, sharing power and setting up learning programmes for marginalised groups to assert greater control over their destinies. Contemporary examples can be found in the work of Dennis Howlett in Canada (Gatt-fly, 1986), the Kirkwoods in Scotland (Kirkwood and Kirkwood, 1989), Ira Shor in New York city (Shor, 1992) and at Highlander in Tennessee (Bell, Gaventa and Peters, 1990). This code of practice is not for the fainthearted. Taken to its logical conclusion, the implementation of such radical programming may call into question the very ethos of many mainstream providers and set the conditions for a redistribution of resources which is incompatible with many fourth sector's providers' philosophies.

Conclusion

This chapter has attempted to convey the complexity of the programming process. The practice of programme development is at the heart of so much fourth sector agency work and is largely undertaken as a pragmatic exercise, sometimes divorced from an espoused philosophy (mission statement). I have outlined some of the conventional models, largely imported from abroad, which can provide guidance for practitioners on the 'how to' side of this work.

Generally, the orthodox models can go only so far. Some critics (Apple, 1981; Giroux, 1979) would argue that practices based on these models reinforce social inequalities in society. The questions raised within the context of the sociology of knowledge point to the need for a more critical stance if there is genuine concern for social justice within the fourth sector. In particular, the work of people like Paulo Freire and Myles Horton of Highlander have established a basis for more liberatory models which may provide adult educators with principles for action. The impact of this kind of emancipatory action may not only challenge practitioners' ideologies but the actual distribution of power and knowledge in society more generally.

Notes

1. Much of the controversy derives from the need for planners or marketing personnel to procure sufficient numbers of students to keep programmes financially viable. This 'bums on seats' mentality lies behind a good deal of the uncritical programming which occurs in today's competitive environment. The drive is to get the numbers to the detriment of critical reflection and effective evaluation.

References

Apple, M.W. (1981), 'Reproduction, Contestation and Curriculum: An Essay in Self-Criticism', *Interchange*, vol. 12, no. 2–3, pp. 27–47.

Bates, R. (1978), 'The New Sociology of Education: Directions for Theory and Research', *New Zealand Journal of Educational Studies,* vol. 13, no. 1, pp. 3–22.

Bell, B., Gaventa, J. and Peters, J. (eds) (1990), *We Make the Way by Walking: Conversations on Education and Social Change (Myles Horton and Paulo Freire),* Philadelphia: Temple University Press.

Benseman, J. (1980), *The Assessment and Meeting of Needs in Continuing Education,* Stockholm: Department of Educational Research, Lärerhögskolan Stockholm Institute of Education.

Boone, E.J. (1985), *Developing Programs in Adult Education,* Englewood Cliffs, New Jersey: Prentice-Hall.

Boshier, R. (1978), 'Adult Education Programme Planning and Instructional Design', *Continuing Education in New Zealand,* vol. 10, no. 1, May, pp. 33–50.

Boyle, P.G. (1981), *Planning Better Programs,* New York: McGraw Hill.

Darkenwald, G.G. and Merriam, S.B. (1982), *Adult Education: Foundations of Practice,* New York: Harper and Row.

Findsen, B. (1992), 'What Really Counts as Knowledge? A Sociological Approach to the Certificate in Maori Studies at the University of Waikato', *New Zealand Journal of Adult Learning,* vol. 20, no. 1, pp. 51–64.

Findsen, B. and Lomas, G. (1993), 'Programming Issues in a Community Learning Centre: The Case of Rutherford High School', *New Zealand Journal of Adult Learning,* vol. 21, no. 2, pp. 43–74.

Freire, P. (1984), *Pedagogy of the Oppressed,* New York: Continuum.

Gatt-fly. (1986), *Ah-hah! A New Approach to Popular Education* (2nd ed.), Toronto, Ontario: Between the Lines.

Giroux, H.A. (1979), 'Toward a New Sociology of the Curriculum', *Educational Leadership,* December, pp. 248–253.

Harré Hindmarsh, J. (1993), 'Community and Continuing Education in 1992: Trends and Issues', *New Zealand Annual Review of Education,* no. 2, pp. 179–204.

Hirst, P.H. and Peters, R.S. (1970), *The Logic of Education,* London: Routledge and Kegan Paul.

Jarvis, P. (1983), *Adult and Continuing Education: Theory and Practice,* London: Croom Helm.

Jarvis, P. (1986), *Sociological Perspectives on Lifelong Education and Lifelong Learning,* Athens, Georgia: University of Georgia.

Kirkwood, G. and Kirkwood, C. (1989), *Living Adult Education: Freire in Scotland,* SIACE and the Open University, Milton Keynes.

Knowles, M.S. (1980), *The Modern Practice of Adult Education,* New York: The Adult Education Company.

Knowles, M.S. (1984), *Andragogy in Action: Applying Modern Principles of Adult Learning*, San Francisco: Jossey-Bass Publishers.

Knowles, M.S. (1990), *The Adult Learner: A Neglected Species* (4th ed.), Houston: Gulf Publishing Co.

Peters, R.S. (ed.) (1967), *The Concept of Education*, London: Routledge and Kegan Paul.

Shor, I. (1992), *Empowering Education: Critical Teaching for Social Change*, London: The University of Chicago Press.

Spicer, E.H. (ed.) (1952), *Human Problems in Technological Change*, New York: John Wiley and Sons.

Thompson, J. (ed.) (1980), *Adult Education for a Change*, London: Hutchinson.

Tyler, R.W. (1949), *Basic Principles in Curriculum and Instruction*, Chicago: University of Chicago Press.

Young, M.F.D. (ed.) (1971), *Knowledge and Control*, London: Collier Macmillan.

18

Participation in the Fourth Sector

John Benseman

Introduction

The issue of who participates in adult and community education is much more commonly debated in this sector of education than any other. While there are periodic debates and reviews of equity of access to preschool, tertiary and even compulsory sectors (see for example NZCER's review of the research literature done for the Royal Commission on Social Policy, Parts 1 and 2, 1987), a far higher proportion of the research carried out in adult and community education has centred on who participates and to a lesser extent, who does not. As Houle (1961: 7) said:

> No other subject is more widely pondered and discussed by people interested in the education of adults than the motives which lead men and women to introduce systematic learning into the patterns of their lives. Legal requirements reinforced by social expectations no longer apply to them. Yet in the years beyond compulsory schooling and amidst all the pleasures and duties of responsible maturity, many people are moved to devote part of their time to the development of their potentialities. They either go seeking for an activity or somehow become aware that one exists and are led by impulse, often obscure to themselves, to take part in it. Many other

people never seek, are never aware of opportunity or, if it does come to their attention, are apathetic or negative to it.

Participation and Equal Opportunity

At the heart of the issue of participation in adult and community education is a concern for equality of opportunity, or equity of access to a range of educational provision. While equality of access does not necessarily translate into equity of outcomes, democratic ideals underpin a concern that education can be shown to be available, if not used, by a reasonable cross-section of the population. As Jarvis (1985: 199) points out, '... it is politically appropriate to demonstrate that access to the educational system is open to everyone throughout their lives, so that an appearance of egalitarianism occurs'. In a political system where social mobility is perceived as the means whereby individual merit is recognised and 'wins through', it is important to show that all sectors of the population have equal access to the means for achieving social mobility. Thus, a cross-representation of the population participating in adult and community education programmes constitutes a form of 'proof' that a society is functioning efficiently, with individuals, irrespective of their social origins, using the educational resources available to realise their full potential.

Like poverty, concern over equality of access to education waxes and wanes with the political moon. From Peter Fraser's famous dictum that education would be available to every person 'whatever his (sic) level of academic ability, whether he be rich or poor, whether he live in the town or country' through to the present, political manifestos of both major political parties have periodically picked up the torch of equal opportunity and run with it in elections. For example, in the mid-1980s both Labour and National included statements about equality of opportunity in their manifestos and National also professed an aim of achieving equality of outcomes – 'Equity has become an important issue in education ... . Fairness must be measured by both opportunities and outcomes; the guarantee that opportunity and outcome won't be dictated by gender, race, by learning disabilities, by geographical or socioeconomic circumstances' (National Party, 1987: Section 16). Key documents preceding the writing of the Education Act in 1990 included not only statements of equal opportunity, but also statements about attracting '... those who have not traditionally participated in the post-school sector' (see Ministry of Education, 1989: 9).

Current concern over participation in education however, has centred more commonly on our low *rate* of participation in tertiary education in comparison with other OECD countries and equality of opportunity, or the analysis of participation patterns has largely disappeared off the agenda of most politicians and consequently, most educational groups.

It is also interesting to note that most statements about equal opportunity in education are primarily aimed at the compulsory and tertiary educational sectors, less often at the preschool sector, and rarely at the adult and community education sector. Nonetheless, it has historically been a strong element in adult and community education – whether in provider groups' philosophies and policies, or individual adult educators' personal beliefs (for a fuller discussion see Benseman, 1989a).

Participation Research

Although adult and community education is significantly under-researched in comparison with other educational sectors, studies of who participates in the various providers' programmes has generated a disproportionately high amount of the research carried out in the sector to date. New Zealand research has included a national study of participation across all forms of provision (Bird and Fenwick, 1981), studies of participation within a region (see Waghorne, 1975), studies of individual providers (see Benseman, 1980; Coleman, 1992; Horton, 1976), comparisons of participants in several institutions (see Boshier 1970 and 1971; Wagemaker, 1978) and studies of particular social or professional groups (see Barham and Benseman, 1984; Benseman, 1989b; Richmond, Hannan and Hunter, 1984; Tobias, 1988).

Participation analyses are generally of two main types: studies which draw on psychological models of behaviour to analyse participation in terms of the individual motivations of people to participate or not; and sociological analyses which look at participation in terms of social groupings and the social functions that the patterns of participation they reflect (see Courtney, 1991; Merriam and Caffarella, 1991; and Rubenson; 1989 for a fuller discussion of these approaches).

Most of the research on individual motivation has been derived from Cyril Houle's 1961 typology of learners:

- *goal-oriented learners* who use education as a means of achieving some other goal
- *activity-oriented learners* who participate in education for the sake of the activity itself and the social interaction
- *learning-oriented learners* who seek knowledge for its own sake.

Later researchers, including Roger Boshier, have developed this typology into a more elaborate scale called the Education Participation Scale (see Merriam and Caffarella, 1991). Most participation research to date in New

Zealand has been oriented towards a sociological analysis, concentrating on which social groups are represented among participants and conversely, which are not.

The results of the research to date have shown a reasonably consistent picture, as is the case internationally. As Roger Boshier (1970, 1971) concluded in his study of three Wellington adult and community education groups, the participants represent a narrow *crème de la crème* group drawn disproportionately from New Zealand's social élite.

Participants in adult/community education programmes include disproportionately high numbers of:

- those who have attended school more than an average amount of time and passed formal qualifications
- women (although men tend to be in a majority in more vocationally oriented courses)
- those under 40 years of age
- Pakeha
- those who have above-average incomes
- people who are in full-time work and most often in a white-collar occupation.

Conversely, those underrepresented disproportionately include:

- the elderly
- ethnic minorities
- immigrants
- those who left school early
- those on low incomes
- people who are unemployed or work in semi- or unskilled jobs
- women with dependent children.

In a word, the marginalised.

It is interesting to note several additional points about the participation issue. Rubenson (1989: 64) points out that a closer look at participation within different forms of adult and community education shows that '... the better an education pays off in terms of income, status, occupation, political efficacy, cultural competence and similar patterns, the greater the differences in socioeconomic status between participants and non-participants'.

Second, it appears that variations of participation within socially homogeneous groups varies according to the same variables that distinguish between participants on a broader social scale. In a study of medical general practitioners' (GPs) continuing medical education (Barham and Benseman, 1984) for example, participation in educational programmes was shown to vary according to where GPs stood in relation to the professions dominant characteristics. Peripheral GPs such as part-timers, those living in isolated areas, those working in solo practices or who did not have postgraduate qualifications all had lower rates of participation than GPs who conform to the mainstream patterns of the profession – working in group practices, especially in urban areas, in full-time practice, aged between 30 and 50 years of age and so forth. In other words, even within a socially élite group like medical practitioners, there are variations in rates of participation which vary according to indices of social status that operate within that group.

Third, the rate of participation for the total population is a useful benchmark to use in comparisons of provision internationally. For example, participation rates vary from 25–30 per cent of the total Swedish population at any one time, to 13 per cent in the U.S.A. (see Benseman, 1989a). The only national survey of participation in New Zealand (Bird and Fenwick, 1981) used a definition of adult learning which incorporated individual learning projects and cannot be compared directly with these figures. They estimated that approximately 30 per cent of all adults were involved in agency-directed learning activities (which includes activities like tennis lessons at the local tennis club) in 1977.

Fourth, individual learning projects are sometimes seen as one area of adult learning where a full range of social groups can be said to be participating. This type of learning received great impetus from the research work of Canadian Allen Tough (1971) and led for example to the development of learning exchanges in this country. More recently however, a large-scale study of Swedish adults (Borgström, 1985) has cast some doubt on the ubiquity of independent learning projects and shown them to reflect similar patterns to participation analyses of formalised learning provision.

Non-participation

The converse side of this issue – non-participation – has received far less attention in comparison. In New Zealand only one study has been carried out involving people who have not participated in adult and community education (Benseman, 1989a). This study involved in-depth interviews with 40 adults who had very limited schooling and the great majority of whom had never attended any form of adult or community education programme since leaving school.

The people interviewed in this study were asked how they perceived adult and community education. These perceptions included:

- seeing it as a form of recreation (especially for those who have excess spare time)
- an opportunity for those who want to get on in life and better themselves
- that it is for people with drive and energy
- that it is a means for gaining a broader perspective and deeper understanding of all aspects of life.

In terms of their own potential for participation in adult and community education, the people interviewed could be categorised into the following groups:

- those who expressed no interest in education (or even a strong dislike)
- those who expressed a strong interest in education but only in terms of formal schooling and therefore irrelevant to themselves as adults
- those who value education and see it as a way of getting on or becoming socially mobile – these people are primarily interested in education with a strong vocational orientation, although they usually have little knowledge of how to turn their aspirations into reality
- those who have an interest in education in a broad sense and are often already active in educational activities in various cultural and social settings somewhat removed from conventional adult and community education groups.

Most writing on non-participation however, analyses the issue in terms of barriers that prevent people from making use of the educational provision available (see McGivney, 1993; Merriam and Caffarella, 1991). These usually include situational barriers such as time, distance and costs; institutional barriers where educational providers fail to maximise their programmes' availability physically and psychologically to all sectors of a community; and dispositional barriers which include learners' attitudes, perceptions and expectations. Most research points to this last group of barriers as being the most powerful deterrents, but they seldom operate in isolation, so that the young mother with hostile attitudes towards education because of negative school experiences will almost inevitably encounter a whole range of other impediments such as costs, lack of childcare and red tape requirements if she were to make the effort to reboard the educational train as an adult.

While the identification of barriers to participation is unlikely to change the practices of adult educators overnight, they are nonetheless a useful tool for sensitising programme administrators to factors which influence the make-up of their programme's clientele.

Changes in Adult and Community Education Participation

Most participation analyses were carried out in the 1970s and early 1980s, starting with Boshier's study of the participants in three Wellington adult/community education programmes in 1970. As I have argued elsewhere (Benseman, 1992), there have been significant changes in the nature of some adult and community education groups since that time, with the development of a number of new forms of provision that differed significantly from the traditional range of provision which had been dominated hitherto by the universities, secondary school programmes for adults and the WEA.

The Adult Reading and Learning Assistance (ARLA) Federation was formed as an umbrella organisation for some 70 adult literacy groups that had developed since their inception in Hawke's Bay and Auckland in 1974. This period also saw the formation and development of 13 Rural Education Activities Programmes (REAP) aimed at increasing educational provision in rural areas where there had been little or no adult and community education provision historically; Te Ataarangi developed for the teaching of te reo Maori; and in the work sphere, ACCESS, MACCESS, TOP and the Trade Union Education Authority (TUEA) had no historical equivalents. While this last group of programmes were designed primarily for vocational purposes, many of them have been much broader in their scope, both in terms of their programmes and the types of people who attended them.

What is particularly interesting in the context of this discussion is that all of these programmes have focused specifically on groups which the earlier research showed to be underrepresented in adult and community education. Te Ataarangi for example is primarily for Maori people; ACCESS and its successors has brought post-school educational opportunities to unemployed people that they would have been extremely unlikely to have had previously; ARLA's recent extension of provision in workplaces and its strong commitment to literacy appropriate to Maori contexts are without precedent and TUEA's efforts in involving large numbers (in excess of 30,000 participant days per year – see Lowe, 1991) of adults, most of whom have below-average schooling, is one of the more significant achievements of the recent educational past.

The research documentation of these achievements however, is still somewhat limited. The 1990 review of REAP (Rivers *et al.*, 1990) for example, makes some reference to the nature of the REAP clientele but it is based on casual observation and hearsay rather than research documentation.

There has been some documentation of ARLA's clientele in its collection of annual statistics (Benseman, 1991, 1992 and 1993) and in a study of the Auckland scheme (Benseman, 1989c). These show, for example, high participation rates of people in low-status, low-income occupations, unemployed or on a benefit – groups who have rarely been represented in adult and community education previously.

Although the achievements of these providers represent a significant development in the history of adult and community education in this country, there is still an urgent need to further document these activities, both in the nature of the changes brought about and the means by which they were achieved.

Similarly, there is also a need to re-visit the more traditional adult and community education providers, for there have been considerable changes with many of these groups since the research studies of the 1970s. Several of the old university extension departments have disappeared totally, been reduced in size or expanded into new programme areas such as New Start for people with minimal school qualifications and provision for the elderly. The community colleges of the 1970s have transmogrified into polytechnics, invariably with an accompanying reduction in their community education provision (see Chapter 13). Community education programmes in secondary schools have enjoyed the biggest increase in funding of any provider group over the past decade. While some of these groups' programmes and the ways they operate appear to have changed little since the days of the technical class era, others are very innovative and participatory in their operations.

Participation in Other Fourth Sector Programmes

While most participation research has traditionally focused on providers such as community-based education in schools, formal education institutions such as polytechnics and universities and community groups such as the WEA, the issue is also important to other groups which come under the umbrella of the fourth sector.

Continuing professional education providers have long had a concern that their programmes involve a reasonable number of their members and in particular, their less competent members. As Colin Gunn has argued in Part 3 of this book, public education continually faces the issue of whether its programmes reach the targeted audiences; programmes such as anti-racism education have the perennial problem of where to aim their recruitment for the maximum effect – those who are already sympathetic to bicultural ideals, those who are most likely to have ongoing influence, or those who are seen as racist; community development literature is peppered with discussions of how to reach those in greatest need.

Concluding Comments

Participation is a central issue for adult and community education. Because it does not deal with a captive audience of learners as occurs in compulsory schooling or the 'like it or lump it' attitude of some of the tertiary sector, most fourth sector groups have a central concern over the issue of participation in their programmes. Whether they are catering for sufficient numbers of participants, who their participants are, how they match with the total population make-up or the subgroups of the population being targeted, recording and monitoring of participation is an essential element in the overall planning and operation of any adult and community education programme.

While it is naïve to argue that any achievements in the extension of provision will necessarily mean changes in the life chances of these 'new' participants, changes in patterns of participation are nonetheless an important first step in achieving a more equitable educational system.

References

Barham, P. and Benseman, J. (Nov. 1984), 'Patterns of Continuing Professional Education and General Practitioners', *Journal of Medical Education*, vol. 59, no. 6, pp. 446–447.

Benseman, J. (1980), 'The Community College as an Extension of Educational Provision', *Continuing Education in New Zealand,* vol. 12, no. 2, pp. 49–68.

Benseman, J. (1989a), 'The View from the Other Side of the Educational Door: Adult Education from the Perspective of People with Low Levels of schooling', Wellington: Department of Education.

Benseman, J. (1989b), 'In Pursuit of Excellence – a Study of Continuing Dental Education in New Zealand', Auckland: New Zealand Dental Association.

Benseman, J. (1989c), 'Taking Control of their Own Lives: a Study of the Auckland Adult Literacy Scheme, Students and Tutors', Auckland: Auckland Adult Literacy Scheme.

Benseman, J. (1991, 1992, 1993), 'ARLA National Statistics', Wellington: ARLA.

Benseman, J. (1992), 'Participation Revisited – Who Gets to Adult and Community Education 1970–1990?', *New Zealand Journal of Adult Learning,* vol. 20, no. 1, pp. 11–20.

Bird, K.A. and Fenwick, P. (1981), 'Continuing Education Survey', Wellington: Department of Education.

Borgström, L. (1985), 'Self-directed Learning and the Reproduction of Inequalities', Unpublished manuscript, Department of Educational Research, Stockholm Institute of Education, Sweden.

Boshier, R. (Nov. 1970, Apr. 1971), 'The Participants: a Clientele Analysis of Three New Zealand Adult Education Institutions', *Australian Journal of Adult Education,* Part 1, vol. X, no. 3, pp. 131–142; Part 2, vol. XI, no. 1, pp. 20–44.

Coleman, B. (May 1992), 'Canterbury WEA – Participants, Activities and the Implications for Future Planning', *New Zealand Journal of Adult Learning,* vol. 20, no. 2, pp. 21–30.

Courtney, S. (1991), *Why Adults Learn: Towards a Theory of Participation in Adult Education,* New York: Routledge, Chapman and Hall.

Horton, C. (1976), 'University Extension Participants: their Characteristics and Attitudes', Hamilton: University Extension.

Houle, C.O. (1961), *The Enquiring Mind,* Madison: University of Wisconsin Press.

Jarvis, P. (1985), *The Sociology of Adult and Continuing Education,* London: Croom Helm.

Lowe, D. (7–9 June 1991), 'The Role of Trade Union Education in Empowering Workers and their Unions', Paper presented to *Union and Tertiary Research Conference,* Victoria University, Wellington.

McGivney, V. (1993), 'Participation and Non-participation – a Review of the Literature', in Edwards, R., Sieminski, S. and Zeldin, D. (eds), *Adult Learners, Education and Training,* Milton Keynes: Open University.

Merriam, S. and Caffarella, R. (1991), *Learning in Adulthood,* San Francisco: Jossey-Bass.

Ministry of Education (1989), *Learning for Life: Two,* Wellington: Government Printing Office.

National Council of Adult Education (1985), 'Action for Learning and Equity – Opportunity for Change' (also known as the 'He Tangata' report), Wellington: NCAE.

National Party (1987), 'A Nation at Risk' (education policy statement), Wellington.

NZCER (1987), *How Fair is NZ Education? Parts I and II,* Wellington: NZCER.

Richmond, D.E., Hannan, S. and Hunter, J.D. (Oct. 1984), 'A Survey of Participation of Physicians in Continuing Medical Education', *New Zealand Journal of Adult Learning,* vol. 16, no. 2, pp. 164–179.

Rivers, M.-J., Dewes, C. and Drumm, B. (1990), 'Review of the Rural Education Activities Programme (REAP)', Wellington: Ministry of Education.

Rubenson, K. (1989), 'The Sociology of Adult Education', in Merriam, S. and Cunningham, P. (eds), *Handbook of Adult and Continuing Education*, San Francisco: Jossey-Bass.

Tobias, R. (1988), 'Participation by Older People in Educational Activities in New Zealand', *Educational Gerontology*, vol. 17, no. 5, pp. 409–421.

Tough, A. (1971), *The Adults Learning Projects: a Fresh Approach to Theory and Practice in Adult Learning,* Toronto: Ontario Institute for Studies in Education.

Wagemaker, H. (1978), 'Participation in Three Adult Education Institutions in Dunedin', Unpublished MA thesis, Dunedin: University of Otago.

Waghorne, M. (1975), 'Adult Learning Activities in the City of Christchurch', Christchurch: Department of Extension Studies.

19

The Experience of Adult Learning

Colleen Mills

Introduction

The quantity and diversity of formal and non-formal educational opportunities in New Zealand are remarkable for a country of 3,600,000 people. As well as those available through the well-known providers such as universities, polytechnics, Workers Educational Association (WEA), Rural Education Activities Programme (REAP), churches and community divisions of secondary schools, there are a wide array of less well-known opportunities such as farmers' discussion groups, rural field days, marae-based education programmes, programmes provided by the Adult Reading and Learning Assistance (ARLA) Federation, drug rehabilitation programmes, Toastmasters Clubs, private sector ESOL (English for Speakers of Other Languages) courses and classes run by Family Planning Clinics. What is surprising, given this plethora of educational activity, is that we know very little about the actual learning experiences of the adults who participate in them.

Learners interact with the social, psychological and physical environment or learning milieu (Boud and Walker, 1991: 13) to create their learning experience. This chapter explores the state of our local knowledge of adult learning experiences before examining a range of factors that learners and researchers suggest are important for understanding these experiences. The chapter concludes by describing a change in perspective for adult educators that could increase the available local knowledge on adults' learning experiences.

The State of our Knowledge

Several factors have contributed to the lack of local knowledge about adult learners' experiences but undoubtedly the most significant factor is the scant resources available for research in adult education (Thorburn, 1986). There has been a tendency for the limited resources to be invested in studies of adult education from an historical, sociological or political rather than psychological perspective. The consequence has been that the bibliographies on New Zealand adult education contain very few studies that address learning processes. The adult educator who wishes to understand how adults feel, the perceptual processes they use and how they create meaning must either access literature from abroad or restrict themselves to insights and understandings gained from their own learning experiences and those of their students. The understandings about the experience of adult learning gained from the latter, anecdotal, approach are seldom documented, which is a further contributing factor to the impoverished state of the local database of research on adult learning processes.

The lack of psychological studies on adult learning has meant that the literature is liberally sprinkled with characterisations of the adult learner that draw on demographic studies which have looked for patterns rather than idiosyncrasies. The result has been the creation of 'the typical adult learner' who is portrayed as a person beyond the grasp of compulsory education who is self-directing, has a wealth of experience, seeks participatory learning experiences and has an instrumental, problem-solving approach to learning that is often directed by developmental issues. Such profiles are often presented by contrasting adults' learning with that of children (e.g. Boshier, 1980: 29–30) and in so doing, the view that adult learners have a great deal in common is encouraged.

These profiles characterise the adult learner in terms of typical circumstances the adult faces, their backgrounds and preferences rather than their cognitive, affective or social behaviour when learning. When adult educators assume that such profiles, either personally constructed or sourced from the literature, provide an adequate basis for curriculum decisions, then the point where learners' individuality is most powerfully expressed – the learner-task interface – is likely to be neglected. This neglect is most apparent when a group of learners are given the same activities, provided with the same explanations and assumed to be capable of or comfortable responding in the same way.

The Learner-task Interface

Overseas, over the last three decades various studies have revealed the highly individual nature of both the behaviour and experiences of adult learners. Their findings suggest that two important points must be borne in mind when designing or managing adult learning activities. First, even when two people are engaging in the same learning task, in the same setting and at the same time, their experience will be unique at an interactive, perceptual, cognitive and affective level. Second, a person's learning experiences from one learning event to the next may have little in common with each other. In other words, learning must be viewed as individually and contextually situated.

An individual brings a unique frame of reference to each learning activity. This is a blend of motivations, attitudes, expectations, styles, strategic knowledge and ability, constructs, understandings and anxieties and with each experience these will be reinforced or modified. It is the unique and dynamic nature of this interplay between these factors and the learning context that presents the greatest challenge to the usefulness of generalised profiles of adult learners. It also provides the rationale for grounding explanations of learning in specific situations with specific individuals (Entwistle, 1988: 56).

Learners' Reflections

The following quotes are from adult learners reflecting on factors they consider had a significant impact on the nature of their learning experience in particular formal and/or non-formal programmes.

The first, from a postgraduate student, is about her learning experience at a New Zealand university. It illustrates the situational nature of learning experiences, the way an individual's frame of reference is modified by experience and how this in turn impacts on the next experience.

> My undergraduate degree was undertaken by correspondence, the only contact with other students occurring at vacation courses. Working in isolation, for the 8 years it took to obtain that degree had a definite effect on me I found, when I began to take Masters classes at Canterbury where weekly tutorials were the operational mode.
>
> I am now in my 3rd year with this degree and these are my experiences now. How I feel and how I learn have been considerably affected though by those formative years with the undergraduate degree. I have noticed that I am one of the quieter members of the

group and don't have the skills (or lack of courtesy) to interrupt when others are speaking to voice my opinion. As this seems to be the accepted norm I am quite often unheard, again, this alters my experience. ... I feel as though I need to be heard sometimes because this helps me link into the topics and to apply meaning.

(Part-time masters student)

This case describes a learner's experience in a formal educational programme. It is likely that the same individual would report markedly different experiences in the non-formal programmes she has participated in. The explanations for the limited parallels between these forms of education are various, not least being the relative prominence and style of the assessment procedures. In formal education the primacy of assessment has a significant effect on the learner-task interface, moulding and limiting the relationship between teachers and learners and providing an extrinsic focus to motivate students.

One adult learner made the following comparison between her university and night school hobby classes, illustrating how the assessment can affect motivation:

I am always looking for the most economical means of passing the university classes I'm enrolled in. When I'm doing a course at the local [night] school though it's different. Then I get carried away and let interest direct me. I find myself going much deeper into things, asking more questions. At uni [sic] ... all I want to do is pass. I only ask if I think I'll need to know for an assignment or exam. Sometimes I get interested but I never have time to get into it.

(Full-time undergraduate university student)

This learner is behaving quite differently in her university classes compared to her hobby class. For her, the motivation to pass her university courses has supplanted the desire to pursue an interest in what she is learning and has contributed to the creation of two distinct learning experiences.

Other elements of the learning context, such as the teacher, also have an important influence on an individual's learning experience. When the teacher's behaviour is not consistent with the learner's expectations this can engender responses from the learner that either directly or indirectly reduces the quality of the learning experience. Morrison's (1992) study of 449 adult learners involved in teaching either in a tertiary institution or in the community in Auckland provides an insight into some of the dimensions of teacher behaviour that learners perceive as either positively or negatively influencing their learning experience. His study does not explore the specific effects of each dimension on the experience of learning but the following comments made by learners in various adult education programmes in Christchurch illustrate some of the ways the teacher's behaviour affects the learning experience:

> It's good the way the tutor just let's you get on with it. You have room to work at your own pace and just get help when you need it. I feel like I'm in control – it's a project I'm doing rather than a class I'm attending. I set my own goals and then break these down into tasks for each night. I really use the tutor as a resource, you know, someone to check my work or suggest the best technique to use.
> (Student attending a polytechnic year-long craft course)

> I went along to this Introduction to Computers class but I found I just didn't get anything out of it. The guy running it seemed to be such a disorganised thinker. He jumped all over the place and I just couldn't make sense of it all. I couldn't put the ideas together so I'd go home with words like RAM and bits and bytes running around in my head but they didn't mean anything. And he gave such long-winded explanations to the few people who bothered to ask questions. I gave up in the end ... it was easier than feeling frustrated and confused.
> (Student attending a polytechnic short course)

> The two group leaders were great. They would explain a skill and then role play how it could be used. I was able to grasp the technique so much better when they did that. It gave me something to remember ... something I could keep in my mind's eye. If they just talked and then got us to role play the technique it was never as easy. When they did a role play I could use it as a model for my behaviour in our role play.
> (Participant in a community-based assertiveness course)

> I get really scared when the lecturer says 'you'll find this straightforward' and then I don't. I feel I must be dumb and maybe I'm out of my depth and shouldn't have come anyway.
> (Mature, full-time, undergraduate, university student)

These accounts illustrate the powerful influence the person facilitating a learning experience can have on how the adult learner feels and acts. They also make an important point; that learners are able to reflect on their experience when learning. This is a valuable source of data which is often overlooked. It is the author's view that research should seek to elicit these reflections and provide frameworks for interpreting them. The next section looks at three factors that research suggests should be included in such frameworks.

Three Key Factors from Research

Learning Approach

Overseas, over the last three decades, a number of researchers have pursued idiographic explanations of adult learning, examining the learner-task interface from the learner's perspective. In so doing they have sought to understand the uniqueness of learners' experiences rather than derive general laws and conclusions (Ramsden, 1985: 52) and have contributed to a renewed interest in the experience of learning.

The most widely quoted studies were undertaken by a group of researchers at Gothenburg University in the early 1970s (e.g. Fransson, 1977; Marton and Säljö, 1976a; 1976b). These studies found a relationship between a learner's level of processing and their intention in a particular learning situation. When a learner's intention was to remember what was studied, surface-level[1] processing was employed. In contrast when their intention was to understand what was being studied, deep-level[2] processing was employed. The combined intention and processing level was termed an approach, either surface or deep.

It was found that the different approaches produced different learning experiences as well as qualitatively different outcomes. Deep approaches achieved more complex learning outcomes than surface ones. The findings of a study at Lincoln University (Mills, 1991) confirmed this relationship between approach and outcome but suggested that, for individual learners, the relationship was mediated by a number of personal and situational factors such as those addressed in the quotes on pages 287–289 of this chapter.

Over the last 20 years, studies at Lancaster University and several universities in Australia have also examined adult learners' levels of processing and learning approaches, although questionnaires rather than the phenomenographic[3] techniques used in the Gothenburg studies were generally used. One such questionnaire, the ASI (Approaches to Studying Inventory) (Ramsden, 1983) has been used in several studies of adult learners in New Zealand. Willis (1989) used it to classify students' learning approaches in a study which examined the relationship between learning approach and involvement in academic study. This study found that a learner's learning approach, as defined by the ASI, has an important influence on the type and level of involvement the student has in their courses and therefore the nature of their experiences.

In another study of adults enrolled in two diploma courses and one certificate course at the Central Institute of Technology, Clift and Willis (1986) investigated the relationship between motivation and the predisposition to use deep or surface processing which suggested that motivation and quality of approach appear to be related through a complex relationship with a number of other factors.

A similar questionnaire, the Study Process Questionnaire (SPQ), developed by Biggs (1987) in Australia, was used in a study by Nuich (1990) of the effect of vocational motives on the study strategies of first-year students at Auckland University. Nuich found that, contrary to expectation, these motives were not necessarily associated with surface approaches (as defined by the SPQ). She found that other motivational variables, but notably the assessment methods and the demands associated with these, were significant in promoting surface approaches.

Notions of Learning

One factor deserves to be singled out from the many that influence learning experiences because of the powerful effect it has on many of the other factors, including learning approach. This is the notion a learner has about the nature of learning and knowledge. Van Rossum and Schenk (1984) found that those learners who saw learning as a process of remembering and reproducing knowledge were more likely to report a surface learning approach than those who saw learning as a constructive process, involving the abstraction of meaning or interpretation. This relationship between notions of learning and approach was also detected in the Lincoln University study (Mills, 1991). In this study, the link was not as consistently demonstrated, however, suggesting that other factors modify the effect of a learner's notion of learning on their approach to learning.

In the United States, two notable studies by Perry (1970) and a team including Clinchy (1989) have shown that not only do students' hold different notions of learning and knowledge, these notions change as an individual progresses through their studies. Furthermore, Clinchy has shown that the process of change and the notions cannot be assumed to be the same for men and women.

In New Zealand, Baer-Doyle (1991) examined the nature of a group of women studying extramurally through Massey University and found that for some of these women their notions of knowledge and learning resulted in learning experiences which actually marginalised them as learners. She also found that these learners' notions of knowledge and learning could not be understood without understanding the learner's life history.

Similarly, in a study of retired couples in a middle-class suburb of Christchurch (Mills, 1989) it was found that the participants' notions of learning in formal educational settings effectively prevented them from accessing such educational opportunities. In the course of 114 learning projects, nine non-formal educational activities were undertaken but not one formal programme.

Just as Baer-Doyle found her respondents, behaviour was shaped by epistemologies that were defined by their life histories, so too was the behaviour of the respondents in this study. These retired New Zealanders' notions about learning was greatly influenced by their previous formal educational experiences. For several these experiences had been curtailed by World War II, while for others the war had provided educational opportunities that they would not otherwise have had. Even for those who had positive memories of what they had achieved in their formal studies, the images they carried with them were incompatible with how they perceived they could best achieve their learning goals. For this reason, fulfilment of learning goals almost invariably involved informal means; a finding which supports findings from an earlier New Zealand study by Battersby (1986).

Learning Style

Learning style has been defined as 'an individual's characteristic and consistent approach to organising and processing information' (Tennant, 1988: 89). Over 21 different style dimensions have been identified, often in the form of polar opposites (e.g. categoriser-conceptualiser). The identification of each dimension has usually been accompanied by the development of an inventory which purports to measure the degree to which an individual exhibits behaviours which correlate with that particular style dimension. Many adult educators have been drawn to the inventories as a means of identifying individual differences in information processing among their students.

Such inventories receive favourable reviews from educators and learners alike (e.g. Wicks, 1989; 1991). However, they can be a 'double-edged sword.' They have the advantage of producing information which has considerable intuitive appeal and which is relatively easy to relate to observable behaviours in a way that highlights individual differences. However, by emphasising the consistencies in learning behaviour (Ramsden, 1985), they provide limited scope for capturing the way learners' behaviour varies according to the situation in which they are learning. Because they also tend to address only a few dimensions when in fact a person's learning style is an aggregation of many stylistic dimensions (Dixon, 1985; Eison, 1984), they also encourage a simplistic view of learning processes. There is also doubt about the construct validity and reliability of some inventories (Ferrell, 1983; Perry and Delahaye, 1987).

Style inventories may have limitations but this does not mean that learning style dimensions should be ignored. There is general acceptance that they are important factors in creating a person's learning experience and that they are not incompatible with the view that learning behaviour is context specific (Wapner, 1978: 75–76). What is needed is further research on the interplay between style and specific contexts.

Style, like learning approach and notions of learning, is a useful window through which adult educators and learners can observe the experience of learning. The various views these concepts offer need to be integrated into a framework which addresses the range of factors that impact on the learner-task interface. This would ensure a comprehensive and balanced view is obtained which takes into account the individual and contextually situated nature of learning.

Summary

This chapter has suggested there is a need to go beyond the generalised profiles of the adult learner and seek an understanding of learning at an individual and contextual level. It has explored a number of factors identified by learners and researchers which affect how individual and contextual factors interact at the learner-task interface to create the learning experience. In so doing, the intention has been to highlight the need for more research activity at this interface so that more meaningful frameworks for understanding learning can be created. This is particularly desirable in New Zealand given the state of our literature-base on adult learning processes.

Future Directions

To pursue frameworks which address the individual and contextual nature of learning, a reorientation of the way research is conducted is called for. Research will need to be situated in classrooms, workshops and studios so that the dynamic interplay between context and individual can be accessed. The adult educator is ideally placed to undertake such research. For many this would require a major shift in perspective but in reality it may require little more than renaming or refining aspects of their current practice.

Many aspects of teaching involve gathering data on students' learning experience. Teachers regularly ask students to give their views and interpretations, explain what they are doing or how they arrived at a particular outcome or identify problems they are encountering. These views, interpretations, explanations and concerns are data which, when systematically collected within a coherent research framework, could contribute greatly to our understanding of the experience of learning.

The best opportunity for educators to collect data on learning is the course evaluation. In many instances, because of the scope such evaluation provides for focusing on learning behaviour, it would require very little to mould evaluation activities into a deliberate, research programme that tapped into the learner's experience. Because course evaluation is now a feature of many adult education programmes throughout the fourth sector, this would save considerable amounts of potentially valuable data from going to waste. It would also encourage adult educators to cast themselves as researchers and 'scholars of their students' learning' (Ramsden, 1988: 13).

Notes

1. Surface approaches are characterised by a focus on the detail (i.e. the sign), an intention to memorise what is being studied, reproductive strategies and extrinsic motivation.
2. Deep approaches are characterised by a focus on what is signified (i.e. the meaning), an intention to understand, transformational strategies and intrinsic motivation.
3. Phenomenography is a situation-based approach to learning research which involves examining the learning behaviour associated with a particular task from the learner's perspective.

References

Baer-Doyle, T.F. (1991), 'Correspondence Education, Personal Epistemologies and Curriculum Initiatives', Paper presented at the Annual Conference of the Distance Education Association of New Zealand, Wellington.

Battersby, D. (1986), 'Continuing Education for the Elderly in New Zealand', *New Zealand Journal of Adult Learning*, vol. 18, no. 1, pp. 22–32.

Biggs, J. (1987), *Study Process Questionnaire (SPQ), Manual*, Hawthorn, Victoria: ACER.

Boshier, R. (1980), *Towards a Learning Society: New Zealand Adult Education in Transition*, Vancouver: Learningpress Ltd.

Boud, D. and Walker, D. (1991), *Experience and Learning: Reflection at Work*, Geelong, Victoria: Deakin University Press.

Clift, J. and Willis, D. (1986), 'How Do Your Students Study?', *Tutor*, vol. 33, pp. 14–20.

Clinchy, B.M. (1989), 'Issues of Gender in Teaching and Learning', *Journal of Excellence in College Teaching*, vol. 1, pp. 52–67.

Dixon, N. M. (1985), The implementation of learning style information. *Lifelong Learning,* vol. 9, no. 3, pp. 16–18, 26–29.

Eison, J. (1984), 'Researchers Examine Learning Styles', *APA Monitor,* vol. 15, no. 5, p. 34.

Entwistle, N. (1988), *Understanding Classroom Learning,* London: Hodder and Stoughton.

Ferrell, B.G. (1983), 'A Factor Analytic Comparison of Four Learning Style Instruments', *Journal of Educational Psychology,* vol. 75, no. 1, pp. 33–39.

Fransson, A. (1977), 'Qualitative Differences in Learning: Effects of Intrinsic Motivation and Extrinsic Test Anxiety on Process and Outcome', *British Journal of Educational Psychology,* vol. 47, pp. 224–257.

Marton, F. and Säljö, R. (1976a), 'On Qualitative Differences in Learning: I – Outcome and Process', *British Journal of Educational Psychology,* vol. 46, pp. 4–11.

Marton, F. and Säljö, R. (1976b), 'Learning Processes and Strategies: – II Outcome as a Function of the Learner's Conception of the Task', *British Journal of Educational Psychology,* vol. 46, pp. 115–127.

Mills, C.E. (1989), 'Learning Projects of Retired Couples', Unpublished dissertation.

Mills, C.E. (1991), 'The Nature and Variability of Tertiary Students', Learning Approaches and Test Outcomes When Learning from Text', Unpublished MA thesis, University of Canterbury.

Morrison, A.A. (1992), 'Learner's Perspectives of Teacher Quality', *New Zealand Journal of Adult Learning,* vol. 20, no. 1, pp. 65–76.

Nuich, S. (1990), 'The Effect of Vocational Motives Upon Study Strategies of First Year University Students', Unpublished MA thesis, University of Auckland.

Perry, C. and Delahaye, B. (1987), 'Learning Styles and Student Experiences in Management Courses. *Higher Education Research and Development,* vol. 6, no. 2, pp. 175–184.

Perry, W.G. (1970), *Forms of Intellectual and Ethical Development in the College Years: A Scheme,* New York: Holt, Rinehart and Winston.

Ramsden, P. (1983), *The Lancaster Approaches to Studying and Course Perceptions Questionnaire,* Oxford: Paul Ramsden and Educational Methods Unit, Oxford Polytechnic.

Ramsden, P. (1985), 'Student Learning Research: Retrospect and Prospect', *Higher Education Research and Development,* vol. 4, no. 1, pp. 51–69.

Ramsden, P. (1988), 'Studying Learning: Improving Teaching', in Ramsden, P. (ed.), *Improving Learning; New Perspectives,* Great Britain: Kogan Page.

Tennant, M. (1988), *Psychology and Adult Learning,* London: Routledge.

Thorburn, R. (1986), 'Research Revisited: A Departmental Look at an Ongoing Research Problem in Continuing Education', Paper presented at 1986 NZARE Conference.

Van Rossum, E.J. and Schenk, S.M. (1984), 'The Relationship Between Learning Conception, Study Strategy and Learning Outcome', *British Journal of Educational Psychology*, vol. 54, pp. 73–83.

Wapner, S. (1978), 'Process and Context in the Conception of Cognitive Style', in Messick, S. and Associates, *Individuality in Learning,* San Francisco: Jossey-Bass, pp. 79–89.

Wicks, A. (1989), 'Use of the Learning Styles Questionnaire with Tutors', *Industrial and Commercial Training*, vol. 21, pp. 24–25.

Wicks, A. (1991), 'Learning Styles and Distance Educators', *Industrial and Commercial Training,* vol. 23, pp. 8–9.

Willis, D.M. (1989), 'Involvement in Academic Study: An Investigation of the Nature, Effects and Development of Involvement in University Courses', Unpublished PhD thesis, Victoria University of Wellington.

20

The Education of Adult and Community Educators

Brian Findsen

Introduction

This chapter entails a description and analysis of selected features of the 'education' (predominantly 'training') of adult educators in this country. In particular, a recent historical perspective of the training of adult educators is presented (using the 1977 National Council of Adult Education Working Party Report as its benchmark), a snapshot of current practice is portrayed and selected issues analysed.

The title for this chapter is by no means uncontentious. I have used 'education' in preference to 'training' for several reasons. First, the term education suggests that adult learners are concerned about developing themselves holistically (intellectually, emotionally, cognitively, physically, spiritually) rather than in a specific technical domain. Second, the term training is too narrow and too mechanistic to encompass the diverse array of activities in which adult educators engage. Third, education subsumes training. Adult and community education is a vast field which includes training and human resource development among its subfields. The position is well encapsulated by Jahns (cited in Grabowski, 1982: 99):

> Training encompasses those acts, events and episodes in which people engage to improve their performance in specific job-related

tasks. Education prepares people for relatively undifferentiated roles, positions and work settings; training is concerned with an individual's performance in a specific position at a given work setting.

Hence, while this chapter deals with the education of fourth sector workers, much emphasis is given here to training as this domain has received most attention by both practitioners and scholars.

As indicated in earlier chapters, the term 'adult and community education' is problematic too. It needs to be acknowledged that adult and community educators are a very diverse subpopulation of society. Educators in this fourth sector are not easily characterised, but are frequently categorised according to their primary role – tutor (facilitator, teacher); programme planner (curriculum developer); administrator; counsellor (Darkenwald and Merriam, 1982). In reality, most adult educators occupy several roles simultaneously especially in a country such as New Zealand where specialisation within a profession has been slower to materialise. There are very few full-time 'professionals' who consciously perceive of themselves as adult and community educators and fewer still who have undertaken systematic training for these positions. Many practitioners in this sector are oblivious to the fact that they are part of a large social movement. Houle (1970) recognised that workers in this diffuse field could be categorised and represented diagrammatically, in terms of actual numbers, into a pyramid as follows (cited by Caldwell in Grabowski, 1982: 2):

> Divided horizontally into three levels, the pyramid has as its base the largest group of people, those who serve as volunteers. At the intermediate level of the pyramid, Houle identifies a smaller group of people who, as part of their paid employment, combine adult education functions with other responsibilities. The smallest group of people at the apex of the pyramid are the full-time specialists whose primary concern and occupation is adult education.

This situation is not unique to the United States. Universally the fourth sector is dependent upon a vast range of volunteers, primarily women, whose labour is provided free and is largely hidden from society. (Most governments are happy to leave this situation unhindered since it saves the state from facing financial and moral responsibility for many initiatives in welfare and social support.) Given the three-tiered nature of the sector, what are the implications for education of its workers? Before addressing this question, I will provide an historical backdrop of recent developments in the education and training of adult and community educators in Aotearoa/New Zealand.

The Education of Adult and Community Educators

Historical Antecedents

Training and the Nature of the Sector

There is scant literature on the education of workers in this field. Busy practitioners have seldom taken the time to write about their 'training needs'; much of the development of staff has been in-house and inaccessible to others; the need for adult and community educators to keep themselves refreshed professionally has not been a high priority, given that the ethos of most workers in the sector is to serve others first and to look after one's own educational needs second. Whatever the reasons, the development of training and professional development for adult educators has been haphazard and poorly documented.

In the New Zealand context, the most significant endeavour to get to grips with education and training for practitioners in this sector took place in 1975 when the then National Council of Adult Education (NCAE) convened a working party to analyse the plight of the education of adult (or continuing) educators. In his preface to the 1977 Report, John Clift identified that the conditions for inquiry were ripe:

> It was perhaps providential that the Working Party was not convened earlier. It was only since about 1974 that tertiary education has been clearly seen as part of continuing education; only since 1972 that the apparent division between vocation and non-vocational continuing education has been considerably eroded; only since then that the sense of common purpose within the field of continuing education has begun to outgrow old distinctions.

Clift rightly observed that the sector had begun to crystallise as a separate entity from compulsory schooling and that the links with higher education were at a crucial stage in terms of leadership in the provision of learning and training opportunities for sector workers. In retrospect, it is possible for us now to look back at the mid to late 1970s as a time of optimism and positive anticipation for the sector – the advent of Community Colleges (later to shrink back into a narrower technical orientation); the beginnings of the Rural Education Activities Programmes (REAP); the experimentation with Community Learning Centres in selected secondary schools – in which this Working Party played a significant role. In short, the education of adult and community educators must always be seen in the context of the development of the field itself and the wider social milieu of which it is part (Brookfield, 1988: 279).

The Working Party on Training of Continuing Educators

Context

The terms of reference for the *Working Party on Training of Continuing Educators* were as follows (Clift, 1977: 4):

- review provisions for organisers and teachers in continuing education (including industrial training) at present available in New Zealand
- relate needs for training for continuing education to needs and current provision for training in similar fields including other sectors of education, community work and recreation
- make recommendations to the National Council for the development of training programmes to meet present and likely future needs in continuing education.

Given that the terms of reference were very broad, it is not surprising that 44 recommendations were made to cover areas of tutor training, programme planner training, awards and qualifications, resources and incentives and career opportunities. In addressing the responsibilities of then existing providers, the report traversed the tasks ahead for secondary school extension, universities (internal and extension departments, including Massey University's extramural operation), technical institutes and polytechnics, the Correspondence School, Radio New Zealand (through the now-defunct Continuing Education Unit) and public libraries. In terms of identifying key voluntary organisations in which training was to be promoted, the Report specified the Workers' Educational Association (WEA) (now without government funding), Countrywomen's Co-ordinating Committee, the Playcentre Movement, Marriage Guidance Council, Wairarapa Community Action Programme (now defunct) and Nelson Community Education Service (since subsumed by Nelson Polytechnic) and Learning Exchanges (now largely defunct). Within vocational training, the possible roles for the Industrial Training Service, the Ministry of Defence and the Ministry of Agriculture and Fisheries were also discussed. In the economic and social reforms of the 1980s and 1990s some of these players have ceased to exist; others have significantly changed their character in response to New Right ideology and demands; others have continued but struggled through lack of funding (e.g. the WEA). Perhaps most importantly, the National Council of Adult Education itself was crippled by the National government of the early 1980s and today only survives in remnants (in part through the functions of the National Resource Centre for Adult and Community Learning (NRC).

Levels of Training

I believe that a very important conceptual aspect of the working party's deliberations was the identification of a four-tier training schema: induction; initial training; basic training; and post-basic training. These four stages of training for sector workers roughly matched the continuum from volunteer worker, to paraprofessional to full-time professional. The first two stages for new recruits were geared at equipping the tutor with the rudiments of the adult teaching situation and would most appropriately be undertaken within an organisation usually using its own personnel and resources. Post-basic training 'would be more substantial than initial training with a minimum of 40 hours course contact' and would normally equip the individual to work 'effectively without requiring supervision' and to have the capacity to work across a variety of agencies (Clift, 1977: 46). The final tier of 'post-basic training' would be more explicitly linked to a credentialling structure. In the Working Party's view (1977: 48):

> Qualifications should be available to teachers of adults who wish to develop their competence to an advanced stage without necessarily abandoning teaching for administration. Such qualification would normally be offered by a tertiary institution.

So the stage was set by the Working Party for a multi-level system of training for adult and community educators but its implementation was to be hindered by political manoeuvrings and inadequate resourcing.

Development Officer Position

One of the positive consequences of the Working Party's Report was the establishment by the National Council of the Training Development Officer position, occupied by Ron Hoskin from 1978 into the early 1980s. (The Report had advocated the appointment of at least two such positions.) This was a time of considerable optimism and innovation in the fourth sector. One of the initiatives developed by the Training Officer was the development of the trainer of trainers model for regionally based workers. For example, the Centre for Continuing Education, University of Waikato, helped to organise an annual series of programme planners' workshops in Rotorua during August, the impetus of which was derived from the NCAE and local networks. These regional workshops, with regional variation, were successfully conducted across other regions of Aotearoa/New Zealand but came to an end when resources dried up nationally.

The impact of the Training Development Officer's work was felt beyond the immediate home context as he cemented international relationships principally through workshops such as those conducted with the International Council for the Education of Adults (ICEA) or with the Asian South Pacific Bureau of Adult Education (ASPBAE). Since the demise of the NCAE and the four specialist officers (other appointments had been made in Maori language development, adult literacy and broadcasting), the opportunities for sustained international involvement in the training of adult educators have been left to sporadic contact via executive members of the New Zealand Association for Community and Continuing Education (NZACCE) and intermittent contact through visiting academics. A lack of funds has prevented any real constancy in relationships to develop and thus benefit the sector since that time.

A flurry of activity around the training of adult educators eventuated in the mid-1980s (as the NCAE realised it was on its last legs). In July of 1986, the National Council convened a workshop to identify current issues in the training of adult educators, the participants emerging from principal providers: universities, community colleges, high school community education, REAPs, Work Skills programmes, Te Ataarangi, the Adult Reading and Learning Assistance Federation and the Voluntary Welfare Agency Training Board. At the heart of the workshop (Galloway and Gordon, 1986: 3) was a review of practice in the training of fourth sector workers since the 1977 Report. Amid the 18 emergent recommendations (many of which echoed the earlier report), there were signs of significant social change. Two important recommendations were pinpointed: the need to develop guidelines on bicultural issues; and the growing centrality of distance education as an effective mode of training, especially for fourth sector personnel, many of whom work in relative geographical and professional isolation. While the recommendations of this workshop were positive, the mechanisms for their achievement were vague. As with many sets of recommendations which personnel within this field have established for future action, they are seldom supported at the national level either through a sufficiently strong infrastructure or through policy related to government's priorities. Too often, recommendations amount to statements of idealism unsupported by effective mechanisms to deliver social action.

Resources

One recommendation – to prepare a 'map' of adult learning, training and development opportunities which exist in New Zealand and the Pacific – was partially implemented just prior to the workshop through the publication of *Training Tracks* (NCAE, 1986: 9). This publication was 'a directory of development and training opportunities for adult educators and voluntary agency personnel throughout New Zealand', the result of a joint initiative between the NCAE and the Voluntary Welfare Agency Training Board. Its contents included regional listings of providers, national organisations (e.g. New Zealand Association of Training and Development, Race Relations Conciliator), a list of trainers and consultants, resources, youth training, peace education (and the promise of women's opportunities and Maori skills development). This publication was commendable as an example of organisational collaboration but unfortunately not much time had to pass to render it outdated.

Specific printed or audiovisual resources geared for the education of fourth-sector educators have been intermittent and seldom integrated into a more comprehensive plan. However, for many years the NCAE demonstrated considerable leadership in this arena, especially as publisher of the popular *Paragraphs About Continuing Education* (*PACE*) and the more academic journal, *Continuing Education in New Zealand*. These two publications, operating in tandem, provided the scattered populace with invaluable information and views about developments throughout the country. During the 1980s and 1990s, the NZACCE through its annual conference and regular publication of *Akina* has provided a necessary supplement. In more recent times, this publication has assumed a more regional character (sometimes based around a theme) as its editorship has circulated through branches. For a period in the mid-to-late 1980s there was little available on a consistent basis at a national level after the dismantling of the NCAE until the subsequent (slight) rise of the National Resource Centre (NRC).

One of the successes of the NRC has been the responsibility it has taken for the publication of *Lifelong Learning in Aotearoa*. While similar in some ways to *PACE,* it has brought a definite 1990s look to portrayal and analysis of the fourth sector. Unfortunately, due to financial constraint, it has been replaced in 1996 by a newsletter. Nevertheless, the rebirth nationally of a more academic avenue for informed discussion in *The New Zealand Journal of Adult Learning* has created a situation of at least three sources of information and debate for people in the field.

During the period since the 1977 Report, the training of fourth-sector educators has followed pathways similar to those advocated, although the distribution of opportunities has been uneven. At the induction and initial levels most agencies have provided elementary or survival skills and knowledge to their personnel, and many have successfully instigated their own training and development (such as Marriage Guidance, renamed Relationship Services in 1995, with government support). However, as the level of sophistication of professional development increases, it is less likely that providers can or should meet these demands. Costs of training professionals can be prohibitive and there is considerable wisdom in professionals meeting across discipline boundaries (Yerka in Grabowski, 1982: 66).

Expansion of Training Provision

At a more advanced level, the tertiary education sector has provided many programmes of either pre-service or in-service varieties, predominantly the latter. This proliferation of providers has been given tacit encouragement by government in allowing 'consumers' choice in the free market. Opportunities for courses in adult and continuing education exist in many locations: Centres for Continuing Education at universities; polytechnics (e.g. the Centre for Professional Development at the Auckland Institute of Technology); the Open Polytechnic of New Zealand; Massey University's Extramural Studies; the Advanced Studies for Teachers Unit; Colleges of Education (e.g. the Performance Improvement Centre at the Auckland College of Education). These programmes vary in emphasis and goals, but there appears to be no systematic inventory of these post-basic programmes in existence. In fact, it is long overdue that a survey of training opportunities in the fourth sector be undertaken. At the more advanced level of full degree and masters level programmes, there are varying components available in the university system, most often located in education departments.

Issues in the Training of Fourth Sector Educators

What is Appropriate Training for Educators?

Conceptual Models

One of the few attempts to develop a conceptual framework for analysing the training of trainers and fourth-sector educators belongs to Boshier (1985: 9) in a special issue of *Convergence*. The purpose of this model is explained as:

> The intent of the model is not to diminish commonalities that pervade the training of all educators, nor to diminish the extent to which socio-cultural factors shape training content and processes. It merely provides a framework within which to consider issues that impinge upon the training of those in different parts of the field who occupy different roles.

In essence, Boshier's model classifies adult educators according to the following:

1. The outcomes engendered by the education they sponsor or work with [i.e. whether the educator is concerned primarily with technical competence

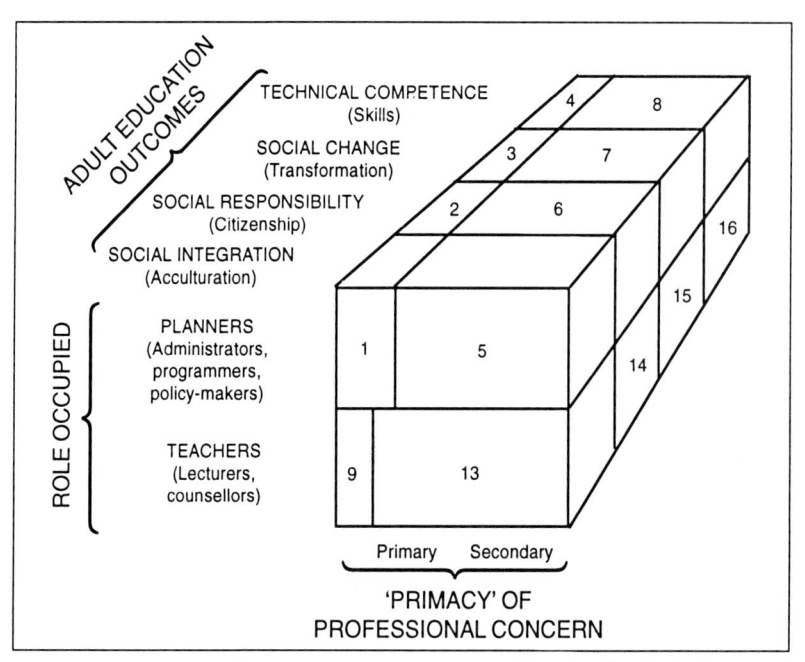

Figure 21.1: Conceptual Framework for Analysing the Training of Adult Educators.

```
                    TECHNICAL COMPETENCE
  ADULT EDUCATION       (Skills)
     OUTCOMES       SOCIAL CHANGE
                     (Transformation)
                 SOCIAL RESPONSIBILITY
                      (Citizenship)
                 SOCIAL INTEGRATION
                    (Acculturation)

                    PLANNERS
   ROLE           (Administrators,
 OCCUPIED          programmers,
                   policy-makers)

                    TEACHERS
                   (Lecturers,
                   counsellors)

                Primary    Secondary
                    'PRIMACY' OF
                PROFESSIONAL CONCERN
```

(Cells numbered 1–16 in the 3D grid.)

(Reproduced from Boshier, R., 1985: 10)

(skills), developing social responsibility (citizenship), social integration (acculturation) or social change (transformation)].
2. The role they play in the field (planner or teacher).
3. The extent to which adult education is their primary or secondary professional concern.

Significantly, Boshier sees the training of educators in a very broad context with special reference to the philosophical basis of the institution, programme or educator as a fundamental thread to incorporate in an appropriate curriculum.

Training Content – What is to be Taught?

Given the array of volunteers, part-time paid workers and full-time professionals in this fragmented sector, what constitutes appropriate training and education?

Should each niche within the sector (e.g. adult literacy; school-based community educators) have its own programme? Should there be deliberate mixing of people from different subcultures within the sector in training? Questions like these have been asked around the Western world (for example Boshier, 1985; Candy, 1981; Elsdon 1975, 1984; Grabowski, 1982; Jarvis and Chadwick, 1991) without definitive answers. At a pragmatic level, as the 1977 Report confirmed, the high costs of training usually mean that educators miss out altogether or receive rudimentary training in their own settings, perhaps bringing in 'outside experts' as necessary. Philosophically, it makes good sense to prepare educators in the immediate context where they work. Jarvis and Chadwick point out (1991: 3) that since the majority of adult educators are part-time workers or volunteers, this arrangement is hardly likely to be otherwise. Importantly, too, educators of adults are often members of other occupations and professions and may not perceive training in this sphere as a professional activity.

At a post-basic (advanced) level of training it is quite common for people from different locations in the fourth-sector matrix to be 'professionally developed', 'trained' or 'educated' together. In my own experiences of this level of provision (in the Certificate in Continuing Education at the University of Waikato and the Certificate in Adult Education at the University of Auckland) the mixing of people has both advantages and limitations but usually the benefits are considerable. More specifically, there are at least two broad types of adult learners in such programmes:

Type 1: Those who work as volunteers or paid part-time workers in an adult/community education agency (e.g. community house). Usually, but not always, this person will have no or minimal familiarity with 'university culture'. This is a disadvantage in terms of meeting the academic demand of certificate programmes but frequently these people have extensive grounded experience.

Type 2: Fully paid professionals (e.g. trained nurses who find themselves in a Human Resource Development (HRD) role) who hold a first or subsequent degree who find themselves in a position of responsibility in an educative role. Such people often have confidence in their study skills ability but need more critical reflection on their work.

The motivation and goals of these two types of educators are frequently quite different, but they are united in their quest for a credential and they have a common footing in the sector. The former person can bring plenty of grassroots experience and informal learning into the situation; the latter person may more readily grasp theoretical issues which can be shared with others.

Assuming that the above scenario still applies, what is the 'right' content and 'best' methodology for the situation? In response to the first question, Elsdon (1984: 29) after his extensive research in Britain of equivalent training programmes, remarked that the content is usually based on:

(a) the development of knowledge of psychological, conceptual and sociological and philosophical principles of adult learning and of a personal and operational understanding of their relevance to and implications for the practice of work with adults
(b) studies in the characteristics and motives of learners and their relation to subject content and group relationships
(c) curriculum planning and course design
(d) studies of the significance of interpersonal relationships in the learning context and of the formation of attitudes in teachers and learners and of their influence.

As a New Zealand point of comparison, the Certificate in Continuing Education (University of Waikato) offers the following core modules:

- Adult Learning and Group Dynamics
- Foundations of Adult/Continuing Education
- Teaching and Learning Methods
- Programme Planning

Thereafter adult students choose two of the following three modules to complete the six-paper qualification:

- Community Development
- Issues in Continuing Education
- Individual Project.

The point is that what constitutes the essence of a study of adult and community education as an area of study is not as controversial as it might first appear, providing that local conditions and interpretations prevail, i.e. the above skeletal framework provides the parameters in which New Zealand knowledge may be constructed and made culturally relevant.

Methodology – How is it Taught?

Given the above views on the curriculum for the education of fourth-sector educators, the accompanying major issue resolves around appropriate methodology. Again, Elsdon (1984: 31–32) provides insightful comment. In his survey of the methodologies used in situations such as the above certificate, he refers to three broad tendencies, abbreviated here:

(a) *Concept-led* courses will tend to follow a programme that begins with the consideration of concepts underlying adult learning, teaching and training. They will usually do this through the study of key texts, their translation into the course members' own practical experience and their field problems.
(b) *Experience or problem-led* courses will tend to take their inception from the analysis of members' own practical experience as adult learners and educators and from the particular problems related to learning and training which they identify in the process.
(c) *Process-led* courses tend to concentrate on the actual training group of course members and on the interpersonal and individual processes within this as a paradigm of any learning or training group.

Each of the above tendencies, if used unwisely or in extreme ways, is likely to highly distort the value of the learning experience. A balance of these tendencies is likely to achieve better results; an emphasis on one methodology in a particular circumstance may be merited.

Principles of 'Best Practice'

In an ideal situation, Elsdon argues that 'best practice' in training occurs under certain conditions:

- if methods are *experiential* then they are not just talked about but experienced, practised, observed, evaluated
- there needs to be a clear *articulation* by learners of their knowledge or understanding, i.e. it is a conscious adoption of 'new learning'
- learning should be *field-related* so that participants have the opportunity to undertake practical work amidst the programme
- courses need to be *intensive* if appropriate attitude change is to occur; trainers often achieve this through demanding involvement, effort and active input from learners.

In support of Elsdon's case (especially the second point), Candy (1981: viii) argues that traditional adult teacher training has suffered from the following weaknesses:

1. It fails to account for individual predispositions, informal preparation for teaching for new entrants into the service
2. Too often it is carried out at the intellectual, cognitive, 'public' level; not allowing participants to inspect their own beliefs and assumptions about teaching and learning
3. Knowledge about how adults learn is not carried out in practice.

Candy develops the thesis that programmes such as the certificates should place greater emphasis on 'the phenomenological universe, or personally constructed reality, of the individual teacher' (1981: 12).

While principles espoused by Elsdon (1975, 1984), Candy (1981) and Boshier (1985) can be useful at multiple levels of training, ultimately what is appropriate to teach and how it is to be taught are judgements made in the light of numerous factors which would normally include: prevailing societal/ organisational conditions; the goals of the programme; the expressed needs of learners; the expertise available in content and process knowledge of trainers; and the existence of suitable back-up resources.

Much of the valuable training of adult educators in Aotearoa/New Zealand already employs many of the effective principles espoused by Elsdon (1984). This observation is reinforced by Boshier and Horton's remarks about the training of adult educators in Australasia (1985: 112):

> The most innovative work appears to be in sub-degree or non-credit programmes. Short programmes designed to train aboriginal [sic] educators, literacy workers, Maori community development workers, community educators, distance educators and Third world educators occur independently of each other, but exemplify the best of the do-it-yourself and egalitarian ethos which is congruent with the ideas of Freire and advocates of participatory research and training.

Training and Professionalisation

The need for greater education and training of fourth sector workers is almost self-evident. As Boshier points out (1985: 3):

> The plea for properly trained personnel has become a full-fledged chorus in most parts of the world. Even recalcitrant governments are coming to see that an educated citizenry is an essential corollary of economic development, national unity and cultural wellbeing.

But what is feared by many is that the heightened need for qualifications will push the sector into a credentialled profession. Some might argue that to deny anyone the right to practise as an adult or community educator because of a lack of training or credential is tantamount to destruction of the collaborative humanistic base of the movement. It might also be argued that the credentialling structures (as exemplified by the Framework of the New Zealand Qualifications Authority) set in place are thinly disguised mechanisms for social control and are largely self-serving for the increasing array of providers.

The hallmarks of a profession are delineated by Yerka (1981: 51) as the control of the content, if not the terms of the work; substantial autonomy and self-direction; control of the production and application of knowledge and skills; the adoption of a code of ethics in practice. If increased professionalisation leads to fewer people controlling the status and exchange of knowledge in the sector, then it should be resisted on the basis of upholding democratic ideals. On the other hand, if the professionalisation of the sector (in which training has a prominent role) leads to more ethical practices, then is it a negative trend? Given the proliferation of agencies involved in the training of fourth sector workers, how can people wanting such services be protected against 'charlatans', 'instant experts' and 'interlopers'?

My own position is that workers within the sector in Aotearoa/New Zealand need to be vigilant about creeping credentialism or educational inflation but also recognise that to deny opportunities for the education of its own workers is contrary to the whole notion of lifelong learning which the sector is trying to create for the entire society. One of the precious gifts the sector possesses in this country (as opposed to the situation in most others) is the immediacy of contact between academics and practitioners, volunteers and paid professionals, policy-makers and grassroots workers. Within the sector itself, stratification is minimal. Training and development of the sector's workers is now receiving a higher profile (in parallel with the situation in Australia – see Chapter 9 in *Come in Cinderella: The Emergence of Adult and Community Education*, 1991) though not as yet supported in legislation, at least for the industrial sector. While credentialism is almost inevitable throughout New Zealand society in line with government initiatives, it needs to be tempered by the continued valuing of non-credit courses and local education initiatives which do not translate into qualifications.

Conclusion

This chapter has identified many of the significant developments in the education and training of adult and community educators in Aotearoa/New Zealand. It has not been possible to be comprehensive. (See, for example, Walker, 1985, for discussion on the training of Maori adult educators. See, also, chapters in Part 1 of this book.) In particular, it has focused on the pivotal Working Party Report of 1977 as a benchmark for changes since then. While some of the recommendations have been implemented (usually in spite of government policy, for the sector has been perceived as an irritant in the education system), there is much yet to be actioned and reflected upon.

Two of many possible issues concerning the education and training of adult educators were selected for analysis. Given the growing number of providers of training opportunities, the question of what might constitute an appropriate curriculum is relevant, whatever the level of provision. The professionalisation of the sector, welcomed by some and resisted by others, remains a controversial issue. The role of training in this scenario is questionable – is it liberating or controlling in its effect or an exercise in compromise? Other important issues persist – to whom should priority of resources be allocated? What role is there for pre-service education and training? Should the training of fourth sector workers be competency-based? How does national policy in the sector promote or impede training? How do (lack of) career structures in the sector affect commitment to training? These are questions not addressed here but are open for future discussion and research.

References

Boshier, R. (1985), 'Conceptual Framework for Analyzing the Training of Trainers and Adult Educators', *Convergence*, vol. 28, no. s 3–4, pp. 3–22.

Boshier, R. and Horton, C. (1985), 'Training of Adult Educators in Oceania', *Convergence*, vol. 18, no. s 3–4, pp. 109–115. Caldwell (p. 2 of text), xxxx.

Brookfield, S.B. (ed.) (1988), *Training Educators of Adults*, New York: Routledge.

Candy, P.C. (1981), *Mirrors of the Mind: Personal Construct Theory in the Training of Adult Educators*, University of Manchester: Department of Adult and Higher Education.

Clift, J.C. (ed.) (1977), *Report of the Working Party on Training of Continuing Educators*, Wellington: National Council of Adult Education.

Darkenwald, G.G. and Merriam, S.B. (1982), *Adult Education: Foundations of Practice,* New York: Harper and Row Publishers.

Elsdon, K.T. (1975), *Training for Adult Education,* University of Nottingham: Department of Adult Education.

Elsdon, K.T. (1984), *The Training of Trainers*, Huntington Publishers Limited in conjunction with the University of Nottingham: Department of Adult Education.

Galloway, I. and Gordon, C. (1986), 'Report of the Workshop on the Current

Issues in the Training of Adult Educators', Wellington: National Council of Adult Education.

Grabowski, S.M. (ed.) (1982), *Preparing Educators of Adults*, San Francisco: Jossey-Bass.

Houle, C.O. (1970), 'The Educators of Adults', in Smith, R.M., Aker, G.F. and Kidd J.R. (eds), *Handbook of Adult Education*, New York: Macmillan.

Jahns, I.R. (1981), 'Training in Organisations', in Grabowski, S.M. (ed.), *Preparing Educators of Adults*, San Francisco: Jossey-Bass.

Jarvis, P. and Chadwick, A. (1991), *Training Adult Educators in Western Europe*, New York: Routledge.

National Council of Adult Education (NCAE) (1986), *Training Tracks*, Wellington: National Council of Adult Education and the Voluntary Welfare Agency Training Board.

Senate Standing Committee on Employment, Education and Training (1991), *Come in Cinderella: The Emergence of Adult and Community Education*, Canberra: Senate Printing Unit, Parliament House.

Walker, R. (1985), 'Training Maori Adult Educators in New Zealand', *Convergence*, vol. 18, no. s 3–4, pp. 123–125.

Yerka, B.L. (1981), 'Training Paraprofessional Instructors of Adults', in Grabowski, S.M. (ed.), *Preparing Educators of Adults*, San Francisco: Jossey-Bass.

21

Research and Evaluation

John Benseman

Definition and Purposes of Research

Research can be broadly defined as 'systematic or disciplined inquiry; that is, it is a purposeful, systematic process by which we know more about something than we did before engaging in the process' (Merriam, 1991: 43). As research knowledge is generated by a systematic process of documenting evidence (whether using qualitative or quantitative data), it is more likely to be informative and enlightening than knowledge generated from individual or even group opinion. While it is accepted that not all research is inherently insightful, educators of adults who make changes based on research evidence are much more likely to produce more effective practice than practitioners who base their practice on personal opinion about what might or might not be a 'good idea'. An important quality of research therefore lies in its ability to bring about improved practice and increased professional competence.

Given the potential contribution that research can make to the fourth sector of adult and community education, what has been achieved to date and what is the potential for its future development? This chapter provides an overview of these topics in relation first to research generally and then to evaluation.

Review of Previous Research in the Fourth Sector

Reviewing the research on continuing education (defined as educational provision for people who have left school, but excluding higher education) in 1980, Garrett, Paterson and Wagner concluded (1980: 357), 'From our point of view, the chief conclusion to be drawn is that the research available looks at best like a pattern of islands scattered in unknown seas ... we have merely begun to scratch the surface and to establish parameters within which future research can be carried out'. Some 16 years on, these authors would find little evidence to change their opinions. Educational sectors like preschool education and Maori education, which once had status comparable to adult and community education, now consistently win sizeable research grants and have been able to compile the knowledge base needed for generating policy and informing practice in their respective fields. But like the field itself, adult and community education research remains piecemeal and marginal in comparison to almost all other educational sectors.

Since the review of research by Garrett, Paterson and Wagner in 1980, the New Zealand Council for Educational Research (NZCER) has published its Continuing Education Bibliography (Elizabeth Wagner, 1990) which complements the main reference used in the 1980 review, Roger Boshier's *Adult and Continuing Education in New Zealand* (1979). Even though the NZCER bibliography's 347-page bulk is initially impressive, closer examination shows that original research studies are clearly in a minority alongside the personal opinions, programme descriptions and prescriptive writings documented. While the future continuation of the NZCER database is uncertain, it has been invaluable in locating much of the field's fugitive research and further documenting the field's research literature to date.

Analysis of the NZCER and Boshier bibliographies and publications such as the *New Zealand Journal of Adult Learning* and *Lifelong Learning in Aotearoa* (the latter has recently ceased publication due to a lack of funding) over the past few years shows a number of clear patterns in the adult and community education research over recent decades:

- most of the research is largely descriptive and atheoretical
- most of the research studies listed are based on limited samples of individuals or settings
- the research is derived predominantly from psychological or historical perspectives
- quantitative studies are much more common than qualitative studies
- the most commonly researched topic areas are analyses of participants in programmes or institutions, needs assessments (including feasibility studies)

at various levels, evaluations of courses/programmes, historical analyses and adult literacy
- the amount of research carried out on the various topics does not reflect the relative weightings of the various forms of provision in terms of either their budgets or size of programme (e.g. given their relatively high levels of funding, school-based community education programmes are under-researched in comparison with some of their counterparts such as the WEA).
- research of Maori adult education is very limited; documentation of education among Pacific Island groups is virtually non-existent.

Researchers

The majority of the research to date has been generated by a handful of researchers, most of whom are university-based academics. Most of these university-based researchers have been based in centres for continuing education and in a few cases now, education departments, but these latter departments are still overwhelmingly staffed by researchers whose interests and knowledge are centred on formal schooling or tertiary education. Increasingly, research is also being generated by masterate students (usually in education departments) and people completing Certificates in Adult Education, but there has also been a significant contribution made over recent years by people from some of the more marginal educational groups. The Adult and Reading Learning Assistance Federation (ARLA) has employed a part-time research officer since 1987, which has undoubtedly led to the increase in adult literacy research now being carried out, both by the ARLA researchers directly and indirectly through other researchers, although of all the university-based researchers currently active in the area of reading in the country, none has worked actively in New Zealand adult literacy research.

Apart from the large proportion of research studies carried out by this small number of university-based researchers, most of the other studies have been carried out by practitioners who do a single piece of research, or researchers who have soon moved on to research in other areas – and in the case of researchers such as Roger Boshier, David Battersby, Barry Cocklin and Richard Bagnall, to other countries.

With the steady rise of professional development departments in polytechnics over recent years, there has been a corresponding increase in interest in adult education research topics related to adult learning in this context and in some instances, community contexts. While the volume of research from this sector is still fairly modest, the push for polytechnics to be involved in research as part of their educational mission will undoubtedly mean that there should be an increasing volume of research originating from this source in the future. The adult education component of the New Zealand Council for Educational Research's work has included the research bibliography mentioned earlier in this chapter and a small number of research studies on topics relating to the fourth sector, but its focus has largely been on aspects of vocational education.

Funding

Acquiring funding for research remains one of the main stumbling blocks to expanding the store of research on adult and community education. With most of the groups and institutions in the field facing decreasing budgets, it is not surprising that only one group (ARLA) has consistently ear-marked a proportion of its budget for research. NZCER has also faced budget cuts over recent years and uses most of its funds for internal research staff. When the 1989 report *Learning for Life: Two* recommended that a National Resource Centre for Adult Education and Community Learning be set up (Section 3.6), it was envisaged that the Centre would act both as a funder and promoter of research in the field. The subsequent reality of the Resource Centre never receiving funding in keeping with its functions has meant that it has never been able to fund any research and has only functioned as a publiciser of research through its publication *Lifelong Learning in Aotearoa* and research workshops run in conjunction with annual New Zealand Association for Community and Continuing Education (NZACCE)[1] conferences. Apart from a very occasional grant from groups such as the Health Research Council or the Foundation for Research, Science and Technology where the educational aspects of the research need to be related to services such as health, the main source for research funding remains the Ministry of Education.

The Ministry's Research Division prioritises the allocation of both its internal and external research budgets according to policy set by the Minister and Ministry officials. Over recent years, these have rarely included adult and community education topics. It is not surprising therefore to find that the number of research grants for adult and community education given by the Ministry has been minimal. Of the 427 external research contracts and the 83 internal research studies financed by the Ministry of Education's Research and Statistics Division since the late 1970s (Donn, 1993), only 11 (2.1 per cent) are related in any way to the fourth sector. While this paucity of grants undoubtedly reflects Ministry priorities, it is also probably due at least in part to the small number of applications from researchers working in the fourth sector.

Issues and Solutions

The most obvious issue in relation to research of adult and community education is the low volume of research which is attributable to a number of factors. First, there are too few researchers active in the field. The solution to this issue lies in the first instance with the universities. While most of the present research is associated with university academics and students, historically most academics in centres for continuing education have been primarily involved in other disciplines and their research activities reflect this. With so few academic appointments left now in adult and community education, it is essential that future appointments be given to researchers who can continue the build-up of graduates with research skills as well as their own research studies. Further appointments of people with adult and community education backgrounds to education departments would also be beneficial because of these departments' less marginal status and more direct involvement in university activities.

Second, because there is so little research being undertaken, it is essential that national priorities be set and that research activities be carefully co-ordinated among those people with an interest in research. There are signs that this is increasingly happening, for example within the structure of research workshops at ACEA conferences, the drafting of a national policy using a UNESCO grant and the formation of a national research network under the National Resource Centre.

Third, research in the field of adult and community education needs to raise its public profile within the education and research communities and with the public at large. This would probably be most easily achieved by several large research studies involving a co-ordinated team of researchers and practitioners. While such studies would obviously not be justified on publicity grounds alone, it is important to realise that research can play an important role in raising the field's profile as well as inform those involved in its practice and policy. Given its potential public profile, one example of this type of study is an incidence study of literacy skills in the national adult population. There is also potential to increase the field's profile within the New Zealand Association for Research in Education (NZARE) to the level that it achieved in the 1980s by ensuring that its conferences include an adult and community education stream for presentations.

Fourth, it is important that the links between researchers and practitioners be strengthened both nationally and regionally. There is little point in increasing the amount of research if it lies unused on library shelves. Practitioners must be involved in the research process and be acquainted with research findings in ways that ensure that their practice and professional development are constantly informed and challenged. Well-planned and executed research is a necessary, but not sufficient, condition to achieving excellence in the field.

Finally, while it is obvious that any list for future research needs ultimately to come through the various policy-making bodies in the field, it is worth mentioning some specific topics I believe need to be researched in adult and community education:

- studies that document and analyse the long-term impact of participation in adult learning opportunities and in particular, their links with people's working lives
- research on how adult and community education groups have implemented their commitment to biculturalism and the subsequent effects of these changes (especially the realities of these effects, beyond the rhetoric being espoused)
- documentation of adult learning in Maori and Pacific Island communities and their perceptions of present organised learning opportunities
- the role and performance of voluntary organisations in the fourth sector
- the potential impact of the new information technologies on adult learning
- historical and international analyses of policy and funding
- the formulation and implementation of statistical methods appropriate for recording and analysing programmes
- description and analysis of how curricula are devised for programmes
- research on the teaching/learning environment including teaching effectiveness and its implications for tutor education
- documentation of non-participants' knowledge and perceptions of learning opportunities for adults and their patterns of decision-making in relation to these opportunities.
- analysis of the macro social, political and economic contexts and their effects on individual learners, groups and agencies.

Evaluation – Definitions and Purposes

As an area of applied research, evaluation has increasingly come to be seen as a discipline in its own right over recent years with applicability to all human services. Traditionally evaluation in an educational context has been understood as the measurement of the attainment of objectives, usually at programme or course level – how well did the learners learn? This form of evaluation is now usually referred to as the assessment of learning and is a component or type of evaluation. Evaluation is now seen as a much broader concept '... a process of determining the merit, worth or value of something, or the product of that process' (Scriven, 1991: 139). Evaluation literature abounds with various classificatory systems for evaluation, but three commonly accepted categories (Turner, Dehar, Casswell and Macdonald, 1992) are:

- *formative evaluation* – 'the collection and feedback of information relevant to programme planning and operation, for use in developing and improving the programme as it is designed and developed' (p. 8). Conducted during the 'forming' of a programme (especially with new or trial programmes), the main intention of formative evaluation is to ensure that it is as successful as possible by evaluating its progress while it is still being developed, rather than waiting until its completion. Formative evaluation includes needs assessments, specification of overall goals and specific programme objectives, development of performance indicators, literature searches, testing programme materials, piloting of strategies and assessing short-term impacts.
- *process evaluation* – 'providing clear information of what the programme consisted of in practice and answering the questions of how and why a programme produced the results it did' (p. 9). It includes documenting details of what was done in the programme (especially in relation to what was planned), how it was perceived by those involved or affected by the programme and what resources were required to implement it.
- *outcome evaluation* – 'the assessment of programme effects, allowing judgement on whether the programme objectives have been achieved' (p. 10). Outcome evaluation includes the collection of baseline data, developing outcome indicators of programme effectiveness and success and the collection and interpretation of the outcome data.

While the most common purposes for evaluations are to improve standards of practice and public accountability, Thomas and Robertson (1991: 199) quote Rutman who identified five additional, covert purposes for evaluations:

- eyewash – an attempt to justify a weak or bad programme by deliberately selecting or allowing access to only those aspects which 'look good' on the surface
- whitewash – efforts to cover up programme failure by having subjective appraisals
- submarine – the use of evaluation to purposefully destroy a programme, regardless of its effectiveness
- posture – an attempt to use evaluation as a gesture of objectivity or professionalism
- postponement – delay of immediate action by pretending to wait for the facts.

Hence, in any evaluation exercise it is important to recognise that there can be latent political functions in addition to the official, stated purposes.

Development of Evaluation as a Distinct Field

The development of evaluation as a field in its own right with a distinctive knowledge base and literature can largely be traced to the 1960s when the American Congress demanded evaluation techniques appropriate to monitor the large-scale social programmes in the U.S. such as *Head Start* and *War on Poverty* (see for example Rossi and Freeman, 1989). The use of evaluation processes has been somewhat slower to take hold in New Zealand, but has been given greater impetus by the far-reaching political reforms of the past decade and in particular, the accountability requirements that were introduced in the State Sector Act of 1988 and the Public Finance Act of 1989 (for a fuller discussion see Trlin and Barrett, 1993).

With growing pressure on government at all levels and organisations to 'do more with less' in public expenditure (cynically known as the rubber band principle – 'it didn't break last time we stretched it, so let's stretch it again'), evaluation in the 1980s was seen as an important way of identifying the gaps and overlaps in service provision and increasing public accountability, especially in social welfare and health. Alongside these pressures have been the moves to contracting out services which were formerly the domain of government departments. These contracts for services (known as POBOCs – payments on behalf of the Crown) now typically incorporate evaluation provision as a matter of course to review the effectiveness of the contractor's work.

Evaluation of Adult and Community Education

The education sector generally and adult and community education in particular, have not been confronted with the same pressure to evaluate services until recently. While *Learning for Life: Two* included provision for the review and audit of educational institutions (Section 3.3), most of this demand has withered away with a series of budget cuts to the body responsible for these functions, the independent Education Review Office. It may also have been because there is a stronger tradition of evaluation in education generally, albeit mostly at the micro level of assessing learning.

The main difficulty with identifying what evaluation of adult and community education has been carried out is that much of the literature is 'fugitive' – not made public. Because evaluations of institutions' or groups' activities often include critical elements, the evaluation reports are often kept in-house or have limited circulation. Also, people seldom see the reports as comparable to other publications and do not submit them to libraries where they are documented and thereby become available through Interloan and various publicly accessible bibliographies such as Kiwinet.

Probably the institution with the longest tradition of being evaluated in the broadest sense of the term are the university centres for continuing education. These reviews are carried out periodically by a group of academics from other departments, continuing education staff from other universities and, in some cases, community representatives. The evaluation process is comprehensive and incorporates process evaluation elements of recording the centre's current activities and structures, an outcome evaluation of a centre's work and recommendations.

One of the most comprehensive evaluations of a fourth-sector group over recent years was the 1990 *Review of the Rural Education Activities Programme (REAP)* prepared by Rivers, Dewes and Drumm for the Minister of Education. The review looked at all 13 REAPs throughout the country and concentrated especially on their 'effectiveness and efficiency' as service providers. Other evaluations over recent years include Hermansson's work with the Wairarapa Community Action Programme (CAP) in 1987, Rivers' review of the Trade Union Education Authority (TUEA) in 1989 and my evaluations of the Northern Region Tutor Training Centre, the Workplace Literacy pilot project at Bluebird Foods, the Manukau City Council Community Houses, the West Auckland WEA Adult Literacy Scheme and the Open Learning Centre in Palmerston North (Benseman, 1990, 1992, 1993, 19996a, 1996b).

With the increasing pressure to demonstrate service effectiveness, a number of groups have begun to develop their own evaluation methodologies in preference to the methods used by evaluators in the large accountancy firms who are increasingly involved in evaluation of social services. These groups include adult literacy (Benseman 1993b), polytechnics (School of Humanities, Carrington Polytechnic, 1992) and community groups (see Anderton and Darracott, 1991; Coup, de Joux and Higgs, 1990).

Funding and the Future

Until recently, funding for evaluations has rarely been apportioned from groups' budgets on a regular basis, unless stipulated by their funding agencies. The reality is that few organisations will readily spend scarce resources on evaluation at present, although there are signs that some groups are entertaining its use more seriously, such as ACEA including it as an integral part of its national policy. The long-term likelihood of evaluation becoming more widely used in adult and community education therefore will most probably depend on the degree to which funding agencies include it as a condition of funding. Given the general direction of public expenditure appropriation patterns in all social services both here and overseas, calls for evaluation will, in all probability, increase.

A second issue to be resolved is the suspicion some administrators and practitioners have towards evaluation, assuming it to be a precursor to cuts in funding or unwanted change. Steele (1989: 264) argues that the credibility of evaluators working in adult and community education is greatly helped by their having a thorough knowledge of programme theory – the evaluator's credibility is enhanced by their perceived legitimacy.

Third, many adult and community education organisations still do not have the necessary administrative and policy structures in place which are conducive for undertaking effective evaluations such as statements of philosophy, programme aims and objectives, annual plans and reports and job descriptions. Evaluability assessments (determining if programmes are in shape for an evaluation) will help ensure that these requisites are met. Most of the requirements are prerequisites for an effective organisation irrespective of any evaluation.

Finally, there is a case for diversifying the range of evaluation techniques used. In particular, the potential of formative evaluation in helping ensure the success of pilot or new programmes remains largely untapped – most evaluations to date have been outcome or process evaluations. Also, it is important that groups undertaking evaluations make their studies publicly available so that they can contribute to the further development of evaluation methods suitable to the sector and promote the concept of evaluation as an integral part of the education process.

Both research and evaluation of adult and community education are still in their infancy of development in New Zealand. While some progress has been made in mapping the activities and achievements of the field over recent decades, the results to date are both few in number and thin in quality. Difficulties in attracting funding, educating sufficient researchers and improving the dissemination of findings in particular need to be improved if research and evaluation are to provide the insights and challenges that they are capable of providing.

Note

1. Now known as Adult and Community Education Association Aotearoa/New Zealand (ACEA).

References

Anderton, J. and Darracott, P. (1991), *Assessing Changing Communities – a Practical Guide to Studying a Community, its People, their Needs and Human Services*, Wellington: Department of Social Welfare.

Benseman, J. (1990), *An Evaluation of the Northern Region Tutor Training Centre*, Auckland: Auckland Institute of Technology.

Benseman, J. (1992), *Workplace Literacy in Bluebird Foods Ltd Evaluation Report*, Auckland: Adult Reading and Learning Assistance Federation.

Benseman, J. (1993), *The Development and Trialing of a Methodology for Reviewing Adult Literacy Schemes*, Wellington: Adult Reading and Learning Assistance Federation.

Benseman, J. (1996a), 'Cinderella's Red-haired Child: Community Houses in Aotearoa', *New Zealand Journal of Adult Learning*, vol. 24, no. 1, May.

Benseman, J. (1996b), 'Adult Literacy and Libaries: The Meeting of the Twains', *New Zealand Libraries*, vol. 48, no. 5, March, pp. 94–97.

Boshier, R. (1979), *Adult and Continuing Education in New Zealand*, Wellington: National Council of Adult Education.

Coup, O., de Joux, M. and Higgs, G. (1990), *We Are Doing Well – Aren't We?*, Wellington: Department of Internal Affairs.

Donn, M. (1993), *Annual Research Report*, Wellington: Research Section, Ministry of Education.

Garrett, D., Paterson, A. and Wagner, G. (1980), 'Research on Continuing Education in New Zealand', in *Research in Education in New Zealand*, Palmerston North: NZARE/Delta.

Goff, P. (1989), *Learning for Life: Two*, Wellington: Government Printer.

Hermansson, G. (1987), *Community Education and Development: the Wairarapa Community Action Programme (CAP), Experience*, Wellington: NZCER.

Merriam, S. (1991), 'How Research Produces Knowledge', in Merriam, S. and Cunningham, P. (eds), *Handbook of Adult and Continuing Education*, San Francisco: Jossey-Bass.

Research and Statistics Division (1990/91 and 1992/93), *Annual Research Reports*, Wellington: Ministry of Education.

Rivers, M.-J. (1989), *Trade Union Education Authority: Independent Review*, Wellington: TUEA.

Rivers, M.-J., Dewes, C. and Drumm, B. (1990), *Review of the Rural Education Activities Programme (REAP)*, Wellington: Ministry of Education.

Rossi, P. and Freeman, H. (1989), *Evaluation – a Systematic Approach*, Newbury Park: Sage.

School of Humanities (1992), *Self Study Report*, Auckland: Carrington Polytechnic.

Scriven, M. (1991), *Evaluation Thesaurus*, Newbury Park: Sage.
Steele, S. (1989), 'The Evaluation of Adult and Continuing Education', in Merriam, S. and Cunningham, P. (eds), *Handbook of Adult and Continuing Education*, San Francisco: Jossey-Bass.
Thomas, D. and Robertson, N. (1991), 'Evaluation of Human Services: Conceptualisation and Planning', in Thomas, D. and Veno, A. (eds), *Psychology and Social Change*, Palmerston North: Dunmore Press.
Trlin, A. and Barrett, P. (1993), 'Evaluation Research in New Zealand: Taking Stock of the Last 12 Years', Paper presented at 'Evaluation in the Public Sector' conference, 29–30 March, James Cook Centra Hotel, Wellington.
Turner, A., Dehar, M.-A., Casswell, S. and Macdonald, J. (1992), *Doing Evaluation: a Manual for Health Education Workers*, Auckland: Alcohol and Public Health Research Unit, University of Auckland.
Wagner, E. (1990), *Continuing Education Bibliography 1970–1990*, Wellington: NZCER.

Part 5

Educating Adults and Social Justice

22

Bicultural and Treaty Education

David James

Introduction

When as a raw recruit from England I began work in adult and community education in Aotearoa/New Zealand, just after Labour Weekend 1961, the model for teaching that I knew was that of the university. There was no training for adult and community education available then, until it was begun by Jack Shallcrass for the Wellington Workers Educational Assocation and then by Denny Garrett and I for Wellington High School Evening Institute, but that was still years in the future. So my original model was one of lecturing from a position of detached impartiality (I was very young). It went on like that for a long time. People seemed to respond and in general my courses ran in the marketplace for individual learners that was adult and community education in those days.

A later glimpse: in the mid-1980s, at the polytechnic where I then worked, a group of us had joined forces to run our first public course on bicultural issues for tauiwi (non-Maori in an inclusive sense). Once again it was advertised to attract individual enrolments. One of the older male participants – predictably – in a position of some influence, ex-Army, was unimpressed. Rather than raise his concerns with us, he rang the more senior colleague to whom I was ultimately accountable. We were then told that we had transgressed by becoming advocates for change rather than impartial educators.

These days, on beginning a Treaty workshop with my partner Jillian, we usually begin by acknowledging our lack of impartiality and that we see ourselves as allies to Maori who are calling for change. (We also reassure the group that it is possible to be both pro-Maori and pro-tauiwi.) It has been a long road from the start to this point, with the help of many friends, colleagues and more remote influences.

But then, not only the field of adult and community education – this corner of it at least – but the whole nation as well has changed. In 1972 the National Council of Adult Education published a report on *Maori Adult Education*. It was created by a working party with a variety of distinguished Maori names on it and one or two Pakeha. They were certainly not invited for their conservatism. But what is immediately striking about the report now, apart from its exclusively male language, is that there is not a single reference to Treaty concerns. Not that the working party members would have been oblivious to it; but the Treaty connection with adult and community education was not as obvious then as it would be now. A different place, a different time.

For the past six years, since moving to Wanganui, Jillian and I have been freelance trainers, consultants and mediators. The larger part of our work, covering virtually every region of Aotearoa/New Zealand, is now Treaty education (more properly decolonisation education, but the Treaty is a framework and a symbol for that). When we are at home, we are also members of our local Network Waitangi group and have other Treaty commitments as well. Being based in Whangarei and then in Wanganui, we missed some of the key developments that happened in Auckland and Wellington, so this chapter does not attempt a complete history of Treaty, anti-racism and bicultural education. The only such account that I have seen is Mitzi Nairn's short paper (1993: 3–5), where she does describe the beginnings in the 1970s which led to such important programmes as the Programme on Racism, now part of the new Conference of Churches in Aotearoa/New Zealand, and Project Waitangi, both of which were starting points for Jillian and me in this learning journey – or at least they offered ways to make sense of earlier experiences and learnings which had not until then come together for me.

Above all, the increasing amount of reliable research and publishing on the Treaty of Waitangi, Treaty-related events and other New Zealand historical material, made it possible for all of us to be clearer about the institutionalisation of racism and deprivation in Aotearoa/New Zealand. Paulo Freire had provided a conceptual background (1970), followed by local facilitators of structural analysis such as Jim Greenaway and Michael Elliot (Yarwood, 1986) and reinforced by the several visits made by Philippe Fanchette (a Catholic priest from Mauritius) to enable Maori and some Pakeha to extend their structural analysis work. The historians and the writers on the politics and economics of the period since 1984 put the local flesh on these conceptual bones.

Racism Awareness Training

This was all vastly different from anti-racism training as I had experienced it. I had been part of a stimulating and well-run workshop in Auckland in the early 1970s. But led by a team of visitors from the U.S.A., it naturally did not relate very specifically to events in this country. Later my attention was caught by an article published by Ahmed Gurnah (1984) in the United Kingdom. His criticisms of the Racism Awareness Training (RAT) movement, and his call to address issues of structural rather than individual racism, led me while on leave in England to take part in a RAT workshop which I was told would indeed address structural issues. It was for local body community workers in Birmingham. It was led by three black people from different parts of the world. What happened was that in turn, as group members responded to exercises and events in the group, one after another would be turned on by the leaders and other members of the group until they broke down and confessed their racist guilt, often in tears. After a day and a half of this and no sign of any move to structural issues, I left, being predictably clobbered on departure. The experience left me with an abiding conviction that guilt is no way to work for justice and with a distrust of whites who out of their own sense of guilt are prepared to induce it in others.

In Treaty training, as we have inherited it from others' practice and fitted it to what works for us, we do not in fact focus directly on learners' feelings at all, but on factual historical and current information, ways to interpret that information, issues to be resolved in society and in organisations and planning for action for change. Feelings emerge in some participants in response to that information and we acknowledge them, encourage them to grapple with them and move on.

Treaty Education and Stopping Violence

To avoid dealing at length with feelings is strange behaviour in principle for educators who in other parts of our facilitation practice work in the field of human relationships, where dealing appropriately with feelings is a vital and central part of the processes of learning. The reason why it is appropriate in Treaty education finally crystallised for us after participating last year in an excellent workshop for counsellors on stopping male violence. The facilitators pointed out that in counselling violent men to focus on their feelings invites those men to dramatise themselves as the victims of circumstance, or in other ways to divert themselves from what is actually happened and their responsibility for it. They are inclined to tell the story of a violent episode in an abbreviated way that minimises the violence and often blames the victim. The counsellor's task, by rehearsing the man through the complete story frame by frame, is to get him to acknowledge the truth (Jenkins, 1990: 75–76). The next step is for the counsellor to invite the man to take another look at the belief system that licenses the violence, that women or children are inferior and to be controlled – and then to explore possibilities for change.

We are dealing as a nation with the effects of what has also been a violent and abusive relationship between a dominant Pakeha group and Maori as oppressed peoples and some of the same processes apply in learning to stop that structural violence. Without attributing personal racism to the majority of those we meet in workshops, we are inviting them to consider the full truth of the course of the Maori/Pakeha relationship and the thinking that appeared to legitimise it – and to consider where they themselves now choose to stand in relationship to that history and those patterns of thought and the small privileged group who instituted them (whom we also avoid demonising). Hence, for example, the spelling out in varying amounts of detail some of the many pieces of legislation which have subordinated and colonised Maori, which is the precise equivalent of the frame-by-frame telling of the male violence.

In Freire's terms, we are engaged in raising critical consciousness, encouraging learners to move beyond awareness of their thought and behaviour patterns into evaluating them against their appropriateness and their congruence with the person's values, and beyond that again into the influences that have shaped them, the assumptions that are built into them and how well those fit the observable world.

In doing this we are generally also working with either a whole organisation or a significant group from within an organisation, so the intention is to influence the system and to visualise the organisation as the learner, through the collective responses of the individual learners.

Tauiwi to Tauiwi

As tauiwi facilitators, we encourage organisations to engage Maori facilitators to train their Maori members or staff in the early stages, while not ourselves excluding those who identify as Maori and make a deliberate choice to take part with us. What we want is to avoid exposing Maori to 'racist Pakeha tapes' unless they are prepared for that, especially those who are new to this learning. As the extent of the injustices of the past and present are laid bare, their feelings can make them extremely vulnerable and a mainly tauiwi group is not usually going to be a safe environment for them to have that experience.

Besides, they do not need a continuation of models from the formal education system in which Pakeha are predominantly the educators and Maori a minority among the learners. I remember an experience in working with a City Council's members and managers, at a stage where it was appropriate for co-facilitation by Maori and tauiwi, so Jillian and I were working with Irihapeti Ramsden. The iwi had sent observers and with them was a young woman in her teens. We watched her visible response to Irihapeti's skills and presence and to her interaction with the managers and others there; for the young woman it was decolonisation education in action, in the whole situation as much as in the words. But it was also built on earlier work that we had done alone, including a torrid time with the usual hard core of male power-brokers which would have done nothing for her spirit.

Mitzi Nairn notes (1993: 5) that the Pakeha anti-racism praxis that developed during the 1970s was in part shaped as a response to challenges from groups like Nga Tamatoa for Pakeha to work with our own people while Maori did what they needed to with theirs. As she says, those of us who became active during the 1980s have inherited frameworks and approaches that were originally created jointly but have been mediated to us mainly through other Pakeha workers. There is a challenge now to maintain or rebuild the links and to share resources without encroaching on Maori time and space. Working alongside Maori co-facilitators on the implementation of change, once the first spadework has been done with an organisation, has always been enriching for us. At the same time we know that Maori colleagues are using some of the materials we have written or adapted.

Meeting Challenges

I would like to return to the overt resistance to Treaty issues from a few workshop participants. It is something that all facilitators meet and have to deal with. The immediate temptation is to use the power vested in a facilitator by the group and to blame and put down the person concerned. Paradoxically, that can be a triumph for them. It reinforces their polarised view of the world and of how people relate in it; it makes them the centre of attention; it diverts attention from the issues and the need for change; and it may gain them sympathy from those who are uncommitted. (It reminds me greatly of the *Star Wars* sequence in which the Emperor taunts the hero Luke Skywalker, inviting Luke to be angry and to attack him and in so doing to put himself into the power of the Dark Side.)

This is where facilitation demands self-awareness. It is easy to be self-righteous on behalf of the cause we are working for but to act out of personal confusion about power, projection onto others and a cultural legacy of dominator/oppressed modes of relating. As William Ury puts it in a different context (1991: 145), what we are on about is not winning over people, but winning them over. Adam Curle, the English Quaker mediator who is also one of our constant reference points, has worked a great deal with leaders of opposing violent groups who have ordered or at least countenanced appalling atrocities. In that situation, he reminds himself, 'Finally I know that she or he is someone just like myself, that we are both in our different ways up against the same fundamental problems, needing each other's help, respect and compassion and only damaged by each other's contempt or anger' (1986).

Such people are not going to alter their orientation in a single short workshop, but facilitators can make a path towards change or, more probably, to their standing aside from actually blocking change, in such ways as:

- enabling them to feel heard and respected, without absorbing too much group time
- sharing our different viewpoint as one that deserves equal consideration
- maintaining the good name of the oppressed groups they are putting down, by providing clear accurate information to support our viewpoint
- helping others in the group to develop knowledge and approaches to exert sustained pressure for change
- affirming the resisters' right to their views and the right of others not to have those views imposed on them
- modelling among the facilitators, as well as with the group, a 'peaceful relationship' (Adam Curle's phrase).

Just as Ahmed Gurnah criticises Racism Awareness Training for its focus on the individual because 'racism is a relationship' (1984: 13), so Adam Curle regards peace not as an entity but as a quality of relationship, one where each party is enabled to become fully who they are capable of being and where each is committed equally to their own and the other party's full development (1971: 15–16). Such a relationship is characterised by high awareness, a balanced power distribution and experience of negotiating for equity. (By the way, we do not claim to be able to operate that way all the time by any means – such things fluctuate a good deal and need constant renegotiation.)

In an 'unpeaceful relationship', on the contrary, the parties are blocked in their development by the relationship. Part of the blockage will be an uneven distribution of power in which one party is 'oppressed', whether consciously and intentionally or not, and the other enjoys more of the power but is also damaged by the skew in the relationship. The model holds for relationships at all levels, from individuals to nations. That is how the way that facilitators operate as a team in workshop practice, in our relationship to one another and our joint relationship with the learning group, comes to be relevant to the issues of building an equitable and negotiated relationship between tangata whenua and tauiwi in this country.

Cultural Safety

This emphasis on self-awareness and the quality of relationships is also part of the current debate on 'cultural safety'. We see this as a second stage of learning, following work on Treaty and structural issues. It is not solely a concern for Maori. There are issues of cultural safety and risk in all interactions where there are differences of power – between young and mature and elderly people, between people in poverty and those who are economically secure, between those with accredited information and those without it and so forth. Along with structural change in organisations, there is also a need for individual workers to create safe interactions and procedures for Maori and for all other people who are at risk. This requires them to be non-judgemental, to empathise, to be aware of some of the main pitfalls and how to avoid them and above all not to take shelter in institutional roles but to meet others fully in their humanity.

This would provide a safe background in turn for further work on tikanga Maori so far as that is appropriate, keeping in mind the comment that 'cultural safety is based in attitude change. If safe attitudes are held by ... practitioners they will be able to work with the continuum of Maori people from traditional practitioners of the culture to those of us who have been denied any information about our Maoritanga. Tikanga Maori will not help with caring for street kids, history and analysis of power relationships will' (Ministry of Education, 1991: 4).

Finding and Training Facilitators

In all of this there is a huge amount of work to be done, more than can be encompassed by the people who are available at present. Project Waitangi had some government funding; now that 1990 is past there is none and the former Project is now Network Waitangi, consisting of self-funded small local groups in a limited number of centres. In addition, there is a number of private training agencies like ours. Presumably the others, as we do, use Robin Hood tactics to work with groups that cannot pay, or that iwi want us to work with for them, while charging others what they can afford. It is a strange situation for people who still see themselves as involved in adult and community education.

It would help if government were to take responsibility for funding some co-ordinated basic Treaty information through TV. The majority of tauiwi, even of those who come voluntarily to workshops, have no substantial background at all and government ministers have acknowledged (Doug Graham and Doug Kidd, TV1, 5 February 1993, programme *The Treaty of Waitangi/Te Tiriti o Waitangi*) that one of their problems is that the public do not understand the grievances and the issues.

There is a growing need for training teams within organisations, particularly the larger voluntary organisations, to keep up the work and spread it right through. The difficulty, when we begin to think it through, is the varied and extensive demands on the facilitators. Someone said the other day, after an introductory workshop, 'If this had been a training for trainers, would it have been different?'. Well, yes.

I recently tried to outline for a group wanting to develop its training skills the areas that seem important, as a menu from which they could identify what was most immediate for them. It included:

Attitudinal Prerequisites

- personal commitment to justice for the tangata whenua
- being 'relatively free of distress' so that one is not as a facilitator dealing with one's own pain, guilt or disempowerment
- compassion.

Cognitive Learnings

- some familiarity with the history of Aotearoa/New Zealand and how it relates to the history of England and other colonising powers and other colonies (especially colonies of settlement)
- knowledge of Te Tiriti o Waitangi, what led up to it and what happened to the Treaty and its undertakings afterwards
- some of the specifics of the legislation and policies that broke the Tiriti guarantees
- understanding of the terms and concepts that occur in Treaty and justice debates and how they shift over time as they get worn out through co-option
- structural analysis of society and awareness of the links between different aspects of oppression
- basic processes of government
- some of the dynamics of organisations and how they can be changed
- some of the basic structures and processes of Maori society and the contact points within it, including knowing what one does not know and what it is not appropriate for Pakeha even to try to explain
- resources of exercises and materials.

Skills

- all the usual skills of course and session design
- exercise facilitation and processing
- explaining, using models, clarifying and story-telling
- acceptable pronunciation of Maori words and names
- listening and conflict resolution skills
- ability to confront in ways that do not damage relationships.

The problem is that to develop all of this to a moderate but safe extent takes a long time and much diverse experience and it cannot be imparted instantly even in a planned training programme. Yet current expectations as well as practical constraints are always pushing for quick solutions.

And no one who knows anything of the situation can doubt the urgent need for change, given the social disasters being created and multiplied by colonisation leading to poverty and racism and by the dumping of so many, especially of Maori and Pacific people, into long-term unemployment over the past 15 years. Despite all of these difficulties, there is hope in the resilience and creativity within the iwi and the city communities. So, for would-be allies, there is no way to stop trying to help organisations to adapt to the requirements of the oppressed and particularly of tangata whenua, whether the requirement is to make equitable provision or to remove the blocks to Maori self-help.

Acknowledgements

It seems improper to end without acknowledging the people who in conversation, writing and action, were important influences on the journey that has led to my present involvement. Some of them were:

Before 1988: Ewan MacColl and Peggy Seeger, Matiu te Hau, Joan Metge, the Pitman whanau, Selwyn Wilson, Arnold Wilson, Koro Dewes, Ngapare Hopa, Ranginui Walker, Roger Oppenheim, Denny Garrett, Wiremu Parker, Jack Shallcrass, Paulo Freire, Turoa Royal, Mike Law and Linda Sissons, Peter Rutherford, Jim Greenaway, Michael Elliot, Philippe Fanchette, Toka Totoro, Hana Tukukino and Adam Curle.

Above all, since 1980, my partner Jillian Wychel, who planned the outline of this chapter with me and would have been working on it in more detail except that she was overseas. Other influences and colleagues have multiplied so much that it would be impossible to list them all.

References

Curle, A. (1986), *In the Middle: Non-Official Mediation in Violent Situations*, Bradford Peace Studies Papers, New Series no. 1, Berg.

Curle, A. (1971), *Making Peace*, London: Tavistock.

Freire, P. (1970), *Pedagogy of the Oppressed*, republished in 1972, Harmondsworth: Penguin.

Gurnah, A. (1984), 'The Politics of Racism Awareness Training', *Critical Social Policy,* other details unknown.

Jenkins, A. (1990), *Invitations to Responsibility,* Adelaide: Dulwich Centre.

Ministry of Education (reprinted 1991), 'Kawa Whakaruruhau/Cultural Safety in Nursing Education in Aotearoa', Wellington.

Nairn, M. (1993), 'Notes on the Programme on Racism', Tamaki-Makau-Rau/Auckland: Programme on Racism, Box 9573.

National Council of Adult Education (1972), *Maori Adult Education,* Wellington.

Ury, W. (1991), *Getting Past No: Negotiating with Difficult People*, Auckland: Random Century.

Yarwood, V. (ed.) (1986), 'Tools for Analysis', *Infact,* no. 12, Auckland: Christian Action.

23

The Invisibility of Women's Studies

Margot Roth

Introduction

Although Women's Studies has built up a strong following in the last 20 years, it has been largely marginalised or ignored in the publications and by the policy-makers of adult and community education. Nevertheless, the Women's Studies Association has provided a forum for discussion and research which underpins innovations in educational theory and practice that aim at promoting genuine equality.

Useful contributions to women's studies (WS)[1] came from some activities included in the centenary of the 1893 legislation when New Zealand women won the vote. Women's past and present lives were creatively celebrated and documented and while much research remains to be done, there is now plenty of soundly based information about women's participation in the country's development. Most of the publicity over the course of the year was favourable, but there were a vociferous few (mostly male) commentators for whom designating 1993 as Suffrage Year was an invitation to denigrate feminism and individual feminists. This is nothing new – our nineteenth-century grandmothers and great-grandmothers who worked so hard for the franchise would have recognised both the words and the spirit of the sneers and jeers.

Yesterday's advocates of equal voting rights were condemned as 'unwomanly'. Today, the word 'feminist' in popular speech and writing is an insult, with the result that: 'Informal surveys of women ... indicate that many of them would not enrol for any course that advertises itself as feminist: either they do not feel personally disadvantaged or they feel it would inhibit their chances of employment ... perhaps, in the austerity of the nineties ... they must learn to conform for success' (Alcorn, 1992).

Similar inhibitions affect some adult and community educators, so common myths about feminism, which flow on to WS, have tended to colour their perceptions of the nature and status of WS. In fact, some members of the fourth sector have always been ambivalent about programmes which might, like WS for instance, or trade union education or anti-racism, offer an analysis of the unequal distribution of power – especially where the distribution of resources is dependent on the power of particular funding bodies.

One interesting result is that publications featuring community and adult education in New Zealand have generally ignored WS, although WS courses and classes, in one form or another, have been offering fresh perspectives on modes and content of teaching for 20 years.[2] The relevant chapter in the 1993 *Annual Review of Education* (for example, Harré Hindmarsh, 1993) points out that women adult learners outnumber men in all categories, but has no reference to WS. Actually, in the period covered by Harré Hindmarsh there was an issue of the *Women's Studies Journal* featuring the special topic 'What is Women's Studies?' (Cooper, 1992), but apparently the official reviewers of the country's instruction do not believe that WS has any bearing on the activities of the fourth sector's female majority.

Another instance of this blind spot was a book review in *Lifelong Learning in Aotearoa* (Stalker, 1992).[3] Stalker was reviewing *Learning Liberation: Women's Response to Men's Education* (Thompson, 1983) an old favourite of many participants in WS for its feminist arguments in support of freeing women from male educational traditions. Stalker claimed that the importance of the book 10 years on was '... in its ability to illuminate for us how little progress had been made on addressing the issues ... raised ...' – an assertion that may be true in some quarters, but is hardly an accurate picture if the debates contained in the publications of the Women's Studies Association (WSA) are examined. Stalker's suggestion that '... the field ... has not confronted the complexities of addressing women's issues in terms of class, race and sexual identity' indicates that 'the field' (whoever or wherever it may be) has been left behind not only by the WSA but also by texts like those edited by Middleton (1988) and Middleton and Jones (1992). Two issues later *Lifelong Learning* published another review of a 10-year-old book (Slusarki, 1993) in which the reviewer drew adult educators' attention to 'the significance of the differences between men's and women's perceptions' as though 'the field' had, all this time, remained as unaware as Stalker's lot of the importance of this kind of analysis as a fundamental component of sound educational practice.

Broadly speaking, it was the recognition of such 'significance' that was one of the main factors in sparking off this century's 'second wave' of the women's liberation movement in the late sixties and early seventies. The absences and silences of women in historical records and policy-making – in all branches of education as well as everywhere else – drew women together in groups scattered over the country, not only to uncover the achievements of their foremothers, but also to establish the reasons for their overall invisibility and how it had affected the opportunities and ambitions of the post-World War II generations.

As educators and reformers, New Zealand women of all ethnic backgrounds have worked together at different times in groups of various sizes and interests to improve the female lot in some way (Coney, 1986; 1993; Else, 1993; Te Awekotuku, 1991). In the 1970s this missionary position was transformed by the sheer numbers of a younger generation who were impatient with the staid procedures of formal organisations and used imported liberation language to express themselves in flamboyant words and deeds. The rapid spread of television accompanied the people growing up in the sixties and seventies so that the activities of the more youthful section of the population were given some international validity in quite a new way for New Zealanders, as they saw and heard some of their concerns being aired simultaneously by their peers overseas. In addition, words like 'community' and 'grassroots' filled the educational air as a relatively untapped source of commercial reward – adults – were encouraged back or 'targeted' into schools, community centres and the like.

Association's Beginnings

So the scene was set for the various kinds of activities in different places which laid a solid foundation for the setting up of the WSA. The Dunedin Women's Collective began in 1971 (Harrison, 1993); in 1972 the indestructible feminist magazine *Broadsheet* was established (Rosier, 1992); in 1973 the Auckland Workers' Educational Association (WEA) sponsored the first groundbreaking United Women's Convention (Roth, 1983); while in 1974 Rosemary Seymour, of the University of Waikato, began to circulate a nation-wide appeal for New Zealand material about women (Roth and McCurdy, 1993). The meetings, the debates and the publications spoke for and to the women who found that they had not only been left out of the textbooks, but, on closer enquiry, saw that they were also excluded from access to education and employment on equal terms with men. From the start the Dunedin Collective had embarked on a variety of feminist educational activities; in 1974 the first long-term courses in WS began both in Hamilton and Auckland – at the University of Waikato and under WEA auspices respectively – and started in Wellington at Victoria University in 1975.

The WSA began in 1976, its membership based on '... an informal network of correspondents who had been answering Seymour's 1974 appeal ...'. The response was 'a deluge indicative of the vital interest women now showed in something previously denied to them, their own heritage' (Roth and McCurdy, 1993). The WSA's first national conference and annual general meeting took place in Hamilton in 1978 and, like its successors, was marked by lively arguments as well as considerable consensus and the participants' eagerness to learn from one another. What could be called the recurring Man Question entered these first discussions, as a conventional, complex draft constitution presented to the meeting proposed that men should be admitted as equal members to the new association. The majority at the meeting disapproved of the draft and the proposal and the next conference in 1979 adopted a simpler constitution which accepted men as associate members only.

The WSA originally stated that it was 'a feminist organisation formed to promote radical social change through the medium of women's studies'.[4] Diversity and debate have always been features of feminism, so that WS could be set in different contexts ranging from the general ('Women in society') to the more particular ('the political economy of Maori women') and in miscellaneous environments. In fact, the setting up of this organisation was at the beginning of what Dalziel (1993) describes as the fragmentation of the women's movement into groups with more specific aims. The annual conferences are an important focus for members and some of the discussions sparked off there carry on into the quarterly newsletter – in fact the increasing popularity of the conferences has presented some logistical problems to the organisers but 'reflects the rare excitement of a woman-supportive setting for intellectual debate' (Roth and McCurdy, 1993). The emphasis on research, on analysing 'commonsense' assumptions, on providing facts and figures and on keeping as many women as possible up-to-date with such developments stems from Seymour's belief that women needed to communicate about 'problems associated with the research, techniques, results, the availability or otherwise of data and its interpretation'.

The WSA's advocacy of social justice, together with its members' tendency to monitor all organisations, including their own, for deficiencies in this area, were manifested in the early existence of a lesbian caucus at conferences. Later, after much brisk discussion about the hows and whys of bicultural practice and theory, the aims were widened to: 'We believe that a feminist perspective necessarily acknowledges oppression on the grounds of race, sexuality and class as well as gender'.

New Approaches

From 1978 onwards, the proceedings of the conferences have been printed in the Conference Papers which provide a useful information base about publications and ongoing research and also give an interesting picture of how feminist theory and practice have developed in New Zealand. A 1980 national survey revealed that the number of WS programmes had approximately tripled since a similar survey covering WS in 1977–1978, with 50 per cent in 1980 run by voluntary organisations compared with 20 per cent two years before (Sissons, 1982). Early on there were considerable exchanges of questions and answers about educating women in a non-threatening, collective way. In 1978, the Auckland WEA introduced tutor training (McCurdy, 1983) and in 1981 its WS subcommittee won the Public Service Association's Equal Opportunities Award for its WS tutor kit. Forty kits were tested in a pilot scheme, with a spread of testers from Invercargill to Whangarei, most operating in some form of community education, with a few intending to introduce the kits into more formal structures (Craven *et al.*, 1984). The WS handbook (Craven *et al.*, 1985) was based on a revised, updated and expanded version of the kit after its trial and evaluation by the first users. However, WEAs outside Auckland remained largely uninterested in WS for some time; while as for 'the field':

> New approaches to learning involving interdisciplinary content, student-centred courses, participatory planning, training of tutors of adults and a national exchange of resources are items on liberal agendas that lip-service has been given to for ages. None of the big guns with the huge salaries has noticed yet that all these things are actually happening now, carried out on a shoe-string with the highly skilled labour of largely unpaid women. The main recognition so far has been the derecognition of withdrawing ... government funds from the WEA ...
>
> (Roth, 1983)

The rationalising and romanticising of voluntary work into one of the philosophical tenets of community education has particularly affected women as the majority of volunteers are female – who very often buy into the notion of no pay or low pay. Sometimes this is because, as in early childhood education – or WS – '... the service provided is ... for a cause the volunteers believe in and have a high commitment to' according to the Social Advisory

Council (1987: 28). And, said the Council: 'much of the innovative development work being done in some schools could not take place without the involvement of volunteers working from community houses, drop-in centres and neighbourhood centres'. The Council also points out (1987: 13): 'The frequent lack of any realistic alternatives to voluntary work can make the concept of "choice" meaningless'.

Bleak Prospects

Since that discussion paper appeared the prospects for both volunteers and non-conforming community education projects are much bleaker as access to resources becomes increasingly restricted and competitive. Existing non-formal programmes for women are unlikely to come under the WS title, which has been largely taken over by the formal tertiary institutions. so: '... [P]rojects originally supported by boundless enthusiasm and unpaid (or for which there was token payment) female labour have tended to run out of steam, especially if the enthusiasm has not been sustained by a clear theoretical framework under close, continuing and collective scrutiny' (Roth, 1986).

Although a few university WS courses have been offered for some years, it is only fairly recently that all universities have (reluctantly) recognised WS as a separate interdisciplinary subject. Its existence has never been assured for:

> Women's Studies has been subject to hostile rhetoric from both the Old and New Right and the Old and New Left outside and inside the University. It has suffered the silent indifference of much of the staff and student body. As embodied in university courses it has sometimes provoked the distrust of committed women teachers and activists outside the university who believe that the academy corrupts absolutely ... academic opponents of Women's Studies dismiss it as a Minnie Mouse subject but are apprehensive of its consequences.
>
> (Matthews, 1992)

Despite the conflicts and the never ending obstacles, WS programmes survived in polytechnics and universities, almost invariably because supportive women have been prepared to spend (unpaid) overtime and energy in organisational and maintenance activities. In 1978 Massey University began a second-year course called 'Women in Society'. After appropriate evaluations and revisions, it was also offered extramurally in 1984 and then became part of a postgraduate Diploma of Social Sciences in WS first established in 1988. In 1986 the pioneering Waikato University's Women's Studies Centre had opened and Ritchie spoke for many beleaguered WS teachers:

> We were marginal because we were not a regular subject protected by a recognised status. We were marginal because we were feminists operating within a patriarchal institution. We were vulnerable, because for many years it was doubtful, from year to year, whether we would have sufficient tenured women staff remaining on campus to be able to continue to offer our programme of courses.
> (Ritchie, 1986)

Canterbury University began in 1988 with students and overburdened staff working as a collective to introduce what the founders insisted on calling feminist studies 'to make it clear the courses ... would not just be about women, but would be based in feminist philosophy and methodology' (O'Connor, 1989). In 1990 Otago University made its first WS appointment and Victoria University, with another first, offered a lesbian studies course as part of its regular WS programme. That same year Auckland University's Centre for Continuing Education (which had included a number of WS classes and forums in its general programme since 1983)[5] established its Certificate in WS which became available nationally in the form of distance learning a couple of years later. Some university departments were also offering WS papers and in 1991 Auckland finally joined the other universities in setting up a separate WS department.

International Argument

In addition to all the current uncertainty about educational funding and staffing, there are conflicts and tensions over the tertiary teaching of WS which are not peculiar to New Zealand (e.g. Gaidzwana, 1993; Joeres, 1992; Mother Jones, 1993; Stratford, 1993; the *Women's Review of Books,* 1993). National arguments surfacing at WSA conferences and in its newsletter still include the Man Question (his status as student/teacher/contributor to the *Journal*), the niceties of bicultural theory and practice and the content and politics of WS teaching. Lately there has been controversy over university appointments, as WSA members argue ideologically and intergenerationally about what WS and its practitioners should be and do (Frye, 1994; Roth, 1993).

While some of these debates may be cloaked in academic terms, they really reflect widespread attitudes: the educational world, claiming to be 'objective' and 'non-political' does little to disturb the status quo and is suspicious of WS which openly advocates educational change to promote equality – although the concept of equal opportunity surely lurks beneath the rhetoric of 'second chance' or 'flaxroots' or 'lifelong'. Even after two decades of WS and its accompanying proliferation of scholarly writing, research shows that women and girls still experience discrimination at all levels and in all facets of learning (see Middleton and Jones, 1992, Te Awekotuku, 1991; Smith, 1992). At the same time these additions to a growing body of knowledge – 'important and valuable and not being done anywhere else' (Rosier, 1986) – make WS participants particularly well-informed about women's and men's location in New Zealand and the rest of the world.

The development of WS has perhaps not featured strongly in the fourth sector's annals, but because it has a clear framework intellectually based on ideas of social justice, its proponents have made significant contributions to both educational and political thought.

Notes

1. The two words women's studies will be used throughout this article as a singular noun: WS.
2. See, for example, Craven *et al.* (1985), a compilation of 10 years' national discussion of the theory and practice of WS.
3. The year of this issue was wrongly printed as 1993.
4. The Association's objects are included in every WSA newsletter and *Women's Studies Journal*.
5. The WSA newsletter, in the March and July issues of 1982 includes early, standard arguments about WS in correspondence between the WSA and Continuing Education (Haines, 1972).

References

Alcorn, N. (1992), 'Women's Studies: Influencing Practice in Continuing Education', *Women's Studies Journal of New Zealand*, vol. 8, no. 1, pp. 47–59.
Coney, S. (1986), *Every Girl*, Auckland: YWCA.
Coney, S. (1993), *Standing in the Sunshine*, Auckland: Penguin Books.
Cooper, A. (ed.) (1992), *Women's Studies Journal of New Zealand*, vol. 8, no. 2.
Craven, C., McCurdy, C.-L. and Roth, M. (1984), 'Women's Studies Tutor Kit: A Workshop', in Haines, H. (ed.), *Women's Studies Conference Papers '83*, pp. 130–131.
Craven, C., McCurdy, C.-L., Rosier, P. and Roth, M. (1985), *Women's Studies: A New Zealand Handbook*, Auckland: New Women's Press.
Dalziel, R. (1993), 'Political Organisations', in Else, A. (ed.), *Women Together*, Wellington: Daphne Brasell Associates, Historical Branch, Department of Internal Affairs, pp. 55–69.

Else, A. (ed.) (1993), *Women Together*, Wellington: Daphne Brasell Associates, Historical Branch, Department of Internal Affairs.

Frye, M. (1994), 'Marilyn Frye and the University of Auckland', *Women's Studies Association (New Zealand), Newsletter*, vol. 14, no. 3, Autumn, p. 37.

Gaidzwana, R.B. (1993), 'Women's Studies in Zimbabwe: Towards the Year 2000', *Australian Feminist Studies,* no. 18, Summer, pp. 191–204.

Haines, H. (1982), 'Women's Studies '82', *Women's Studies Association (New Zealand), Newsletter*, vol. 3, no. 2, March, pp. 12–13.

Haines, H. (1982), 'Continuing Saga of Continuing Education', *Women's Studies Association (New Zealand), Newsletter*, vol. 3, no. 3, July, pp. 9–16.

Harrison, E. (1993), 'Dunedin Collective for Women 1971–1982', in Else, A. (Ed.), *Women Together*, Wellington: Daphne Brasell Associates, Historical Branch, Department of Internal Affairs, pp. 96–98.

Harré Hindmarsh, J.H. (1993), 'Community and Continuing Education in 1992: Trends and Issues', in Manson, H. (ed.), *New Zealand Annual Review of Education 2,* Wellington: Faculty of Education, Victoria University of Wellington, pp. 179–204.

Joeres, R.-E.B. (1982), 'On Writing Feminist Academic Prose', *Signs,* vol. 17, no. 4, Summer, pp. 701–704.

Matthews, J. (1992), 'Reflections and Recollections of a Retiring Woman', *Women's Studies Journal of New Zealand,* pp. 1–15.

McCurdy, C.-L. (1983), 'Tutor-Training for Non-Formal Women's Studies Courses', in Haines, H. (ed.), *Women's Studies Conference Papers '82,* pp. 143–150.

Middleton, S. (ed.) (1988), *Women and Education in Aotearoa,* Wellington: Allen and Unwin/Port Nicholson.

Middleton, S. and Jones, A. (eds) (1992), *Women and Education in Aotearoa 2,* Wellington: Bridget Williams Books.

Mother Jones (1993), 'Backtalk', *Mother Jones,* November/December, pp. 4–10.

O'Connor, N. (1989), 'Feminist Studies, University of Canterbury', *Women's Studies Association (New Zealand), Newsletter,* vol. 10, no. 2, February, pp. 17–23.

Ritchie, J. (1986), 'Women's Studies at the University of Waikato: Progress, Problems and Prospects', *Women's Studies Association (New Zealand), Newsletter,* vol. 7, no. 3, May, pp. 8–14.

Rosier, P. (1986), 'Rethinking our Aims', *Women's Studies Association (New Zealand), Newsletter,* vol. 8, no. 1, November, pp. 19–22.

Rosier, P. (1992), *Been Around for Quite a While,* Auckland: New Women's Press.

Roth, M. (1983), 'Women's Studies and WEA (Auckland)', *Women's Studies Association (New Zealand), Newsletter*, vol. 5, no. 1, August, pp. 24–28.

Roth, M. (1986), 'Because We're Talking Past Each Other', *Women's Studies Association (New Zealand), Newsletter*, vol. 8, no. 1, November, pp. 14–17.

Roth, M. (1993), 'Women's Studies: Tried and True', *Women's Studies Association (New Zealand), Newsletter*, vol. 14, no. 2, Summer, pp. 20–21.

Roth, M. and McCurdy, C.-L (1993), 'Women's Studies Association', in Else, A. (ed.), *Women Together*, Wellington: Daphne Brasell Associates, Historical Branch, Department of Internal Affairs, pp. 366–369.

Sissons, L. (1982), 'Women's Studies Programmes in New Zealand: 1980', in Haines, H. (ed.), *Women's Studies Conference Papers '81*.

Slusarki, S. (1993), 'In a Different Voice', *Lifelong Learning in Aotearoa*, no. 5, August, p. 21.

Smith, A.B. (1992), 'Women in University Teaching', *Women's Studies Journal of New Zealand*, vol. 8, no. 2, pp. 101–128.

Social Advisory Council (1987), *Working with Volunteers in Government Departments: A Discussion Paper*, Wellington: Ministry of Social Welfare.

Stalker, J. (1992), 'Learning Liberation', *Lifelong Learning in Aotearoa*, no. 3, p. 13.

Stratford, E. (1993), 'Happy Anniversary? A Retrospective on the 1983 Women's Studies Campaign at Flinders University', *Australian Feminist Studies*, no. 18, Summer, pp. 205–213.

Te Awekotuku, N. (1991), *Mana Wahine Maori*, Auckland: New Women's Press.

Thompson, J.L. (1983), *Learning Liberation: Women's Response to Men's Education*, London: Croom Helm.

Women's Review of Books (1993), 'From Theory to Practice', *Women's Review of Books*, vol. X, no. 5, February, pp. 17–30.

24

Public Issues and Adult Education

Robert Tobias and Judy Henderson

Introduction

In Chapter 2 of this book, attention was drawn to the fact that at certain historical moments adult and community education has been closely linked with a range of social and political movements. The rise of modern movements of adult and community education in the nineteenth and early twentieth centuries took place in part as a consequence of attempts by disenfranchised and exploited groups to mobilise politically, economically and culturally. Popular education which sought to provide 'really useful knowledge' (see Johnson, 1988) was promoted and provided by a wide range of groups, organisations and individuals. The question may be asked whether these traditions of movement-based education are still alive today and if so, what forms they may take.

This chapter seeks to throw some light on these questions by looking at trends in movement-based education in Christchurch between 1983 and 1991.[1] More specifically, it examines trends and patterns in the development of programmes of adult and community education focused on public issues, and documents some of the ideological struggles as the New Right sought to gain acceptance for its programme and implement its policies. Programmes addressing a range of issues are discussed with a more detailed discussion of economic policy, social policy and health.

Background

Ever since the election of the fourth Labour government in mid-1984, New Right ideologies have dominated the development of economic and social policies by successive Labour and National governments (see for example Holland and Boston, 1990; Boston and Dalziel, 1992; Kelsey, 1993; Rice, 1992). This has resulted in the break-up of the welfare state compromise (Law, 1993) which had been in existence over the previous 50 years. New Right ideologues draw their strength from several sources. They occupy positions of power in business, in government and in key state bureaucracies such as Treasury. In addition, at an ideological level, they have been able to reinterpret the arguments and policy initiatives taken to support the interests of multinational capital in ways which make it appear that these interests are the same as, or at least are consistent with, the interests of ordinary working people (see Douglas, 1993).

Despite this undoubted strength, New Right ideologues have not had things all their own way. At a political level, alliances and some compromises have had to be made, especially with traditional conservatives who have historically also opposed the welfare state, not least because of its perceived secularising tendencies, and because they argue that it reduces the sphere of personal moral responsibility. Such alliances and compromises have also been made with some Maori interest groups as well as groups within the feminist movement. In both cases, the common ground lay in the failure of the welfare state over the past 50 years to address gross inequities. This was combined with a belief that, with appropriate targeting of assistance to the least advantaged groups in society, the 'free market' would be more responsive to the needs of these groups and would deliver services more equitably than the state could ever do.

Of course it has not been possible for the New Right to develop alliances with all interest groups – especially those whose interests have been threatened by the political agenda of the New Right. Forthright opposition and resistance has come from various sources including social democrats, socialists, feminists and the Maori community. These groups have been at least as critical as their opponents of the failure of the welfare state to address gross inequities. However, they have rejected utterly the notion that problems of inequity are likely to be solved more effectively within the context of a 'free market'. Instead they have argued that these inequities can only be understood within the context of a wider historical and contemporary analysis of the nature and politics of race, gender and class and that they can only be addressed by means of collective cultural, social, political and economic action.

In a report on Trade Union and Workers' Education in 1987, a task force appointed by the Ministers of Education and Labour undertook a critique of the field of adult education. It suggested that, although the range of activity that constitutes adult education is impressive:

> ... the cultural and educational aspirations of working people have been poorly attended to ... . Social equity in adult education is not simply about access, participation and outcomes. It is also about defining the knowledge base, setting the goals and planning the learning process. In this sense it is about power (and) the relationship between citizens and a state-funded educational service ... . Historically there has been continuing tension between workers' self-education, which is often linked with causes and campaigns and rooted in the pressing demands of everyday life and those forms of education which are provided for working people by state-funded educational institutions.
> (Law, 1987: 63–64)

The report suggested that the predominant focus of mainstream, traditional adult education is on the provision of leisure-oriented programmes which in mode and content appeal most to middle income, suburban, Pakeha New Zealand, an observation that is borne out by most participation analyses of adult education providers (see Chapter 18). The report identified three significant trends in adult education. First, it maintained that there is an increasing emphasis on narrow vocational education. Much tertiary education currently seeks to satisfy this demand which, within a context of high unemployment, tends to be driven by the short-term requirements of the labour market. Second, it suggested that there is an emergence of adult education 'welfarism' – a mix of social work and the development of coping skills, coupled with a tendency to define social and economic issues such as unemployment as educational problems. The third trend, it argued, is a reaction to the former two and consists of a resurgence of collective self-education generally taking place within the context of social movements and independently of educational institutions. Within the context of this third trend however, the report did not discount the role of educational institutions, but rather suggested that the interaction between social movements and educational institutions can be highly productive (Law, 1987: 64–65).

Purpose

As indicated earlier, the purpose of this chapter is to examine some aspects of this movement based education. More specifically, it is intended to illuminate recent trends in public issues programmes of adult and community education and to document some of the ideological struggles as the New Right has sought to gain acceptance for its programme and implement its policies. Thus, the chapter addresses the following kinds of questions:

- what trends and patterns of public issues programmes emerged during this period of very rapid and fundamental change?
- what kinds of issues predominated?
- what movements and groups were active in organising these programmes?

'Public issues programmes' are defined as programmes which are intended primarily to promote, inform, analyse, critique, challenge, or raise public consciousness about any social, economic, cultural or political policies or issues of public concern. For purposes of analysis, the issues addressed by programmes have been classified into the following groupings: social policy; health and disabilities; economics, employment and trade unions; gender; peace and violence; biculturalism and racism; the environment; education; the media; party politics; local and regional issues; and international issues (although detailed discussion is included in only the first three of these categories in this chapter). In many cases, programmes could be located clearly and unambiguously in one of these groupings. In many more cases however, the issues addressed were relevant to more than one of these groupings (e.g. Maori employment and women's health). In these cases, programmes were classified into two or more of the above groupings.

'Programmes' have been defined very broadly to include courses, classes, workshops, seminars, hui, conferences, summer schools, field trips, study-tours, discussion, study and support groups, distance learning opportunities, one-to-one tuition, talks, lectures, symposia, forums and public meetings and gatherings to protest or advocate change. Thus the programmes discussed include a wide range of activities from single public lectures or protest gatherings to full-time, one-year courses.

Despite this breadth of scope we were not able to cover all aspects of movement-based education, or indeed all forms of education about public issues within educational institutions. Much of this education takes place away from the attention of the mass media, in small groups, in classrooms and at meetings that are not reported in the newspapers. Our focus was on those activities which were open to the public and our primary source of information was *The Press*. A systematic search was undertaken of every issue of this newspaper published in the following years: 1983, 1985, 1987, 1989 and 1991. Our aim was to identify every programme that fitted our definition and that was referred to in any of the columns of the newspaper. In addition, further interviews with organisers are being undertaken where necessary in order to obtain additional information.

For the purpose of this chapter, we will be looking at programmes organised by the following kinds of organisations:

1. public educational institutions, including schools, polytechnics, colleges of education and universities
2. voluntary organisations and groups with adult education as a primary function, including the Workers Educational Association (WEA) and several other special interest adult and community education groups
3. other voluntary organisations, community groups and individuals
4. state organisations and local authorities.

General Trends and Patterns

In the first place, our data suggest that the task force on trade union and worker education was correct in arguing that there has been a resurgence in movement-based education. The overall number of public issues programmes increased substantially over the period, from 269 in 1983 to 525 in 1991 (see Figure 24.1). The pattern of growth was, however, not uniform over the period. In the mid-1980s growth was slow, so that by 1987, 297 programmes were organised – an annual growth rate of nearly 2.6 per cent over the four-year period. From then on the rate of growth accelerated, with 390 programmes being identified in 1989 and 525 in 1991, giving an annual growth rate of 19.2 per cent.

This picture of a resurgence in movement-based education is reinforced when one looks at the increase in the number of programmes organised by voluntary organisations and community groups, especially in the latter part of the period. Between 1983 and 1987 the number of these programmes grew from 197 to 221 – a relatively small increase especially in view of the fact that 1987 was an election year. By 1991, however, the number of these programmes organised by voluntary organisations and community groups had increased to 382.

There was also a substantial increase in the number of public issues programmes organised by educational institutions and by state and local authority organisations between 1987 and 1991. In general, it would appear that the momentum of debate and protest over the changes in economic and social policy grew very slowly in the mid-1980s and then with increasing rapidity in the late-1980s and early 1990s as the impact of these policies on every aspect of the social fabric became clearer.

Figure 24.1: Public Issues Programmes, 1983–1991

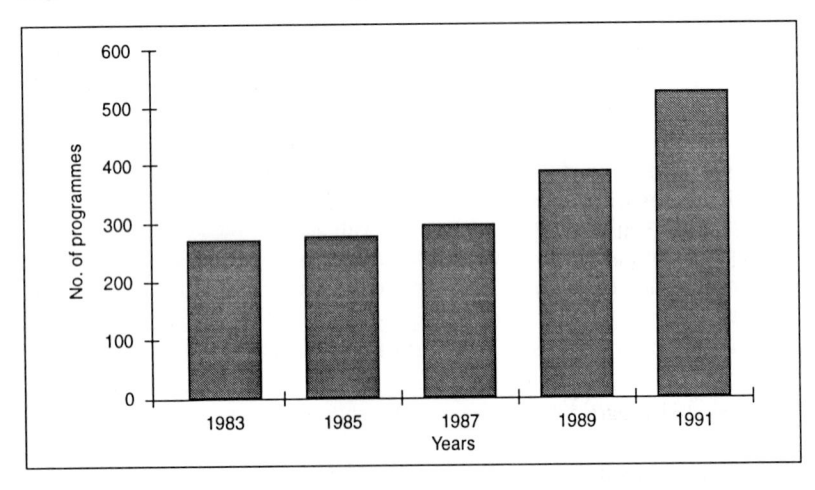

Figure 24.2: Number of Public Issues-oriented Programmes in Selected Areas, 1983–1991

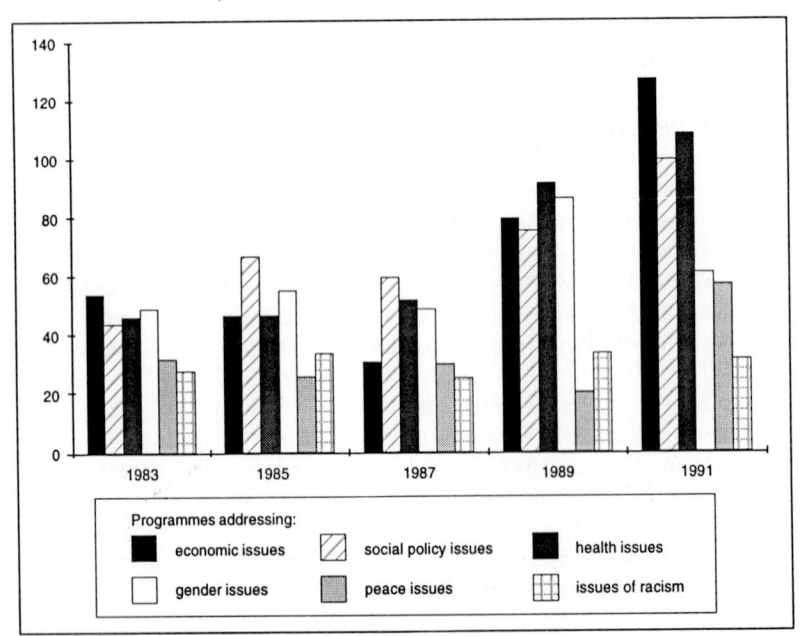

Issues

What kinds of issues were discussed and debated over the period? What forms did the ideological struggles take? It is clear that these struggles can only be understood within the context of the real economic, social, cultural and political changes taking place. Unfortunately, within the space of this chapter it will not be possible to describe and analyse these changes. Nevertheless, where necessary, brief references will be made to key events and trends that had a direct impact on the ideological struggles.

When one looks at the overall picture (Figure 24.2), it appears that programmes dealing with social policy issues (342 programmes), issues of health and disability (341 programmes) and economic, employment and trade union issues (335 programmes) were the most common. These were followed by programmes dealing with gender issues (297 programmes), peace and violence (162 programmes) and biculturalism and racism (148 programmes). Other kinds of issues were also reflected in the programmes. These included environmental issues, education, the media, party political issues, local and regional issues and international issues. In addition a small number of programmes dealt with general issues or current affairs that could not readily be classified. To illustrate what happened with these programmes during this period, the rest of this chapter looks at three of these issues in more detail.

Economic, Employment and Trade Union Issues

Between 1983 and 1987 there was a consistent falling away in the number of programmes dealing with economic issues. By way of contrast, between 1987 and 1991 there was a very sharp and dramatic increase. Although some of this increase can be attributed to a small growth in the number of programmes offered by educational institutions and by state and local authority organisations, the major increase was in programmes organised by voluntary organisations and community groups. In very broad terms, over the entire period there was a shift in emphasis from issues dealing with narrower sectoral interests and industrial relations to those addressing broader trade union and poverty matters and the political economy and economic policy directions in general.

Economically 1983 was a bad year for New Zealand. The economy was contracting; the number of unemployed was increasing rapidly to a total of 80,000, or 5.4 per cent of the paid workforce; the balance of payments deficit was continuing to grow; and there was evidence that the gap between rich and poor was also growing. One measure that had been taken by the state in June 1982 in the hope of countering the runaway inflation of over 16 per cent per annum was the institution of a 'wage-price freeze'. This remained in operation throughout 1983.

Not surprisingly therefore, 1983 was characterised by a large number of programmes addressing issues of employment and unemployment. These ranged from meetings to look at job promotion and worker co-operatives to meetings to form a local branch of the unemployed workers union. Given the increasing unpopularity of the policies of the Muldoon government it is not surprising perhaps that there were also a number of programmes which examined economic policy directions. Programmes also focused on trade union and/or industrial relations issues as well as issues affecting particular agricultural, industrial or services sectors of the economy.

Fourth Labour Government

When the fourth Labour government was elected to office in mid-1984 it was widely believed that the economy was in crisis. The incoming government took a number of immediate steps including a 20 per cent devaluation of the New Zealand dollar and a short-term price freeze to stabilise the situation. However, it did little to dispel the sense of crisis which provided the political climate within which it was possible for the neo-classical economists in Treasury and in Government to take a number of initiatives during 1985 which transformed the political economy. These measures included the floating of the New Zealand dollar, the lifting of foreign exchange controls, the abolition of limits on foreign ownership of financial institutions, the removal or reduction of export subsidies and import tariffs, duties and restrictions, the broadening of the tax base with the introduction of GST, the reduction of marginal tax rates and the reduction in the scope of the provision of a wide range of state services and of state expenditure for the provision of these goods and services.

Whether or not the negative evaluation and sense of economic crisis was warranted must remain a matter for debate. What is clear is that the immediate measures taken do seem to have been successful in stabilising the situation. 1985 saw a growth of 5 per cent in real Gross Domestic Product and a fall to 4.7 per cent in the rate of unemployment.

Perhaps reflecting this more positive economic climate, 1985 saw a lower overall number of programmes in this area. In particular, the number of programmes addressing issues of employment and unemployment fell by a third and there were fewer programmes dealing with economic policy directions. Not surprisingly however, in view of the changes being made in the tax structure, the number of programmes dealing with taxation issues and especially with GST rose substantially to their highest level over the entire period. With the establishment of a Ministry of Consumer Affairs several programmes were identified dealing with consumer issues. The number of programmes focused on trade union and/or industrial relations issues and on issues affecting particular agricultural, industrial or services sectors of the economy remained about the same as in 1983.

If 1985 provided some evidence of increased economic stability and growth arising in part out of the short-term measures taken by government in 1984, it would seem that the medium-term outcomes of the measures adopted by the New Right ideologues from early 1985 were by no means as successful. By 1987, the growth in real GDP had dropped to 2.5 per cent – half the rate of growth in 1985 – and this rate continued to fall to -1.4 per cent in 1989 and -1.8 per cent in 1991. In addition, the rate of unemployment had increased again to 5.2 per cent in 1987 and then to 9.0 per cent in 1989 and 10.2 per cent in 1991.

Re-election of Labour Government

In view of this and especially since 1987 was an election year, it is surprising to find that the number of programmes addressing economic issues was at such a low ebb – only 30 programmes were identified, compared with 53 in 1983. During the latter part of the year, however, following the re-election of the Labour government with a very much reduced majority, there was some increase in activity. This was lead by such groups as the WEA, the Women's Economic Awareness Group, the Kitchen Table and the Otautahi Women's Labour Pool. Nevertheless, over the entire year fewer programmes addressing economic issues were organised than in either of the previous years. Moreover, educational institutions and state and local authority organisations offered very little.

By 1989 a significant change had taken place. The number of programmes focusing on economic, employment and trade union issues had increased to 79 – more than double the 1987 figure. This included an increased involvement by educational institutions, as well as in the number of programmes organised by state and local authority organisations. These latter programmes addressed such issues as tourism, exporting, innovations in business and women's unpaid work. The biggest increase in 1989, however, was in the number of programmes organised by voluntary organisations, community groups and individuals. They organised a total of 51 programmes – more than double the 1987 figure. The dominant themes of the programmes were those of employment and unemployment as well as wider issues of economic policy. There was also an increase in programmes dealing with trade union and industrial relations issues.

Election of National Government

In November 1990, the National government was elected to office and in December it introduced a package of measures cutting benefits significantly and extending the stand-down period for the unemployment benefit to six months. This was followed in May 1991 by the enactment of the Employment Contracts Act – a measure designed to increase 'labour market flexibility' – to do away with national negotiations and awards on wages and conditions of employment and to encourage work-based negotiations and agreements and individual employment contracts. In a situation of high unemployment, it constituted a direct attack on the trade union movement since under the Act trade unions had no greater rights than any other agent. In particular it threatened the wages and conditions of service of the least powerful and lowest paid segments of the labour market. Then in July 1991 the Budget sought to introduce a wide range of further cost-cutting measures and measures designed to reduce the size of the welfare state.

Not surprisingly in light of this, the number of programmes focusing on economic, employment and trade union issues increased dramatically to a total of 127. The number of programmes provided by educational institutions fell away to eight, and state and local authority organisations organised only six programmes – very small contributions at a time of rapid change. Much of the increase consisted of protest meetings and gatherings called to discuss, debate and/or protest against the benefit cuts, the Employment Contracts Act 1991, the Budget cuts to education, the announcement of further radical changes to the health system and the surcharge on superannuation.

Voluntary organisations and community groups active in organising programmes included the WEA, the Kitchen Table, the Council of Trade Unions, a number of individual trade unions, the Public Service Association, the Christchurch Unemployed Rights Centre, the National Council of Churches, the Conference of Churches in Aotearoa/New Zealand, the Women's Refuge movement, the Christian Family Movement Solo Parents' Support Group, the National Superannuitants' Federation, Grey Power and Age Concern. Overall, the focus of the majority of programmes was on broad issues of economic policy as these were manifested in the key measures taken by government. These of course related to concerns about the survival of the trade union movement and for the first time a number of programmes focused on issues of poverty in Aotearoa/New Zealand.

Issues Concerned with Social Policy and the Social Services

Between 1983 and 1989, the increase in programmes focusing on various issues of social policy was small and fluctuating. In 1983, 43 programmes were organised. This increased to 66 in 1985, followed by a slight decrease to 59 in 1987 and then an increase again in 1989 to 75. Between 1989 and 1991 however, the increase was substantial, with the total rising to 99 programmes in 1991. The number of programmes addressing issues of social policy organised

Public Issues and Adult Education

by educational institutions and by state organisations and local authorities remained more or less constant. The growth can therefore be attributed entirely to the increased activity by voluntary organisations and community groups. What kinds of issues were addressed in these programmes? And how do we account for or explain the increase in activity?

In 1983 a number of programmes dealt with issues concerning children, young people and the family and sexual abuse, domestic violence and rape legislation. In addition the first National Disabled Person's Assembly was held in Hamilton in May. In 1985 programmes focused on such issues as smoking, alcohol, drugs and solvent abuse, AIDS counselling, pornography, housing, homosexual law reform, abortion and rural stress.

In 1987 programmes continued to focus on a number of similar issues to those identified in 1983 and 1985. However, there were also programmes focusing on adoption changes organised by the National Organisation for Women, homelessness organised by the YWCA and the Christchurch Shelter for All, and on the funding crisis facing voluntary groups organised by the District Council of Social Services and the Methodist Central Mission.

Programmes organised in 1989 focused on many similar issues to those in previous years. These included substance abuse, housing, children and young people and the family. However, programmes of resistance to the application of New Right ideologies to social policy began to emerge. These included protest action against the erosion of benefits organised by the Christchurch Unemployed Rights Collective, a public meeting to oppose the privatisation of public assets organised by the Public Service Association, a seminar on 'Building base communities' organised by the Anglican Social Responsibility Commission and a discussion on recent social policy changes organised by Presbyterian Support Services.

As in previous years, programmes organised in 1991 addressed a very wide range of issues. However, the number of programmes of resistance to the application of New Right ideologies to social policy increased substantially. At least 20 of the programmes organised by voluntary organisations and groups consisted of public meetings, marches, demonstrations and other gatherings opposing the benefit cuts and the Employment Contracts Act or engaging in a critique of policies. Towards the end of the year, meetings were held to set up a People's Select Committee on Welfare Benefit Cuts which was to gather data and seek submissions in 1992.

Issues Concerned with Health and Disability

Between 1983 and 1987 there was little change in the number of programmes focusing on health and disability issues. In 1983, 45 programmes were identified.

Between 1987 and 1989 the total number of programmes jumped dramatically from 51 to 91, and then rose again in 1991 to a total of 108. This increase can be attributed primarily to the increase in activity by voluntary organisations, community groups and individuals. In 1983, 37 programmes were organised by these groups; by 1991 this had grown to 88. What kinds of issues were addressed in these programmes? And how do we account for or explain the increase in activity in the latter part of the period?

Each year programmes focused on a wide range of health issues. In 1983 a number addressed the concerns faced by people with various disabilities. They included a course on 'Sociological aspects of disability' offered by the Centre for Continuing Education of the University of Canterbury and the New Zealand Conference of the Intellectually Disabled. In 1985 there was an increase in the number of programmes focusing on solvent and alcohol abuse. These included two public forums organised by the Canterbury Community Council on Alcohol and other Drugs – 'Should alcohol be sold in supermarkets?' and 'Merry Christmas for Everyone?'. In addition, there was an increase in the number of support groups, such as ADARDS, Women for Sobriety and the AIDS Support Network, which were formed to provide support and information, as well as to undertake political lobbying. Issues of solvent and alcohol abuse were addressed again in 1989, with several groups focusing exclusively on women with drug or alcohol problems.

The development of awareness weeks to raise public consciousness of health issues, was a noticeable trend throughout our period of study. In 1985 there was an increase in the number of these weeks, organised by such diverse groups as the Diabetes Society, New Zealand Home Birth Association, Canterbury Asthma Society, the Hearing Association and Raja Yoga Centre. By 1991, open meetings, health festivals and awareness weeks appeared to have become an established method of raising the level of public knowledge and understanding of particular health issues.

By 1989 the process of restructuring of the health system was gathering momentum. This process had been initiated by the Area Health Boards Act of 1983 which provided for the replacement of the 27 Hospital Boards by 14 Area Health Boards, responsible for public health, hospitals and some primary healthcare services. This was completed by 1989. In 1988 the report of the Taskforce on Hospitals and Related Services (Gibbs *et al.*, 1988) was published. Few of the recommendations of this report, which was one of a number of reports that were driven by New Right libertarian ideologies, were implemented by the Labour government. Nevertheless, under pressure from Treasury, 1989 and 1990 did see a number of changes which were consistent with the demands of the New Right. These included the restructuring of the Department of Health, changes in the management of Area Health Boards, the introduction of performance indicators and the contracting of services. However, none of these changes were as fundamental as those proposed in the 1991 budget policy statement on reforms.

The rapid increase in programmes addressing health and disabilities issues from 1989 can undoubtedly be attributed in large part to the activity of voluntary organisations and community groups in organising various kinds of public meetings and seminars to discuss and protest against the changes taking place in the health system. In 1989 the groups involved included the Canterbury Health Coalition, the Save Christchurch Women's Hospital Action Group and The Health Alternative for Women.

The number of programmes organised by state and local authority organisations also grew significantly. In 1983 only two such programmes were identified, whereas seven or eight programmes were organised each year in 1987, 1989 and 1991. Most of these were organised by the Canterbury Area Health Board as part of the process of public consultation on policy issues such as the proposed closure of hospitals and priorities in health expenditure. In 1983, 1987 and 1991 the Canterbury Area Health Board also organised programmes addressing questions concerning the health care needs of an ageing New Zealand population.

On the other hand, the number of programmes offered by public educational institutions did not grow much over the period. These programmes fluctuated from a total of six in 1983 to one in 1987 to eight in both 1989 and 1991 and no trends could be identified in the kinds of issues dealt with. In 1983 the Christchurch Clinical School of Medicine organised programmes on health economics and the counselling of sexually abused women. In 1989 the Next Step Centre of the Christchurch Polytechnic offered a number of programmes addressing health issues specifically for women and in 1991 the Christchurch Clinical School of Medicine held a public forum on the future of Canterbury's mental health services.

Conclusion

At the beginning of this chapter we pointed out that at certain historical moments adult and community education has been closely linked with a range of social and political movements. We also drew attention to the view that, in the face of powerful conservative forces affecting educational institutions and leading to the mushrooming of private education and training providers, the 1980s and early 1990s saw a resurgence of collective self-education taking place within the context of social movements and independently of educational institutions.

Our findings summarised in this chapter support this view. Issue-oriented movement-based adult and community education appears for the most part to have been at a relatively low ebb in Christchurch in the mid-1980s. The number of programmes focused on public issues ranged between 268 in 1983 and 297 in 1987. The measures taken by the Labour government between 1984 and 1988 to open the New Zealand economy to the forces of international capitalism appear to have been undertaken with little attempt being made to engage the public (of Christchurch) in any popular education programmes. Even the devastation wreaked upon many rural areas by the sudden withdrawal of agricultural subsidies and the large-scale redundancies that followed the restructuring of a number of state departments and agencies, seem to have provoked few issue-oriented programmes in Christchurch. However, by the time that the policies driven by the New Right were beginning to have a significant impact on the lives of a larger number of people in the late-1980s and early 1990s, the forces of popular resistance began to take shape and influence developments in movement-based adult education. The number of issue-oriented programmes rose to 390 in 1989 and then dramatically to 525 in 1991 following the election of the National government and the renewed assault on the welfare state.

This chapter has summarised some of the key trends and patterns in movement-based adult and community education. Some movements and groups appear to have been more successful and/or active in organising programmes at certain times. Thus, in 1983 various oppositional groups were active in organising educational programmes focusing on economic policy issues. In the mid-1980s, however, these groups were less active in organising public programmes and it was only in the late 1980s and early 1990s that there was a regrouping of oppositional forces and the establishment of a number of campaigns and programmes to debate and challenge the assumptions underlying economic policies. A similar pattern is also discernible when one looks at programmes focused on health and social policy issues. Here too, it was only in the late 1980s and early 1990s that there was a resurgence of programmes focused on these issues.

In our analysis of other areas (not detailed in this chapter), somewhat different patterns emerge. The peace movement appears to have been most active in organising educational programmes in 1983 (when nuclear disarmament was the predominant issue) and in 1991 (at the time of the Gulf War). On the other hand, more programmes addressing issues of racism and biculturalism were organised in 1985 (when sporting contacts with South Africa provided the key focus) and in 1989 (when the 1990 commemoration of the Treaty of Waitangi was the predominant issue) than in any other years. The high point in the organisation of programmes to raise public consciousness of gender inequities appears to have been reached in 1989, with a subsequent decrease in programmes in 1991. One interpretation of this is that, in the face of a conservative onslaught and economic pressures in the 1990s, the women's movement has been in retreat. Further research is, however, necessary to examine this thesis, as well as to examine in greater detail the economic, social, cultural and political changes and their impact on adult and community education.

In this chapter we have also documented the key role played by a very wide range of voluntary organisations and community groups in promoting discussion and debate on public issues, in responding critically to agendas developed by powerful public and private interests and in keeping alive alternative philosophies and agendas. In particular, we have noted the small but important contributions made by voluntary adult education organisations such as the WEA to issues-oriented adult and community education. The roles played by state organisations, local authorities and educational institutions were far more limited and ambiguous than those of voluntary organisations and in a further article we will examine more closely the roles of the various organisations and in particular the roles of schools, colleges and universities in this field.

We believe that too few adult and community educators – and too few educational institutions – take sufficiently seriously their roles in maintaining links with voluntary organisations, community groups and social movements and in raising public policy issues for discussion and debate. They all too readily acquiesce in responding to such issues and in performing ameliorative functions required of them by the state. If this chapter succeeds in documenting and raising questions about modern social movements and their links with adult and community education, it will have served its purpose.

Notes

1. It is based mainly on data gathered for the Christchurch Adult Education Curriculum Project, which will be reported on more fully in a series of monographs to be published in 1996. As a report on work in progress, the findings are still tentative, but it does provide a picture of some of the major trends in issue-oriented adult and community education in Christchurch between 1983 and 1991. We wish to acknowledge the assistance of a number of people, especially Lynda Gill and gratefully acknowledge the financial support of the University of Canterbury from its Research Funds.

References

Boston, J. and Holland, M. (eds) (1987), *The Fourth Labour Government: Radical Politics in New Zealand*, Auckland: Oxford University Press.

Boston, J. and Dalziel, P. (eds) (1992), *The Decent Society? Essays in Response to National's Economic and Social Policies*, Auckland: Oxford University Press.

Cartwright, Silvia (1988), *Report of Committee of Inquiry into Allegations Concerning the Treatment of Cervical Cancer at National Women's Hospital and into Other Related Matters*, Auckland: Government Printing Office.

Coney, Sandra and Bunkle, Phillida (June 1987), 'An "Unfortunate Experiment" at National Women's', *Metro*, pp. 46–65.

Douglas, R. (1993), *Unfinished Business*, Auckland: Random House.

Gibbs, A. et al. (1988), *Unshackling the Hospitals: Report of the Hospital and Related Services Taskforce*, Wellington: Government Printer.

Holland, M. and Boston, J. (eds) (1990), *The Fourth Labour Government: Politics and Policy in New Zealand* (2nd ed.), Auckland: Oxford University Press.

Johnson, R. (1988), '"Really Useful Knowledge" 1790–1850: Memories for Education in the 1980s', in Lovett, T. (ed.), *Radical Approaches to Adult Education*, London: Routledge.

Kelsey, J. (1993), *Rolling Back the State: Privatisation of Power in Aotearoa/New Zealand*, Wellington: Bridget Williams Books Limited.

Law, M. (Chairperson) (1987), *Second Report of the Task Force on Trade Union Education – Trade Union Education: Directions for Change*, Wellington: Government Printer, March.

Law, M. (1993), 'The Changing World of Worker Education', *New Zealand Journal of Adult Learning*, vol. 21, no. 1, pp. 7–33.

Rice, G.W. (ed.) (1992), *The Oxford History of New Zealand* (2nd ed.), Auckland: Oxford University Press.

Roper, C. (1987), *Report of the Ministerial Committee of Inquiry into Violence*, Wellington: Department of Justice, March.

Part 6

Bringing it Together

25

New Zealand Adult and Community Education:

An International Perspective

Joyce Stalker

Throughout this book, the authors have grappled with issues and dilemmas which confront adult educators in Aotearoa/New Zealand. They give timely and useful insights into the history, the development and the contours of adult and community education. In this chapter, I hope to locate these stories within an international context. This is not an easy task, given the extremely complex, ever changing nature of international politics, economies, societies and cultures. This chapter is thus restricted to a brief snapshot of some current international forces which influence adult educators. Indeed, it is more a black and white photograph than a coloured one which catches the many nuances and shades of the issues discussed. Nonetheless, I hope that by raising these issues, I can help to contribute to discussions on the role of adult educators in Aotearoa/New Zealand.

This chapter is presented in three sections. First, it explores three major international forces which currently create the context within which adult educators undertake their practice, create policies and conduct research and theorisation. Second, it presents the traditional responses of the field to these forces and argues for a new approach of appropriation. Finally, the chapter explicates this approach and considers the unique Aotearoa/New Zealand location which must be considered as this response is activated. The chapter finishes with a brief summary and concluding statements.

The Current Context: Major International Forces

It seems that for at least the last decade, it has been impossible to read an article that did not include some comment on the 'rapid social changes' which faced adult educators around the world. At a minimum, these were identified as 'technological advances' and 'the entry or re-entry of women to the paid work force'. Today, although these factors still face adult educators there are forces emerging which although not new, are more frequently visible and more sharply felt. Three of these forces – globalisation, market orientation and fundamentalism – increasingly define the context within which adult educators undertake their practice, create policies and conduct research and theorisation. In reality, of course, these forces are inextricably interwoven and dependent upon each other. For the purposes of clarity and analysis, however, they will be treated as discrete phenomena within the discussions below.

Globalisation

Although the task of defining major international forces seems as impossible as that of defining adult education, this first factor helps to explain the possibility of the task. *Globalisation* is a complex phenomenon which at its most basic can be said to foster homogeneity rather than diversity, sameness rather than difference and unity rather than variance. Its impact is independent of national boundaries. The result of many factors, among them 'technological advances' in communications and transport, its influence is most clearly seen in the areas of knowledge, culture and economic policies and practices. These areas have a symbiotic relationship with globalisation for they both experience and maintain globalisation. Knowledge shared internationally, for example, fosters homogeneity and at the same time globalisation fosters the sharing of knowledge. The following discussion focuses on the impact of globalisation on these areas.

Knowledge

Although some might define *knowledge* as equivalent to the attainment of skills and technical information, I take a more holistic view. Here, knowledge corresponds to the ways in which we understand our worlds. These understandings in turn shape our attitudes and actions. Where once this knowledge was influenced primarily by local social, economic, political and cultural contexts, a much more homogenised global knowledge now is evolving.

Although some might identify television or the information highway as the major purveyors of globalised knowledge, Apple and Christian-Smith (1991) make a persuasive argument that texts hold that role. Altbach (1991) goes on to note that the centralised publication of texts in the United States and other major industrialised countries ensures that the international discourse, although contested, excludes countries on the periphery.

The preferred knowledge within this discourse has an identifiable character. Since its epicentre is located in industrialised 'first' worlds, it corresponds to the needs and demands of the urban, white, able-bodied, heterosexual and for the most part male, leaders of those countries. That location defines what counts as knowledge, which knowledge is valued or deemed to be appropriate and which knowledge is not made available. The resultant homogenisation of ideas, imported through a preferred language, values and norms is interwoven with the globalisation of cultural and economic factors.

Culture

If we define *cultures* as distinguishable systems of values, norms, attitudes and social structures as acted out by individuals within those systems, then the globalisation of culture has profound ramifications. The generation of a mass, standardised consciousness is a cornerstone of such a reconstructed, homogenised system. Given the nature of globalisation as discussed above, it should be clear that this consciousness is of a particular kind; one which is derived from and defined by the industrialised 'first' worlds. The ideology of consumerism dominates and in some instances replaces, more localised cultures. The possibility of a diversified society is replaced by shared understandings of life worlds as defined by that 'first' world.

For indigenous cultures, the consequences of globalisation are particularly serious. As the 'first' world culture permeates their cultures and redefines what are legitimate and relevant values, norms, attitudes and social structures, indigenous peoples may break away from their 'ancient but fragile chain of oral traditions' (Linden, 1991: 45). Since these traditions may hold the knowledge upon which the culture is based, the hegemonic interference of the 'first' worlds can prove destructive to the culture as a whole.

Economic Policies and Practices

Although it is beyond the parameters of this chapter to define the complex nature of economics, it is important to include this dimension of globalisation. After all, some would argue that economic policies and practices are the fundamental processes which lead to globalisation and that the homogenisation of knowledge and culture are merely their byproducts. Basically, these factors involve monetary relationships which shape the growth and interdependence of countries. At a micro-level they are measurable in the health and development of industries and firms. At the macro-level, they involve the national income and gross national product.

As noted above, the study of the impact of globalisation on knowledge, culture and economic policies and practices is muddied by the role of those areas in maintaining globalisation. Bearing that in mind, evidence of the impact of globalisation on economic policies and practices is evident at several levels. At one level, nations are increasingly bound together economically by their shift or increased commitment to some form of a capitalistic economic system. At other levels, globalisation is evident through the developing and defining power of multinational corporations and their associated international managerial class; through the increasing involvement of the World Bank and the International Monetary Fund in the economic lives of all countries; through the compartmentalised production of single items shared among different nations; and through the binding and decisive role of multilevel trade agreements among countries. Given the strength and activities of these factors, it becomes a moot question as to whether it is possible for any economic policies and practices to operate independently of global forces.

Market Orientation

Market orientation is a second major international force which defines the context within which adult educators work. It fosters globalisation and fundamentalism and is simultaneously sustained by them. To best understand this force, it is important to examine the perspective which forms its cornerstone: the New Right. Indeed, it is the New Right perspective which guides the globalisation of economic policies and practices examined earlier.

This perspective exists in a variety of forms and is known by a variety of names, for example: neo-conservatism, neo-liberalism, Thatcherism, Reaganism, Rogernomics and structural adjustment. It has been extensively explored in numerous books and articles (e.g. Levitas, 1986; Green, 1987; Manne, 1982; Coghill, 1987; Jesson, Ryan and Spoonley, 1988). This paper identifies and briefly discusses six of the elements which revolve around the notion of market orientation: privatisation; open competition; consumerism, user-pays; flexibility of the workforce and workplace; and rationality.

A basic premise of this view is that the state has no role intervening in the conduct of society, that a healthier society results when it is market- rather than state-driven. Thus, New Right proponents support the privatisation of state services in, for example, the areas of health, transport and communication.

They believe that corporate freedom will ensure that only those providers who offer services which meet the market demand for quality outputs will survive. They argue that the quality and nature of these services will be regulated naturally by a marketplace in which there is open competition among many providers. This notion of open competition is comprehensive, for it includes the concept of individuals competing against individuals with nations competing against nations in the global marketplace.

The sovereignty of the individual plays an important role in this configuration, for it neatly links the concepts of privatisation and open competition. Since the New Right emphasises the *absolute* freedom of individuals within society, this supports their distaste for interference in the lives of individuals (for example, through benefits for the unemployed or union-negotiated contracts) or the false protection of particular interest groups (for example, Maori and women) who are in competition with other interest groups (for example, Pakeha and men).

Simultaneously, the emphases on these three elements fosters both consumerism and a user-pays approach. The assumption in a New Right environment is that individuals have absolute, unrestricted freedom to make choices suited to themselves and thus to achieve their goals. It follows that they are believed to make better choices for their circumstances than the state and thus to be active consumers who are uncontaminated, unrestrained and unhampered by state intervention. Given this scenario, it is argued, it makes more sense that individuals accept a user-pays model in which they pay relative to what they use. Since the user-pays model is a natural consequence of privatisation, these elements weave together nicely.

Since the New Right prefers an unfettered marketplace, it follows that it requires a corresponding flexibility in the workforce and workplace. The workforce and workplace must be able to make rapid responses to shifts in micro-level consumer demands or in macro-level international policies. Part-time workers, a large cadre of skilled unemployed willing and able to work short-term and employer-defined contracts, ensure that the New Right sustains a flexible workforce and workplace.

Underlying these six elements of market orientation is a strong emphasis on rationality. There is a strict logic which rejects contradictory views or actions. Individuals, organisations and social structures are subject to measurement and control in relation to this market orientation. Ideally, decisions are based on empirical, 'objective', instrumental deduction, yet there is little attempt to appraise the rationality of the ends themselves. Ultimately, actions are deemed to be rational if they effectively and efficiently meet the needs of the marketplace.

Fundamentalism

Fundamentalism is a third force which creates the context within which adult educators work. It is interesting to note that fundamentalism originally referred to American Protestantism in the early twentieth century. Today, it includes many communities, the most visible being the Islamic and Judaic communities. Concurrently its association with democracy and progress has disappeared and now often it is viewed as 'just another synonym for religious dogmatism or ideologically rooted authoritarianism' (Davidson Hunter, 1990: 56).

Basically, fundamentalism is a movement which emphasises the importance of the literal tenets of a particular religious doctrine (Marsden, 1991). It seeks to restore the traditional values based on the tenets drawn from historical religious texts. Its objective is to recreate an original moral, cultural and religious base. In 'first' worlds, this is often evidenced in fundamentalists' attempts to make abortion illegal, to retract social, educational and health regulations which conflict with 'family values', to return to the practice of Christian prayers in public schools, to elect Christian politicians and so on.

Fundamentalism is also based in a belief that the material world of modernity and modernism, its complementary ideology, has gone awry. Fundamentalists thus see their task as the recreation of their religious historical worlds and ideologies. They question the modernists' view of the world – a world which they assume to be one of an 'enlightened', secular leadership and direction – which modernists prefer to a religiously led leadership and direction. They counter reason with faith, and scientific rationality with universal norms drawn from a religious doctrine (Lawrence, 1989). Their questioning of liberal convictions places issues of social conscience on the social agenda. These multiple challenges often result in fundamentalists' separation and isolation from the surrounding modern society.

At first glance, fundamentalism would appear to create fragmented rather than homogenous cultures and to counter the effects of globalisation. After all, Christian, Islamic and Judaic fundamentalisms have distinctive historical, geographical and doctrinal characteristics. It seems that antagonisms between the 'remarkably dense networks of interactions ... and the demand for the recognition of identity' (Larochelle, 1992: 150) are inevitable. It can be argued, however, that fundamentalisms share basic characteristics as outlined above and further that they seek to promulgate their religious ideologies at a global level. Some also argue that because some configuration of modernity exists globally, then its antithesis, fundamentalism, must also exist globally (Lawrence, 1989). At any rate, although fundamentalism creates a theoretical tension with globalisation, they nonetheless coexist simultaneously.

Recalling the previous section, it is important to note that the promulgation of fundamentalist norms, values and attitudes often complement a market orientation. The withdrawal of public support for health, education and transportation, for example, is sustained by ideologies which argue for 'traditional' morals in which family members are responsible for many aspects of their own welfare. State restraints also mesh neatly with voluntary involvement in the community encouraged by a return to 'traditional' morals. The impact of this convergence of fundamentalism and market orientation falls particularly heavily on women who traditionally have carried the responsibility for the care of those most affected by the withdrawal of state support (e.g. children, sick and elderly family and community members).

Summary

This section has discussed three major international factors which create the context within which adult educators undertake their practice, create policies and conduct research and theorisation. It is clear that they affect Aotearoa/New Zealand adult educators. A careful reader would have found them woven throughout the previous chapters in both explicit and implicit ways. For example, several authors link the origins of some of our adult education organisations to overseas organisations, a survey of the articles' references speaks to the issue of knowledge and culture imported from industrialised 'first' worlds; various authors address the New Right and the impact of its market orientation on vocationalising the field and in ensuring its underfunding; several authors express a concern for the survival and strengthening of Maori protocols and traditions.

Given this orientation, how can adult educators respond to globalisation, market orientation and fundamentalism? In all these cases, positive as well as negative consequences are possible. In the case of globalisation, for example, there is a tendency to assume imperialistic and colonialistic consequences and to decry the sacrifice and exploitation of those on the periphery to the imperialistic tendencies of those 'at the centre' who shape the process. As well, it is common to highlight the shallowness of societies which might be stripped of their social differentiation, diverse ethnicities, class structures and regional variations.

Globalisation may have more positive impacts, however. For example, some applaud the advance of globalisation and focus on the possibilities for a harmonised and unified macro-society with reduced conflicts among subcultures. They suggest that globalisation may encourage us to take responsibility for oppressions beyond our national borders (Giroux, 1992). Others point to the emergence of global social movements such as the peace movement and the campaign against the apartheid system. These movements are applauded for creating 'new civil solidarities across boundaries' (Hegedus, 1990: 274).

In view of these theoretical hopes for positive impacts the key question becomes 'How can we best respond to major international forces in order to counter their negative impact and yet simultaneously foster their positive effects?'. The next section addresses this question.

Potential Responses by Adult Educators

Traditionally, the adult education literature has provided two models of response for adult educators to implement when faced with the challenge of action: the consensus and the conflict models (e.g. Jarvis, 1985; Rubenson, 1980; Thomas, 1982). More recently, contemporary responses which loosely fit within an interpretivist view have emerged (e.g. Collard and Law, 1990; Welton, 1994; Wildermeersch and Jansen, 1991; Westwood, 1991). Although the adult education literature seldom promotes a purely New Right response, some insights about it can be gained by those who critique it directly (e.g. McIlroy and Spencer, 1988; Newman, 1994). As one might imagine, each of these perspectives is complex, with subtle and intertwined characteristics. Thus, the following discussion introduces these views only briefly,[1] before moving on to recommend a new model of response: appropriation. (Since the New Right perspective was explored fully above in relation to globalisation, it will not be presented again here.)

Consensus

A basic characteristic of the consensus view is that society is a harmonious, stable, balanced and static entity which functions successfully. It is similar to a smoothly operating, living organism in which each element is unique, but interdependent on each other element. For adult educators responding from this perspective, continued equilibrium and survival of the whole are of paramount importance.

Adult educators who hold this viewpoint accept a society in which some individuals and groups of individuals have much more power, authority and control relative to other groups. They see this hierarchical relationship as normal. There is a sense that 'the poor will always be with us'. Furthermore, the differential power is perceived as essential for the continuance of a smoothly operating society in which some are more able to lead and others more suited to follow.

This analysis is congruent with a strong concern for 'society's good' rather than for the good of the individual. This is not to say that the individual is ignored, for adult educators who hold the consensus view stress the role and responsibilities of the individual. In particular, they emphasise the multiple and equal opportunities available to individuals. They point to the rewards which are achievable and deserved by those who work hard and apply themselves. There is a strong sense that 'you can make it if you try'.

Consensus adult educators respond to issues like poverty, for example, from a charitable base. Frequently, they apply a top-down approach and focus on remedial activities designed to improve the attitudes and behaviours of those individuals who have 'failed'. They focus their practice, policies and research agendas on 'helping' and 'motivating' adults to adapt, adjust, cope and harmonise with their environments. In other words, they accept, maintain and perpetuate the existing social, political, cultural and economic structures.

Conflict

In contrast to the consensus viewpoint, the conflict view basically stresses the dynamic, ever-changing nature of society. Unlike the harmonious, balanced and static society of the consensus perspective, the conflict society is viewed as volatile and energised. It is an unstable form within which different kinds of groups exist in states of tension and confrontation.

Adult educators who theorise their worlds from a conflict viewpoint, like those who hold the consensus view, note that there are groups which have more power, authority and control relative to other groups. Those with a conflict perspective, however, respond to the situation by labelling the differentials of power and authority as *un*acceptable. They judge inequalities to be the unjust expression of a society in which the élite class creates, manipulates and maintains the lower classes' powerlessness in order to benefit themselves.

Their analysis is congruent with their concern for 'group interests' rather than for individuals' interests. They see society in terms of groups of élite and powerful who control the social, political, cultural and economic structures in order to ensure the perpetuation of less power among groups such as the working class, the poor and women. It follows that adult educators with a conflict perspective presume that the solutions to poverty, for example, do not rest with the effort of the individual. Neither do they blame the individual for the situation. Rather, they consider the 'oppression' which groups of the poor suffer at the hands of the groups who hold the resources. They emphasise the rightful claim that the oppressed have to the power, control, authority and resources of the élite.

Adult educators from this perspective focus their practice, policies and research agendas on promoting group activities which collectively challenge the existing social, political, cultural and economic structures. They are involved in raising group consciousness about inequitable social structures, injustices and violation of rights. In other words, they challenge the status quo.

Interpretive

Those holding an interpretive perspective view the world as a complex place of negotiated understandings. Within it, groups and individuals create and maintain shared rules. These are influenced by social, political, cultural and economic contexts. Thus, in one context, a set of keys may indicate wealth, while in another it may represent the torture associated with imprisonment.

From this viewpoint, groups with differential power are not about a social structure required to make society function well, nor are they about overcoming the oppression of some to the disadvantage of others. Rather, these groups represent complex structures which are linked and constantly interact to form the particular nature of a society at a particular moment. Interpretive adult educators respond to these interactions and the changes they may engender with interest and curiosity. They seek to uncover the shared practices, beliefs and spoken and unspoken agreements among groups and individuals which guide society.

As one might expect, these adult educators have a unique interpretation of and response to, an individual's or group's situation of, for example, poverty. They suggest that this situation should be understood by exploring the subjective experiences of those involved. Solutions to situations of poverty, are similarly subjective and notions of charity, justice or rights are deemed to have different meanings and different levels of desirability in different contexts.

In other words, one can say that while consensus adult educators respond by maintaining the status quo and conflict adult educators challenge it, interpretive adult educators seek to understand, analyse and reveal common-sense understandings of people's life-worlds.

Discussion

The above three models of action are not without their critics. The consensus and conflict models are often dismissed for their simplistic, reductionistic and deterministic views of society and conflict. Both these models are criticised also for their abstract and macro-level analyses which are impractical and do not adequately explain or resolve problems. This latter criticism is also directed at the interpretivist response which often is said to suffer from paralysis by analysis. The New Right model offers a framework for response which, as we have seen in the discussions above, is embedded within the very forces which we may wish to change. It appears that a new model of action is required.

A New Model of Action: Appropriation

For many adult educators, their dissatisfaction with the models runs deeper than criticisms of abstract analysis or simplistic views. In this volume, for example, most of the authors either explicitly or implicitly embedded their writing within a social justice agenda. The perplexing dilemma for adult educators is to find a way to retain and realise that agenda, given the potency of international forces. A new model of action is necessary; one which ensures that we can remain 'gloriously one-sided' (Newman, 1995, page not numbered) in our commitment to an agenda for social justice.

I suggest that a more powerful model of response is based on the notion of appropriation. While the other models function to accommodate, resist or understand, a model of appropriation would redirect energy to capturing individuals, organisations and social structures. Such a model views society as dynamic, flexible and somewhat chaotic. This view of society as fluid and unpredictable offers adult educators different kinds of opportunities. Chaos, after all, suggests that there are unmonitored spaces and cracks into which we can insert our social agenda. In addition, as discussed earlier, it is clear that international forces have both positive and negative impacts. This model allows adult educators to work in both dimensions; to accommodate and facilitate positive elements, yet to resist negative ones.

This model accepts most adult educators' lived experiences in which they accommodate oppressive individual, organisational and societal systems, yet counters them by highlighting the potential to create change from within. It replaces the notion of co-operation with one of capture. It identifies resistance to oppression as a multifaceted, multidimensional activity which can be carried out at many levels and uses an understanding of the system to further its capture. Most importantly, this model retains a clear, urgent drive toward a society in which resources, power, control and authority are equally allocated.

In summary, this model is about finding the cracks and spaces, the interstices, where social changes can be made. It is a model guided by a sense of urgency to accomplish a social agenda for justice. This model used in the particular Aotearoa/New Zealand context has interesting possibilities. I undertake an initial exploration of those possibilities below.

Appropriation in the Aotearoa/New Zealand Context

Elsewhere in this book, Findsen and Harré Hindmarsh have referred to Snook's (1989) identification of three characteristics which make Aotearoa/New Zealand unique. While not disagreeing with these characteristics, as an emigrant of five years and a new Aotearoa/New Zealand citizen, I see them somewhat differently. I believe that the unique nature of Aotearoa/New Zealand can be identified as its struggles over the Treaty of Waitangi, its peripheral location and its history as a social laboratory. In the discussion below, I begin to explore the possibilities that these unique features offer adult educators who respond to major international forces from an appropriation perspective.

Struggles Over the Treaty of Waitangi

The struggles over the Treaty of Waitangi provide an ideal environment in which adult educators, both Maori and Pakeha can strive to accomplish an agenda of social justice. The ongoing negotiations, the constant interpretations at many locations and many levels all suggest a society which is dynamic, flexible and somewhat chaotic. Within this energy and movement, adult educators can seek out, at many levels, the cracks and spaces.

The struggles give us the opportunity to counter the negative and select the positive elements of globalisation, market orientation and fundamentalism. The Treaty can strengthen and legitimate adult educators' defence against globalised knowledges and cultures. Since it defines Aotearoa/New Zealand's knowledge and culture in a unique way, it potentially gives us a strong basis from which to capture only those aspects which are congruent with the Treaty.

A market orientation and its congruent economic policies and practices can be captured and used to further Maori economic independence. We have already seen Maori educators use the privatisation principles to create whare wananga, health centres and training organisations. As well, to the extent that the Treaty emphasises non-objective, non-measurable phenomena such as the spirituality of the land, it helps us in our fights against the stark rationality of a market orientation.

The Treaty also offers us educative possibilities in terms of fundamentalism. We can create new possibilities if we rethink its current pejorative connotations and its strictly theological emphasis and retain its stress on tradition, belief in fundamentals related to spirituality and a willingness to take a stand against modernism (Marsden, 1987). We can visualise a movement which might result in positive effects. After all, and of particular importance to those who live in Aotearoa/New Zealand, there are elements within fundamentalism which suggest an attempt to reinstate spirituality which was held and valued in the past. It follows that particular elements of fundamentalism might encourage the revitalisation of indigenous cultures and traditions in Aotearoa/New Zealand. As well, if globalisation and fundamentalism do exist simultaneously, it is possible that revitalised indigenous cultures may create alliances linked to the attainment of world-wide political power and social justice.

Peripheral Location

Adult educators in Aotearoa/New Zealand occupy a unique site. To some extent this has to do with its geographical isolation, but it is also clear that we are peripheral to major international game playing in the social, political and economic arenas. There is a sense that such a position guarantees that either our uniqueness is subsumed and consumed by, or marginalised and separated from, the major forces. The task for adult educators is to use the appropriation model in this location to advance an agenda for social fairness and equity.

This seems possible, for we are in a position of being able to both understand and oppose hegemonic international forces. It is possible that as adult educators we are more able to select and adapt imported knowledges and cultures precisely because of our peripheral location. This suggests the possibility of recreating and reforming the role of adult educators based on the best of the traditions which are imported to us. This could be linked to our study, from a distance, of the impact of market orientation and fundamentalism. In Britain, for example, we can see that privatisation is faltering as the number of agencies interested in purchasing government services decrease, as leaders of privatised industries are brought to trial on fraud and embezzlement charges and as the middle class begins to feel the social ramifications of the New Right's privatisation of social services. As adult educators, there is much to learn from these scenarios, much which can help us to be proactive in shaping an alternative path towards a neo-New Right environment. Similarly, we can look at the militant Christian fundamentalism in the United States around issues like abortion and act, in advance of similar hostilities, to resolve the issue in more productive ways. We can, in other words, appropriate these discourses and direct them in ways which are useful in this environment.

History as a Social Laboratory

Aotearoa/New Zealand has a history of being a social laboratory. The task is for adult educators to anticipate, initiate or guide the social experiments so that they foster a more just allocation of social, political, economic and cultural resources in our society.

Thus, as adult educators in the country which has gained a reputation as a 'pure' New Right nation, we need to anticipate the future shape and form of globalisation, market orientation and fundamentalism. Informed by global shifts in the New Right situation, we can help to shape neo-New Right economic policies and practices which are emerging. Energies can still be spent in combatting the negative impact of the current policies and practices, but we need to strategise to capture the emerging paradigm.

Mixed Member Proportional (MMP) government and referenda offer adult educators other opportunities to further our social agenda. Although not unique to Aotearoa/New Zealand, both have the potential to bring deep changes to our political structure. The fragmentation of political parties under MMP suggests a shifting balance of power which could give the field of adult education scope for more serious lobbying. Similarly, adult educators can play an important role in the definition of and education around referenda topics. As well, the malcontent and votes of resistance which seemed to drive both the institution of MMP and referenda results, offer us cracks and spaces within which to foster changes.

Conclusion

This paper has examined three major international forces which influence adult educators in Aotearoa/New Zealand. It has presented the traditional responses of the field and formulated a new model of appropriation. The possibilities for that model were explored within the unique Aotearoa/New Zealand context.

A model of appropriation acknowledges the day-to-day experiences of many adult educators who work within oppressive systems. It emphasises the notion of capture and is guided by a sense of urgency to accomplish a social agenda of justice. This model offers an alternative view which can reform the role of adult educators into more proactive agents of change. The task for both Maori and Pakeha is to use it in partnership in productive and imaginative ways.

Note

1. For a fuller discussion of these perspectives, see Stalker, J. (forthcoming), 'Sharing the Secrets of Perspectives: Operating Honestly in the Classroom', in Boud, D. and Miller, N. (eds.), *Working with Experience: Promoting Learning,* London: Jossey-Bass (pp. unknown).

References

Altbach, P. (1991), 'The International Dimension', in Apple, M. and Christian-Smith, L. (eds), *The Politics of the Textbook,* New York: Routledge.

Apple, M. and Christian-Smith, L. (1991), 'The Politics of the Textbook', in Apple, M. and Christian-Smith, M. (eds), *The Politics of the Textbook,* New York: Routledge.

Coghill, K. (ed.) (1987), *The New Right's Australian Fantasy,* Victoria: McPhee Gribble.

Collard, S. and Law, M. (1990), 'Universal Abandon: Postmodernity, Politics and Adult Education', Proceedings of the 31st Adult Education Research Conference Atlanta, Georgia: University of Georgia, pp. 54–58.

Davidson Hunter, J. (1990), 'Fundamentalism in its Global Contours', in Norman, J. (ed.), *The Fundamentalist Phenomenon: A View from Within, a Response from Without,* Grand Rapids, MI: Eerdmans Publishing.

Giroux, H. (1992), *Border Crossings: Cultural Workers and the Politics of Education,* New York: Routledge.

Green, D. (1987), *The New Right: The Counter Revolution in Political Economic and Social Thought,* Sussex: Wheatsheaf Books.

Hegedus, Z. (1990), 'Social Movements and Social Change in Self-creative Society', in Albrow, M. and King, E. (eds), *Globalization, Knowledge and Society,* London: Sage.

Jarvis, P. (1985), *Sociology of Adult and Continuing Education,* London: Crumb Helm.

Jesson, B., Ryan, A. and Spoonley, P. (1988), *Revival of the Right: New Zealand Politics in the 1980s,* Australia: Heinemann Reed.

Keddie, N. (1992), 'Adult Education in the Marketplace', Proceedings of the 11th Annual Conference of Canadian Association for the Study of Adult Education, Saskatoon, Saskatchewan: University of Saskatchewan, College of Education.

LaPlante, E. (1991), 'Lost Tribes, Lost Knowledge', *Time,* September, pp. 44–56.

Larochelle, G. (1992), 'Interdependence, Globalization and Fragmentation', in Milinar, Z. (ed.), *Globalization and Territorial Identities,* England: Avebury.

Lawrence, B. (1989), *Defenders of God,* San Francisco: Harper and Row.

Levitas, R. (ed.) (1986), *The Ideology of the New Right,* Cambridge: Polity Press.

Linden, E. (1991), 'Lost Tribes, Lost Knowledge', *Time,* September, pp. 44–56.

Manne, R. (ed.) (1982), *The New Conservatism in Australia,* Melbourne: Oxford University Press.
Marsden, G. (1987), *Reforming Fundamentalism,* Grand Rapids, MI: Eerdmans Publishing.
Marsden, G. (1991), *Understanding Fundamentalism and Evangelicalism,* Grand Rapids, MI: Eerdmans Publishing.
McIlroy, J. and Spencer, B. (1988), *University Adult Education in Crisis,* Leeds: Studies in Adult and Continuing Education.
Newman, M. (1995), 'Locating Learning in Social Action', Proceedings of the Trade Union Training in Australia, Asia and the Pacific Conference, Sydney: Australian Trade Union Training Authority:
Rubenson, K. (1980), 'Background and Theoretical Context', in Höghielm, R. and Rubenson, R. (eds), *Adult Education for Social Change: Research on the Swedish Allocation Policy,* Lund: Gleerup.
Snook, I. (1989), 'Educational Reform in New Zealand: What is Going On?', Paper presented at the New Zealand Association for Research in Education, Trentham.
Thomas, J.E. (1982), *Radical Adult Education: Theory and Practice,* Nottingham: University of Nottingham.
Welton, M. (1994), in *Defence of the Life World,* New York: Suny Press.
Westwood, S. (1991), 'Constructing the Future: A Postmodern Agenda for Adult Education', in Westwood, S. and Thomas, J. (eds), *Radical Agendas: The Politics of Adult Education,* London: Billing and Son.
Wildermeersch, D. and Jansen, T. (1991), *Adult Education, Experiential Learning and Social Change: A Post-modern Critique,* Gravenhage, Netherlands: VUGA.

Glossary

Access – a government-funded training programme for unemployed, particularly youth, to equip them to return to the workforce.

Adult and Community Education Association Aotearoa/New Zealand (ACEA) – refer to the New Zealand Association for Community and Continuing Education (NZACCE)

Adult Reading and Learning Association Federation (ARLA) – this federation of adult literacy schemes in Aotearoa/New Zealand was set up in 1982. In 1990, in recognition of the Treaty of Waitangi, it developed two sections with equal funding – the original Pakeha arm and the newly established Te Whiri Kaupapa Ako (TWKA). See Chapter 3 by Jennie Harré Hindmarsh for further details.

Committee for Community Learning Aotearoa/New Zealand (CLANZ) – set up in 1989 as a national advisory committee on non-formal learning. Originally it advised the Minister of Education on significant events/issues for the fourth sector but this role was later withdrawn by the Minister. CLANZ disburses very modest funds to community groups in the field.

Community Learning Centres (CLC) – in 1974 the government, subsequent to the Educational Development Conference, initially targeted four schools for extra resources to boost community education initiatives. The additional resources consisted of extra staffing allocation (at least one full-time organiser) and a grant for administration. Subsequently the scheme was expanded to other schools.

Declaration of Independence (1835) – this document, which predated the signing of the Treaty of Waitangi by five years, was signed by 35 northern Maori chiefs to create a confederation of the chiefs and tribes of New Zealand. It soon languished because of a lack of support from the British Government.

Education and Training Support Agency (ETSA) – a government-sponsored agency which focuses its effort on skills development for work. It consults with industry sectors to identify training needs and develop training systems. Major training initiatives include the new Industry Training Strategy, traineeships and Training Opportunities Programmes.

Education Review Office (ERO) – an autonomous agency established by government to monitor and review the financial and educational performance of educational institutions as stated in their charters.

Educational Development Conference (EDC) of 1972–1974 consisted of a major review of the directions of New Zealand education through consultation with citizens and through participation by international experts in conferences. See chapters by Jim Dakin (Chapter 1) and Robert Tobias (Chapter 2) for further discussion.

Employment Contracts Act 1991 (ECA) – established by the National government, this Act provides for employers to arrange individual contracts with employees. In effect, it treats unions as third parties, not as a collective agency working for and with, workers. For its effects, see Chapter 10 by Michael Law.

Industry Training Act (ITA) of 1992 – this Act sets the directions for industry training, including the establishment of Industry Training Organisations. See chapters by Michael Law (Chapter 10) and Liz Moore (Chapter 11).

Industry Training Organisations (ITO) – recently established industry-based organisations formed to co-ordinate and articulate the special training and development needs of that industry. ITOs set standards for the industry training in accord with the NZQA framework. Refer to Chapter 11 by Liz Moore for more discussion on ITOs.

Mixed Member Proportional Representation (MMP) – a system of voting which combines candidate and party selection in electorates to replace the former 'first-past-the-post' regime. MMP will come into force in the 1996 national elections.

National Council of Adult Education (NCAE) – established by the Act of 1947, its primary aim was to co-ordinate and promote the field of adult education nationally and in its earlier period to make recommendations to the Minister of Education for the disbursement of funds. It went into recess in 1986 and eventually disappeared in 1990 (see Chapter 1 by James Dakin).

National Resource Centre for Adult and Community Learning (NRC) – established in 1989 as a national co-ordinating body but with minimal funding from government. In July 1990 it took over the assets from the NCAE when the latter was legally disestablished.

New Zealand Association for Community and Continuing Education (NZACCE), now renamed the Adult and Community Education Association Aotearoa/New Zealand (ACEA), is the umbrella membership organisation for the fourth sector. It is an independent organisation which fosters the development of the fourth sector through regular conferences, publishing of *Akina* (its newsletter) and other appropriate activities. Refer to James Dakin's chapter (Chapter 1) for further detail.

New Zealand Qualifications Authority (NZQA) – through the Education Amendment Act (1990), this authority was established with the following functions: to co-ordinate all qualifications in post-compulsory education and training from upper secondary school to degree level; to set and regularly review standards for qualifications; to ensure that New Zealand qualifications are recognised overseas and vice versa; to administer national examinations.

New Zealand Qualifications Authority Framework – an eight-level framework which includes both vocational and general education from senior secondary school (level 1) to graduate degrees (level 8). Broadly speaking, achievements from levels 1 to 4 can lead to a 'National Certificate'; levels 5 to 6 can lead to a 'National Diploma'.

Playcentre Movement – with the absence of many fathers because of World War II, mothers organised a co-operative preschool effort to share their knowledge and resources. A co-operative educational movement was born wherein parents, predominantly mothers, could learn about childrearing practices through their children playing together. Hence, Playcentre is simultaneously a preschool educational service for children and a non-formal adult learning context for parents.

Private Training Establishments (PTE) – as a result of privatisation in education, there have been many small providers establish themselves to provide educational programmes for specific groups or needs (e.g. unemployed; religious education). Most of these agencies have sought registration from the NZQA and accreditation to offer education programmes through the framework.

Project Waitangi – an educational project initiated by Pakeha to familiarise people with the Treaty of Waitangi and its implications for daily life. Now known as Network Waitangi.

Regional Health Authorities (RHAs) – these organisations, established as a result of health 'reforms', receive funding from government to contract Community Health Enterprises (CHEs) and other health agencies for specified health outputs in their regions.

Rogernomics – a slang term coined to encapsulate the New Right economic directions (market liberalism) developed by Sir Roger Douglas, the Minister of Finance in the fourth Labour government, 1984–1990. Roger Douglas is touted as the architect of New Zealand's financial reforms.

Rural Education Activities Programme (REAP) – these consist of government funding for staffing and educational resources for selected small towns in New Zealand. First appearing in 1979, each REAP included an adult education component wherein community education organisers were appointed who acted as catalysts for adult learning in their communities. Refer to Chapter 3 by Jennie Harré Hindmarsh for additional information.

Study Right – a term used to describe a subsidy from government for those students straight from secondary school who qualify for a greater level of support for their tertiary fees. (Non-study right students, typically mature-age students, pay a higher level of the real costs of their education. Some universities have 'smoothed over' the differences in these categories so that all students pay the same fee.)

Te Ataarangi – a Maori organisation, developed in the 1970s, which works to develop speakers of te reo (Maori language) throughout Aotearoa, primarily through oral competency. See Chapter 3 by Jennie Harré Hindmarsh for more detail.

Trade Union Education Authority (TUEA) – this publicly funded organisation was established in 1986 by the fourth Labour government to foster trade union education throughout the union movement. In setting up a wide variety of programmes for and about unions it was hugely successful (see Chapter 10 by Michael Law), until it was abolished by the National government in 1992.

Training Opportunity Programme (TOP) – a government-funded training programme of short duration geared at unemployed individuals gaining vocational skills to enhance their employment prospects.

Treaty of Waitangi (Te Tiriti o Waitangi) – the foundation document signed in 1840 between the Crown (represented by Governor Hobson) and many tribes of Aotearoa. There are two versions of the document – one printed in English; one printed in Maori. The articles expounded within these documents have formed the basis for relationships between tangata whenua (the indigenous Maori or literally 'people of the land') and tauiwi (Pakeha descendants of the signatories to the Treaty).

Union Representatives Educational Leave Act (UREL) – passed in 1986, this Act established a publicly funded Trade Union Education Authority (TUEA) and provided some paid educational leave for trade union education.

Unit Standards – these are effectively 'units of work' on the Qualifications Framework, expressed in terms of learning outcomes and 'standards' of competency to be achieved by the learner to earn 'credit'. A unit standard can stand alone or be combined with other unit standards to make up a qualification.

Waitangi Tribunal – is a standing commission of inquiry into Maori grievances under the Treaty of Waitangi and operates as part of the Department of Courts.

Glossary of Maori Terms

Words/Concepts

ahuatanga Maori	Maori tradition
ako	learn/teach (in a holistic sense)
akonga	learner, pupil, disciple
Aotearoa	New Zealand
aroha	love, compassion
hapu	pregnant, sub-tribal group
harakeke	flax
He Tangata	a man, human being, people; title of the report by IAGNE
huarahi	road, highway, pathway; method, procedure
hui	gathering
iwi	tribe
kai	food
kaiawhina	assistant
kaiwhakaako	coach, educator
kaiwhakarite	person who arranges, provides opportunity for
kaumatua	respected elders
kaupapa	policy, topic
kawa whakaruruhau	cultural safety
Kingitanga	Maori King movement
korero	talk, discuss(ion)
koro	form of address for a respected male elder
kura kaupapa	primary school
Kura Kaupapa Maori	Maori primary school

…

mahi	work
Maori	indigenous people of Aotearoa
Maoritanga	process of being Maori
mana	power, authority, prestige
mana whenua	power associated with the possession of lands, the power associated with the ability of the land to produce the bounties of nature (Barlow, 1994: 61)
manaakitanga	hospitality
matua	parent(s)
mauri	life principle, essence of self, life-essence
me	and (conj.)
mihi	greeting
mo	for (conj.)
Otautahi	Christchurch
Pakeha	fair-skinned New Zealanders of European descent
pepe	baby
rangatahi	young people, youth
rangatiratanga	evidence of breeding and greatness, kingdom, principality, often used to denote self-determination
raranga	weaving
rohe	district, tribal area
runanga	tribal council, assembly
taha hinengaro	emotional side/part
taha Maori	Maori side/part
taha tinana	physical side/part
taha wairua	spiritual side/part
take	subject/topic (of discussion)
tamariki	children
tangata whenua	people of the land, i.e. Maori (as opposed to Pakeha)
taonga	property, treasure, artefact, relic
tauiwi	non-Maori in the inclusive sense, strange, foreign race
taurahere	bound by a rope or cord symbolising affinity to a group that is outside of the area, therefore the person is not tangata whenua
tautoko	support, advocate
Te Kohanga Reo	Maori preschool movement to preserve and foster the use of the reo (Maori language)
te iwi Maori	the Maori people
te reo	the Maori language
Te Tiriti o Waitangi	The Treaty of Waitangi

tikanga Maori	Maori custom
tino rangatiratanga	sovereignty, self-determination, control of resources
tohunga	expert (in a particular field)
tumuaki	leader
tupuna	ancestor
utu	reciprocity
waiata	song
wananga	esoteric learning, learning
whakahihi	make vain, boastful
whakakotahitanga	process of unifying (making one)
whakawhanaungatanga	dynamics of familial relationships
whanau	extended family group
whare	house
whare kura	school house, often used to represent Maori secondary school
whare wananga	house of special learning, now denotes tertiary level educational institution (especially Maori)

People

Apirana Ngata	Ngati Porou leader and politician
Papatuanuku	Earth mother, mother of the gods
Rua Kenana	Tuhoe religious/resistance leader
Ruataupare	Ngati Porou ancestor
Tuwhakairiora	Ngati Porou ancestor

Organisations

Te Ataarangi	formed to train teachers in the reo (Maori language), particularly by using the rakau (stick) method
Te Puni Kokiri	Ministry of Maori Development
Te Whiri Kaupapa Ako	Maori Development Committee of the Adult Reading and Learning Assistance Federation Aotearoa/New Zealand (ARLA)
Whakapakari	Maori Women's Business Enterprises Project

References

Barlow, Cleve (1994), *Tikanga Whakaaro: Key Concepts in Maori Culture*, Auckland: Oxford University Press.

Ngata, H.M. (1995), *English-Maori Dictionary*, Pocket Edition, Whanganui a Tara: Learning Media Limited.

Ryan, P.M. (1989), *The Revised Dictionary of Modern Maori*, Auckland: Heinemann Education.

Te Taura Whiri i te Reo Maori (Maori Language Commission) (1996), *Te Matatiki: Contemporary Maori Words*, Auckland: Oxford University Press.

Williams, H.W. (1975), *A Dictionary of the Maori Language*, Wellington: Government Printer.

Contributors

Julie Barbour is the Director of Community Education at Rutherford High School in West Auckland. As a teacher, a student who has recently finished a Masters of Education in Adult and Higher Education, and a Preschool licensee, she is keenly aware of the challenges lifelong education offers. Teaching and learning are her passions which she loves to share with her family and friends.

John Benseman has been involved in a wide range of adult education activities as a teacher, administrator and researcher. After completing his university and teacher education, John taught in a primary school where his disillusionment with formal structures led him to pursue an interest in adult education. He then spent a year with an adult education research group in Sweden and on his return to New Zealand, worked as a researcher in continuing medical education for general practitioners and as the tutor-organiser for the Auckland Workers Educational Association. For the past seven years he has worked as a self-employed researcher and evaluator on more than 60 projects, primarily concerning the education of adults. He recently took up the position of Senior Lecturer in Adult Education at the University of Auckland.

Wendy Craig has been the Director of Student Services at the University of Waikato since 1991. From 1985 to 1990 she lectured in social and community work, social change and feminist studies at Massey University. Prior to this, she was the Co-ordinator of Community Volunteers in Palmerston North and was actively involved in initiating and implementing an extensive range of community work projects. Her doctoral thesis captured her 20 years of involvement in community work.

Jim Dakin received his university education at the universities of Otago and Oxford and joined the British Colonial Administrative Service in Uganda in 1933. He retired in 1953 as Commissioner for Community Development in Uganda. Returning to New Zealand he worked as tutor-organiser in adult education for Otago and Auckland Universities before being appointed Director of Adult Education at Victoria University of Wellington in 1959. He served in that capacity until retirement in 1974. He had been made an Associate Professor in 1969 and in 1973 published *Education in New Zealand*. Since retirement he has engaged in research activity in adult education and has published various articles and two books – *The Community Centre Story* (1979) and *Focus for Lifelong Education: the National Council of Adult Education 1938–1988* (1988).

Brian Findsen is currently a senior lecturer in adult education at the University of Auckland. Previously he spent many years at the Centre for Continuing Education at the University of Waikato. During this period Brian went on leave (1985–1987) to North Carolina State University in Raleigh where he completed a doctorate of education, majoring in adult education and sociology. On returning to Hamilton he helped to establish the Teaching Development Unit at Waikato prior to spending three years in the Education Department teaching in the sociology of education. In 1992 he commenced work at the University of Auckland where his main interests are in the sociology of adult education and international adult education. In 1994 he spent most of his research and study leave at the University of Warwick, England, as a Visiting Fellow.

Colin Gunn is employed by Nelson Polytechnic to promote and support community education and non-formal learning. As such, he has worked with numerous community organisations and community workers, advising and supporting them and assisting new groups and new services to develop. He has been a member of a number of national working parties including the Interim Advisory Group on Non-formal Education (IAGNE), Learning for Life Working Party: Non-formal Learning and the NZQA Standing Committee on Non-formal and Community Education. He is currently a Trustee of the National Resource Centre for Adult and Community Learning (NRC). Colin is the editor of the book *Seizing the Moment II* – a practical how-to guide for community organisations and workers.

Judy Henderson graduated from the University of Otago with a BA in anthropology. She is currently a Regional Adviser for Massey University, based in Christchurch (and advising extramural students in Canterbury, the West Coast, Nelson and Marlborough). From 1991 to 1994 she worked as research assistant to Robert Tobias on his Christchurch Adult Education Curriculum Project (and prior to that was involved in the establishment of the Gore Outpost of Southland Polytechnic).

Jennie Harré Hindmarsh, a Pakeha, has been Senior Lecturer in Continuing Education at Victoria University of Wellington since 1987. This position was located in the Centre for Continuing Education from 1987 to 1993 and since 1994 has been located in the Department of Education. Jennie is a graduate of Massey, London and Victoria Universities. Her degrees and work experiences are in the fields of education and social work. In more recent years Jennie has researched, published and been involved as a consultant regarding community and continuing education policy and practices issues, bicultural development and adults' learning pathways. Jennie spent her early years in a rural area of the Manawatu and since then has lived and worked in London, Palmerston North and Wellington.

Christine Herzog originally trained as a social planner in the United States. While she had always preferred 'planning with people' to 'planning for people', a major change came with the realisation that community development is 'planning by people'. Her work in the areas of social change for women and for tangata whenua had been based on Freirean models; thus the fourth sector was a natural extension. She began in the heady days when the Community Education Department at Manukau Polytechnic was more like the fourth sector than the tertiary. Her next involvement was and continues to be, with Auckland Workers Education Association. Woven throughout have been ad hoc experiences with community groups, primarily in the areas of structural analysis and Treaty of Waitangi, but also in sharing house-painting and small business skills. Currently, she spends most of her time as a Pakeha tutor in the Maori Education Department (which sits somewhat uncomfortably between tertiary and fourth sector) at Manukau Institute of Technology.

David James was born and raised in England of Welsh and English descent. His entire career since 1961 has been in adult and community education in Aotearoa/New Zealand, with Auckland University Extension, National Council of Adult Education and Northland Polytechnic. Abandoning his career in 1988, he moved with partner Jillian Wychel to Wanganui for the proximity to Quaker Settlement. David and Jillian now work as the Rowan Partnership, on invitation throughout the country. Concerns apart from Treaty issues are peace-making – mediation, conflict resolution, communication, social justice and spreading those skills. David is a singer of traditional folksongs, a Quaker and a planter of green dollar exchanges.

Maarie McCarthy is of Ngati Porou, Ngati Tuwharetoa and Te Arawa descent and is currently employed as a lecturer in the Department of Education, Victoria University, Wellington.

Huhana Mete

Historical Background of Writer

Whakapapa

Ko Whakapunake te maunga.
Ko Wairoa te awa.
Ko Takatimu te wake.
Ko Ngati Kahungunu te iwi.
Ko Rongomai Wahine te tipuna.
Ko Ngapuhi te iwi.
Ko Ngati Kahu te hapu o toku matua tipuna.
Ko Ruataniwha te marae.
Ko ahau te mokopuna a Eru raua ko Ani Hohaia Mete.
Ko ahau te tamahine a Wiripo Mete raua ko Marie Rose Conroy.
Ko ahau te mama o Lisa, ratouko Ryan, Taniora, Rihara, Harata.
Ko Huhana Mete taku ingoa.

Mahi

Huhana Mete has taught at all levels of the education system. More recently she worked as a Personnel Consultant, specialising in sales and marketing. In 1991 Huhana began work in the Maori literacy field on contract to ETSA for TOP, MACCESS and school programmes. From 1991 to 1994 she worked for Te Huarahi Education Trust and then in 1994 initiated Tumanoko Enterprise, a national Maori educational management consultancy.

Colleen Mills is a lecturer in Communication and Learning at Lincoln University and Assistant Director of the Kellogg Rural Leadership Programme. Her degrees in education are from Massey (BEd) and Canterbury (MEd).

Previously Colleen was Massey University's Regional Extramural Co-ordinator for the top half of the South Island and before that the founding director of the South Island Tutor Training Centre which trained teachers in the South Island's polytechnics. Recently she has been working on an ASEAN project which aims to develop training programmes for sustainable, integrated rural development in the five participating Asian countries. Her primary research interest is studying how the individual nature of adult learners' behaviour and the communication processes encountered in adult learning activities affect the understandings learners gain.

Liz Moore has worked in adult literacy education for 15 years, both in Britain and Aotearoa/New Zealand. Liz taught adult literacy in the British tertiary sector, co-ordinated the literacy and ABE service of a large local education authority and worked on several government-funded, national development projects. In Aotearoa/New Zealand Liz set up and managed Workbase, the new workplace literacy unit of the Adult Reading and Learning Assistance Federation (ARLA).

Robyn Munford lectures in the Department of Social Policy and Social Work at Massey University. Her teaching and research interests focus on disability studies, feminist research, social policy analysis, social work practice and community development. She is active in advocacy organisations for people with disabilities and their families. She has recently completed an edited text with Mary Nash entitled *Social Work in Action*. A companion volume to *Superwoman Where are You? – Social Policy and Women's Experience* and is currently co-writing a book documenting the work of community development workers.

Margot Roth was a founding member of the Women's Studies Association (NZ), the first editor of its *Journal* and its first honorary life member. As an active member of the Auckland Workers Educational Association for over 20 years she was also involved in the general provision of adult education and was herself a mature university student who graduated with an MA in Sociology in 1981. She was a consultant with the group which set up the Women's Studies Certificate for Auckland University's Centre for Continuing Education and makes regular contributions to the Women's Studies Association *Newsletter* and *Broadsheet*.

Miriama Scott of Ngati Kahungunu, Rangitane descent is working at Te Whare Takiura o Manukau towards a Diploma in Social and Community Work.

Contributors

Joyce Stalker is a senior lecturer in the Department of Education Studies at the University of Waikato in Hamilton, New Zealand. She emigrated to New Zealand/Aotearoa in 1991. She has a master's and doctorate in adult education from the University of British Columbia. She worked in the field of adult education in Canada, Australia and Sweden and travelled extensively in England, Europe, Central America, Thailand and the U.S.A. Her research interests focus on issues of equity and social justice and on sociological and feminist approaches to the field. She keeps sane by running, writing poetry, sewing, tramping and boogie-boarding.

Robert Tobias who is a graduate of the Universities of Cambridge and Chicago was formerly at the University of Cape Town where he was Director of Extramural Studies. In 1978 he moved to New Zealand to take up the position of Senior Lecturer in Continuing Education at the University of Canterbury, a position he still occupies today. He is interested in all aspects of adult learning and education but his special interests are concerned with the impact of social, economic and educational policies on popular and community education and the effects of race, gender and class on adult learning and education.

Bronwyn Yates of Te Arawa, Rongowhakaata and Ngai Tangamahi descent is the Apiha Kaiwhakahaere o te Motu (National Co-ordinator) of Te Whiri Kaupapa Ako, which is the Maori Development Committee in partnership with Adult Reading and Learning Assistance Federation Aotearoa/New Zealand (ARLA).

Nick Zepke started his working life as a farmhand. After eight years' teaching children, he taught history at Auckland University and Social Studies at Hamilton Teachers' College. Then after three years as a researcher with the Commission for the Future, he joined the polytechnic sector as a teacher educator, first with the Tutor Training Unit then with the Tutor Education Centre (Central). Between 1988 and late 1992 he was the foundation principal of Wairarapa Community Polytechnic, a small regional provider which championed adult and community education – until it was forced to shed many of its guises by the forces described in his chapter. He currently works in academic and staff development at Wellington Polytechnic.

Index

(Italicised numbers are in glossary)

Adult and community education
- as a social movement 45–47
- categories 45–58, 66
- definitions 39, 41
- evaluation of 320
- functions of 43–45
- funding 67, 152
- international developments in 50–53, 366–371,
- nature and functions 43–45
- perspectives and traditions 45, 372–378
- policy 71–74
- research 74, 314–315
- school-based 248–249
- tertiary institutions 70, 120
- in universities 193

Adult and Community Education Aotearoa/ New Zealand (ACEA) – see also NZACCE 34, 74, 316, 318, *381*

Adult Education Act (1947) 26, 49

Adult Education Bill (1963) 29

Adult educators
- history of training for 299
- levels of training 301
- marginal status 298
- professionalisation of 309
- response models of 372–378
- roles of 298
- Working Party report on training 300

Adult learning
- action-based 154–155
- approaches 290–291
- formal 58
- independent 155
- informal 58, 155
- in the community 150, 153
- knowledge about 286
- learner reflections 287–290
- non-formal 57–58, 153
- notions of 291–292
- styles 292–3

Adult literacy
- definitions of 104–105
- evaluation of 321
- funding 108
- Maori and 104, 124, 125
- National Council of Adult Education role 32
- incidence of difficulties in adults 184
- national campaigns 179
- workplace 178, 185

Adult Reading and Learning Assistance (ARLA) Federation 68, *381*
- formation of 32, 35, 49
- participation 280–281
- research 315
- Te Whiri Kaupapa Ako 68, 121, 124

Index

- the Treaty of Waitangi and 105–106
- Workbase 181

Athenaeums 22

Biculturalism
- courses on issues about 327
- identity and cultural safety 136
- implications of 73, 141
- in ARLA 105–106
- models of relationships 128–130
- strategies 132

Book Discussion Scheme 32

Box scheme 24

Community Action Programme (CAP) 321
Community centres 26
Community colleges 31, 211
Community development
- definition 58, 224–225
- feminist 227
- Maori 226–227
- models 225–229
- principles underpinning 225
- relationship with adult education 223–224
- women 227–230
- working class 228–229

Community education
- definitions 57
- in polytechnics 211
- trends in 150
- types of learning 153–155

Community houses 321
Community Learning Aotearoa New Zealand (CLANZ) 33, 59, 66, *381*
Community learning centres 250, *381*
Continuing professional education
- administration of 242–243
- curriculum 237
- effectiveness of 240–241
- justification for 234–235
- models 235–236
- participation 238–239, 281

Country Library Service 25
Country Women's Co-ordinating Committee 35
Country Women's Institute 49

Credentialism 52, 71, 255, 310
Cultural identity 136–138
Cultural safety
- programmes 333
- tauiwi and 40

Currie Commission on Education 28

Education Amendment Act (1938), (1974), (1990) 31, 33, 54, 82, 91
Education and Training Support Agency (ETSA) *382*
- funding programmes 116, 120
- workplace 170, 182

Education Development Conference 31, 53, 54 250, *382*

Education of adult educators
- content 305–307
- history of 299
- levels of 298
- methodology for 307–308
- models 304
- National Council of Adult Education 301–302
- principles of best practice 308–309
- resources 302–303
- Working Party report 300

Evaluation
- continuing professional education 240–241
- covert purposes 319
- definitions 318
- funding 321–322
- methodologies 321
- types 319

Feilding Community Centre 26, 49
Fourth Sector 40–42
- categories 66
Fundamentalism 370

Garrett, Denis 30, 249
Globalisation 366–368

Hely, Arnold 30
Herbert, Charlie 249
'He Tangata' report 33, 35, 67, 216

Industry Training Act (1992) (ITA) 159, 170, 180, 182, *382*
Industry training boards 161
Industry training organisations (ITO) 170, 182, 190, *382*
International Labour Office (ILO) 162
International Standards Organisation (ISO) accreditation 179
Interim Advisory Group on Non-formal Education (IAGNE) 36, 73

James, David 30

Labour government 25, 53–55, 160, 162, 164–165, 195–197, 248, 348, 354–355
Learning for Life: Two 72, 212, 215
Literary institutes 22

Manual and Technical Instruction Acts (1895 and 1900) 23, 26
Maori adult education
- community development 226
- National Council of Adult Education 27, 32, 55, 328
- pre-European 39
- report on
- tino rangatiratanga 96
- universities 204, 206–207
Market orientation 368
Marshall, Russell 33
Martin Smith, Bob 30
Mechanics' Institutes 21
Ministry of Education 316
Mutual improvement societies 22

National Council of Adult Education 28–30, 56, *382*
- abolition 33, 36, 55, 59
- broadcasting liaison 31–32
- establishment of 26, 49
- legislation 56
- Maori Advisory Committee 69
- special projects 32, 55
- training development 301–302
- working party 31, 297, 300
National government 55, 165, 169–170, 348, 355

National Resource Centre for Adult Education and Community Learning (NRC) 33, 59, 74, 316, *382*
Native Schools Act (1867) 102
Needs analysis
- defining needs 268–269
- in continuing professional education 237
Nelson Community Education Service (NCES) 55
New Right
- dominance by 169, 360
- effects on education 139, 195–196
- influence in polytechnics 212
- influence on universities 195
- influence on whare wananga 82–90
- policies 85, 139, 159, 163–165, 169–170, 195–196, 348, 360, 368
- resistance to 348
New Zealand Association for Community and Community Education (NZACCE)
– see also ACEA 34, 74, 316, *381*
New Zealand Council of Trade Unions (NZCTU) 68, 171, 184
New Zealand Employers' Federation (NZEF) 172
New Zealand Qualifications Authority (NZQA) *382*
- community education 150
- Framework *382*
- impact of 72
- polytechnics 213
- school based programmes 256–257
- workplace 180, 183
Non-formal education/learning 149
- defining 57
- funding 152
- problems and prospects 152

Organisation for Economic and Cultural Development (OECD) 50, 162, 164

Paid educational leave (PEL) 162, 171
Parents Centres 68
Parry Report (1959) 28
Participation
- barriers to 279

Index

- continuing professional education 238–239, 281
- equal opportunity 275
- mandatory 239
- non-participation 238–239, 278
- research of 276–278
- school based programmes 250
- typology of participants 276
- university programmes 205–206

Pewhairangi, Ngoingoi 32, 35

Polytechnics
- community education models 216–217
- degree developments 214
- funding issues 214–215

Private Training Establishments (PTEs) 116, 214, *384*

Professionalism
- continuing professional education 243–244
- non-formal education 150

Programme planning
- case study 267–268
- models 264–267
- process 264

Racism awareness training 328–329

Radio New Zealand Continuing Education Unit 31

Research
- analysis of studies 316–317
- bibliography 314, 316
- definition and purposes 313
- funding 316
- need for 319
- whare wananga 91

Response models by adult educators
- appropriation 375–376
- conflict 373–374
- consensus 372–373
- interpretive 374–375

Rural Education Activities Programme (REAP) 32, 49, 55, 68, 280, 321, *384*

School based programmes 31, 70
- community learning centres 250, *381*
- current issues 255–257
- current practice 250–251

- history of 28, 248–249
- participation 250
- theoretical perspectives on 251–254

Social movement education 45–48
- issues in 353–359
- programmes 349–351

Somerville, Rosalie 32, 35

Study Right *384*
- in polytechnics 215
- in universities 196

Te Ataarangi 32, 35, 49, 69 254, *384*

Technical institutes 29, 211

Te Huarahi Trust
- achievements 123–125
- development of 113
- issues 115–123
- staffing and management 122–123

Tertiary education
- community education 70
- identity and cultural safety in 139
- the Treaty of Waitangi and 139
- Women's Studies and

Thomas Report (1939) 248

Tino rangatiratanga (self-determination)
- case for 132–134
- definitions of 96–98
- impact of 73, 109
- Te Huarahi Trust and 113

Trade Union Education Authority (TUEA) 30, 71, *385*
- abolition 159, 171–172
- achievements 167
- evaluation of 321

Trade union education
- centres for labour and trade union studies 167
- Task Force on Trade Union Education 57, 166–167, 349

Trade union movement 46, 170

Trade Union Training Board (TUTB) 163

Training Opportunities Programme (TOP) 214, *385*

Treaty of Waitangi 99–101, 139–143, *385*
- agenda for social justice 376
- ARLA and 105–107
- attitudes for training about 334

- education about 330
- impact of 73
- material about 328
- Project Waitangi 69, 328, *384*
- resistance to 331
- tertiary education 139

UNESCO, National Commission for
- Committee for Lifelong Education 30, 54
- 'lifelong learning' 50, 162, 166
- Nairobi conference 31, 51
- Tokyo conference 51

Union Representatives Educational Leave Act (1986) (UREL) 166, *385*

Universities
- centres for continuing education 193
- curriculum and provision 199
- historical developments 28, 30, 194–195
- labour studies 204
- mainstreaming vs marginalisation 200
- Maori programmes 204
- models 201–203
- participation 205–207
- staffing 198
- university extension 27, 30, 53, 193
- women's studies 204

Vocational Training Council (VTC) 29, 31, 53, 161

Vocationalism 52

Wairarapa Community Action Programme (CAP) 55, 321

Wairarapa Community Polytechnic 210, 215, 218–220

Welfare state 160, 163

Wellington, Merv 33

Whare wananga
- autonomy of 89
- commodification of knowledge 90
- curriculum 89–91
- features of 81
- funding issues 87–89

- ideological conflicts in 82
- research 91
- the State and 86

Women's Division, Federated Farmers 49

Women's studies
- conflicts and tensions 343
- ignoring of 337
- programmes 341
- reflecting feminist theory and practice 340
- tertiary education and 342–343

Women's Studies Association 338–341

Workbase (ARLA) 181

Workers' education 160, 162

Workers Educational Association (WEA) 25–26, 35, 48–49, 69
- book discussion scheme 32
- funding for 25, 34, 55
- origins 23–25, 35, 48
- in rural areas 24
- Trade Union Postal Education Service 30
- Treaty of Waitangi 133
- tutors 24
- worker education 162

Workplace education
- and the 'learning organisation' 179
- Australia 165–166, 182,184
- Britain 165, 182, 184
- evaluation of 321
- features of 185–191
- literacy provision 181, 185, 187
- Maori workers 184
- overview 71, 177–179
- 'skill crisis' 180
- training 161